The Strangl

At the Interface

Series Editors

Dr Robert Fisher   Lisa Howard
Dr Ken Monteith

Advisory Board

An *At the Interface* research and publications project.
http://www.inter-disciplinary.net/at-the-interface/

The Evil Hub
'Trauma: Theory and Practice'

2013

The Strangled Cry:

The Communication and Experience of Trauma

Edited by

Aparjita Nanda and Peter Bray

Inter-Disciplinary Press

Oxford, United Kingdom

© Inter-Disciplinary Press 2013
http://www.inter-disciplinary.net/publishing/id-press/

The *Inter-Disciplinary Press* is part of *Inter-Disciplinary.Net* – a global network for research and publishing. The *Inter-Disciplinary Press* aims to promote and encourage the kind of work which is collaborative, innovative, imaginative, and which provides an exemplar for inter-disciplinary and multi-disciplinary publishing.

British Library Cataloguing in Publication Data. A catalogue record for this book is available from the British Library.

Inter-Disciplinary Press, Priory House, 149B Wroslyn Road, Freeland, Oxfordshire. OX29 8HR, United Kingdom.
+44 (0)1993 882087

ISBN: 978-1-84888-204-1
First published in the United Kingdom in Paperback format in 2013. First Edition.

Table of Contents

Foreword

Peter Bray

It is no secret that trauma is a deal-breaker. It leaves sudden, deep, visceral scarring that changes everything. In her introduction to *Trauma and Recovery*, Judith Lewis Herman writes, 'The conflict between the will to deny horrible events and the will to proclaim them aloud is the central dialectic of psychological trauma.' The manner in which we individually or collectively respond to the experience of trauma, interpret and remember its power over us, critically defines, directs and continues to ascribe meaning to our lives and to the lives of others.

This volume is one outcome; proceedings have been published electronically elsewhere, of the Inter-Disciplinary.Net's Second Global Conference: 'Trauma: Theory and Practice', convened in March 2011 in Prague, Czech Republic. The conference, purposefully intended to facilitate inter-disciplinary exchange, brought together artists and performers, writers and philosophers, therapists, psychologists, and survivors, and many others whose interests lie in furthering the scholarly understanding of our troubled relationship with traumatic events. The following papers invited for inclusion in *The Strangled Cry* have been considerably expanded for this collection and are shamelessly rendered to 'proclaim...aloud' the unspeakable, easy deniability, and wounding mechanism of trauma. From their diverse scholarly perspectives our contributors offer fresh interpretations of current theories, sensitive and thought-provoking narratives, and cutting-edge research that anticipate new and emerging trends in trauma studies – covered in more detail in the Afterword.

The third in its series, this collection represents and samples evolving perspectives in academic expression, research, and lived experience that cannot fail to impress upon us the inescapable reality, and all-pervasive influence of trauma's power to irrevocably change the lives and development of individuals and communities across time. As each international contributor shares his or her unique perspective they suggest that on occasion these painful and unasked for experiences can potentially become sustainable bridges between those lives fractured by trauma and those, through the resilient tendency toward survival, meaning-making, and actualisation, that are remade. Notably, in every instance where people bring themselves together in communities of attachment we are reminded as readers that they are seeking a context for healing. That it is in relationship – the seedbed of recovery and the ultimate source of comfort and long-term healing – that we regroup and share our struggles with traumatisation, carry, integrate and mourn our losses, and re-create life-stories that make these devastating experiences matter.

As a snapshot, this book represents a significant and useful resource but its intrinsic value is in its sharing. From its shared proclamation of despair and of hope, its fruitful analysis and hard questioning, its original viewpoints and profound perspectives it carries one solitary and very human concern – that all of us at some point in our lives will be directly or indirectly altered by an experience of trauma. In all likelihood some of us, already profoundly touched by experience, will be challenged, affirmed, reminded or activated by something in this collection. Trauma, it seems, implicates us all. It challenges us as it compels us to hear and to voice the strangled cries of the traumatised, to freely admit their experiences into the secret and silent places of our own violations. To do so even for a moment is to step beyond its gagging conspiracy. To have the capacity to share, witness, and acknowledge, to hear and then to speak back to the trauma of our times is a hope worthy of resolution.

Introduction

Aparajita Nanda

The word trauma traces its etymology back to the Greek word meaning wound – a result of bodily injury. The Greek sense of trauma was singularly focused on the physical nature of injury. However, in its psychoanalytical sense, trauma is mental, not corporeal. Trauma refers to a psychic injury caused by extreme emotional shock, which often leaves a repressed, metaphorical wound. This initial shock destabilizes the mental well-being of the subject, resulting in a traumatic neurosis. Trauma theory has evolved dramatically, from a focus on childhood sexuality and sexual exploitation to a modern multi-disciplinary field that explores trauma throughout human culture in numerous studies and media.

This new primarily psychological interpretation of trauma was commonly associated with witnesses of horrific, scarring events. In response to what they saw, these witnesses often developed a debilitating neurosis that was inherently paradoxical: they typically could not recall the source of the trauma, but were simultaneously plagued by a series of repeated flashbacks of the event. As the medical world and the general public began to recognize that the victims of traumatic events were not limited to those who experienced them firsthand, but also included those who witnessed them, the definition of trauma began to broaden greatly.

One of the first professional psychoanalysts who addressed this new manifestation of trauma was none other than the founding father of psychoanalysis himself: Sigmund Freud. Initially following Charcot's theory of hystero-trauma, Freud defined trauma as the result of a physical violation or breach. Later he began to recognize the psychological repercussions of horrific events and observed that the victims of such events initially responded to their experiences by repressing the event. After this repression, however, the repercussions of the traumatic event later surfaced as external reactions or neuroses. Freud recognized two primary types of traumatic neuroses: one where the victim experienced hysteria without a discharge of the accumulated emotions, and the other characterized by a delayed emotional discharge long after the actual event took place.

By 1893 Freud made a transition from the theory of hystero-trauma to the theory of sexual trauma when along with Josef Breuer, he published 'On the Psychical Mechanism of Hysterical Phenomena: A Preliminary Communication' and followed this up, two years later with the jointly written 'Studies in Hysteria'. He perceived sexual trauma to be divided into two parts: first, the initial sexual aggression of an adult on a child, and second, the child's later recognition of the event, typically after the child experienced puberty. This second revelatory moment served as a catalyst for recovery, requiring the reenactment of the sexual exploitation in order to let the repressed emotions finally surface. As he diagnosed more patients, Freud stretched the parameters of his theory, including a patient's individual history, the time and circumstances of the traumatic incident, and any element of personal fantasy as key factors in determining the effects of sexual trauma.[1] For Freud, however, prompt discovery remained paramount in the treatment of trauma; either premature or delayed diagnosis could lead to a setback. Concerned as he was with childhood seduction and its psychological manifestation at this point paid little or no attention to sexual seductions in adulthood and their traumatic aftermath.[2]

The notion of Freudian trauma acquired a new dimension during the two World Wars as cases of war neuroses or 'shell shocked' soldiers were reported. The symptoms ranged from instant amnesia to compulsive syndromes. In 'Beyond the Pleasure Principle', Freud equates these syndromes to an essential death wish in the person – a desire to be free of the traumatic experience.[3] The syndrome creates interplay between the death wish and the desire to survive, providing symbols in dreams that lead to a resolution of anxiety. In this revised theory of anxiety, the patient remains a helpless victim in the throes of an ego overwhelmed by the traumatic event – one that he is powerless to understand, much less contain. This inability of the ego to deal with repetitive hauntings in the form of personal ruminations or repetitive dreams is the foundation of narcissistic trauma.[4] Narcissistic trauma is generally categorized by a failure, due to a sense of self-love overwhelming the ego to control the traumatic trigger. Such an understanding of trauma expands the category from an intermittently appearing phenomenon to one that fundamentally alters a victim's worldview.

This broadened concept of trauma, which tended to downplay the specificity of a traumatic event and yet accept the presence of resultant fear or other pathological developments, thrived in the post-World War II era. Trauma theory in the aftermath of World War II had to address victims of mass trauma –survivors of the Holocaust or the atomic bombings of Hiroshima who developed post-traumatic stress disorder (PTSD). The severity of these excruciating events stymied the victims' articulation of the impact of the loss simply because of their unparalleled nature.[5] Thus a narration of historical events became imperative: the sharing of the narrative by the victim with later generations was vital for these recipients of 'postmemory' to establish a bridge between those who survived and those who followed after them, a bridge that was essential if the trauma was to be resolved.[6]

These tales, like PTSD, have been subject to much criticism and controversy. Even as diagnoses of PTSD have drawn worldwide sympathy for the patients and humanitarian organizations have provided them with help, it has been alleged that people have often misrepresented the disorder and elicited sympathy (and often financial help) where the symptoms have been misconstrued. Even as one recognizes these pitfalls, one needs also to understand the variety of PTSDs. And while PTSD is a phenomenon usually linked to war victims or tied to personal tragedy, protracted homelessness, unemployment, or political exile or oppression could result in similar symptoms.

Many factors influence one's experience of trauma, including, but not limited to, one's gender, race and age. According to Breslau et al., gender plays a key role in determining one's exposure to trauma.[7] While women are more commonly victims of rape, sexual molestation, and abuse, men are more likely to experience trauma as a whole. Race is also a factor in trauma studies; some studies claim higher rates of trauma among the white race whereas others claim the same rates for non-whites as minorities. However, age has the clearest impact on trauma. Older people are much less likely to experience new trauma due to previous experience dealing with it. The elderly are much more likely to come to terms with traumatic incidents in their lives. While it is not without exception, statistics strongly support that one is much more likely to experience serious trauma during childhood than during adulthood.[8] While gender and race often affect one's likelihood to experience trauma, one's age has the greatest impact in determining the level of trauma experienced.

Additionally, social and cultural contexts play important roles in the lives of traumatized people. Often, people who have been the victims of excessive parental discipline and physical abuse react differently than those who were raised by parents who frown upon the use of physical force as a form of discipline. Also, certain cultural beliefs and rituals play a vital part in precipitating traumatic events, particularly if they involve a high degree of violence and repression. Genital mutilation of African women and the burning of young Indian women in their husbands' pyres are examples of cultural practices that have traumatized millions throughout the ages.

In the face of such multifaceted factors of trauma, concern has grown in recent decades as to what therapeutic approaches can allow for successful healing of trauma. A 'one size fits all' approach to the relief of trauma proves elusive due to both the varying sources of trauma and varying factors that affect the internal processing of trauma. For example, soldiers in combat often become hardened to the on-going trauma of death and do not immediately appear to need the process of grieving as such. However, for people exposed to a traumatic event once in their lifetime, such as a death of a child, the grieving process requires considerable time and support from friends and relatives. A form of grief that defies open acknowledgement may be even harder to deal with. Such diverse needs have led to a multitude of trauma therapies.

Judith Herman highlights the need for recovery to be viewed as a three-phased process – rather than a single effort. The first step is to make the patient feel safe, to make them feel like a survivor and to build up a level of confidence that would enable them to take control of their life. The second phase involves a recall of the past that 're-constructs' the event so that the patient can relive it and interpret it in such a way as to reach a level of comfort with it that allows the memory to remain accessible to the survivor. This is the most difficult phase, as it is fraught with anxiety and resurgences of memory which at any point could become hazardous barriers to recovery. The third and final phase in this model of therapy involves helping the survivor find new meaning and create a new life. However, one must keep in mind that this process of healing may never provide a feeling of absolute release from the trauma.[9]

Another commonly recommended pathway to surviving trauma is logotherapy, in which a subject is encouraged to follow an expressive pursuit related to their traumatic experience. Therapists do not provide solutions but instead encourage patients to find 'meanings' in their lives. Telling or writing stories about an originary loss in one's life often helps the patient understand, or even connect to, others' losses, setting up an empathetic network that could provide strength to others as well as to oneself. In this way, a primary loss can be transformed into a positive space, providing regenerative feelings that heal others. Expressing one's pent-up emotions is vital in the healing process. However, repetitive pondering of the loss, what Nolen-Hoeksema calls 'ruminative coping', causes logotherapy to fail its therapeutic effect by instead pushing one to recycle the loss, leading to negative mood cycles.[10] Crucially, therefore, patients must negotiate a thin line between embracing and discharging their traumatic experience so that they obtain social support without trapping themselves into the syndrome of loss.

While some studies espouse complete distraction from trauma as a successful therapeutic strategy, most therapeutic strategies incorporate some degree of the mourning process. Mourning for a lost loved one is complete when one can move away from the memory to find a substitute or find meaning and reinvest oneself in a totally different context. Oftentimes, the transition to mourning is slow, begun with merely envisaging different pathways to express and endure grief. To truly embark on a trail of mourning, one needs to recognize, acknowledge and even accept grief, as doing so looks ahead at moving beyond grief. However, during therapy the patient may encounter a number of setbacks such as denial, withdrawal, and aggression accompanied by a sense of shame, helplessness and hopelessness. In 'Mourning and Melancholia', Freud explains that mourners can be at risk of melancholia, a protracted period of mourning where one refuses to let go of one's loss.

It is important to note that all loss is relative to other aspects of a person's life. Indeed, putting any loss in perspective helps to situate it in the larger context of life. This perspective, or what John Harvey calls 'cognitive framing', helps one to look into oneself and reconsider one's own interpretation of the situation. This often results, via a relational realization, in a feeling of compassion for others. Often the feeling of being shattered, of being a fragmented remnant of life in the aftermath of trauma, can be slowly transformed. One needs to be realistic in one's appraisal of life and to match one's actions to one's beliefs. To make this transition happen, one must pursue this philosophy of living. But to abide by this philosophy, one needs to realize the magnitude and the effect of the loss. This effect often becomes part of a cumulative life history of loss, as the close inspection of loss inherently pushes one to recall earlier losses in one's life. This aggregation of loss begins to set off an overwhelming, heart-wringing realization of the full extent of the losses. Ultimately, one must expend a focused effort to accept and begin to deal with these moments by means of what Harvey calls 'memoralization': when one needs to focus on the blessings in life – on whatever one considers are the highlights of his or her life – and cherish the moments by recalling them. This is not a pathway that, when pursued, will help one gloss over one's losses. Rather the loss needs to be recognized and not suppressed – maybe put beside the good moments of one's life to be understood better. Anger, revenge, and hatred are often the outcomes of violent losses in life. The only antidote to these feelings is learning to forgive and to try to find peace where earlier there was none.

The stakes of overcoming trauma have been the focus of much contemporary research. Recently in academia there has been a shift away from solely studying the mental effects of trauma, like PTSD, to researching the physical effects that multiple exposures to trauma have. This research has shown that people who struggle with adversity and remain victims to an on-going traumatic situation often fare better in the long run, improving their overall functionality.[11] However, these conclusions remain highly controversial and require further research to be proven unquestionably true. Research is also needed to deal better with the outcomes and repercussions of public trauma. How do large groups of people react to natural disasters or terrorist attacks? Who is more vulnerable to these exigencies and what aftereffects do they suffer mentally and physically? There is an attempt today to prevent posttraumatic disorders. But exposure to trauma in many cases is inevitable, thus prevention of secondary issues that may emanate from trauma is far more viable than nullifying the primary issue. For example, early medical intervention to treat trauma patients is highly effective in diminishing negative responses to the trauma. As research on trauma and post-traumatic disorders improves, scholars and doctors keep discovering new methods of preventing negative side effects in response to horrific events.

Two recent books have critically expanded the horizon of trauma studies. In *Haunting Legacies*, Gabriele Schwab uses psychoanalysis and trauma theory to understand 'transgenerational' trauma: collective horrors such as the Holocaust and slavery that impact more than a single generation. She focuses on literary texts, believing that they stand witness to 'unarticulated' trauma that society fails to directly address.[12] Schwab follows in the footsteps of her predecessors in the field (Cathy Caruth, Dominick La Capra, Soshana Felman and Dori Laub to name a few) by focusing on the critical role the unconscious plays in the transference and transmission of trauma to future generations. This transmission acknowledges the 'subject position of the analyst' – a position determined by the experience of the writer.[13] However, whatever influences Schwab's experiences might have played in its development, her theory is instrumental for the modern understanding of trauma. Schwab professes a need of a 'syncretistic memory that operates at the intersections of different violent histories' and admits a 'transgenerational' transfer of these scarred legacies to descendants of the original victims.[14] The 'creative rewritings' by these descendants would establish a path for collective mourning that looks ahead to future reparations. Schwab also understands the importance of recognizing the suffering of not only the victims but of the perpetrators as well. Once torture and suffering has been sanctioned, it kills the victim physically while simultaneously killing the perpetrator spiritually. The other book, *Interrogating Trauma*, a collection of essays by leading trauma theory scholars edited by Mick Broderick and Antonio Traverso, considers traumatic histories internationally through a broad range of artistic and media representations. Though they do not reject the dominant modern theories, the duo remains concerned about how any examination of trauma ignores the cultural underpinning of those who experience it. They seek to develop alternative conceptualizations of trauma studies that recognize, even as they constitute, 'thematic and cross-cultural epistemologies that deepen the discussion about the relationship between individual memory/trauma and collective or cultural memory/trauma'.[15]

The present collection, *The Strangled Cry*, born of the second Interdisciplinary Conference on Trauma held at Prague in March of 2012, brings together international scholars from different disciplines in order to address the primary issues of trauma studies in its multiple branches. This book examines the trauma from the standpoint of various disciplines ranging from history and literature to sociology and critical theory, and suggests therapeutic avenues to tackle the issues presented in these studies. The presentations combine incisive personal insights with theoretical knowledge.

All the chapters of this collection seek to set up meaningful dialogue between scholars in the field. The goal is to create conversations that add to a critical appraisal of the primary theme. Communication being crucial in this context, the intention of this compilation is to reflect in its chapter divisions an exchange of ideas about a crucial topic in human history. By *history* is meant not only knowledge dealing with past events related to the human race but also history as 'his-story' – the personal narrative of a particular person. Hence the fifteen chapters, divided into three sections, move from the individual response, which often seeks a collective voice, to a search for resolution of trauma. A detailed description of this process follows.

Part I. The Individual Response explores the multiple impact of trauma while demonstrating the revelatory role of literature in trauma studies. Jessica Aliaga Lavrijsen's deconstructive reading of Janice Galloway's *The Trick is to Keep Breathing* in this volume introduces trauma fiction studies as a fertile field, an ideal field for the exploration of identity and formal experimentation. Aliaga Lavrijsen argues that Galloway explores the inherent form of the genre while analysing the play of the conscious and the unconscious in the construction of the primary narrator's identity. This performativity of the text, which asks readers to actively participate in the construction of meaning, is enhanced by the experimental narrative techniques appropriated by the author to rewrite trauma fiction studies. Simon Bacon talks about the vampire as a cinematic representation of bodily and psychological response to individual trauma in Matt Reeves *Let Me In*. Bacon traces a symbiotic relationship between the vampire, Abby, and Owen, the young boy whose trauma the vampire embodies by focusing on Abby's need for reparation and individual continuance with and through Owen. The function of performance as a therapeutic tool is at the core of Oliver Bray and Peter Bray's chapter, which incorporate Shakespeare's *Hamlet*, Tim Crouch's *The Author* and Franko B's *I Miss You.'* These three case studies are used to illuminate and address questions of the effect of 'performed' trauma on the performer, the audience and the maker, and to examine the complex implications for the ethical issues and psychological safety of the parties involved.

Part II. The Collective Voice moves from the individual responses of Part I to the emergence of collective voices that represent responses to traumatic experiences. The collectivity of trauma theory is reflected in countless different areas of human culture, ranging from feminist literature to accounts of genocide. Majda R. Atieh and Ghada Mohammad, in their chapter, writes of a lacuna in those Middle Eastern and African narratives that deal with the trauma of female non-combatants during wartime. Atieh and Mohammad's intertextual read of Hanan al-Shaykh's *The Story of Zahra* and Chimamanda Ngozi Adichie's *Half of a Yellow Sun* addresses the attempt made by collective female voices for recovery from trauma, while it also admits that total recovery may be impossible. Yet it is hope that drives the author's rendering of these women's ability to make substantial progress, often through narration and scriptotherapy, toward individual and collective changes. Aparajita Nanda studies Lilith Iyapo as a mother figure in Octavia Butler's science fiction trilogy *Lilith's Brood*, noting Lilith's fragmentation of self-wrought by the traumatic loss of her son in an accident. The loss resonates in her psyche and becomes a trigger for her re-living the 'motherhood' story in different milieus and different time frames. Drawing on the different possibilities of these retold stories, Lilith seeks a release from her traumatic memory. Bridget Haylock picks up Barbara Baynton's novel *Human Toll* to discuss it as a feminist inroad into the genre of bildungsroman, initiating a collage of genres, from melodrama to romance, that disturbs the status quo of social 'patriarchal' strongholds and creates an empowered space of unique feminine subjectivity. Filiz Celik focuses on intergenerational transmission of what he calls 'human made' trauma, such as that of genocide or ethnocide, which not only precipitates the horror of collective human violence during its time but also percolates down to later generations in various forms that affect the sense of human dignity. Documenting interviews with second and third generation survivors of the 1937-38 Dersim massacres, Celik focuses on the collective impact of ancestral trauma. Patricia Varas argues that the Guatemalan indigenous activist and Nobel Peace Prize winner Rigoberta Menchú adopts different genres – from the testimonio to the memoir – to articulate her personal trauma that coalesces with that of her community. Varas talks about Rigoberta Menchú's choice of different narratives to give shape to her personal and collective memories and insists that the ritualistic roots of cultural memory provide an aid to the narration of intergenerational trauma and heal one of painful memories.

Part III. Prevention and Reconciliation speaks to both Parts I and II, as it suggests prevention of, and reconciliation with, traumatic events. Yao Xu, Helen Herrman, Atsuro Tsutsumi and Jane Fisher's chapter concerns itself with long-term depression, anxiety, and PTSD originating from the loss of a child to a natural disaster. Findings endorse that women who lost a child in the May 2008 earthquake in Sichuan, China often became the victims of multiple psychological disorders. Xu et al., encourage further research into the issue and advises that better health care facilities are needed to cope with the crisis. Evgenia Troshikhina encourages sandplay as a form of therapy, one often more potent than talk therapy. The silent space of hands-on action provided by sandplay allows the patient to deal with the trauma without having to talk about it. By expressing themselves creatively through sandplay, the patient gives voice to the otherwise 'verbally blocked' trauma that now, through visual display, liberates and heals itself. Moara Crivelente considers the traditional Rwandan courts of reconciliation, small community courts called Gacacas, where victims confront the perpetrators of violent crime and the latter seek forgiveness. Once forgiven, the perpetrators are integrated back into society. Despite criticism of this mode as insufficient to deal with the perpetrators of genocide Crivelente promotes the traditional Gacacas, albeit as a transformed path to recovery from collective trauma. Beverly Ayling-Smith speaks of cloth as a metaphorical representation of traumatic memory, a memory of grief, mourning and melancholia that persists in mourning but is not exclusively defined by it. She cites the art works of Michelle Walker, Anne Wilson, and Chiyoko Tanaka along with her own to illustrate how textiles stand as memorial to loss and yet facilitate the work of mourning. Johanne N. Fleming-Saraceno argues that Indigenous girls in Canada have historically been victims of sexualized and racialized violence that has perpetrated in them an intergenerational collective trauma. Her chapter brings to the fore avenues through which these girls could map out, strategically resist and begin to disrupt these horrific practices in their own communities.

As the range and scope of the chapters in this collection show, trauma studies has emerged as a rich and complex field that needs to consider the proliferating violence and brutality in human life. The twenty-first century comes with its own share of trauma: the effects of the terrorist attacks of September 11th as well as issues of the Iraq War, the Israeli occupation and blockade of Palestine, homeland security, and human rights. In this reality, memory and trauma have to move from comparatively simple interpersonal dynamics to an admission of an intrapersonal one, wherein the 'intra-' acknowledges the presence of the other *in* the self, where the self and the other are both the victim and the perpetrator of trauma. Reconciliation and resolution of trauma therefore need both the victim and the perpetrator to partake in the recovery process. Initiation of this process is hard. The process is long and demanding; at this point a strangled cry at best – one that in the future seeks an articulation and a communication of the traumatic experience that would ultimately bring on a healing.

Notes

[1] Sigmund Freud, 'Three Essays on the Theory of Sexuality', in *The Standard Edition of the Complete Psychological Works of Sigmund Freud*, ed. James Strachey (London: Hogarth Press, 1966-1974), 123-243.

[2] Ibid., 209-253.

[3] Karl Abraham, 'The Experiencing of Sexual Traumas as a Form of Sexual Activity', in *Selected Papers on Psychoanalysis*, trans. Douglas Bryan and Alix Strachey (New York: Basic Books, 1968), 47-63.

[4] Freud, 'Inhibitions, Symptoms and Anxiety', 87-172.

[5] Cathy Caruth, ed., *Trauma: Explorations in Memory* (Baltimore: John Hopkins Press, 1995), 3-12; 151-157.

[6] Marianne Hirsch, *Family, Frames: Photography, Narrative and Postmemory* (Cambridge, MA: Harvard University Press, 1997), 17-40.

[7] Naomi Breslau, et al., 'Trauma and Post-Traumatic Stress Disorder in the Community: The 1996 Detroit Area Survey of Trauma', *Archives of General Psychiatry* 55 (1998): 626.

[8] Shalon M. Irving and Kenneth F. Ferraro, 'Reports of Abusive Experiences during Childhood and Adult Health Ratings: Personal Control as a Pathway?' *Journal of Aging and Health* 18 (2006): 458-485.

[9] Judith Herman, *Trauma and Recovery* (New York: Basic Books, 1997), 7-95, 115-129, 133-154, 175-236.

[10] Susan Nolen-Hoeksema, 'Ruminative Coping and Adjustment to Bereavement' in *Handbook of Bereavement Research: Consequences, Coping and Care*, ed. Margaret S. Stroebe et al. (Washington, D.C.: American Psychological Association, 2001), 545-562.

[11] Alex Linley and Stephen Joseph, 'Positive Change following Trauma and Adversity: A Review', *Journal of Traumatic Stress* 17 (2004): 11-21.

[12] Gabriele Schwab, *Haunting Legacies: Violent and Transgenerational Trauma* (New York: Columbia University Press, 2010), 1-32, 36-38.

[13] Dominick LaCapra, *Representing the Holocaust: History, Theory, Trauma* (New York: Cornell University Press, 1994), quoted in Gabriele Schwab, *Haunting Legacies*, 9.
[14] Gabriele Schwab, *Haunting Legacies*, 9.
[15] Mick Broderick and Antonio Traverso, eds., *Interrogating Trauma: Collective Suffering in Global Arts and Media* (New York: Routledge, 2011), 11.

Bibliography

Abraham, Karl. 'The Experiencing of Sexual Traumas as a Form of Sexual Activity.' In *Selected Papers on Psychoanalysis*. Translated by Douglas Bryan and Alix Strachey. New York: Basic Books, 1968.

Breslau, Naomi, Ronald C. Kessler, Howard D. Chilcoat, Lonni R. Schultz, Glenn C. Davis and Patricia Andreski. 'Trauma and Post-Traumatic Stress Disorder in the Community: The 1996 Detroit Area Survey of Trauma.' *Archives of General Psychiatry* 55 (1998): 626.

Broderick, Mick and Antonio Traverso, eds. *Interrogating Trauma: Collective Suffering in Global Arts and Media*. New York: Routledge, 2011.

Caruth, Cathy, ed. *Trauma: Explorations in Memory*. Baltimore: John Hopkins Press, 1995.

———. *Unclaimed Experience: Trauma, Narrative, and History*. Baltimore: The John Hopkins University Press, 1996.

Felman, Shoshana and Dori Laub. *Testimony: Crises of Witnessing in Literature, Psychoanalysis, and History*. New York: Routledge, 1992.

Freud, Sigmund and Josef Breuer. 'On the Psychical Mechanism of Hysterical Phenomena: A Preliminary Communication.' *The Standard Edition of the Complete Psychological Works of Sigmund Freud*. Translated by James L. Strachey. London: Hogarth Press, 1966-1974.

———. 'Studies in Hysteria.' *The Standard Edition of the Complete Psychological Works of Sigmund Freud*. Translated by James L. Strachey. London: Hogarth Press, 1966-1974.

Harvey, John H. *Perspectives on Loss and Trauma: Assaults on the Self*. Thousand Oaks: Sage Publications, 2002.

Herman, Judith. *Trauma and Recovery.* New York: Basic Books, 1992.

Hirsch, Marianne. *Family, Frames: Photography, Narrative and Postmemory.* Cambridge, MA:Harvard University Press, 1997.

——. *The Generation of Postmemory: Writing and Visual Culture after the Holocaust.* New York: Columbia University Press, 2012.

Irving, Shalon M. and Kenneth F. Ferraro. 'Reports of Abusive Experiences during Childhood and Adult Health Ratings: Personal Control as a Pathway?' *Journal of Aging and Health* 18 (2006): 458-485.

LaCapra, Dominick. *Representing the Holocaust: History, Theory, Trauma.* Ithaca, NY: Cornell University Press, 1994.

——. *Writing History, Writing Trauma.* Baltimore: John Hopkins University Press, 2001.

Linley, Alex and Stephen Joseph. 'Positive Change following Trauma and Adversity: A Review.' *Journal of Traumatic Stress* 17 (2004): 11-21.

Nolen-Hoeksema, Susan. 'Ruminative Coping and Adjustment to Bereavement.' *Handbook of Bereavement Research: Consequences, Coping and Care*, edited by Margaret S. Stroebe, Robert O. Hansson, Wolfgang Stroebe, and Henk Schut. Washington, D.C.: American Psychological Association, 2001.

Schwab, Gabriele. *Haunting Legacies: Violent and Transgenerational Trauma.* New York: Columbia University Press, 2010.

Part I

The Individual Response

The Trick is to Keep Breathing: Female (Scottish) Trauma

Jessica Aliaga Lavrijsen

Abstract
In the late twentieth-century, Scottish trauma fiction becomes a field for exploring the forms of the novel and further analysing the complexity of consciousness, feelings, and identity construction – a quite problematic issue in Scotland. Besides, literal representations of the displaced experience and non-linear narratives are further explored, since the narration of a traumatised subject, who may suffer from gaps in memory, repetition compulsions, sense of fragmentation of the self, and other PTSD symptoms, requires a further exploring of narrative techniques by the writer. Among the many representations of traumatised characters in the fiction written in the last decades, we find Janice Galloway's novel, *The Trick is to Keep Breathing* (1989). The novel presents a homodiegetic female narrator who is suffering from a serious depression after the accidental death of her lover, and who desperately tries to find reasons to keep herself alive. Since the narrator-focaliser is a woman, the question of gender is very much present in the novel. The book uses different graphic modes of representation of the narrator's trauma, as there are incomplete sentences written in the margins of some pages, blank spaces, and columns splitting the narrative in two. Some of these experimental techniques ask readers to actively participate in the construction of the meanings of the texts, to enter a dialogue with the different voices presented (and hidden) in the texts, as they have to interpret/create these writerly texts, to use Barthes' term. They demand as well new identitarian reconfigurations in their bordering or liminality, which can be seen both in terms of nationality and of gender.

Key Words: Scottish fiction, trauma fiction, gender, nation, formal experimentation, identitarian reconfiguration.

*****

Sometimes, a collective trauma can conceal the expression of an additional and more particular and individual trauma, both in literature and in real life. This is especially the case when dealing with traumas affecting people who are less visible in a given society, such as children or women in a patriarchal community. This fact might lead us to the conclusion that there seems to be a hierarchy of trauma, a pecking order of suffering. A thorough questioning of how power relationships work inside 'trauma studies' and how trauma is represented in art becomes then an obligation. It seems to me that an over-generalizing approach to a text in which some kind of trauma is represented in might lead us to paying too much attention to the more general issues related to trauma – what was the original traumatic event? What were the consequences of it? How is it represented here? etc – and to ignoring the more specific and materialistic reality of individual trauma – Why is this character traumatised? What is specific about his or her trauma? How is it represented and contextualised? – which actually can be shared by many other individuals, and thus be individual and shareable or communal at the same time. Sometimes, when using a certain theory or theories which is broadly defined, such as trauma studies, we run the risk of attempting at extracting universal truths from precise traumatic experiences, which might lead us to a superficial reading of trauma, as the specific elements that can determine or influence the effects of a terrible event on a given individual, are over-looked. So, if not all human being react in the same way in the same circumstances, then, particularities are essential to understand the workings of trauma in more depth. My aim in this chapter is to see how a collective 'trauma' – the history of the Scottish nation from 1707 – can hide an individual trauma – the personal experience of a female Scottish character – because of the workings of the above-mentioned power relationships that are present in trauma studies and in life. Firstly, I will present a brief overview on what has been interpreted as the Scottish national trauma and on how historic and political circumstances have affected Scottish cultural identity. According to this pessimistic view that perceives the Scottish past as being traumatic, the artistic production in Scotland would be damned, as the creation of a healthy national culture is rendered impossible – 'Scotland [is] unrelatable, unnarratable.'[1] However, after the 1980s the nation's cultural spirit becomes more optimistic and self-assured, and trauma, as well as mental illnesses and other liminal states, become tropes for exploring narrative techniques and for further analysing the complexity of consciousness, feelings, and identity. It is in this context where we find Janice Galloway's first novel, *The Trick is to Keep Breathing*, which will be developed in the second section. In the third section, the focus moves onto more specific characteristics that have made Galloway a reference in women's writing in Scotland. This will serve me as a starting point to unveil the more particular elements, related to feminine problems and interests, which have been usually ignored by mainstream criticism. These issues reveal themselves as being both individual and communal, since they may affect a single person,in this particular case it is the novel's protagonist Joy who is traumatized, but they are also socially constructed as the roots of her identitarian struggles and her specific traumatic situation are in the larger social context.

1. Scottish (Collective) Trauma and the Nation

The illusion of national cohesion has been unattainable in Scotland, which has been 'doomed' to a permanent status of ethnic and linguistic fragmentation since the Union in 1707. The lack of historical and political cohesion of the many Scotlands of the past (and I would say, also of the present) made it almost impossible to construct a neat central unifying myth. Some critics have seen this lack of linguistic cohesion and political independence as the source of a national 'squizophrenia' or 'trauma' – that is, the emotional and cultural responses to the distressing events that were related to the move in 1707 of the centre of political dominance to London, from the imposed Highland Clearances during the 18th and 19th century, to the prohibition of the use of Scots in schools and other official institutions in 1761, when David Hume, Adam Smith, John Home and Allan Ramsay formed, 'The Society for Promoting the Reading and Speaking of the English Language' – that would have accompanied the Scots since the Union, when Scots language was relegated to the poetic imagination, and English became the language used for intellectual and institutional matters. Edwin Muir was among the thinkers of the Scottish Renaissance that lamented the 'wedge' they saw in Scottish culture between thought and feeling.[2] Muir believed that the Scots were in a sense estranged from themselves, since they were condemned to 'think in one language and feel in another': 'Scots has survived to our time as a language for simple poetry, and the simpler kind of short story. [...] [A]ll its other uses have lapsed, and it expresses therefore only a fragment of the Scottish mind.'[3] In keeping with his argumentation, Muir asserted that 'its very use is proof that the Scottish consciousness is divided,' and he termed this problematic issue as 'the Scottish predicament.'[4]

As Cairns Craig has stated, Scottish history could not work as the medium through which the nation could rediscover and redesign its identity, since Scottish history did no longer exist as such, it 'had ceased,' it had been obliterated.[5] This erasure has been said to have negative consequences for the cultural production in Scotland, which was then contemplated as a 'damaged land'. Some writers and critics such as T. S. Eliot argued that Scottish literature was an appendage to English Literature. As the poet argued in his 'Tradition and the Individual Talent', the significance of an individual work of art must reside in its place within an identifiable literary tradition, written, of course, in a single language, and not several – Gaelic, Scots and English in the case of Scotland. Consequently, he argued, Scotland could not be said to have a 'proper' tradition of its own. It is, thus, not difficult to deduce from this position that, since, according to Eliot, every great work has to be in contact with its tradition, no great work of art could be born in Scotland. This critical thinking lead later writers and critics, such as Edwin Muir, to continue this pessimistic and essentialist or monologic critical trend that condemned Scottish literature to non-existence. This view does not allow literary, linguistic and identitarian hybridism, even if Eliot's essay has been taken as one of the hallmarks of dialogism – the poet states: 'the past should be altered by the present as much as the present is directed by the past,'; but he seems to ignore the inevitable hybrid linguistic forms of the present, as well as the power relationships that operate in the construction of the literary canon.[6]

All the differing factors involved in the definition of Scotland deny the reality of national ideals. Between the end of the nineteenth century and the beginning of the twentieth, 'Scottishness' started to be re-defined against 'Englishness' and became 'England's alter ego.'[7] As Angus Calder has stated: 'We define ourselves by what we are not. We are not English,' so national identity was structured around an absence, that is, around this 'what we are not.'[8] Still, the fact remains that this vision of the Scottish past as being erased and of the Scottish national identity as being 'traumatic' has been very common. Sarah M. Dunnigan, for example, explicitly refers to the Scottish 'practice of forgetting or ignoring unresolved conflicts' and 'unacknowledged desires' as part of Scotland's 'traumatic past.'[9] In a sense, the definition of the Scottish past as 'traumatic' is adequate, as trauma breaks the experience of time and distorts or even erases a difficult past event, without the possibility of simply leaving it behind. As Cathy Caruth has put it, trauma is a 'wound of world', a split or break.[10] And this could be applied to national identity at that time, as Edwin Muir's above-mentioned statement suggest. Actually, the subject of trauma is so common in Scottish literature that Douglas Gifford has even stated that 'a predominant theme of current Scottish writing, [is] that of the emergence from a traumatised personal – and modern Scottish – past.' [11]

Moreover, liminal states of mind, such as schizophrenia, trauma and other altered psychological states have been one of the fields where writers could explore identity more profoundly. Furthermore, these transitional or liminal states where contrast and contradictions dwell are, according to Gregory Smith, essential to the Scottish literary mood. As he states:

> There is more in the Scottish antithesis of the real and the fantastic than is to be explained by the familiar rules of rhetoric. The sudden jostling of contraries seems to preclude any relationship by literary suggestion. The one invades the other without warning. They are the 'polar twins' of the Scottish Muse. [12]

This 'individual and alien' mood seems to have slipped into 'the plain tale of experience,' and the fluctuating world between the fantastic and the real finds its expression in the in-between.[13] Scottish fiction dwells thus in the in-between and it has also been characterised as focusing on social pessimism and personal trauma, because of the mentioned erasure or splitting of a coherent identity.

It is not necessary to explain that this trauma-linked perspective was quite pessimistic, and that it did not allow much space for the search of a Scottish voice, and that in fact it worked to prevent it. Nevertheless, Scottish fiction began in the closing decades of the century to move from bleakness and trauma to regeneration.[14] According to critics such as Douglas Gifford, Sarah Dunningham and Alan MacGillivray, Scottish writing became more optimistic and self-assured after the 1990s, when the moods and possibilities of the fiction had changed profoundly.

2. Contemporary Explorations of Scottish Trauma

The feeling of the 'Second Scottish Renaissance,' that is, the period starting in the decade of the 1980s, was more optimistic, and the earlier complaints about the lack of a homogenous language that seemed to doom Scottish literature started giving way to a much more positive perspective, where linguistic diversity was pictured as an ideal tool for the development of a plural and rich literature. In contemporary Scottish literature we no longer find Scots and English, but rather a variety of different voices unfolding and competing with each other in dialogic texts. Writers such as Iain Banks, Janice Galloway, Alasdair Gray, Jackie Kay, James Kelman, A. L. Kennedy, Brian McCabe, Ali Smith, Alan Warner, and Irvine Welsh, among others, show how rich and multiple Scottish literature can be. Aspects such as class, race and gender have come to the fore, and many different groups are set on the exploration of the representation of their own voices and languages from a non-nationalistic centred perspective.

Moreover, the (re-)opening of the Parliament in Edinburgh in 1998 demanded a imaginative future projection of a nation where the government has been located in London during the last three centuries. There is, however, a difficulty in this reconfiguring or reconstruction of the nation's imagination, as a homegeneous and settled tradition is not available, because of the above commented problem of dislocation. Therefore, it should not surprise us to see that identity continues to be a central interest in Scottish literature. Hence, the narratives of the fragile self are one of the central leitmotifs of much of contemporary Scottish fiction, and it has often been read as an examination of identity crisis. We can, for example, find plenty of works that present focalisers who are in a coma, as in Iain Bank's *The Bridge* or Irving Welsh's *Marabou Stork Nightmare*; who are drunk, as in Hugh MacDiarmid's classic poem 'A Drunk Man Looks at a Thistle' or Ron Butlin's novel *The Sound of my Voice*; under the effects of drugs, as in Irving Welsh's *Trainspotting*; and characters who are mad and suffer crises or nervous breakdowns, or who are terrified by something, whether real or not, as in Brian McCabe's short stories 'Conversation Area One', 'A Breakdown', 'The Lipstick Circus'. More specifically, we can also find many representations of liminal and traumatised characters in late twentieth-century Scottish fiction, as for example, Ian Banks' acclaimed novels *The Wasp Factory* (1984) and *Espedair Street* (1987), Alan Warner's *Morvern Callar*, A. L. Kennedy's *So I Am Glad* and *Everything You Need* and Janice Galloway's *The Trick is to Keep Breathing*.

In the light of these novels, it could be argued that in contemporary Scottish fiction, trauma is not so much a topic in itself, but rather a field for exploring the forms of the novel and further analyse the complexity of consciousness, feelings, and identity construction – a quite problematic issue in Scotland. Literal representations of the displaced experience and non-linear narratives are further explored, since the narration of a traumatised subject – who may suffer from gaps in memory, repetition compulsions, sense of fragmentation of the self, and other

PTSD symptoms – requires new narrative techniques. Use of flashbacks, repetitions and also of typographic experimentation are quite common in contemporary Scottish literature. And, as Craig has pointed out, there is a Scottish edge to this:

> For a culture whose whole experience since 1707 has been shaped by the medium of a learned written language which displaced its own oral cultures, and whose native languages were never properly standardized within the domain of type, typography becomes the symbol of its own culturally repressed condition: to overthrow the rule of type is synonymous with overthrowing the type of rule under which the culture has struggled for self-expression.[15]

The use of playful layout may be or not be linked to a nationalistic statement – this will depend on the work – , but it is undeniable that this special use of typography, in its deviation from the norm, demands from readers an active effort to re-enact the actions of writing/reading, as well as provides them the *jouissance* of *writerly* texts.[16]

3. Galloway and a Feminine Perspective on (National) Trauma

Janice Galloway's first novel, *The Trick is to Keep Breathing*, was shortlisted for both the Whitebread First Novel Award and the Irish Times International Fiction Prize, and won the Mind Book of the Year Award. The international impact of her work has led Margery Metzstein to describe her as a writer "'nurtured' in Scotland', who has however become 'important in the context of a wider history of women's writing, one which resists definition by mainstream culture.'[17]

The novel presents a homodiegetic female narrator who is suffering from a serious depression after the accidental death of her lover, a married husband who drowned in a swimming-pool whilst on holiday, and who desperately tries to find reasons to keep breathing, to keep herself alive. The novel adopts a first-person diary style stream of consciousness, which brings the reader into a closer relationship with the main character, Joy Stone. Throughout this narration, there are some analepses or retrogressions to the moment when her lover died: nineteen fragments written in italics haunt the narration, as uncanny intrusions. These fragments could be interpreted as mimicking the symptoms of Joy's emotional trauma, as traumas tend to be partially re-experienced through compulsive or uncontrollable repetitions of this frozen time. As Judith Herman explains: 'It is as if time stops at the moment of trauma.'[18]

The book uses different graphic modes to represent the narrator's trauma, as there are incomplete sentences written on the margins of some pages, blank spaces, and columns splitting the narrative in two. From Alasdair Gray to Irvine Welsh, many Scottish writers have used the appearance of the book page, including drawings, typography, and font, as an expressive means to convey those subsidiary narratives that are hidden in the main text. Some of the experimental techniques used by Galloway ask readers to actively participate in the construction of the meanings of the texts, to enter into a dialogue with the different voices presented, and hidden, in the texts, as they have to interpret/create these *scriptible* texts. They demand as well new identitarian reconfigurations in their bordering or liminality. As Bernand Sellin points out, Galloway 'is aware of her position as a female writer and especially shows interest for the most innovative techniques of presentation, techniques which become appropriate to render the sense of fragmentation and the difficulties of adjusting to the modern world.'[19]

The novel's emphasis on the relevance of the specific circumstances of Joy's experience demands both a subject centred reading and a more political one, that focuses on both individual and social matters. Here it could be argued that the Scottish interest in fiction dealing with traumas is mostly presented from a masculine point of view, involving traditionally Scottish and male issues such as visiting the pub, working in the pits or in factories, etc. In contrast, Galloway is more concerned with more traditionally feminine interests. As she explained in a recent interview: 'I'm interested in writing stories about problems which don't necessarily have answers, which is I think more of a female concern than a male one.'[20]

In this novel, Joy's trauma is not just an individual trauma, in the sense that it is also related to feelings of guilt and shame, which are socially oriented feelings. The narrator-character has suffered a big blow when her lover dies. However, it is not the event of his death that traumatises her, but rather, and as Dominic Head has stated, her condition of mistress and her effacement by social institutions, as the clergyman's speech at the funeral illustrates:

ESPECIALLY OUR LOVE
a split-second awareness that
something terrible was about to
about to
TO HIS WIFE AND FAMILY happen

Half-way into the silence for Norma Fisher, my arms were weightless.
The rest came piecemeal as the moral started to compute.[21]

Not being able to mourn and work through her traumatic experience, Joy falls into a severe depression. This inevitably reminds us of Kenneth Doka's concept of disenfranchised grief, that is a grief that has not been acknowledged by society, and that, consequently, might add an extra layer of stigmatization related to the incapability of mourning and, hence, of healing naturally.[22] Therefore, trauma, like grief, seems to be linked to socially constructed phenomena and processes. Joy's invisibility or absence in the public act of mourning is reflected in her own invisibility, in her physical deterioration and also in her mental weakening which even leads to dissociation. In the novel there are plenty of scenes where Joy does not recognise herself, such as in a scene that takes place in her bathroom, when she is taking a bath while observing herself from outside. As Stefanie Lehner has pointed out, this scene 'evoques Jacques Lacan's notion of the mirror stage' but ironically inverted, reflecting her *corps morcelé*:[23]

> It is difficult to pull the thing together, to see all the offering and not a jumble of different parts. [...] I smile at the woman in the mirror. Her eyes are huge. But what looks back is never what I want. Someone melting. And too much like me.

> She switches out the light and opens the door.[24]

It seems here that Joy's dissociation is related to her feeling of abjection, as can be seen in many other passages when she obsessively cleans her home or prepares herself for public appearance or male company, since society has rejected her in her role of illegitimate widow.

As the novel advances, readers get to know that she was mistreated by her sister Myra – 'I've been afraid of Myra ever since I remember. [...] She could have been my mother [...] Myra's baby died. I didn't. Maybe that was why she hit me so much' – , and the abuse by Tony, who fucks her without her consent, as she is more a lifeless robot than a person, does not contribute to her well-being. Besides, and as can be read on the pages where the rape is narrated – pages 174 and 175 – , as the reader puts together the fragmented and incomplete sentence written on the margins, – 'often we (ignore) the warni(ngs) (so) when the w(orst) hap(pens) we can on(ly) blame our(selves)' – we get to know that she blames herself for this. [25] In a sense, this marginalisation of her thoughts during this violent act could be read as abjection of her text, of her as a text. It is here where the typography of the novel, where the materiality of words, makes its highest statement: words are power, and, as such, they can also be used subversively, to give voice to certain silenced events that take place everyday.

In relation to this abjection we find a strong presence of elements related to physical perceptions and to the body in Joy's narration. But these reinforce her feeling of grotesque presence, as something unnatural that should be hidden, and her desire to be erased – she mentions suicide several times – , to be annihilated. It could be interpreted that her desire to be wiped out is in fact a re-enactment of a previous wiping out, when at the memorial service for Michael, she is completely ignored in favour of her lover's former wife: '[...] the stain was me. I didn't exist.

The miracle had wiped me out.'[26] According to Cathy Carruth, trauma 'is always the story of a wound that cries out, that addresses us in the attempt to tell us a reality or truth that is not otherwise available.'[27] Therefore, symptoms could be read as a narrative of the unsaid or unsayable.

Another possible symptom of this traumatic erasure could be Joy's refusal to eat. It is not by chance that she refuses to eat, as at a certain point she has an argument with her lover, whom she has been trying to satisfy by being the perfect housewife and an excellent cook, and he tells her that he doesn't need her for a thing, not even to eat. Some time later, she comes to the conclusion that she actually does not have to eat. Her anorexia should then be understood as a symptom of her desire to regain some control over her own body, over her own life. It could also be construed as a punishment, where food could be interpreted as a metaphor for the relationship or domesticity that failed to be satisfactory to her.

As the abovementioned passage suggests, Joy's body and the domestic are very closely related, as in many gothic stories. The house she used to share with her lover, Michael, is quite unhomely. The domestic sphere in *The Trick is to Keep Breathing* is seldom seen as a safe place. On the contrary, Joy's house seems to be a menacing place: in the past, with Michael, mushrooms threatened to destroy their love nest, as if reflecting the nature of their 'unclean' or illegitimate relation; later people such as the health visitor or her sister Myra erupt into her peacefulness; then Tony, her boss, forces her to have sex with him in her dormitory; and at a certain point Joy is even forced to leave her home in order to spend some time in a mental hospital. Besides, these uncanny places are always related to personal relations and social conventions. Homi Bhabha states that the 'unhomely moment relates the traumatic ambivalences of a personal, psychic history to the wider disjunctions of political existence.'[28] And, as Stefanie Lehner has pointed out, it is precisely this that indicates how the domestic is not a uniquely private space, but rather socially mediated and inscribed.[29] Hence the necessity of understanding Joy's particular story in a broader social context, and her traumatic symptoms as potentially universally readable.

Galloway's narrative, which mimics the mental state of psychological trauma, exploits the capacity of the novel to articulate individual identity with larger social systems. As Dominic Head states, 'Joy's dissolution represents an uncertainty about national belonging, and the textual materials that might compose it.'[30] The title of the novel, *The Trick is to Keep Breathing*, could indicate, thus, 'the textual trick that permits the breathing of life into a character, and the preservation of the sickly [sic.] national self' as has been stated.[31] But yet again, this statement, which might suggest that Joy's suffering is a metaphor for the national self, seems to take the Scottish 'sickness' of schizophrenia or its traumatic symptoms for granted, a tendency that reveals itself as an oversimplifying and misleading theory, since Scottish culture is not damaged at all, as the quality and quantity of Scottish contemporary works – widely translated – , shows.

If we understand that the novel emphasises the link between social systems and the domestic, then we might be inclined to interpret Joy's personal problems as the symptoms of a certain social (national) social discomfort. It must be bore in mind that this novel was published in 1989, the year that Margaret Thatcher left the government and Scotland had yet to live the cultural explosion and optimism of the 1990s. However, national issues should not hide from view gender issues, which in the case of Galloway's novels are revealed as essential concerns.

As commented above, Joy's mental and physical breakdown is related to the fact that she has no social space, position or role to grieve for her dead lover, Michael. She is not allowed to have any position in this particular social context: she is not a wife, she is not a beloved sister, as her fraternal relationship with Myra is based on fear and violence, she is no longer a dearly-loved daughter, as her parents are dead, she is not even a girlfriend or a respectable widow; instead, she is the mistress, the 'prostitute'. Logically, having become a 'misfit', a person without a place or healthy social relationships, she senses a loss of identity. Identity, as contemporary thinkers propose, is something dialogically constructed. It can no longer be understood as something monologic, fixed and isolated, as Cartesian thinking stated. The traditional monologic conception of identity, which follows a unitarian logic, understands the self as an individualistic, independent and self-contained exclusive entity, or, as Edward Sampson puts it, 'a kind of bounded container, separate from other similar bounded containers and in possession or ownerships of its own capacities and abilities.'[32] This conception does not allow for a positive view of Scottish identity, as it is necessarily founded on an implicit in-group *vs.* out-group distinction, often based on un equal relations: the dominant self or group *vs.* the submissive or excluded.[33] In contrast, a dialogic conception of the self implies that it the individual is constructed through a multiplicity of self-positions, that is, by means of his or her selves-in-action or selves-in-context, rather than as essential and self-contained individuals who can entertain dialogical relationships with each other. Since this dialogic understanding of identity recognises and stressed the social aspect of the individual self, the dialogic model demands a renewed focus on social interactions and also opens up possibilities of reconfiguring these power relations.

So, when Joy stops behaving 'properly', that is, adjusting to one of the restrictive feminine roles mentioned above and when she decides instead not to assume any stereotypically female role, she is considered to be ill, insane, by the rest of the community. Therefore, it could be argued that her illness or traumatic state is in a sense a symptom of her disengagement with strict societal norms that are based on the idea that an individual's identity should be static and selfcontained rather than negotiable and mutable: she cannot engage 'normally' – that is, following the norms set by the dominant group – , so she must be mad. Pursuing this line of argument, it would not be too farfetched to suggest that her 'trauma' is also the symptom of a social malfunctioning, especially regarding gender issues: it is not her fault that she is not allowed a proper space/role to assimilate her terrible experience and be comforted. Her hope in society has thus been shattered, and she will need others to establish a dialogic relationship with, to find her place in society, and to re-establish her faith. Only then, after she has positively renegotiated her identity, will Joy feel ready and strong to breathe. But of course this is not a task that should be accomplished by a single individual, as it is the community who has the strength to help her in the renegotiation of identity. By examining Joy's personal and intimate life, the reader is forced to examine what are the motives of her state of mind, and maybe, even, what could make her feel a bit better. Therefore, we could state that the problem of contemporary (Scottish) patriarchal society is here exposed through the deep scrutiny and questioning of the real motives of Joy's 'trauma' and her desire to disappear.

The power relations operating in the aftermath of potentially traumatic events, such as the death of a beloved person or family violence, should be scrutinized at all levels: at a national and political level, and also at the micro level of class, gender or sexual orientation, amongst others. There are some factors that might make some individuals more inclined to be affected by a traumatic event, since they might be less protected or recognised by their societies. It is important thus to examine trauma narratives and analyse which structures are operating in them, focusing of course on the social and communal context, but without ignoring the more personal stories of the people who might suffer without being heard.

In conclusion, and as has become evident by now, trauma reveals itself as a social issue, which is very much related to social conventions, taboos, silences and power. Therefore, an ethical approach towards these traumatic texts is required, taking into account that there is no such thing as a hierarchy of suffering, and that national and individual traumas are intrinsically related.

Notes

[1] Cairns Craig, *The Modern Scottish Novel: Narrative and the National Imagination* (Edinburgh: Edinburgh University Press, 1990), 21.
[2] As Muir stated in his poem 'Scotland 1941', the Scots were a sham nation narrated by sham writers: 'Now smoke and dearth and money everywhere; / Mean heirlooms of each fainter generation, / And mummied housegods in their musty nichs, / Burns and Scott, sham bards of a sham nation.'
[3] Edwin Muir, *Scott and Scotland: The Predicament of the Scottish Writer* (London: Routledge and Sons, 1936), 97.
[4] Ibid., 8
[5] Craig, *The Modern Scottish Novel*, 21.
[6] T. S. Eliot, 'Tradition and the Individual Talent', in *The Sacred Wood* (1920) Accessed August 15, 2012.

http://www.bartleby.com/200/sw4.html/

[7] Carla Sassi, *Why Scottish Literature Matters* (Edinburgh: The Saltire Society, 2005), 31.

[8] Angus Calder, 'By the Water of the Leith I Sat Down and Wept: Reflections on Scottish Identity', in *New Scottish Writing. VII*, ed. Harry Ritchie (London: Bloomsbury, 1996), 236.

[9] Sarah M. Dunnigan, 'The Return of the Repressed', in *Beyond Scotland. New Contexts for Twentieth-Century Scottish Literature*, ed. Gerard Carruthers, David Goldie and Alastair Reufrew (Amsterdam: Rodopi, 2004), 114.

[10] Cathy Caruth, *Unclaimed Experience: Trauma, Narrative, and History* (Baltimore and London: The Johns Hopkins University Press, 1996), 3.

[11] Ibid., 961.

[12] Gregory Smith, *Scottish Literature, Character and Influence* (London: MacMillan, 1919), 20.

[13] Douglas Gifford, Sarah Dunningham, and Alan MacGillivray, *Scottish Literature in English and Scots* (Edinburgh: Edinburgh University Press, 2002), 933.

[14] Ibid., 960.

[15] Craig, *The Modern Scottish Novel*.

[16] Roland Barthes, *The Pleasure of the Text*, trans. Richard Miller (New York: Hing and Wang, 1975 [1973]).

[17] Margery Metzstein, 'Of Myths and Men: Aspects of Gender in the Fiction of Janice Galloway', in *The Scottish Novel since the Seventies: New Visions, Old Dreams*, ed. Gavin Wallace and Randall Stevenson (Edinburgh: Edinburgh University Press, 1993), 136.

[18] Judith Herman, *Trauma and Recovery: From Domestic Abuse to Political Terror* (London: Pandora, 2001), 37.

[19] Bernard Sellin, 'Varieties of Voice and Changing Contexts: Robin Jenkins and Janice Galloway', *The Edinburgh History of Scottish Literature. Volume 3, Modern Transformations: New Identities (From 1918)*, ed. Ian Brown, Thomas Owen Clancy, Susan Manning, and Murray Pittock (Edinburgh: Edinburgh University Press, 2007), 234.

[20] Ruth Thomas, 'Janice Galloway Interview', *Textualities*, Accessed 17 September 2011, http://textualities.net/ruth-thomas/janice-galloway-interview/

[21] Janice Galloway, *The Trick is to Keep Breathing* (London: Vintage, 1999 [1989]), 79.

[22] Kenneth J. Doka, *Disenfranchised Grief: Recognising Hidden Sorrow* (Lexington: Lexington Books, 1989).

[23] Stefanie Lehner, *Subaltern Ethics in Contemporary Scottish and Irish Literature: Tracing Counter-Histories* (New York: Palgrave MacMillan, 2011), 137.

[24] Galloway, *The Trick is to Keep Breathing*, 79.

[25] Ibid., 59.

[26] Ibid., 79.

[27] Caruth, *Unclaimed Experience*, 4.

[28] Homi Bhabha, 'The Home and the World', in *Dangerous Liaisons: Gender, Nation, and Postcolonial Perspectives*, ed. McClintock et al. (Minnesota: University of Minnesota Press, 1997), 448.

[29] Lehner, *Subaltern Ethics in Contemporary Scottish and Irish Literature*, 125.

[30] Dominic Head, *Modern British Fiction, 1950-2000* (Cambridge: Cambridge University Press, 2002), 150.

[31] Ibid., 150.

[32] Edward Samson, *Celebrating the Other: A Dialogic Account of Human Nature* (New York: Harvester Wheatsheaf ,1993), 31.

[33] Ibid., 73.

Bibliography

Barthes, Roland. *The Pleasure of the Text*. Translated by Richard Miller. New York: Hing and Wang, 1975 (1973).

Bhabha, Homi. 'The Home and the World'. In *Dangerous Liaisons: Gender, Nation, and Postcolonial Perspectives*, edited by McClintock et al., 445-455. Minnesota: University of Minnesota Press, 1997.

Brown, Ian and Alan Riach eds. *The Edinburgh Companion to Twentieth-Century Scottish Literature*. Edinburgh: Edinburgh University Press, 2009.

Calder, Angus. 'By the Water of the Leith I Sat Down and Wept: Reflections on Scottish Identity'. In *New Scottish Writing. VII*, edited by Harry Ritchie, 218-238. London: Bloomsbury, 1996.

Caruth, Cathy. *Unclaimed Experience: Trauma, Narrative, and History*. Baltimore: Johns Hopkins University Press, 1996.

Carruthers, Gerard. *Scottish Literature*. Edinburgh: Edinburgh University Press, 2009.

Craig, Cairns. *The Modern Scottish Novel: Narrative and the National Imagination.* Edinburgh: Edinburgh University Press, 1990.

Doka, Kenneth J. ed. *Disenfranchised Grief: Recognising Hidden Sorrow.* Lexington: Lexington Books, 1989.

Eliot, T. S.. 'Tradition and the Individual Talent.' *The Sacred Wood: Essays on Poetry and Criticism.* Accessed 15 August 2012. http://www.bartleby.com/200/sw4.html.

Galloway, Janice. *The Trick is to Keep Breathing.* London: Vintage, 1999 (1989).

Goldie, David and Alastair Reufrew, eds. *Beyond Scotland: New Contexts for Twentieth-Century Scottish Literature.* Amsterdam: Rodopi, 2004.

Head, Dominic. *Modern British Fiction, 1950-2000.* Cambridge: Cambridge University Press, 2002.

Herman, Judith. *Trauma and Recovery: From Domestic Abuse to Political Terror.* London: Pandora, 2001.

Lehner, Stefanie. *Subaltern Ethics in Contemporary Scottish and Irish Literature: Tracing Counter Histories.* New York: Palgrave MacMillan, 2011.

Metzstein, Margery. 'Of Myths and Men: Aspects of Gender in the Fiction of Janice Galloway'. *The Scottish Novel Since the Seventies: New Visions, Old Dreams*, edited by Gavin Wallace and Randall Stevenson. Edinburgh: Edinburgh University Press, 1993.

Muir, Edwin. *Scott and Scotland: The Predicament of the Scottish Writer.* London: Routledge and Sons, 1936.

Samson, Edward. *Celebrating the Other: A Dialogic Account of Human Nature.* New York: Harvester Wheatsheaf, 1993.

Sassi, Carla. *Why Scottish Literature Matters.* Edinburgh: The Saltire Society, 2005.

Sellin, Bernand. 'Varieties of Voice and Changing Contexts: Robin Jenkins and Janice Galloway'. *The Edinburgh History of Scottish Literature. Volume 3, Modern Transformations: New Identities (From 1918)*, edited by Ian Brown, Thomas Owen Clancy, Susan Manning, and Murray Pittock, 231-236. Edinburgh: Edinburgh University Press. 2007.

Smith, Gregory G. *Scottish Literature, Character and Influence*. London: MacMillan, 1919.

Thomas, Ruth. 'Janice Galloway Interview'. *Textualities*. Accessed 17 September 2011. http://textualities.net/ruth-thomas/janice-gallowayinterview/.

Wallace, Gavin and Randall Stevenson. *The Scottish Novel ince the Seventies*. Edinburgh: Edinburgh University Press, 2005 (1993).

Watson, Roderick. *The Literature of Scotland: The Twentieth Century*. New York: Palgrave MacMillan, 2007 (1984).

Jessica Aliaga Lavrijsen is Lecturer at the Centro Universitario de la Defensa (Zaragoza, Spain). Her research is mainly focused on Scottish contemporary fiction, and she is a research member in the competitive group 'Narrativa contemporánea en lengua inglesa,' and is currently working on the project 'Ética y trauma en la ficción contemporánea en lengua inglesa' (HUM2007-61035/FILO. Projecto Eje C-Consolider).

'I've been Twelve for a Very Long Time': Trauma, Reparation and Continuance in *Let Me In* by Matt Reeves

Simon Bacon

Abstract

This chapter looks at how certain cinematic representations of the vampire in contemporary popular culture can be seen to correspond to ideas around bodily and psychological responses to individual trauma. In particular, this is configured in the notion of trauma being an event that, through its extreme nature, excludes itself from our everyday memory and experience. However, its unclaimability subsequently causes it to be projected outside of the body, not just onto or into another object but by becoming an actual physical manifestation. Once achieving an external embodiment it then repeats the events that first created it in an attempt to re-claim or remember those original actions. Consequently, there is a symbiotic relationship between the vampire, as a projection, and the person whose trauma it embodies. In *Let Me In*[1] we see this in the relationship between the young boy, Owen, and the vampire Abby who is effectively brought forth by the traumatic events that are happening to him.[2] Once they are together, Abby can then be seen to enact and repeat the violence, both physical and psychological, that is inflicted upon Owen, and which he cannot contain within himself. However, although Abby is aware of her link to Owen and the violence she repeats upon his behalf, she also knows that to stop this re-enact of the original traumatic events that created her would also mean her own dissolution and death. As such, to grow old and re-enter experience, the vampire needs to re-integrate with Owen, which in itself would allow him to re-claim the traumatic events that first created her. Reeves, though, purposely creates a tension between Abby's need for reparation and individual continuance to show the levels of entanglement between memory and identity and self and the lives of others.

Key Words: Trauma, vampire, immortal child, allegory, reparation, Freud, violence, Object Relations.

*****

1. Beginnings

> I am a mirror. When people look at me they see themselves. It is not necessarily a part of themselves that they want to recognise, but it is there.[3]

This chapter will consider the idea that the vampire, at least in certain cinematic representations, can be seen as the physical manifestation of trauma that is a psychic excess made flesh. To do this, it will be necessary to briefly example the various psychoanalytical interpretations of the vampire and the ways that it is fundamentally linked to ideas around an emotional excess that cannot be contained within the self. Consequently, the psyche has to find ways to distance itself from these excessive feelings and so projects them out into the world. It will be argued that the vampire, in certain narratives, can then be seen to be not just the physical manifestation of such a process of projection, but one that is autonomous from the individual psyche that creates it, or brings it forth. Further, this idea of emotional uncontainability can then be linked to another psychically excessive state, that of trauma or the traumatic event. Often described as an event that ruptures our experience of time and our place within the normal flow of memory, it too has a 'life' beyond the control of the subject that cannot contain the emotional excess created during and after the original traumatic event. Just how these processes of excess, trauma and projection come together in the body of the vampire is a fundamental part of the narrative of Matt Reeves' 2010 film *Let Me In*. This features a young human protagonist, Owen, whose own experiences of emotional excess cause him to bring forth a vampire, Abby. Abby, then, manifests the traumatic excess that Owen feels and consequently re-enacts, or repeats, the original traumatic violence that created her. However, it should be noted, that just because Abby embodies the excess that Owen cannot contain, how has no more control over her than he did of the original trauma that created her.

It should also be noted that the narrative of *Let Me In* is strongly related to its more well-known source material, the novel *Let the Right One In* by John Ajvide Lindqvist and the subsequent film of the same name by Tomas Alfredson. However, and as this chapter will show, Reeves' film positions itself as a completely separate and more realistic story in comparison to the earlier dreamlike Swedish narratives which produces a very different relationship between the main protagonist and the vampire. It is the nature of this difference and its dependence upon the continuation of excess and violence that underpins the importance of Reeves' film. Abby, the vampire, is a creature created in and from violence. To deny this violence and return herself to the normative flow of time and memory, that is to allow Owen to 're-claim' his memory of the events that created her, would cause her total destruction and death; but her continued existence means the continuation of the violence from which she was born. This then forms the core of entanglement that beats at the heart of this chapter.

The vampire, whether in popular culture or even psychoanalytic parlance, is a figure of excess. An excess that not only makes it more than human but also the receptacle for all that humanity cannot contain, or accept, of itself. The 'beyond' or even 'super' human qualities of the vampire then can be seen to be manifestations of all those things which normative society deem as transgressive or abject; a defilement or danger that society must necessarily expel from itself. Mary Douglas in *Purity and Danger* and Julia Kristeva in *The Powers of Horror* describe this process, and in particular the correlation between social and individual bodies.[4] As Douglas observes:

> We cannot possibly interpret rituals concerning excreta, breast milk, saliva and the rest unless we are prepared to see in the body a symbol of society, and to see the powers and dangers credited to social structure reproduced in small on the human body.[5]

The vampire here, then, becomes the perfect receptacle of collective and bodily transgression, a figure that embodies the anxiety between individual desire and societal restriction. In a somewhat simple psychoanalytical interpretation, and one initially stated in Sigmund Freud's 1920 essay, *Beyond the Pleasure Principle*, we can say that the vampire is created in the tension between the id, as our individual instinctual desires, and the superego, as the moralistic codes imposed by society. Such a reading is seen in Bram Dijkstra's writing of the fin-de-siecle, where he describes the cultural construction of the female vampire at the end of the 19th century thus:

> ...a polyandrous predator indiscriminately lusting after man's seminal essence...the insatiable soil into whose bottomless crevasses man must poor the essence of his intellect in payment for her lewd enticements...[a] bestial woman.[6]

A similar excess is bestowed upon the male vampire by Montague Summers in his rather florid writings at the beginning of the 20th century:

> Throughout the whole vast shadowy world of ghosts and demons there is no figure so terrible, no figure so dreaded and abhorred, yet dight with such fearful fascination as the vampire, who is himself neither ghost nor demon, but yet who partakes the dark natures and possesses the mysterious and terrible qualities of both.[7]

Psychoanalyst, Ernest Jones, in *On the Nightmare*, written halfway through the 20th century, comments on the 'over determination' of the vampire and that the belief in them 'yields plain indications of most kinds of sexual perversions.'[8] Similarly, he sees that their appearance in our dreams 'has two deep sources both of which originate in childhood...the first...is derived from love, the second from hate.'[9] This then sees the vampire as not just a sexually transgressive figure but an emotionally excessive one, subsequently linking it to ideas around Lacanian jouissance, the irrepressible froth of energy and desire that collects around our inability to grasp or contain the 'Real' within ourselves. As Fiona Peters points out in her article

'Vampire, the Symbolic and the Thing,' the vampire, as a mirror image of humanity, is not just representative of this desire towards the lack, or *objet a*, that humans cannot contain but actually *are* that desire made real. She observes:

> Vampires... don't *desire* in the same way that Lacan theorises this notion, as the endless quest to capture this elusive excess [*objet a*]; they *are* an example of this elusive excess, an *objet a*, a site of fantasy.[10]

Consequently, the vampire can be seen as the embodiment of this inability to contain desire, or an excess so great that it has to be projected out of the body, and not just onto another object as in Kleinian Object Relations, but actually becomes a separate physical embodiment of excess. [11] The excess and over-determination of the vampire then becomes the uncanny double of that which the body of the individual, or society, cannot contain. As Joan Copjec describes it:

> [the] vampiric double is not only a creature with 'too much' body, it is also a 'body too much,' that is, as a double of the subject, it always stands in the way of or crowds out the subject's own actions.[12]

The vampire than becomes a part of ourselves that we not only will not recognise, as seen in the quote from Timmy Valentine, the prepubescent vampire from *Vampire Junction* at the start of this section, but something that we cannot contain.[13] This is largely seen as a sexual excess in many, often Freudian interpretations, of which Jones is an example, but it also speaks of an emotional excess that the body can no longer control or lay claim too. As such, and as this chapter will argue, the vampire can then become the physical manifestation of another psychological, or experiential excess that the body cannot contain, that of the traumatic event. Roger Luckhurst describes such an event as follows: 'a traumatic event is one that exceeds the ability of the mind to assimilate it within the parameters of normal mental functioning.'[14] Trauma, or the traumatic event, is something then, that exceeds the capabilities of the mind, or psyche, to contain; placing it outside or beyond the integrity of the normative body. This can be seen to be part projection and part phantasy where the excess is not put onto another object but actually becomes an entity in its own right which then acts both in connection to but also autonomously from, the person from which it emanates.

This is a point picked up by Cathy Caruth in her book, *Unclaimed Experience*, where she quotes Freud from *Beyond the Pleasure Principle*, where he also writes about such extreme events which affect the individual, and 'which seem to be entirely outside their wish or control.'[15] This idea of excessive events being too much to be contained by the body, and subsequently open for a linkage to ideas of projection, is particularly strong in relation to the configurations of trauma as posited by Cathy Caruth. Here the experience of the traumatic event 'leaves' or is 'missing' from consciousness and consequently removes it from our experience both of ourselves and of time.[16] It quite literally holds the event beyond or outside of time. This then begins to create the framework for looking at the film *Let Me In* by Matt Reeves where the vampire can be seen to be directly related to traumatic events that happen to its young male protagonist, being both the dark reflection of the psychologically uncontainable desires and emotions but also the actual physical manifestation of them. This sees the vampire not just as an 'empowered alter-ego' as Jeffrey Weinstock describes it but rather a more transubstantiative act of trauma made flesh.[17] Not surprisingly, in terms of the film, this has serious consequence for the vampire, Abby, herself. Firstly, it ties her completely to the human from which she 'originates,' in this case the young male protagonist, Owen, but, more importantly, her continued existence is intimately tied to the act of trauma itself.[18] She only remains alive through constant repetition of the violent event that first created her and it is the traumatic nature of it that removes her from both Owen's experience and the passage of time. If this is no longer the case then she re-enters the flow of time, or 'history,' as Caruth calls it, and consequently would no longer exist. Psychoanalytically, this would be seen as a good thing, as it would not only signal reparation between the 'good' and 'bad' parts of the self but also the re-integration of previously 'unclaimed' experience.[19] However, it would also signal the end of the excess that gave autonomy to the projected 'bad' object and the *need* for the vampire would no longer be sufficient to give it life beyond the body or individual memory.[20] To see just how Reeves resolves this dilemma, or whether he does not, it is time to consider the film in more depth.

2. Letting the Vampire In

> Abby: [*touching Owen's bandaged cheek*] What happened there?
> Owen: Some kids from school.
> Abby: I'll help you.
> Owen: But you're a girl.
> Abby: I'm a lot stronger than you think I am.[21]

Let Me In begins not with the vampire but with Owen the 12 year-old-boy. On the cusp of adolescence, events in his life seem to have literally caught him in time. His parents are divorced and he lives with his mother. Neither of his parents, or any other adults for that matter, play any significant part in his life, and he appears locked in a cycle of recurring violence inflicted upon him by a group of bullies at school. He has little authority over his life and even his own body would seem to be beyond his control as he regularly wets himself when confronted by his abusers at school. The traumatic events that recur over and over again would seem to be on the point of overwhelming him when the vampire arrives; it is almost as if the trauma that is engulfing his life has brought the creature to him. Oddly enough, this is not unusual in vampire films and earlier movies such as *Fright Night* by Tom Holland, *Once Bitten* by Howard Storm from 1985 and *Near Dark* by Kathryn Bigelow from 1987 all show the vampire as being brought forward by the angst of the stories young male protagonist. As I have written elsewhere, in these films 'the vampire is not trying to destroy the adolescent hero but is in fact a manifestation brought into existence by him, a product of his psyche.'[22] The vampire than acts as a form of the survival instinct and this connection is seen particularly strongly within Reeves' film, as the vampire appears almost immediately after we see Owen acting out a somewhat sadistic revenge scene in front of a mirror in his bedroom. Semi-naked and wearing a partially transparent mask, which makes him look like he has severe facial burns, he repeatedly jabs the air with a knife, imagining himself stabbing his tormentors from school. It is only after this scene that we see the car arriving, bring the vampire to the block of flats that Owen and his mother live in.

It is worth remembering at this point that Reeves' film is based on an earlier film *Let the Right One In* by Tomas Alfredson from 2008, which itself was based upon an earlier book of the same name by John Ajvide Lindqvist from 2004. All share similar scenes and settings, not least in this opening phase of the narrative. However, *Let Me In* is specifically constructed by Reeves as a separate story which is not connected to the back story or plots of either Lindqvist's or Alfredson's narratives. Also, and more importantly, Alfredson's film, for which Lindqvist also helped write the screenplay, creates a very dreamlike quality throughout. Although the spaces and scenes within Alfredson's film are sparse, or what J. M. Tyree typifies as 'dirty realism... which relies on austerity and a stripped-down language of visual information drawn from ordinary life,' it is a vision of the ordinary turned into the phatasmorgorical.[23] As Tyree goes on to observe: 'It's a banality that gradually turns eerie' but, more than this, it creates an otherworldliness; it maybe a vision or reality, but it a reality in an alternate universe to our own.[24] In contrast, *Let Me In* is set in a very familiar and worldly vision of small town America. Owen too is less dreamlike than Oskar, and is much more the prepubescent boy on the verge of adulthood, as seen in his spying on his next door neighbours' sexual exploits.[25] Consequently, the meaning of the characters and their relationships within Reeves' film is very different to that established within the earlier Swedish narratives. So although the entrance of the vampire in *Let the Right One In* is equally constructed around the young male protagonist's violent outbursts, Reeves' film makes the relationship between Owen and the vampire a far more sinister and symbiotic one. Here Abby is truly a dark double of Owen, a physical and autonomous manifestation of his traumatic and violent excess. Such an idea is not so strange, as Jones observes there are 'beliefs in which the vampire-like spirit emanates not from a dead but from a still living person.'[26] And although Abby would seem to have a story before her meeting with Owen, within the world of the film, their union is one that is configured as totally dependent upon each other.[27] This we see in the way that they seem inevitably drawn together, particularly in the playground area outside the building where Owen and Abby live. Although on their first meeting Abby makes a point of saying, 'Just so you know, I can't be your friend,' they continue to meet there.[28]

What we see of Owen in the film describes him as very disturbed young boy. His parents are separated and take little notice of him. He seems to have few, if any, friends and is only noticed by the bullies that relentlessly pick on him. This distance and separation from the world around him, possibly due to the traumatic events happening to him, is shown in the scenes where Owen spies on his neighbours through a telescope, showing that he can only touch or interact with other people from a distance. Unfortunately for Owen, when the bullies, Kenny, Mark and Donald, do notice him, it is only to intimidate and physically and verbally abuse him. After one such meeting we see Owen urinate on himself and more often than not this is accompanied by the bullies, Kenny in particular, calling him a 'little girl.' This in itself is quite interesting in that it carries on the theme of Owen being emasculated by the bullies – not being able to 'stand up for himself' like a man would and being called a 'little girl' which positions him outside the normal categorisations of identity and sexual development, which is of particular importance during the emotional tumult of adolescence.

This aligns him more strongly with the vampire Abby, when she arrives, than with the 'normal' humans around him.[29] As such, Owen is suffering not just from the trauma of his parents' separation but also the bullying he receives at school. Taken together, these events produce an emotional excess that Owen cannot contain. Again the scene where he wears the mask whilst acting out revenge upon his abusers is instructive. In wearing the mask whilst stabbing his imagined attackers, Owen shows that he cannot accept within himself the violent acts that he wishes to commit, and so he must pretend to be someone else to be able to do it. This, then, identifies a first step in the splitting of Owen's psyche into what Klein would identify as, 'good' and 'bad' parts. The fantasy that Owen is enacting whilst wearing the mask reveals the excessive nature of the emotions that he cannot contain and that are consequently spilling out of, or being projected beyond, his own body. It is no surprise then that it is at this moment that Owen's fantasy, or Kleinian phantasy, undergoes 'concretization' and becomes fully realised in the figure of the vampire that is arriving in the car outside his bedroom window.[30] The meeting between them is inevitable, and again re-iterates the difference between Alfredson's film and *Let Me In*.

In *Let the Right One In* Oskar is blond and very pale, almost ghost-like, whilst Eli, the vampire, is dark, making them alike but opposites. In Reeves' film Owen and Abby have dark hair and light skin; they are reflections of each other and parts of the same person. This is further seen in that they are both trapped at the same age in time. Owen is 12 years old and just on the verge, symbolically that is, of becoming a man, his growing sexualisation revealed in his spying on the sexual activities of his neighbours. However, as mentioned earlier, the bullying and emasculation he receives at school is preventing this process of maturation, effectively locking him in time. Similarly, Abby is locked in time at that exact age as well. We see this early on in the film when Owen questions her about her birthday:

> Owen: When is your birthday?
> Abby: I don't know.
> Owen: You don't celebrate your birthday? Don't get birthday presents?...
> Owen: But how old are you, really?
> Abby: Twelve. But... I've been twelve for a very long time.[31]

Inevitably though, because Abby is the bad excess that Owen cannot contain, it is not long before she is counselling Owen to violent acts. After one incident when they cut Owen's face using a branch as a small whip, the vampire cajoles the boy to fight back:

> Abby: You have to hit back.
> Owen: I can't. There's 3 of them.
> Abby: Then you hit back even harder.[32]

This re-enactment of violence and also the violence that brought forth the vampire in the first place relates directly to Caruth's explanation of trauma and repetition:

> The repetition of the traumatic event – which remains unavailable to consciousness but intrude repeatedly on sight – thus suggest a larger relation to the event that extends beyond what can simply be seen or what can be known, and is inextricably tied up with the belatedness and incomprehensibility that remain at the heart of this repetitive seeing.[33]

Caruth's observation quite usefully ties together the original traumatic event to its later re-enactments and also the way that the vampire, because it manifests an experience that remains incomprehensible, is seen as something other to the subject from which it is projected.

Of equal interest within the film is the need for the vampire itself to enact violence. Not unlike most other vampire narratives, Abby's continued existence is predicated on the need for blood. Again, like many other vampire narratives, within *Let Me In* this is not given up lightly but is forcibly removed. Although the film opens with Abby having to rely on someone else to do this for her, she has a Renfield-like assistant in the character known as the 'Father,'[34] it is not long after meeting Owen that she begins undertaking violent acts on her own behalf.[35] This again indicates the entangled nature of their relationship for although Abby would seem to have had an existence before her meeting with Owen, it was of a different order than it has now subsequently become. As such, the particular Abby we see in *Let Me In* is purely that which was brought forth by Owen. However, it is equally true that the Owen we see in the film is that which was brought forth by Abby. This is a more involved idea to explain and revolves around one particular point in the film, which is consequently worth examining in a little more detail.

3. 'The Choice is Made'[36]

> Hi Owen,
> Good morning. I am in the bathroom.
> Please do not come in.
> Want to hang out with me again tonight?
> I really like you.
> Love Abby[37]

The words above are those on a note that Owen finds in Abby's flat after he has spent the night sleeping on the floor there. In many ways it is a note that he has written to himself, as Abby is very much the unrecognised part of himself which he cannot contain – a message from a forgotten memory. As indicated in the note, although they are in the same flat together and Owen can 'hear' Abby's voice, through the written word, he cannot see her, for she is a thing of the darkness. Like many vampires in popular narratives since Bram Stoker's *Dracula* Abby cannot allow herself to be exposed to daylight or she will be destroyed by it, a point made earlier in the film when a victim of her bite combusts in sunlight.[38] This subsequently constructs the vampire, not just as a nightmare, in that it appears only at night, or the sleeping hours, but also as a disembodied voice, or ghost. In this way the vampire begins to embody a form of what Dominic LaCapra sees as 'hauntology.'[39] He goes on to further describe this effect in terms of the past and the kind of 'uncontainable' memory that was mentioned earlier:

> In more metaphoric terms, one might suggest that the ghosts of the past – symptomatic revenants who have not been laid to rest because of a disturbance in the symbolic order, a deficit in the ritual process, or a death so extreme in its unjustifiability or transgressiveness that in certain ways it exceeds existing modes... of mourning – roam the post-traumatic world and are not entirely 'owned' as 'one's own'... If they haunt a house (a nation or

group), they come to disturb all who live – perhaps even pass through – that house.[40]

What is important here are the ideas of the excessive nature of a past that comes back to haunt the present, but it is a haunting that one does not recognise as one's own. In this configuration of LaCapra Owen then becomes the house, or psychic home, from which the ghost has been expelled, but which it then comes back to haunt, and all those that come into contact, or pass through, that home. What is interesting as the scene develops is that Owen does not exorcise himself of the ghost or 'owns' it but in fact becomes 'owned' by the ghost, in that he becomes controlled by the events that he is not able to contain but without reintegrating them back into his psyche. This idea of the ghost and the ghost house repeats within the film.

Possibly its most striking appearance is at the very end of the story where we see Owen sitting on a train with a large box in front of him. We see him scratching and tapping on the surface of the container, supposedly communicating with Abby, who we are lead to believe, is inside the box. However, what we actually see is something akin to a medium contacting the dead via a ouija board. The Morse code that Owen uses is repeated by an unseen hand; an undead and unseen presence from the other side that impinges upon everyday reality.

Similarly, this notion of the ghost house is shown in the scene in Abby's apartment as we see Owen sleepily wondering around her flat. The interior of the flat is dark and mysterious and somewhat dreamlike, almost as though Owen and Abby are somehow two differing parts of his identity that are living inside the space of his own psyche. This sees the space of the flat in a similar way to Carl Jung's idea of the oneric house where each floor of a house represents different levels of the psyche from our conscious mind in the upper levels to the 'lower' subconscious ones in the cellar. French theorist, Gaston Bachelard, sees this metaphorical mapping of the human mind onto the framework of a house as a 'topography of our intimate being.'[41] This somewhat intimate scene then represents something of an act of recognition between the two parts of Owen's split identity, bringing about the kind of reparation that Klein and others see as necessary to healing the mind; a reintegration of the traumatic event into the flow of memory and consciousness. This does not preclude a certain level of ambivalence within this configuration, for whilst presenting a space for the divided parts of the self to co-exist it does not necessarily mean that they come together as an integrated whole.

Interestingly, Caruth, at the end of *Unclaimed Experience*, describes such an act as 'the imperative of awakening' which is exactly what does not happen in the film. [42] Suddenly, there is a loud knock and we see the Policeman standing outside the door of the flat. This again is one of the fundamental changes that Reeves makes in his narrative to distance it from the earlier Swedish versions. In

Lindqvist's book and Alfredson's film there is no policeman, but Jocke, a friend of the vampire's first victim who tries to track down the person who murdered his associate. Here, in Reeves' film, we have a figure who is only known by the title Policeman and who consequently comes to represent truth within the film. With no connections to any of the characters portrayed, his sole purpose is to provide justice to those who have been murdered and track down who did it: in many ways he is an idealised archetypal figure who represents societal rule, individual morality and truth. In the film Owen backs away from the door but the Policeman breaks down the door and enters the flat, almost literally smashing into the space of Owen's psyche. Unable to see his way around the interior because of paper that has been stuck to the windows to keep out the light, the Policeman begins to tear pieces away letting bursts of sunlight enter the flat. He eventually comes to the bathroom within which we know Abby is sleeping. Within the oneric house of Owen's mind this constitutes the deepest, darkest part, and the violence and trauma that Abby represents is hidden under blankets in a bath tub at its very core. The Policeman begins to uncover Abby, just as he tears pieces of card away from the window above the bath tub. A ray of light hits Abby's skin and it immediately burns and cracks. As if scalded himself, Owen suddenly screams out 'No! No! Stop!'[43] Distracted by this the Policeman stops and turns towards the boy, allowing Abby to leap from the bath and sink her teeth into the Policeman's neck. Owen slowly backs out of the room to the noise of Abby tearing the Policeman apart. This represents, quite literally, the dying of the light in Owen's mind. The justice that is represented by the Policemen, and that is allowing the light of morality and truth enter Owen's mind, is too much and the boy's excessive, dark impulses are unleashed upon them and consumes them. This pact between his good and bad parts, or rather the fact that he has allowed himself to be possessed by the trauma and violence represented by Abby, is shown as the scene reaches its climax. The Policeman, laying in a pool of his own blood, reaches out an imploring hand to Owen. Again we do not see Abby but hear the disembodied sounds of her biting the Policeman. Owen slowly advances towards the Policeman's outstretched hand but rather than holding on to it and pulling him to safety, he closes the door leaving him to be eaten by the all-consuming ghost of the boy's traumatic excess. It is important to note here that whilst all the characters are 'real' in terms of the films narrative, and interact with one another as such, their symbolic meaning is largely only 'seen' by Owen, and us as the audience, who are allowed to 'see' through his eyes.

What is of particular interest here is that Owen's acceptance of Abby as being his projected 'dark self' does not facilitate any kind of reparation between the 'good' and 'bad' parts of his split self. Normally, as Klein would describe it, such acceptance or recognition of this part of the lost self is the basic requirement of a 'working through' which then allows the re-integrated subject to grow. Yet both Owen and Abby disavow this position. [44] This is due in part to how Owen constructs his sense of identity within the film but also the levels of entanglement involved in Owen's trauma and his subsequent relationship to violence. In particular, this relationship is due to how Abby is constructed as psychological trauma quite literally made flesh. As such, Abby exists because of the traumatic excess of an original event and, consequently, only continues to exist through the re-enactment of that violence, equating to the kind of 'repetitions'[45] that Caruth speaks of which necessarily exclude the event and its re-enactments from, as she further notes, 'being experienced in time.'[46] Consequently. Abby remains locked at the age of twelve, the same age as Owen, precisely because of her violent enactments of trauma that exclude her from the normal flow of time. Without this repetitive violence she would re-enter the flow of time and memory, and would age at the same rate as Owen; or even worse – she would be re-integrated back into the traumatic subject and no longer exist as a separate entity. So what this scene finally represents within the film is the point where the divided parts of Owen recognise each other as divided parts of the same subject, but that true reparation would also annihilate the thing, or entity, that they have become together and which neither of them want to destroy. As such, it signals Owens relationship to the excessive violence he feels and the traumatic events that created it, namely that he does not want it to end and that he finds what he, arguably, feels is his 'true' identity in its constant re-enactment. This we see as the scene closes and Abby kisses Owen on the lips for the first time, but her face is smothered in the blood of the innocent Policeman, symbolising the pact made in and of blood and in the necessity of violence.

4. Now and Later and Forever[47]

> Surface and depth exist in a set of relations in which each relies on the existence of the other, in which they are entwined or enfolded, suggestive each of the other, interpenetrating, and separating out at different points.[48]

The relationship between Owen and his trauma, as seen in Abby, and indeed between Abby and her creator, as seen in Owen, becomes one that is increasingly symbiotic and interdependent as the film develops, to the point that one cannot exist without the other. Many therapeutic or psychoanalytic discourses propose some form of 'cure,' and this is specifically shown in the section in this book on 'Reconciliation', and is particularly highlighted in the chapters by Evgenia Troshikhina and Beverley Ayling-Smith, where some form of working through is required.[49] In this process of facilitating a re-experiencing of the original excessive event it is necessary for the subject to re-integrate itself with the 'lost' or traumatic experience or, as Paul Antze comments, 'cure is a matter of extracting or releasing it [trauma] somehow,' here it is more a process of acceptance.[50] What is interesting in Reeves' film, and is more in line with the work on Rwanda by Moara Crivelente, also in the section on 'Reconciliation,' is that continuance is not dependent upon reclaiming what was lost but in accepting or coming to terms with it.[51] This more relational view of trauma and its aftermath, as shown in *Let Me In*, sees acceptance coming from both the subject, Owen, but also from the manifestation of the traumatic moment, Abby, as well; so not just the more traditional view of reconciliation between the victim and the victimiser but the recognition of the entanglement of violence and the subject's identity through time. This sees an interdependence between the subject's new identity and the violence that caused it to be created. Without violence the new identity would be annihilated.

Abby, as mentioned before, is brought forward by Owen's trauma but is also made 'real' by the emotional excess that is produced by that experience. As such, she only has existence by the continuance of that emotional excess and through the re-enactment of that original violence – the 'repetitions' that Caruth speaks of. Consequently, she needs Owen to remain separate from her and to accept violence but not to 'own' it himself, for if he accepts it as his own, she is no longer necessary. Owen's acceptance, therefore, is slightly different. Although Abby is fully aware of the violence and trauma she embodies, Owen is still trying to grasp the true nature of himself. The traumatic events in his life have destabilised his sense of self. As Michael Rosington and Anne Whitehead observe: 'crises of memory have tended to coincide with crises of identity.'[52] The traumatic events in Owen's life are a crisis of memory and, subsequently, cause a crisis in his identity, which we saw at the start of the film when he was wearing a mask and pretending to be someone else whilst acting out his violent phantasies. As the film has progressed, he has managed to form a new sense of self in relation to Abby, specifically, this is a sense of identity separate to the adults around him, who have only ever shown themselves to be ineffectual or missing in his life. As such, his dependence on Abby configures a form of independence from adult control but also one which negotiates a new identity in regard to the traumatic events from his past. He does not accept them but creates a sense of self in relation to them.

What is interesting here is that Owen's reaction to trauma is not to try and go back in time to reclaim either an identity or memory that he has lost, but he constructs a system of continuance to maintain the persona that was created out of that original act or acts. And, in fact, he purposely chooses the agency that he attains from this over the societal or 'normalised' dependence that he was allowed before the traumatic rupture that changed him. As intimated before, this involves a certain sense of what Sarah Nuttall calls 'entanglement.' Although she uses it in terms of literary criticism and geographical space I think it can be, at least partially, applied to the psychological spaces, or what we might term topologies of identity, that are enacted in and around Owen in Reeves' film. Nuttall then sees entanglement as, 'the relationship between the visible and the invisible' which 'gives identity and presence' through 'the interplay between what can be seen and what surmised.'[53] Further the identity that we see is a product, or only part of, those that we cannot immediately apprehend, therefore, as Nuttall continues, the presence, 'that reveals itself and one that inverts into an occult space in which significance overheat and meaning cuts loose from the previously knowable.'[54] Owen and Abby, then, configure an interplay between the seen and the unseen, the violence that destroys but also that which creates, indicating that the identity of the self is never less through change but only ever become more entangled. As Nuttall herself says, within this, 'entanglement is frequently revealed to be a process of becoming someone you were not in the beginning.'[55] Owen, most definitely embodies this idea, in that we can see where he began but exactly how his relationship with the past, and the violence it engenders will affect what he is becoming, we never find truly find out.

The effect of this is to create a certain sense of unease in the characters of Owen and Abby and how the audience can relate to them. Whilst both are seen to be victims of trauma and twelve-year-old children at the mercy of the world, the agency and identity that they have achieved is not a clear-cut one but is permanently and inextricably entangled with the events that created them. More worryingly, their respective becomings, if it is even possible to view them as separate entities, might indicate eternal repetition rather than new possibilities. And in fact, from one perspective, the film can be seen to heavily suggest that Owen could just be another replacement 'Father' for Abby, that the entanglement that he embodies is a trap from which he can never escape. However, we can also see this from Abby's perspective, in that her balancing between being both the manifestation of a particular trauma but also being brought forward by different subjects over time is not an inescapable repetition of trauma but a continuing attempt to become. In this way, her entanglement with Owen, and the acceptance of the violence that created them both, is both knowing and hopeful, and is a way for her to become or re-enter time. This does not necessarily justify the violence that has gone before but rather sees that it is the nature of our relationship to the traumas of the past which affects our ability to 'become' or otherwise remain trapped in a temporal stasis. Consequently, Abby, as representative of a knowing if potentially volatile, ambivalence between the past and the present can be seen to be ever striving to be something other than she is: in being the embodiment of the inevitable entanglements of trauma configures her re-enactments of violence, not as an inevitable continuation of her old self but as the ever-hopeful beginning of a new one.

Notes

[1] Matt Reeves, dir. *Let Me In*. Hammer Films, 2010.

[2] The quote in the title are words spoken by Abby in answer to Owen's question about how old she is in *Let Me In*.

[3] S. P. Somtow, *Vampire Junction* (New York: Berkley Books, 1984), 133.

[4] Julia Kristeva. *Powers of Horror: An Essay on Abjection* (New York: Columbia University Press, 1982).

[5] Mary Douglas, *Purity and Danger: An Analysis of the Concepts of Pollution and Taboo* (New York: Routledge, 1966), 116.

[6] Bram Dijkstra, *Idols of Perversity: Fantasies of Feminine Evil in Fin-De-Siecle Culture* (Oxford: Oxford University Press, 1986), 334-335.

[7] Montague Summers, *The Vampire* (London: Senate, 1955 [1928]), 1.

[8] Ernest Jones, *On the Nightmare* (New York: Liveright Publishing Corporation, 1951), 98.

[9] Ibid., 105.

[10] Fiona Peters, 'Looking into the Mirror: Vampires, the Symbolic, and the Thing', in *Vampires: Myths and Metaphors of Enduring Evil*, ed. Peter Day (Amsterdam: Rodopi, 2006), 184.

[11] Juliet Mitchell, *The Selected Melanie Klein* (New York: Simon & Schuster, 1987).

[12] Joan Copjec, 'Vampires, Breast-Feeding, and Anxiety', *October* 58 (1991): 36.

[13] The character of the vampire in *Vampire Junction* is explicitly linked to psychoanalytical interpretations. Not only is the human focus of much of the vampires attention a Jungian analyst, but he speaks of himself in terms of nightmares, dreams, doppelgäängers and repressed desires. Consequently, he becomes as much a point of phantasy and 'acting out' for the humans he comes into contact with but is, quite literally, a physical manifestation of Freud's 'death drive.'

[14] Roger Luckhurst, *Science Fiction* (Cambridge: Polity Press, 2005), 27.

[15] Cathy Caruth, *Unclaimed Experience: Trauma, Narrative and History* (Baltimore: The Jon Hopkins University Press, 1996), 1.

[16] Ibid., 62.

[17] Jeffrey Weinstock, *The Vampire Film: Undead Cinema* (London: Wallflower 2012), 4.

[18] Within this framework Owen is unable to seek vengeance on the bullies himself and so 'allows' Abby to do this for him. However, in removing himself from active participation in this act he achieves no psychic resolution from it but rather it acts to further entrench the solidity of the division within himself.

[19] Melanie Klein, *Envy and Gratitude and Other Works 1946-1963* (London: The Hogarth Press, 1975), 297.

[20] Klein tends to infer that 'bad' objects are projected out of the subjects psyche to protect, what are conceived of as, 'good' objects. However, the actual nature of these is not so much a 'dark' mirroring of the self, in that it produces a manifestation of evil or pure violence, but rather that of an embodiemnt of difference to the subject.

[21] From *Let Me In*.

[22] Simon Bacon, 'Lost Boys: The Infernal Youth of the Cinematic Teenage Vampire', *Thymos* 5.2 (2011): 157.

[23] J. M. Tyree, 'Warm-Blooded: *True Blood* and *Let the Right One In*', *Film Quarterly* 63.2 (2009): 34.

[24] Ibid., 35.

[25] This again aligns *Let Me In* to earlier American vampire films, as a very similar thing goes on in *Fright Night* from 1985. Where the teenager, Charley Brewster spies on his vampiric nextdoor neighbour, Jerry Dandridge, and his sexual exploits.

[26] Jones, *On the Nightmare*, 106.

[27] This earlier story is shown in a graphic novel *Let Me In: Crossroads* by Marc Andreyko and Patric Reynolds. Released after the film, it acts as a prequel showing Abby's life just before the narrative of the movie begins. Consequently, it also separates *Let Me In* from the earlier Swedish films, a point which is further made by Lindqvist himself as he has since released a sequel to *Let the Right One In*, a short story entitled *Let the Old Dreams Die*, where his two protagonists, Eli and Oskar, are both vampires living in present day Spain.

[28] *Let Me In*.

[29] In Linqvist's book and Alfredson's film, the bullies call Oskar a 'little piggy' which again removes him from normal social categorisation. In this case though it de-sexualises him which corresponds to the de-sexualised nature of the vampire Eli (or Elias) when they arrive.

[30] Melanie Klein as quoted in Julia Kristeva, *Melanie Klein*, trans. Ross Guberman (New York: Columbia University Press, 2001), 141.

[31] *Let Me In*.

[32] *Let Me In*.

[33] Caruth, *Unclaimed Experience*, 92.

[34] Renfield is a character from Bram Stoker's seminal vampire novel, *Dracula*, who is kept in a state of thrall by the Undead Count. Never made into a vampire himself, Renfield acts as a servant and facilitator for Dracula's nefarious deeds. Because of his importance in Stoker's story a Renfield-like character appears in many subsequent vampire narratives.

[35] This point again cites a fundamental difference between Matt Reeves' film and the earlier Swedish narratives. Both Lindqvist and Alfredson give all their main characters names: Eli's 'helper' is called Hakan. In *Let Me In*, certain characters'

are given names which are more place holders: Abby's helper is called 'Father' and the detective that investigates her crimes is called 'The Policemen' which has the result of making the story more archetypal in nature rather than time and place specific, as *Let the Right One In* does.

[36] From the commentary by Matt Reeves of the scene under discussion in this section of the chapter.

[37] Note written to Owen from Abby from *Let Me In*.

[38] Oddly, Stoker's vampire was perfectly fine in daylight, though his powers were somewhat weakened. It is not until the vampire appeared on film in F. W. Murnau's *Nosferatu* that exposure to the sunlight became so destructive upon the undead body.

[39] Dominick LaCapra, *Writing History, Writing Trauma* (Baltimore: The John Hopkins University Press, 2001), 68.

[40] Ibid., 215.

[41] Gaston Bachelard, *The Poetics of Space*, trans. Maria Jolas (Boston: Beacon Press, 1964), xxxii.

[42] Caruth, *Unclaimed Experience*, 112.

[43] *Let Me In*.

[44] Kristeva, *Melanie Klein*, 80-81.

[45] Caruth, *Unclaimed Experience*, 92.

[46] Ibid., 62.

[47] 'Now and Later' sweets are used within the film. They are indicative of the time period that the film is set in, 1980s America, as well as suggestive of the nature of evil within the film. The advertising slogan for the sweets, 'Eat Some Now, Save Some for Later,' which is played during the film, also hints that the violence perpetrated now will be enacted again later.

[48] Sarah Nuttall, *Entanglement: Literary and Cultural Reflections on Post-Apartheid* (Johannesburg: Wits University Press, 2009), 83.

[49] See chapters in this book by Evgenia Troshikhina.'Sandplay Therapy for the Healing of Trauma' and Beverley Ayling-Smith.'Cloth, Memory and Mourning.'

[50] Paul Antze, 'The Other Inside: Memory as Metaphor in Psychoanalysis', in *Memory Cultures: Memory, Subjectivity and Recognition*, eds. Susannah Radstone and Katherine Hodgkin (New Brunswick: Transaction Publishers, 2003), 101.

[51] See chapter in this book by Moara Crivelente. 'Recovery in Rwanda: The Traditional Courts for Reconciliation.'

[52] Michael Rosington and Anne Whitehead, *Theories of Memory: A Reader* (Edinburgh: Edinburgh University Press, 2007), 11.

[53] Nuttall, *Entanglement*, 83.

[54] Ibid., *Entanglement*, 83.

[55] Ibid., 58.

Bibliography

Andreyko, Mark, and Patric Reynolds. *Let Me In: Crossroads*. Milwaukee: Dark Horse Books, 2011.

Antze, Paul. 'The Other Inside: Memory as Metaphor in Psychoanalysis'. In *Memory Cultures: Memory, Subjectivity and Recognition*, edited by Susannah Radstone, and Katherine Hodgkin, 96-113. New Brunswick: Transaction Publishers, 2003.

Bachelard, Gaston. *The Poetics of Space*. Translated by Maria Jolas. Boston: Beacon Press, 1964.

Bacon, Simon. 'Lost Boys: The Infernal Youth of the Cinematic Teenage Vampire'. *Thymos* 5.2 (2011): 152-162.

Caruth, Cathy. *Unclaimed Experience: Trauma, Narrative and History*. Baltimore: The Jon Hopkins University Press, 1996.

Copjec, Joan. 'Vampires, Breast-Feeding, and Anxiety'. *October* 58 (1991): 24-43.

Dijkstra, Bram. *Idols of Perversity: Fantasies of Feminine Evil in Fin-De-Siecle Culture*. Oxford: Oxford University Press, 1986.

Douglas, Mary. *Purity and Danger: An Analysis of the Concepts of Pollution and Taboo*. New York: Routledge, 1966.

Freud, Sigmund. *Sigmund Freud Collected Works: The Psychopathology of Everyday Life, The Theory of Sexuality, Beyond the Pleasure Principle, The Ego and the Id, and The Future of an Illusion*. Seattle: Pacific Publishing, 2010.

Jones, Ernest. *On the Nightmare*. New York: Liveright Publishing Corporation, 1951.

Klein, Melanie. *Envy and Gratitude and Other Works 1946-1963*. London: The Hogarth Press, 1975.

Kristeva, Julia. *Powers of Horror: An Essay on Abjection*. New York: Columbia University Press, 1982.

————. *Melanie Klein*. Translated by Ross Guberman. New York: Columbia University Press, 2001.

LaCapra, Dominick. *Writing History, Writing Trauma*. Baltimore: The John Hopkins University Press, 2001.

Lindqvist, John Ajvide. *Let the Right One In (Låt den Rätte Komma In)*. Translated by Ebba Segerberg, St. Ives: Quercus, 2009 [2004].

————. *Let the Old Dreams Die (Låt de Gamla Drömmarna Dö)*. Translated by Marlaine Delargy. St. Ives: Quercus, 2012.

Luckhurst, Roger. *Science Fiction*. Cambridge: Polity Press, 2005.

Nuttall, Sarah. *Entanglement: Literary and Cultural Reflections on Post-Apartheid*. Johannesburg: Wits University Press, 2009.

Peters, Fiona. 'Looking into the Mirror: Vampires, the Symbolic, and the Thing'. In *Vampires: Myths and Metaphors of Enduring Evil*, edited by Peter Day, 177-188. Amsterdam: Rodopi, 2006.

Rosington, Michael, and Anne Whitehead. *Theories of Memory: A Reader*. Edinburgh: Edinburgh University Press, 2007.

Somtow, S. P. *Vampire Junction*. New York: Berkley Books, 1984.

Summers, Montague. *The Vampire*. London: Senate, 1955 [1928].

Tyree, J. M. 'Warm-Blooded: *True Blood* and *Let the Right One In*'. *Film Quarterly* 63.2 (2009): 31-37.

Weinstock, Jeffrey. *The Vampire Film: Undead Cinema*. London: Wallflower 2012.

Filmography

Alfredson, Tomas, dir. *Let the Right One In*. Momentum Pictures, 2008.

Bigelow, Kathryn, dir. *Near Dark*. Anchor Bay Entertainment, 1987.

Holland, Tom, dir. *Fright Night*. Columbia Pictures, 1985.

Murnau, F. W., dir. *Nosferatu: A Symphony of Terror*. Film Arts Guild, 1922.

Reeves, Matt, dir. *Let Me In*. Hammer Films, 2010.

Storm, Howard, dir. *Once Bitten*. The Samuel Goldwyn Company, 1985.

Simon Bacon is an Independent Researcher based in Poznań, Poland. He is the editor of the journal *Monsters and the Monstrous* and is currently working on the book *Undead Memory: Vampires and Human Memory in Popular Culture*.

'Why me?' Trauma through a Performance Lens: Performance through a Trauma Lens

Oliver Bray and Peter Bray

Abstract
Originally constructed as a performance piece, this work invites discussion of the uncomfortable, but nonetheless delightful, differences and similarities of interpretation of the discipline-specific methodologies of performance and therapy. Using three case studies we consider the performance of trauma: as the replication of experience; it's effect on the maker, the performer and the audience of the work; and questions that touch upon power, perception and interpretation; and, the implication that psychological safety and ethics inherent in the reciprocal sharing of such powerful materials is questionable.

Key Words: Abuse, audience, counselling, Franko B, performance, text theatre, Tim Crouch, trauma, William Shakespeare.

*****

Unsettling Narrative (Part 1)

Are you married? My first wife humiliated me. We had been living together for about a year. We were getting married.... We were in love.... My best man had told me to be careful – it was going to be a disaster. She was living with me and she was having an affair with her best friend. It could have been for months. I didn't see it coming. That morning they had left their lover's bed to be with me at the altar. They both wore white, their hair in golden ringlets, their nails were red. They both smiled...I swear I still had no idea....

1. Contextualising our Trauma

You are witnessing an exercise in style in the service of trauma.[1] How we perceive events is subject to the influence of prior socio-cultural experiences, the way that we have learned to construct our understanding of the world through meaning.[2] Similarly, the work of this chapter came about through a desire to interpret the raw and habitual assemblage of anecdotal and autobiographical texts that gather in the cyberspace between two psychologically attached but physically separated individuals. One of us is a performance maker, the other a counsellor, both have an interest in the work of the other. Our fundamental impulse to be makers, and to make meaning, encouraged some further exploration of found performance and therapeutic texts and materials. This in turn supported the co-construction of ideas and in birthing further questions generated a loose form which appealed to our sense of coherence.

As a consequence, this chapter has assisted two men at different ends of the Earth to continue to develop research interests which are linked not only by the internet but by genetics, memory, creative impulse, ambition, humour and a desire for a close relationship.[3] Originally conceived as a means of communicating and understanding our own experiences of trauma, this research views, observes and presents trauma from our own specialist perspectives of performance and grief research and draws upon insights made in a paper and a performance piece created earlier this year.[4]

Corresponding to the meaning-making experience in the aftermath of trauma, what appears here is simply one attempt to engage with the fracturing and restorative experiences and perspectives of trauma presented by three very different performance case studies and their creators. As bystanders, audiences or performers to the witnessing of traumatic events, we acknowledge that we are simultaneously and vicariously implicated and located within these inescapably traumatic worlds of actual or mimetically shared experiences. However, presented with performance work that has the potential to modify our views of the world we recognise our capacity to understand how these new perceptions will challenge us and that we may choose how to subsequently respond.

The following paper-based reflection of our performance about trauma addresses questions of interpretation, authorship and intention in performance practice. It also notes the significance of memory and traumatic events; the mimesis of traumatic episodes; and, the conscious and unconscious creation of traumatic events both in the performance and in the audience members' minds. Making links between trauma and performance on this 'page-stage' and on the 'inner stage', you the reader are invited to consider, reflect upon, and rehearse your own relationships with trauma in ways that might draw upon implicit memory or nudge those alien and as yet unincorporated experiences that lurk there and repetitively rehearse themselves.

Patrick Duggan and Mick Wallis, linking trauma with performance, hypothesise that the trauma survivor's symptoms are intrusive representations of the original event much like retroactive rehearsals.[5] Similarly, this page-stage discussion of trauma and traumatic moments, constructed from memory, experience, and imagination in imitating or drawing upon the survivor/authors' experiences, re-performs their traumatic experiences. Managing trauma through a performance lens, therefore, becomes an excellent departure point. Through their work artists cannot help but unpack and then construct and share networks of meaning that represent their full experiences.

In our consideration of the three case studies of performance that follow we include reflexive writing about 'reading' – a frank and honest appraisal of what the work meant to us, as influenced by our respective disciplines. Performances may directly address traumatic themes in different ways. When we 'read' performance work there is no right answer and no sanctuary, consequently this is both an impossible and exposing exercise.

Embarking upon this electronic altercation exposed us to a vivid storm of traumatic and discomforting words, images, and ideas that, rendered down, presented more questions about the role of trauma in human affairs than could possibly be answered here. As a result the world had changed for us and there is no useful way back. Trauma, rather than being a painful experience that one ultimately hopes to discretely manage or evade, and that we secretly believe happens to other people, revealed itself to be a universal imperative. Trauma is not the sugar coated exception to the rule, it is the rule. And the existential reality is that most of us will at some time or another be confronted by this phenomenon, and be constrained to struggle with its meaning and feel its powerful influence upon our psycho-social development. At a fundamental level we continue to be challenged by trauma's ultimate cry for coherence – Why me?[6]

Unsettling Narrative (Part 2)

The marriage ended and I was wasted. She made me lonely.... I started meeting women in internet chat rooms. It was innocent. I wanted to share that the world is a bitch and I had to divorce her. It didn't make me attractive and at the time I couldn't care less! Soon I began seeking out bad women – women my mother wouldn't approve of – women who hurt men. It just made things worse. It taught me to feel how dirty they really are.... It hurt me. It was the wrong way round. Do you see? I wasn't naive anymore. It was my time to punish innocence. I was taking control. I met them in the virtual and then took their virtue in reality. I wanted to love them but they were victims too – broken relationships, victim bodies, pathetically hopeful.... It was so easy! Oh, God made it so easy!

2. Case Study One: Why Them?

In his acclaimed masterpiece *The Tragedy of Hamlet, Prince of Denmark* William Shakespeare, through a series of bleakly constructed traumatic events, draws us into a labyrinthine inner world of seemingly inescapable tragedy.[7] His audience is presented with a protagonist, Hamlet, whose immutable beliefs about the world are fundamentally challenged and transformed by tragic circumstances. The playwright's interpretation and translation of this drama makes us curious to know if the nature and power of the seismic events so effectively presented to us also reside within the author's experiences of the world.

On the brink of war, a traumatised adolescent Hamlet returns to his deceased father's fortress to attend his state funeral and face his mother's remarriage to his father's murderer, and brother, Claudius and Claudius's coronation. Believing that he has received damning information from his father's ghost, a psychologically unstable Hamlet sets about proving his uncle's guilt and in so doing becomes a danger to himself and others at court. In a fit of paranoia he murders his girlfriend's father, Polonius, and in an attempt to silence him is in turn exiled by Claudius and then contracted to be killed by his university friends and/or by the King of England. The assassination fails on both counts and he dispatches his would-be murderers instead. Meanwhile, his girlfriend, Ophelia, appears to go mad from her losses and commits suicide. Hamlet returning to a Denmark altered by these events becomes embroiled in a fencing match in which Laertes, Ophelia's brother, guided by Claudius attempts to kill him with a poisoned rapier. Laertes succeeds but in a scuffle the swords are exchanged and Laertes is also stabbed. Simultaneously, Claudius's plans to poison Hamlet's drink back-fires and instead his wife, Hamlet's mother Gertrude, drinks the poison and dies. Poisoned and angry, Hamlet stabs Claudius and they both die. At this point in the play the audience is confronted with the chilling spectacle of a stage littered with corpses of the Danish royal family and the entrance of an amazed Norwegian prince who is able to claim the empty throne in a 'bloodless' coup.

William Shakespeare's *Hamlet, Prince of Denmark*, evokes the traumatic, claustrophobic, and seemingly inevitable demise of a body politic corrupted by secrets, regicide, fratricide and terrifying losses. The disconnected narratives of Denmark's trauma are finally exposed and healed at the tragic expense of its government. The play's traumatic 'reality' observed through its main protagonist Hamlet, exposes the audience to the dual taboos of incest and fratricide. Once these stigmatising infections are made known to Hamlet these dark secrets create an unstoppable flood that permeates the consciousness of the whole play. Allowed to run their course, they produce a broad range of sequelae that affect both the macrocosmic world of the play and its characters and vicariously assist us to review changes to our assumed realities.[8] How is this creative narrative linked to its creator – how does he take the fact, the history, of Hamlet and reassemble it into a performance piece and with how much of his traumatic experiences does he furnish it?

The relationship between the author and his creation interests us. On 11 August 1596, William Shakespeare's heir Hamnet, died. In the same year Shakespeare's powerful patron died and his acting company, the Lord Chamberlain's Men, were forced onto the road by the 'inhibition' of London's playhouses.[9] In the next four years following these considerable personal losses, Shakespeare became powerfully absorbed in his creativity. However, we can never know if he wrote his greatest of works as a direct result of his trauma and can only surmise that they fed his extraordinary creativity at this time. Paul Gaugin's famously 'agonistic and heroicized presentation of the artist's life' obsessively and essentially links traumatic suffering with artistic achievement.[10] Gaugin believed and helped to popularise the myth that suffering of the kind that may follow loss is implicated not only as a resource that enhances the artist's wider view of the human condition but also imbues his creations with greatness. 'Je suis un grand artiste et je le sais. C'est parce que je le suis que j'ai tellement enduré de souffrances.'[11]

As an audience to these works does the inclusion of the artists 'suffering' in the programme notes in some way validate the artistic achievement? If trauma is a catalyst in the conception of exceptional work then it might be accounted for in terms of the artist's personal development – significantly those inner transformations that accompany deeply spiritual journeys or rites of passage.[12] The fact that Shakespeare was formally able to begin *Hamlet* in 1600, establishes that his experiences of traumatic loss were already available to provide the intra-psychic infrastructure and conditions necessary for the building blocks of a psycho-spiritual transformation to be used towards the construction of this new work. Intense experiences of bereavement can trigger inner change. The psyche becomes vulnerable to potentially challenging transformational materials from the (collective) unconscious.[13] The world of the play, the main character and his audience has the potency of a bad dream that one finds hard to wake from, mirroring those experiences that accompany crises of bereavement and psychological crises like spiritual emergency. In both cases post-traumatic coping is associated with the successful integration of these new experiences and information resulting in beneficial psychological outcomes characterised by personal balance, greater wisdom, and overall improved functioning.

Hamlet's journey and his soliloquies replicate features typically found in spiritual emergency and subsequent posttraumatic growth.[14] We share in Hamlet's hero's journey throughout the play. As he traverses those terrifying traumascapes of spiritual emergency we understand as he understands that his world has been irreversibly changed, that inner and outer realities are dislocated and everything is uncertain. We seek with him the unsettling truth that will make meaning of his experiences and stand in his liminal place as he witnesses the chaotic and toxic prison that Denmark has become. Searching for his life and fearing his death we are correspondingly challenged to question our existence. Thus, *Hamlet* the play can be interpreted as a profoundly disturbing transpersonal experience.

The plot contrives to bring together a grieving adolescent and the supernatural presence of his murdered father and suggests that the only possible suspect is Hamlet's new step-father, Claudius. Hamlet's brooding pain finds an immediate focus in proving Claudius' guilt. He re-authors a play to be performed to Claudius in which he features the murder of Old Hamlet and as a result an exposed Claudius storms from the performance. Falling into a detached contemplation of existence, Hamlet plans bloody revenge against Claudius. A dangerous risk to others, he viciously confronts his mother with Claudius's misdemeanours but is stopped by a further transpersonal episode, in which the influence of the Ghost momentarily calms him. Woven into the play, revenge concomitant with trauma holds the possibility of positive or negatively charged intra-psychic outcomes, and/or political and relational decay or stability. In this sense trauma is the agent of catharsis and healing. In *Hamlet* a stage world is created where a comprehension of Shakespeare's experiences of loss and trauma seem possible.

Of course, whether a fiction is created out of 'real life' events, or is purely imagined, in the moment of performance the audience can see no overtly highlighted connection to Shakespeare's actual life. Yet Hamlet's intense inner awareness invites us to explore the potentially vast and complex interiors of Shakespeare's psychology. While interesting, this raises the question as whether performance work, like any art form, should ever ask the audience to consider what is not presented, that which is not immediately accessible in the work itself. Shakespeare is not evident in the live moment of the performance of one of his plays – but, in the context of literary analysis, he's there in the text to be uncovered. The literary text can be positioned as the authentic expression of the writer's inner life – the awareness that what we see in Hamlet belongs to Shakespeare and *vice versa*.

Our desire, as 'readers', to work out, to make meaning, leads to the personalisation of art to such an extent that we are left with the notion that, in order to understand something, we must research more than *it*, know its history and respond to its aura – derived from its authorship.[15] Each instance of this distances us from the work itself. From a historian's perspective *Hamlet* is 'invalid historical material' and consequently fails as an example because he wasn't real and therefore not quantifiable. Historians are probably more pedantic than artists about notions of reality and non-reality. For the rest of us the unpacking of spiritual emergency in Hamlet above allows this 'character', these words on a page, to give us an unexpected insight into the human condition. Perhaps this is the most valuable use of art, using our best, codified communication method (words), together with imaginative interpretation, to inform our understanding of reality (perspective).

A major outcome of Freud's analytic theory is that after hyper-interpretational analysis we can no longer look at Hamlet as just a character in a play. He is 'real' and his pathological behaviour – his attempts to repeat the faulty attunements of childhood in order to master particular traumatic events – is Shakespeare's, a part of 'the poet's own psychology'.[16] The blurring of boundaries between reality and non-reality thus makes us less interested in reading/watching and analysing Hamlet the play and more in seeing *difference* when looking through an alternate lens, with Hamlet positioned in this case as a client.

In the spirit of Plato, since 'imitation has been proved to be thrice removed from the truth', *Hamlet* is an imitative representation of nature and human behaviour in a *mimesis* of tragedy.[17] Readers of *Hamlet* can recognise the psychological and moral struggles that the main character undergoes and, to this extent, some reference to a world of experience beyond the relationship between the signifiers and the signified is inferred. This is, of course, not arguing that Hamlet is a real person. What is read or heard resembles, or imitates what may be thought about. It is in this sense that Hamlet is a 'mimetic character'.[18]

As Hamlet isn't real his possibilities are endless. He may go through anything and everything, and his example is flexible – interrogated without a second thought for ethics or moral considerations. *Hamlet* speaks into aspects of Shakespeare's life that we cannot possibly know about. The Irish playwright George Bernard Shaw, better known for his socialist commentaries and acerbic wit, has posed the simple question – if Shakespeare had been recognised as a despicable human-being would his audience still think highly of him and his work?[19] It is in this tradition of theatrical anthropology that Sigmund Freud, Ernest Jones, Jacques Lacan and many others have found themselves seduced by *Hamlet* and the prospect of discovering its 'true' meaning. Through their psychologising and validation of art as life, they too have become engaged in something of a creative enterprise. Psychotherapists and philosophers turn artist and like artists they exploit/interpret their (and other's) experiences and transmute them into meaningful (for them) expressions of experience and understanding.

The use of mimesis has become a legitimate way to psychologically reflect upon or read the human condition. Consequently, even though *Hamlet* is not a historically legitimate representation of fact, true statements can be made about what happens in it and beliefs directed towards those events can be true or false. As philosopher R. T. Allen has suggested 'once we realize that truth is not confined to the factual, the problem disappears'.[20] However, as art imitates life this process allows its counterfeit to take on a life of its own separate from its creator. It is now a fact that *Hamlet*, irrespective of its resemblance to reality, by itself exists as one of the most formative, analysed, and universally quoted works in the English language.

In the stage world of *Hamlet* the idea of trauma, concomitant to revenge, is thoroughly explored. Through this lens traumatic events hold the possibility of positive or negatively charged intra-psychic outcomes, which makes Hamlet a useful illustration of how the transformational state of spiritual emergency may present itself in reality and provide the conditions necessary for catharsis and the healing potential of intra-psychic change to occur even in the most brutal of circumstances.

Unsettling Narrative (Part 3)
After the first drink, the sleight of hand, the drugs, they wanted to sleep. I went into my work. So much to do! I am not proud of every heaving moment. It was slapdash and artless. Back street quackery – I didn't harm them any more than life had already, did I? I have a code of ethics! When they woke stunned and bruised – I had gone. I am cautious by nature. I was very careful to cover my tracks. Meticulous in my professional relationships and practice – my work goes pretty well now. This really helps! No harm done. It's about balance really. Most of the time, I really feel so much better for it....

3. Case Study Two: Why Us?

Unlike Shakespeare, Tim Crouch is very much alive and literally present in his work. His play *The Author* tells the story of a writer called Tim Crouch, (who is played by the real Tim Crouch in the moment of performance) who has written a successful and savage play about the effects of violent abuse and its impact upon those involved; a man who saw it and two actors who appeared in it.[21] With no conventional stage area, just two banks of seats facing each other, the performers unravel their stories from within the audience. The play is about audience responsibility and it directly implicates them as collaborators in what is seen and unseen.

I sit in the audience, fully lit, with nothing but other audience members to look at. I don't realise that the performers are in the audience too, until they start speaking. The performance style is conversational, but theatrical, I know the actors are following their text but they are also inviting me to participate – they're asking me questions. And I do mean actors, not performers. Although apparently using their real names, they speak like actors, their voices are loud enough to carry, their articulation flawless, their gaze seeing everything but not seeing me. They keep asking me questions, I'm being led to participation, he's inviting me to speak, he's leaving gaps for me to speak...shall I speak? Acts of violence and abuse are being carefully described from perpetrators' and survivors' perspectives, I'm in danger of becoming an object of, and complicit in, these acts of abuse. I'm being invited to speak, shall I speak? I speak. I'm ignored. I'm back in a play again. I feel foolish. Foolish for being 'played'.

The audience is exposed to real people, who as actors are taking the roles of fictional actors performing the roles of real or fictional people, using a prepared text by an author, playing the part of an author, based upon actual or fictional research about people and events who, even though they may or may not be real, are real in that moment. Transparently troubled by the emergence of naturalistically violent plays in contemporary theatre, Crouch challenges his audience with similarly abusive techniques. The actors describe in detail the acts of violence that the 'play within a play' addresses, specifically the somewhat blasé attitude of the actors to their research of atrocities during their creative process (culminating in Crouch's own disclosure of his own act of sexual abuse against a baby). These various verbal descriptions disrupt audience expectation, dislocating the convention of actor and perhaps encouraging a bleeding between expectations of art and life. Oscar Wilde held the anti-mimetic view that 'Life imitates Art far more than Art imitates Life'.[22]

Crouch describes *The Author* as 'a kind of love song to actors – which says "look at what these fuckers can do to you!"', and the trauma inflicted by the theatre upon Crouch as an actor continues to stimulate his angry creativity,

> ...the abuse that I experienced and the abuse that is still perpetrated in the name of art, in the name of theatre – that's something that I still feel fired up by. Abuse inflicting on actors, in terms of power ratios, how powerless an actor can feel – I feel there's a drive in my work about celebrating what an actor can do.[23]

If the creative mind plays with the objects it loves, Crouch plays with the thorny relationship between representational acts of violence and the act itself.[24] 'If we choose to look at it, we are in some way responsible for it.' He suggests.[25] His shockingly dark satire of artistic and creative practices is so genuinely real that the audience may be forgiven for taking it too seriously – 'I have an innate distrust of art that takes itself seriously...you create a false shield of some sort'.[26]

Whilst Crouch's aim may be to celebrate what the actor can do he seems to be blaming his bystander/audience for permitting him to perform. The 'comatose' audience (Crouch's words), willingly shepherded into what they imagine is a conventional drama, find themselves encouraged to participate: to share in accounts of humiliation, depravity and pain; and, to examine their tolerance for such acts – not by graphic representation but by claustrophobic suggestion.[27] The performers, like clients fearful of judgement and re-traumatisation, almost apologetically share their increasingly harrowing stories of how preparing for, and participating in, a shockingly violent play has irrevocably affected their personalities, relationships and views of themselves and the world. The audience is made aware of its powerlessness to respond or to censor what they are exposed to. Meanwhile, Crouch as himself, as the director/actor, and the author conducts the show from within the body of the audience.

The 'audience' experiences the trauma of the work in the same way as an individual – indeed it might be either heightened or mitigated by being in a group. However, the path to the traumatising event is all too well sign-posted: *Essentially we are spectators, not given to action and often not invited to do so. We are the mob, and we don't generally take the law into our own hands. If you rouse us or excite us we will withdraw into ourselves, demand our investment back or ask you to change your behaviour because you are after all the performers. You perform for us, you provide a service, and without us you are nothing! You need us to make sense. So how is it that we allow you, even encourage you, to serve up time and time again dishes of extreme violence and pornography? Clearly, at a basic level this is what we are worthy of, but how did it come to this and what is it doing to us?*

If we are warned that a performance is likely to contain scenes of violence or strong language we may not respond in such a shocked way, we have a choice to enter the performance after all. This foreknowledge of trauma may serve to lessen its impact. We manage the crisis not only because we anticipate it but also because we are often aware of its form and content. Unsafe in ourselves we place our confidence in you – you will not let us down – we have paid you to make our pain plausible. And yet... we enter at our peril?

Crouch's manipulation of theatrical conventions in refashioning the audience's expectations and perspectives, like the traumatic event itself, plays upon pre-existing vulnerabilities creating discomfort, hyper-vigilance, and fear. Which raises the question how does the mechanical reiteration of character and text night after night, like any form of repetitive action, serve to traumatise or re-traumatise the (perception of the) performer? Like any professional practice involving regular exposure to trauma do the actors, as Crouch strongly suggests in his play, become both simultaneously desensitised and overly vulnerable to its affect?

In the live moment of *The Author* the narratives delivered by the actors aren't really shocking to the audience, we've heard and seen it before, and we know that real world can be worse than this. However, it is the discomforting intimacy and design of the space that makes the trauma powerful, it's a question of geography, and it's about proxemics.[28] It's real people looking us in the face and daring us. Although this work seems to push theatrical boundaries, in actuality, it enforces them. Although lit, we are in the dark, we're not allowed to change the rules and play the game, even though, at moments, it seems like we are. Crouch takes our involvement as an audience seriously, 'It's not about making the audience comfortable; it's about responsibility, for me.'[29] Whilst on one level Crouch appears to abuse his audience, he has an expectation that they will have the intelligence to navigate their way through that, perhaps even to forgive him as he breaks the rules and disrespectfully invades their world. He suggests that,

> Theater does all that hand holding, you know, takes care of its audience, explains things to its audience. You wouldn't get that from an intelligent visual artist. They make the audience have to work out their own relationship with the work.[30]

Philosophically, Crouch's desire is to be transparently in relationship with his audiences. Yet the simple fact is that the play is structured in ways that mystify and disorient even a prepared audience. To reflect upon two or more meanings in one sentence multiplied by two or three identities in one actor in an auditorium that is all stage and forces the audience to experience the disempowerment of an abused performer may be just too much to decode or make sense of. Crouch's truth is too artful, too playful, and witty – the conventional theatrical form, in refusing to be subverted, creates a further barrier and he is hoisted upon the petard of his own artifice.

Bad theatre is neither real nor unreal, it nudges us but not far enough, it seems radical because it slips, ever so slightly, away from the expected conventions, which are so tirelessly boring and sensible. It pacifies the liberal theatre-goer with 'radical', yet expected, little moments of subversion. It's a bit naughty, but not naughty enough. Another kind of abuse? 'Every art interaction or intervention should be an experiment' confirms Crouch.[31] But, as he reflects, 'I have no control over it' is an inadequate defence.[32] If the play is therapy intended to confront the audience/client with painful truths about themselves and the world, does Crouch have a responsibility to make it safe? Perhaps the first stage of looking after the audience is to get them to admit that they all have horrific thoughts on a regular basis? Perhaps *everybody* has the most frightful and appalling thoughts. The difference is that Crouch plays them out loud. He puts voice to them and suddenly we're offended. But, one could say that those who walked out at the Royal Court – and many have walked out of this performance – were not the people that were offended. No, they were the people that have convinced themselves they don't, or shouldn't, think the exact same things. Those people weren't offended – they needed to *demonstrate* being offended. The best way to do that? Walk out. How theatrical!

Crouch hides himself in plain sight and exposes *us*. It could be argued that he has unrealistic expectations of his audience and even himself that are not willingly fulfilled. But, his audiences are implicated by his performance of trauma, not only in the fictive universe of the performance but also in the real world where actors and the audiences, and even authors, live as real people – *the guilty audience!* If that is so we are all guilty of supporting a system that makes entertainment from others' pain and fails decisively to redress or resolve it. In his satirisation of the theatre of trauma Crouch re-presents the appalling and unbearable reality of the impact of this corruption and abuse and challenges us to respond.

Or, perhaps it is impossible to make entertainment from real pain. Perhaps, what we represent as real pain is partially constructed from entertainment? The truth is not palatable, it is terrible. The truthful reality of terrible, traumatic pain is not inherently entertaining to anyone. So we take, piecemeal, bits and bobs and string them together into something that makes more sense than the reality it was born of – and watch that instead. The irony is that these mediated, theatrical, fantastical interpretations become the new barometer for measuring what we now recognise as *real* trauma and pain. Has our perception of reality has become irreversibly skewed? Oscar Wilde's anti-mimetic assertion that 'Life imitates Art' mentioned earlier, holds some truth here. Thus, those of us who have never had the unfortunate experience of becoming directly acquainted with trauma can only measure it against the experience of faux-trauma selectively mediated by culture.

Unsettling Narrative (Part 4)

Being a doctor really seems to impress my on-line flock. The questions they ask! They know the risks when they meet me. Of course they do. So hungry in their conceit to trap me (to read me) they ignore the dangers. One day I might write an academic paper on their pliable innocence and their simple greeds. I don't have to use the drugs anymore. Not in that way. But I have kept the arrangement with my medical friend. We drink at his club. I am not a member yet. He supplies me with what I need and I in turn regale him with stories of their pathetic struggling, their sharpening cries and their soiled bodies. We have a drink and he laughs and laughs and laughs and then goes back to his wife! It's good to help. I can see that he finds my stories more than amusing...he thinks we are similar. We are <u>not</u>. We are not even friends!

4. 'Meaning Seminar': Why Not Me?

Since approximately the 1960s, Performance Art has displaced the relationship between the subject and object in performance. This may be a response to late capitalism and the pervasion of reproducibility in art. Physically, the artist herself is not given to being reproduced and so becomes the object of the work to protect it from reproduction and consequent dilution through dispersion.[33] The object of the artist becomes the site for the performance work, no hypothesizing about the author is necessary as she is in the room exposed <u>as</u> the work.[34] Interestingly, contemporary literature has taken a similar departure over the last 30 or so years. Specifically referencing Scottish literature, Jessica Aliaga Lavrijsen, in her chapter in this volume, points out that contemporary writers 'are set on the exploration of the representation of their own voices'.[35] Performance has a seemingly unbreakable historical relationship to literature, in particular literary analysis. For example, Shakespeare is not really seen as a theatre maker (perhaps the most accurate description of what he actually was), but as a writer of plays. Our earlier writing in this chapter is testament to a desire to still prioritise the notion of Author as being inextricably linked to the ability to decode meaning, that there is more to know/understand than the work alone (in the case of Shakespeare, the work is the live performance of his plays rather than the more secondary literary text).. We don't have this issue with other kinds of artwork. While we may pontificate about what Matisse was thinking when he painted, or remark upon how there was 'only one Picasso' – they are not, as people, acknowledged to be necessary subjects of investigation in order to comprehend their work. One does not look at Guernica and exclaim 'I don't care about what I see and what it means to me – what did Picasso want me to think?' The physical performer as the site of the work shakes the conventions of author-function, the creator of the work is in the room with us. Our analysis and rational, person-centred approach to 'reading', learned through our relationship to literature, leads us desperately to the desire to understand what is in the head of the person presenting (the invisible), rather than that which is actually presented (the visible). Without the invisible being made visible, or hidden meaning explained or prescribed, audiences lean to the soft embrace of assumption – hazard a guess, use existing knowledge to inform them as to what <u>might</u> be going on. Performance plays with these kinds of assumptions. The reader of performance work presents their *assumptions to themselves and they are forced to introspect. The 'actor/not actor' problem that the* The Author *presents, destabilizes truth and morality in the live moment. In our next case study, Franko B presents ambiguous meaning coupled with non-ambiguous physical trauma. It's not as simple as saying 'take whatever you want from it' – that's like confessing your abusive history in the italicized text of a chapter in this book and expecting the reader to just deal with it,* '[T]he birth of the reader must be at the cost of the death of the Author.'[36]

Unsettling Narrative (Resolution Part 1)
This is all a story of course – I never did any of these things. I am not that person.... But try as you might to forget, he is now inextricably linked to me.... Look at me spying on my ex-wife! In a dark room, a bending body in the glare of a computer screen. The sad and the hopeful women – shocked and sobbing now, their shaking hands painfully wiping me away like broken glass. The motives, the stories, the man-laughter, the woman at home...all a fiction, a fantasy! None of this happened. I saw it on TV. But it is happening somewhere right now. I am just the messenger. I wasn't even there! This is not my life and I am not responsible!
You are though, aren't you...? Eh? I am in your head now. You need to blame someone...right? Not really! Not really, it's a... joke! A joke! You should see your faces!

5. Case Study Three: Why Him?

Franko B is an artist and a performance maker. In contrast to the other writer/actor/directors here, in his work *I Miss You* he directly and intentionally inflicts trauma upon his own body.[37] In each arm he places a calendula that allows his veins to vent blood down his body and pool onto the floor. Amid a reverential and largely silent audience, this artist, up-lit by fluorescent tubes, naked and painted white, slowly promenades up and down a canvas 'catwalk' to the haunting strains of Diamanda Galas's 'My World is Empty Without You', and the slow, soft punctuating slip-slap of his sticky feet.[38] It is a passionate, overstated, yet impressively honest and unashamed expression of the artist, the performance maker's relationship with self and other. The audience knows what to expect and they know their roles as witnesses to this mute performance event.

Scenographically, *I Miss You* intentionally features a 'catwalk' similar to those used in fashion shows or, in theatrical terms, the 'traverse' stage. This gives the audience a closeness and intimacy to the action. We can see him bleed and it's real. Like a wounded giant white slug, he parades his naked body 'letting' his blood in fine red lines spatter onto the canvas – red on white, like a surgeon/barber's pole, striking, bold and simple. Emotionally as a spectator I am captivated and drawn reluctantly across the boundary of his metaphoric opened body. Flying in the face of Franko B's own resistance to the works rationalisation, I cognitively want to read a meaning into work. But by re-staging it here, I know I am changing it.

I can tell by the way you look at this page that you feel guilty...
The fact that you've chosen this chapter to read at all, tells me you're experiencing relationship problems...
I bet you wish you had met someone special sooner. All that 'fooling around' when you were younger, you regret it now...

Franko B is:
Naked...   Hairless...
Tattooed...   Plump...   Gay...
Italian....
He intentionally wounds himself.
He wants to shock me!
He creates art installations from faecal matter, emissions and other bodily materials.
He clearly gets a deep satisfaction from his Art....

...are you reading me right now?

This exercise is counter-cultural to my person-centred practice. I establish a number of conditions that support the client to engage in meaningful disclosure and self-exploration. What you do here is take an expert, analytical position. In spite of ourselves, we do this cold reading anyway...

In his article *Self Inflicted Wounds: Art, Ritual, Popular Culture*, Richard Schechner argues that the real and make-believe violence presented in media technologies have reduced even the most traumatic and extreme violence to 'spectacle'.[39] In making a distinction between wounding in performance art and the pathology of self-inflicted wounding, he controversially suggests that many artists may 'perform or wound themselves to show off or because they are sick', and asks is 'this kind of art acceptable in "civilized" society?'[40]

By blood-letting, not cutting, Franko B simply becomes the installation that allows himself and his audiences to re-vision relationships and even transcend them through the symbolic language of a blank body/canvas daubed in blood. Blood has a profound effect on an audience in this context. Unless we're a genuine haemaphobe, we are not generally fearful of blood – women are exposed to their own blood during menstruation, men the non-comparable shaving cut, both during the genderless accidental scratch.

> Blood is the body's most ambiguous liquid. Bleeding can be good or bad; in the post HIV-AIDS world, blood can heal or kill... If a vein is cut, blood flows softly; but arterial bleeding can be eruptive, draining a person to death after a few minutes. The only natural and regular flow of blood is menstruation. Menstruation affects only females and only for a portion of their lives. In many cultures, menstrual blood is hidden from men. Women take steps to absorb and get rid of the blood. In surgery, blood is sponged away as it appears. But in art, as in ritual, the blood flows visibly, even triumphantly, and is on display.[41]

Franko B's work is not consciously sadomasochist in its use of blood, but it is concerned with its visual associations and its beauty. What he does may be difficult to look at for some, the overt and intentional bleeding directly problematises the notion that when people bleed – it should matter in a particular way, that when people bleed – it should be either accidental or incidental – *Bleed in private, shame on me? Bleed in public, shame on you?* To bleed purposefully, to bleed as a result of 'artificial' intervention is difficult – the abjection of the inside being brought out, through design, can shock some of the witnesses. 'Abjection [...] disturbs identity, system, order. [That which] does not respect borders, positions, rules.'[42] Abjection and socially digressive representations in art are also addressed within this section in Simon Bacon's chapter, which highlights the cultural figure of the Vampire as 'manifestations of all those things which normative society deem as transgressive or abject'.[43]

The audience is shocked. Even in their civilised detachment they are witnessing something primal. Moving beyond the veil of spectacle they are confronted by the ancient blood metaphors of human existence writ large upon Franko B's body – birth, survival, sacrifice, and death. As Jennifer Doyle has remarked, attending a performance can be a risky business and Franko B's audiences are perhaps more shocked by the idea of what he does than by the act itself. Trained to expect to feel nothing they are fearful that they 'might actually feel something'.[44] But it is just these feelings of fear, Franko B suggests, that prevents us from seeing what is beautiful. In making this act a public spectacle he makes the idea transparent and assists his conception that the human body is even more beautiful in this vulnerable fragility. It is no longer an unspeakably private affair muddied by those psychological vices we associate with covert self-abuse and shame. 'I want to make it bearable; whether you like it or not, you're going to go away with that image in your memory.'[45]

When the language of 'reading' the work is learned, the 'gimmick' falls away we are left with only the beauty of what is presented. Man in space, imperfect and moving gracefully, bleeding, red on white, red on white. Reactions of disgust and repulsion or utterances of disagreement are not surprising, but more arresting are how these sentiments can eclipse the quality of the work. Fixation on one element overshadows the others, the fact of the 'material' becoming all encompassing.

> Michaelangelo's *David*
>
> Male nude, eyes pointed towards Rome, symbolizing the defence of liberties in the Florentine Republic.

> Michaelangelo's *David*
>
> Marble, means that Michaelangelo had a problem with his mother because marble is metamorphosed limestone, which comes from compressed, ancient sea creatures – which are the 'mother' of all living creatures.

Crude perhaps, but the point is the 'material' shouldn't be *the* thing, just *a* thing. By putting aside readings of 'indulging' we may see a more spiritual position emerge. As audience we assist Franko B in the shamanic tradition of ritualised self-abuse to induce a trauma, in order to heighten our own awareness of transcendent states and power. This requires a high level of openness, honesty and acceptance to the experience.

Franko B authors his own work, his body is the canvas, his blood the paint, and he decides the context and location. Thus, he *is* the work and he *is* the body. He is the object and the subject. He has overall control of everything within his control. He presents *himself* and would not claim to manipulate his audience in any particular direction. What the audience does with him, is up to them. If what Franko B does *is* a kind of therapy, it sort of pays off, the context of performance gives him permission to push himself to the limits of his endurance.[46] He achieves this goal because he survives the experience – in front of us – perhaps we want to save him, love him, comfort him? In *I Miss You,* trauma is in the body of the artist and in his audience. It is used to induce catharsis and/or transcendence in both. We begin to believe that if we can get through the shocking reality of the spectacle we might find something better, we might find beauty. Relationships, as he vividly points out, are inevitably painful. *We*, the audience, want to justify *his* pain.

Unsettling Narrative (Resolution Part 2)

Perhaps we can never really 'know' why a performer did this, wrote that. Finding out is subject to an understanding of the individual maker's conceit, context and intention, and myriad other stuff – the reasoning behind a piece of performance making. We might ask them, of course. Analysis suggests that either we don't trust them enough to know themselves or we don't trust them enough to give us the truth. And once explained or shared, what does the answer signify anyway? Would it change your impression of me if I was to tell you that everything I wrote before, all that stuff in italics, everything I claimed was false, was actually true? Would you reassess how you feel about me? I just wonder if it worked for Franko B. Whether he's 'better now'...nicely cured? He doesn't do the blood stuff anymore, perhaps that's why. Perhaps he just got bored with it – exploited it to the point where it was surplus to requirements.

Shakespeare, now he wrote to make money, gain respect and get a coat of arms, keep himself and his colleagues in work, and to feed his family – no artifice with him, it was all about product. Trouble is...I expect Franko B hasn't made very much money from his work – I doubt he's very wealthy. But there's something about 'that moment', that 'live' moment, the dialogic relationship between audience and performer, between writer and reader. The wordless contract between two parties – between you and me.... Trust. Trust that you will safely take me somewhere. You won't abuse my trust, you can't really. You can't be that edgy, not even you Crouch – you can't be. You'd never work again. You haven't *walked again have you Franko B?*

We all agreed didn't we? You decided to read this. And you never even thought, not for one single moment, that you'd be broken.

You knew. And I knew.

And we played.

Didn't we?

Notes

[1] The term 'exercise in style' is used here to illustrate the notion of multiple interpretations. In his book *Exercises in Style*, Raymond Queneau writes the same narrative 99 different ways.

[2] Social constructivists like George Kelly, Bob Neimeyer and Peter Marris, identify 'meaning making' as a central task of grief work.

[3] Peter Bray and Oliver Bray, eds., *Voicing Trauma and Truth: Narratives of Disruption and Transformation* (Oxford: Inter-Disciplinary Press, 2013).
[4] Oliver Bray and Peter Bray, '"Why Can't I Stop Looking?" A Therapeutic and Performative Debate on the Performance of Trauma', (paper presented at *The Second Global Conference. Trauma: Theory and Practice*, Prague, 21-24 March 2012).
[5] Patrick Duggan and Mick Wallis, 'Trauma and Performance: Maps, Narratives and Folds', *Performance Research* 16 (2011): 4-17.
[6] Ronnie Janoff-Bulman, 'Posttraumatic Growth: Three Explanatory Models', *Psychological Inquiry* 15 (2004): 30-34.
[7] John Dover Wilson, ed., *The Tragedy of Hamlet, Prince of Denmark* (Cambridge: Cambridge University Press, 1972).
[8] A useful understanding of the play's complex plot and the traumatic interiority of Hamlet's state of mind may be gained through a thorough reading of his soliloquies and the accompanying book: Alex Newell, *The Soliloquies in Hamlet: The Structural Design* (London: Associated University Presses, 1991).
[9] Fearing plague and the disorderly overcrowding of London's playhouses, in 1596 the authorities prevented the presentation of plays within the city walls. Acting troupes, like Shakespeare's, were forced to find alternative opportunities and create new venues beyond the city limits. Stephen Greenblatt, *Will in the World: How Shakespeare Became Shakespeare* (London: Pimlico, 2005), 289-294.
[10] Abigail Solomon-Godeau, 'Going Native', *Art in America* 77 (1989): 119.
[11] As Paul Gauguin, wrote in a letter to his wife, Mette (Tahiti, March 1892), 'I am a great artist and I know it. It's because of what I am that I have endured so much suffering'. Daniel Guérin, ed., *The Writings of a Savage*, trans. Eleanor Levieux (New York: Viking, 1978), 53-54.
[12] Joseph Cambell conceptualises three stages of the archetypal rites of passage as: 'the hero's journey'; 'separation'; 'initiation'; and, 'return'. Phil Cousineau, ed., *The Hero's Journey: Joseph Campbell on His Life and Work* (Novato: New World Library, 2003), 186-187.
[13] The work of the Grof's outline their concerns about the psycho-spiritual crisis of transformation that they have called 'spiritual emergency'. Christina Grof and Stan Grof, *The Stormy Search for Self: A Guide to Personal Growth Through Transformational Crises*, and Stan's later work, *Psychology of the future: Lessons from modern consciousness research* detail their holotropic philosophy.
[14] Peter Bray, 'Men, Loss and Spiritual Emergency: Shakespeare, the Death of Hamnet and the Making of Hamlet', *Journal of Men, Masculinities and Spirituality* (2008). Viewed 10 January 2012,
http://www.jmmsweb.org/issues/volume2/number2/pp95-115;
Peter Bray, 'Bereavement, Post-traumatic Growth and Psycho-spiritual Transformation', *Journal of Religion and Health* (2011), Viewed 5 January 2012,

http://www.springerlink.com/content/37n011w7463167h4/.

[15] Walter Benjamin, *The Work of Art in the Age of Mechanical Reproduction*, trans. J.A. Underwood (London: Penguin, 2008).

[16] Sigmund Freud, 'Dreams of the Death of Beloved Persons', in *The Interpretation of Dreams: The Material and Sources of Dreams* (1900), 81-88, Viewed 12 August 2012, http://psychclassics.yorku.ca/Freud/Dreams/dreams.pdf.

[17] Plato, *Plato's Republic: Book X*, trans. Benjamin Jowett (New York: Airmont Publishing, 1968), 387.

[18] Bernard Paris, 'The Uses of Psychology: A Psychological Approach to Fiction', in *Contexts for Criticism*, ed. Donald Keesey (Mountain View: Mayfield, 1998), 226-34.

[19] George Bernard Shaw's famously struggles with this and other issues concerning Shakespeare's artistic motivation: 'there is no eminent writer...whom I can despise so entirely as I despise Shakespeare when I measure my mind against his. The intensity of my impatience with him occasionally reaches such a pitch, that it would positively be a relief to me to dig him up and throw stones at him,' in *Shaw on Shakespeare: An Anthology of Bernard Shaw's Writings on the Plays and Production of Shakespeare*, ed., Edwin Wilson (New York: Applause, 2002), 50.

[20] R.T. Allen, 'The reality of responses to fiction', *British Journal of Aesthetics* 26 (1986): 6.

[21] Tim Crouch, *The Author* (London: Oberon Books, 2010).

[22] Wilde, Oscar, *The Decay of Lying: An Observation* (London: Oneworld Classics Ltd, 2008).

[23] Joe Spurgeon, 'Tim Crouch', *Venue*, Viewed 21 January 2012, http://www.venue.co.uk/performance-comedy-features/12231-the-interview-tim-crouch.

[24] Jolande Jacobi, ed., *C.G. Jung: Psychological Reflections: A New Anthology of His Writings 1905-1961* (London: Routledge Kegan Paul, 1971), 200.

[25] Rebecca Kinskey, 'Tim Crouch is "The Author" and the Actor at Kirk Douglas', *LA Stage Times*, 16 February, 2011, Viewed 21 January 2012, http://www.lastagetimes.com/2011/02/tim-crouch-is-%E2%80%9Cthe-author%E2%80%9D-and-the-actor-at-kirk-douglas/.

[26] Siobhan Davies, 'Siobhan Davies and Tim Crouch: Conversations around Choreography', Viewed 21 January 2012, http://www.siobhandavies.com/conversations/crouch/transcript.php.

[27] Kinskey, 'Tim Crouch'.

[28] In a recent discussion Stephen Bottoms quotes Crouch as saying 'I minimise what's happening on stage so I can maximise what's happening in the audience'. Stephen Bottoms, 'Authorizing the Audience: The Conceptual Drama of Tim Crouch', *Performance Research* 14 (2009): 69.

[29] Kinskey, 'Tim Crouch'.
[30] Ibid.
[31] 'Interview: Tim Crouch, Theatre Director', *Scotsman*, 22 June 2010, Viewed 20 January 2012, http://www.scotsman.com/news/interview_tim_crouch_theatre_director_820005.
[32] Davies, 'Siobhan Davies and Tim Crouch'
[33] Lynn Turner, 'Braiding Polyphony: Je tu il elle & lui', *Performance Research* 8 (2003): 93-99.
[34] Rebecca Schneider and Richard Schechner, *Performance Studies: An Introduction* (London: Routledge, 2006), 159.
[35] Jessica Aliaga Lavrijsen, 'The Trick is to Keep Breathing', in this volume.
[36] Roland Barthes, *Image Music Text*, (London: Fontana, 1977), 148.
[37] You Tube, 'I miss you', Viewed January 6, 2012, http://www.youtube.com/watch?v=ic6fOEkpiko.
[38] Diamanda Galas, 'My World is Empty without You', *Malediction & Prayer*, (EMI Europe Generic, 2002).
[39] Richard Schechner, 'Self Inflicted Wounds: Art, Ritual, Popular Culture', *Performance, art et anthropologie*, Viewed August 12, 2012, http://actesbranly.revues.org/445#toc.
[40] Schechner 'Self Inflicted Wounds'.
[41] Ibid.
[42] Julia Kristeva, *Powers of Horror* (New York: Columbia University Press, 1982), 4.
[43] Simon Bacon, 'Trauma and the Vampire', in this volume
[44] Jennifer Doyle, 'Critical Tears: Franko B's "I Miss You"', Viewed 6 January, 2012, http://www.franko-b.com/text3.htm.
[45] Patrick Campbell and Helen Spackman, 'Surviving the Performance: An interview with Franko B', in *Physical Theatres: A Critical Reader*, eds. John Keefe and Simon Murray (London: Routledge, 2007), 109-111.
[46] Nietzche coined the phrase 'What doesn't kill me makes me stronger' in his book *Twilight of the Idols*. His existential philosophy powerfully supports the contestable view that, when pushed to one's limits, individuals develop characteristics that make them stronger. Stephen Joseph uses this as a starting point for his book *What Doesn't Kill Us: The New Psychology of Posttraumatic Growth*.

Bibliography

Allen, R. T. 'The Reality of Responses to Fiction'. *British Journal of Aesthetics* 26 (1986): 64-68.

Barthes, Roland. *Image Music Text*. London: Fontana, 1977.

Benjamin, Walter. *The Work of Art in the Age of Mechanical Reproduction.* Translated by J. A. Underwood. London: Penguin, 2008.

Bray, Peter. 'Men, Loss and Spiritual Emergency: Shakespeare, the Death of Hamnet and the Making of Hamlet'. *Journal of Men, Masculinities and Spirituality* (2008). Viewed 10 January 2012. http://www.jmmsweb.org/issues/volume2/number2/pp95-115.

————. 'Bereavement, Post-traumatic Growth and Psycho-Spiritual Transformation'. *Journal of Religion and Health* (2011). Viewed 5 January 2012. http://www.springerlink.com/content/37n011w7463167h4/.

Bray, Peter, and Oliver Bray, eds. *Voicing Trauma and Truth: Narratives of Disruption and Transformation.* Cambridge: Inter-Disciplinary Press, 2013.

Bottoms, Stephen. 'Authorizing the Audience: The Conceptual Drama of Tim Crouch'. *Performance Research* 14 (2009): 69.

Campbell, Patrick, and Helen Spackman. 'Surviving the Performance: An Interview with Franko B'. In *Physical Theatres: A Critical Reader*, edited John Keefe and Simon Murray, 109-111. London: Routledge, 2007.

Crouch, Tim. *The Author.* London: Oberon Books, 2010.

Davies, Siobhan. 'Siobhan Davies and Tim Crouch: Conversations around Choreography'. Viewed 21 January 2012. http://www.siobhandavies.com/conversations/crouch/transcript.php.

Doyle, Jennifer. 'Critical Tears: Franko B's "I Miss You"'. Viewed 6 January 2012. http://www.franko-b.com/text3.htm.

Duggan, Patrick, and Mick Wallis. 'Trauma and Performance: Maps, Narratives and Folds'. *Performance Research* 16 (2011): 4-17.

Greenblatt, Stephen. *Will in the World: How Shakespeare Became Shakespeare.* London: Pimlico, 2005.

Grof, Stanislav. *Psychology of the future: Lessons from Modern Consciousness Research.* Albany: State University of New York Press, 2000.

Grof, Stanislav and Christina Grof, eds. *The Stormy Search for Self: A Guide to Personal Growth through Transformational Crises*. Los Angeles: J.P. Tarcher, 1990.

————. *Spiritual Emergency: When Personal Transformation becomes a Crisis*. New York: G. P. Putnam, 1989.

Jacobi, Jolande, ed. *C.G. Jung: Psychological Reflections: A New Anthology of His Writings 1905-1961*. London: Routledge Kegan Paul, 1971.

Janoff-Bulman, Ronnie. 'Posttraumatic Growth: Three Explanatory Models'. *Psychological Inquiry* 15 (2004): 30-34.

Joseph, Stephen. *What Doesn't Kill Us: The New Psychology of Posttraumatic Growth*. New York: Basic Books, 2011.

Kinskey, Rebecca. 'Tim Crouch is "The Author" and the Actor at Kirk Douglas'. *LA Stage Times*, 16 February, 2011. Viewed 21 January 2012. http://www.lastagetimes.com/2011/02/tim-crouch-is-%E2%80%9Cthe-author%E2%80%9D-and-the-actor-at-kirk-douglas/.

Kristeva, Julia. *Powers of Horror*. Columbia: Columbia University Press, 1982.

Neimeyer, Robert, ed.. *Meaning Reconstruction and the Experience of Loss*. Washington, DC: American Psychological Association, 2001.

Paris, Bernard. 'The Uses of Psychology: A Psychological Approach to Fiction'. In *Contexts for Criticism*, edited by Donald Keesey, 226-34. Mountain View: Mayfield, 1998.

Queneau, Raymond. *Exercises in Style*. Translated by Barbara Wright. London: One World Classics, 2009.

Schechner, Richard. *Performance Studies: An Introduction*. London: Routledge, 2006.

——. 'Self-Inflicted Wounds: Art, Ritual, Popular Culture'. *Performance, Art et Anthropologie*. Viewed August 12, 2012. http://actesbranly.revues.org/445#toc.

Solomon-Godeau, Abigail. 'Going Native'. *Art in America* 77 (1989): 119.

Spurgeon, Joe. 'Tim Crouch'. *Venue.* Viewed 21 January 2012. http://www.venue.co.uk/performance-comedy-features/12231-the-interview-tim-crouch.

Turner, Lynn. 'Braiding Polyphony: Je tu il elle & lui'. *Performance Research* 8 (2003): 93-99.

You Tube. 'I miss you'. Accessed 6 January 2012. http://www.youtube.com/watch?v=ic6fOEkpiko.

Oliver Bray is a Senior Lecturer in Performance Practice at Leeds Metropolitan University, UK. He is a Performance Artist and the Artistic Director of Until Thursday Theatre Company. His research interests include restriction and constraint in performance, performance pedagogy, contemporary theatre making and self-consciousness and grief in performance practice. www.oliverbray.com

Peter Bray is an Associate Professor in The Faculty of Humanities, Ideas and Trades at the Eastern Institute of Technology in Hawke's Bay, New Zealand. His current research and writing in psychology and counselling reflects his interest in the identification and exploration of connections between loss and grief and the impact of spiritual dimensions of experience upon post-traumatic growth and consciousness.

Part II

The Collective Voice

Post-Traumatic Responses in the War Narratives of Hanan al-Shaykh's *The Story of Zahra* and Chimamanda Ngozi Adichie's *Half of a Yellow Sun*

Majda R. Atieh and Ghada Mohammad

Abstract
This essay extends the focus of wartime trauma scholarship to recognize female non-combatants' variants of traumatic victimization and agency, as presented in the Middle Eastern and African contexts. The agency of such actors, who suffered tragically from the traumas of war, was inexplicably overlooked in both Middle Eastern and African literatures and scholarships. Thus, my essay rectifies this lacuna and presents the significant contributions of two female authors, Hanan al-Shaykh and Chimamanda Ngozi Adichie. And the post-traumatic responses of female non-combatants in the war narratives of al-Shaykh's *The Story of Zahra* and Adichie's *Half of a Yellow Sun* are examined. In particular, I re-address *The Story of Zahra* in light of *Half of a Yellow Sun* that revises the role of traumatized female non-combatants in collective change. I contend that reading traumas in both narratives propounds that traumatic recovery is never complete. However, the impossibility of transcending the 'acting out' of trauma does not necessarily entail the impossibility of the 'working through' strategy. Arguably, traumatized victims may fail to entirely disengage themselves from the traumatic past but they can still be agents of change. As such, *Half of a Yellow Sun* exposes the limitation and the failure of *The Story of Zahra*'s traumatized non-combatant in realizing any social transformation. On the other hand, I demonstrate how both narratives construe narration, scriptotherapy, and psychophysical therapy as modes of re-enactment, in relation to the inculcation of self-reconstruction and instigation of individual and collective change. My argument follows an interdisciplinary approach as it engages cultural studies, psychoanalysis and narratology in addressing trauma. Also, trauma theories by Bessel A. van der Kolk, Dori Laub, Suzette Henke and Cathy Caruth are of substantial significance to this proposed reading.

Key Words: War trauma, post-traumatic response, narration, female non-combatant, 'working through,' 'acting out,' scriptotherapy, agency.

*****

1. Introduction

Wartime literature and scholarship reveal an exclusive focus on the masculine response to combat. War World I, II, and the following wars such as the Korean War and the Vietnam War have attracted a large number of novelists, thus giving rise to the war fiction genre. Throughout history and across cultures, war has been regarded as a gendered event that further deepens the divide between the male and female identified roles. Observing that the diversity proposed by gender norms disappears when it comes to war, Joshua S. Goldstein points out that 'cultures develop gender roles that equate "manhood" with toughness under fire' in order to 'help overcome soldiers' reluctance to fight.'[1] 'Across cultures and through time,' Goldstein indicates, 'the selection of men as potential combatants and (of women for feminine support roles) has helped shape the war system.'[2] A significant feature of the pre-1950s war narratives, mostly written by male veterans, was the exclusive focus on the male war experience. Such experience foregrounds the masculine response to major battles and the depiction of military heroism. John Dos Passos's *Three Soldiers* (1921), Laurence Stalling' *Plumes* (1924), Erich Maria Remarque's *All Quiet on the Western Front* (1929), Hobert Douglas Skidmore's *Valley of the Sky* (1944), Harry Peter Brown's *A Walk in the Sun* (1944), Norman Mailer's *The Naked and the Dead* (1948), and Irwin Shaw's *The Young Lions* (1948) are a few examples of a vast range of war narratives concerned with the male war experience. These narratives portray the impact of war on male combatants, the horror of the battlefield, and the nostalgic reminiscences of home and family left behind.

However, such exclusive focus witnessed a shift and consequent inclusion of women's voices in the war narratives of the 1950s. The involvement of women in public life increased and the need to report and speak the unspoken became, increasingly, a vital necessity. Women started to break the decades of silence. Their voices started to find their way to fiction all around the world. They wrote about war, nation, community, and other crucial issues. In this respect, war narratives by African female writers highlighted peripheral actors in times of war. In particular, they shifted the focus away from the domain of the male combatants to that of victimized female non-combatants. For instance, the Algerian writer Djamila Debeche's *Aziza* (1955) was the first novel about the French-Algerian War. *Aziza* was Debeche's 'fictive articulation of a plea for the integration of the French and Algerian cultures.'[3] Likewise, the Algerian leading female literary figure Fatima-Zohra Imalayen, who used to write under the pen name of Assia Djebar, has earned international attention for her portrayal of the experiences of Algerian women. Her *Women of Algiers in Their Apartment* (1980), for instance, is a collection of short stories narrated as dialogues about the role of women in Algeria's struggle for independence. *Fantasia, An Algerian Cavalcade* (1985), is also an account of the life of a young girl in a story taking place during the War of Colonization in Algeria (1830) and stretching to the Algerian War of Decolonization in 1950s. In West Africa, no work has brought the impact of Nigerian Civil War's atrocities (1967-1970) to light better than Chimamanda Ngozi Adichie's *Half of a Yellow Sun*. The narrative recounts the everlasting trauma, particularly experienced by female civilians, during the Nigeria-Biafra War.

Certain Middle Eastern narratives also present a major focus on women's war experience. In this context, critic Elise Salem demonstrates how the war narratives written by Lebanon's women authors have 'confronted the Lebanese War and explored the psychology of the Lebanese.'[4] For instance, 'Beirut Decentrists,' defined by Miriam Cook as 'a group of women writers who have shared Beirut as their home and the war as their experience,'[5] have contributed to the Lebanese Civil War fiction. This Civil War fiction is enunciated by Ghada al-Samman's *Beirut 75* (1975), the first of a trilogy that has been followed later by *Kawabis Beirut* (1977) (*Beirut Nightmares*) and *Laylat al-Milyar* (1986) (*The Night of the First Billion*). The three novels focus on different stages of the Lebanese Civil War. Other prominent war narratives by Beirut's Decentrists are *Sitt Marie Rose* by Etel Adnan (1977), *Those Memories (Tilka al-Thikrayat)* (1980) by Emily Nasrallah, *Hajar al-Dohk (The Laughing Stone) (1990)* by Hoda Barakat, *Barid Beirut* (1992) (*Beirut Blues*) and *Ya Salaam* (1999) by Najwa Barakat, and *Maryam of Stories* (2002) by Alawiyya Subuh. Being one of Beirut Decentrists, the contribution of writer Hanan al-Shaykh to the civil war fiction is remarkable. Al-Shaykh's *The Story of Zahra* highlights the Lebanese Civil War (1975-1990), and particularly focuses on a Lebanese lady traumatized by the painful memories of the past and the atrocious war of the present. Equally, novels of the Palestinian writer Sahar Khalifa have made a remarkable contribution to the war fiction genre. These works include *Abbad al-Shams* or *The Sunflowers* (1980), which is about the struggle of Palestinian women, and *Bab al-Saha* or *The Door of the Courtyard* (1990), which focuses on the years of the first Intifada in the city of Nablus.

As surmised earlier, the narratives by Middle Eastern and African female writers highlight the peripheral actors in times of war, namely victimized female non-combatants and their suffering from war trauma. However, they do not suggest any therapeutic response. Rectifying this lacuna, my essay proposes a contribution to the wartime trauma scholarship by addressing women's attempt at agency and initiation of healing. As such, the traumatic responses of two female non-combatants in al-Shaykh's *The Story of Zahra* and Adichie's *Half of a Yellow Sun* are explored.

2. Traumatic Symptoms: Victimized Female Non-combatants in *The Story of Zahra* and *Half of a Yellow Sun*

Addressing the experience of female non-combatants during war, both *The Story of Zahra* and *Half of a Yellow Sun* evolve as significant modes of war trauma narratives. *The Story of Zahra* presents a mode of individual trauma, namely pre-war childhood trauma where Zahra, a Lebanese female, experiences domestic violence, alienation from the mother, gender discrimination, and sexual abuse. However, Zahra's traumatic symptoms are all complicated by the escalation of the Civil War. In *Half of a Yellow Sun*, witnessing the Biafran Civil War's atrocities precipitates a collective trauma as several female and male civilians undergo fear and hunger.

The Story of Zahra foregrounds individual trauma as the narrative probes the psyche of a female non-combatant during the times of war. In his book *Everything in its Path*, sociologist Kai Erikson makes a distinction between individual trauma which he defines as 'a blow to the psyche that breaks through one's defenses so suddenly and with such brutal force that one cannot react to it effectively,'[6] and collective trauma, which is 'a blow to the basic tissues of social life that damages the bonds attaching people together and impairs the prevailing sense of communality.'[7] In al-Shaykh's narrative, the distinction between individual trauma and collective trauma is not possible. Individual trauma is integrated here into a collective trauma because the social structure that produced this individual trauma is still unchanged. In particular, little Zahra is raised in a disconnected family where the intimate relationship between her parents is absent. She grows up watching her mother's love affair with an anonymous man outside the house while experiencing emotional abuse, negligence, rejection, and gender discrimination inside. She describes how privilege is granted to her brother Ahmad when food is served:

> Every day, as we sat in the kitchen to eat, her love would be declared: having filled my plate with soup she serves my brother Ahmad, taking all her time, searching carefully for the best pieces of meat. She dips the ladle into the pot and salvages meat fragments. There they go into Ahmad's dish.[8]

Zahra's images of her father are always associated with the khaki suit. His appearance, a 'frowning face, a Hitler-like moustache above thick full lips, a heavy body,'[9] imposes a military-like mood. Such mood of rigidity, discipline, and order brings to mind the political violence that intersects with the gender-based violence. However, Zahra's pre-war childhood trauma is complicated by the escalation of the Civil War. Not yet recovered from pre-war trauma, Zahra leads a devastating life in a war-torn Beirut. As domestic tensions erupt, death rules every aspect of the civilians' lives. Explosions, bombings, religious-based killings, and kidnappings become part of their daily lives. News of abductions, arsons, robberies, and even snipers lurking on the rooftops haunt all their talks. Consequently, Zahra's nervous fits return, especially when she realizes that her brother Ahmad is involved in the war. Not only he but also her schoolmates and other young people are leaving their study and work to fight under the orders of the factions' leaders. Beirut turns into a city where Zahra can see only people fleeing their homes and hear nothing but the shootings and screams of women and children in the streets. She recounts her experience on one of her nights at home in Beirut:

Before I could cry out, an explosion had burst near-by and my heart dropped between my feet. I was left completely empty, except for my voice, but even this I could not control any more.[10]

Similarly depicting the atrocities of civil war, Adichie's narrative presents a collective mode of trauma that shapes the daily life of civilians undergoing fear and hunger. For instance, Olanna, a female professor at Nsukka University in the Igboland, witnesses the murder of some Igbo people, particularly her relatives. She finds their bodies scattered around the ruins of their compound in Kano. Uncle Mbaezi has lain facedown 'in an ungainly twist, legs splayed. Something creamy-white oozed through the large gash on the back of his head.'[11] Aunty Ifeka has lain on the veranda and the 'cuts on her naked body were smaller, dotting her arms and legs like slightly parted red lips.'[12] Shocked by the axes and machetes with Hausa's community, Olanna watches Abdulmalik, her uncle's best friend, stepping over the bodies lying there as dolls made of cloth and announcing that it is Allah's will. On the train back to Nsukka and among the passengers' screams and agonies, Olanna runs into another image that will be stuck in her mind throughout the narrative. This haunting image features a woman holding her little girl's head in a calabash. Olanna sees 'the little girl's head with the ashy-gray skin and the braided hair and rolled-back eyes and open mouth,'[13] while the mother explains how long it took her to plait the thick hair on the head. Kainene, Olanna's twin sister, undergoes a similar traumatic encounter when, in a very horrifying scene, she observes the tragic death of her steward, Ikejide. During an explosion of a mortar, a shrapnel cuts off Ikejide head completely. Kainene watches his body running with only a bloodied neck after the head is gone.[14] In a scene similar to that of the little girl's head in the calabash, Ikejide's head is picked up and put in a raffia bag.

Pre-war sexual trauma features heavily in both narratives. In al-Shaykh's narrative, it is sexual abuse that further escalates Zahra's childhood trauma. The first sexual relation for a grown-up Zahra is with a married man who cunningly takes advantage of her submissiveness to satisfy his needs. Malek, a friend of both her brother Ahmad and the family, finds Zahra a job at al-Régie factory and starts seducing her by talking about friendship then about platonic passion. The seduction ends up on a bamboo bed in a friend's garage room. Though Zahra has her virginity restored after the first terrible abortion, Malek undoes 'the doctor's handiwork in one split second, without it being any pleasure to him since he knew the restoration was counterfeit.'[15] Zahra's sexual trauma is extended through her relationship with her husband, Majed, whom she marries only to veil her loss of virginity. On his part, Majed marries Zahra only to find a legitimate venue for his sexual satisfaction. When Zahra escapes from Lebanon and returns to him trying to keep hidden her feeling of latent hatred, Majed forcefully tries to have sexual intercourse with her. Their intercourse, being non-consensual, is described as a spousal rape by Majed, which is part of an abusive relationship. Zahra even confesses her reluctance to have sex with Majed and how he tries to subdue her forcefully:

> He tried to put his arms around me. I slipped away. He drew
> close. I stepped back. He followed. I screamed, but he ignored
> my cries. I tried to push his hands away, but he was set on having
> a fight. I screamed again, hoping someone would hear, but we
> were alone except for the constantly falling rain.[16]

In Adichie's narrative, betrayal and cheating mark both Olanna's and Kainene's sexual traumas. Olanna's sexual trauma is initiated upon realizing that Odenigbo, her revolutionary lover, has slept with Amala, his mother's village girl, 'after only three weeks away from her.' [17] Kainene also gets severely shocked after discovering that Richard, her English boyfriend, has slept with Olanna. Both drunk and frustrated, Richard and Olanna unintentionally engage in a sexual act that further escalates Kainene's childhood trauma generated from being the ugly twin of the beauty and the favorite.

Though differently presented, the mother's emotional alienation shapes both narratives. While alienation is a strategy by Zahra's mother to escape the father's authority and restrictive religion, it is part of bourgeois attitude in *Half of a Yellow Sun*. The mother's affection, care, and love that usually help develop the child's conscious is absent in Zahra's life. Zahra's need for this affection is revealed through the emotional identification she seeks to establish with her mother. Zahra always feels strong affinity with her mother. This affinity is psychological and reflected in Zahra's perpetual wish to be so close to her mother more than 'the navel is to the orange.' [18] However, the distance between Zahra and her mother grows deeper. Zahra silently observes how her mother abandons and later transforms her into a pretext to initiate an ex-marital relationship:

> The distance between me and my mother grows greater, deeper,
> although we have been as close as orange and its navel... I
> would watch her when she was with me, and study her when she
> was at a distance. I thought all the while, as I looked up at her, of
> how much I wanted to draw her towards me, to draw myself
> close to her, to touch her face and have her eyes peering into
> mine.[19]

Zahra's longing for this close connection with her mother is also expressed in her regression to 'the state of being fetus in its mother's womb.' [20] Whenever Zahra feels troubled, frightened, or insecure, she takes the embryo-like posture. She moves back to this earlier emotional level in an attempt to feel the mother-daughter connection again. Zahra even transforms her mother into a model to achieve her goals. Whenever Zahra and her mother are severely beaten by her father, she imitates the mother's pathetic reaction in such situations: '[s]eeing the blood covering her face, I tore at my hair and beat my chest, exactly as would do herself.'[21]

While Zahra longs for a close connection with the mother, Olanna, in *Half of a Yellow Sun*, practices a kind of emotional cutoff or estrangement from her parents. She refuses to be 'a part of the gloss that was her parents' life.'[22] As such, she abandons Lagos' luxurious and classy life for Odenigbo and a university in a poor town. No proper or normal communication could ever be established between Olanna and her parents, especially her mother. Paradoxically, Olanna enjoys such a communication with Uncle Mbaezi, her mother's brother, as they can discuss different issues of social and political nature. Her affection is also directed to Aunty Ifeka, Uncle Mbaezi's wife, whom Olanna wished were her mother. 'Aunty Ifeka,' Olanna observes, 'was as good as her mother, anyway, since it was Aunty Ifeka's breasts that she and Kainene had sucked when their mother's dried up soon after they were born.'[23] Both Olanna and Kainene realize that their mother's bourgeois mind-set has obliged her to give them to 'a nursing aunt only to save her own breasts from drooping.'[24] Furthermore, the way Olanna treats the family's stewards and servants reflects her attitude towards the proletariats. Olanna's parents believe that it is enough to pay these people good salaries and that 'thanking them would give them room to be insulting.'[25] Defiantly, Olanna believes that thanking servants is the simplest step toward acknowledging their humanity.

Both narratives feature traumatic memories that develop as intrusive recollections, haunting flashbacks, somatic sensations, and other signs. Relating the long term outcome of trauma to the initial somatic response, Bessel A. van der Kolk observes that traumatized people keep experiencing life as a continuation of the trauma, and remain in a state of constant alert for its return.[26] In this respect, al-Shaykh's narrative presents a disturbing memory that retrieves early childhood's images of intense fear, such as a frightened little girl and a mother 'trembling behind the door'[27] hiding from a male chaser, and continues to haunt Zahra whenever under stress. In the same way, Adichie's narrative features traumatic memories and images that persistently haunt Olanna's life. For instance, the hideous image of plaited hair resting in a calabash revisits her whenever she plaits the hair of Baby, the daughter of Odenigbo. Olanna's ability of visualization even becomes dulled by disturbing memories about victimized relatives, such as Arize, Aunty Ifeka, and Uncle Mbaezi.

Traumatic memories in both narratives are marked by 'belatedness.'[28] According to Cathy Caruth's theory of 'latency'[29] or 'belatedness,' the traumatic experience constitutes 'a break in the mind's experience of time.'[30] It is characterized by the 'structure of its experience or reception: the event is not assimilated or experienced fully at the time, but only belatedly, in its repeated possession of the one who experiences it.'[31] This belatedness entails that 'trauma is not locatable in the simple violent and original event in an individual's past,'[32] Caruth explains, 'but rather in the way that its unassimilated nature – the way it is precisely not known in the first instance – retunes to haunt the survivor later on.'[33] Such theory is pertinent to the interpretation of belatedness that shapes the traumatic memories in both narratives. In al-Shaykh's narrative, Zahra's memories of her traumatized childhood are recalled while she is an adult. Book I of the narrative starts with a section entitled 'Zahra Remembers.' As the title suggests, this section presents Zahra's recollections of her traumatic past. In a series of flashbacks and vivid memories, her traumatic childhood constantly revisits a grown-up Zahra living in Africa. Similarly, Adichie's narrative features belatedness in Olanna's traumatic experience. Memories of the victimized relatives and the plaited hair resting in the calabash do not follow the traumatic event immediately. They haunt Olanna later on, provoking pain with the power of the traumatic event itself.

The traumatic signs in both narratives develop into the dissociative inability of communicating trauma. Asserting the limitation of language in communicating trauma, psychoanalyst Dori Laub contends that 'there are never enough words or the right words … to articulate the story that cannot be fully captured in thought, memory, and speech.'[34] In Adichie's narrative, such linguistic limitation is translated into an initial failure of narration. Olanna encounters difficulty verbalizing what she has been through and loses the ability of narrating her trauma to the others. Olanna's verbal failure develops into spatial dissociation that involves her loss of touch with the surroundings or any sense of time, and a failure to engage in the present. As a result, she develops symptoms of conversion disorder as her psychological trauma is exhibited in a physical form. Conversion disorder, according to the Diagnostic and Statistical Manual of Mental Disorders, 'involves unexplained symptoms or deficits affecting voluntary motor or sensory function that suggests a neurological or other general medical condition.'[35] Psychological factors, they add, 'are judged as being associated with the symptoms or deficits.'[36] In Adichie's narrative, such disorder is developed into a movement disorder. Olanna suddenly becomes unable to walk or move upon returning home from Kano:

> Her legs were fine when she climbed down from the train and she did not need to hold on to the blood-smeared railings; they were fine as she stood for the three-hour drive to Nsukka in a bus so crowded she could not reach out to scratch her itching back. But at the front door of Odenigbo's house, they failed.[37]

Though her condition has the characteristics of physical disease, no organic cause is found. This is why Olanna's inability to walk has been diagnosed by Dr. Patel,

Odenigbo's friend, as psychological. A main feature of the conversion disorder is the appearance of certain symptoms affecting the patient's senses or voluntary movements such as the ability to walk, swallow, see, or hear. However, such symptoms suggest a neurological or general medical disease or condition. Such disorder affects Olanna in Adichie's narrative. Olanna suffers from a failing in both her legs and bladder: '[t]here was the melting of her legs, and there was also the wetness of hot liquid running between her thighs.'[38] Olanna has swallowing difficulty as well. She could hardly take 'the pills Odenigbo slipped in her mouth.'[39] In al-Shaykh's narrative, Zahra is presented as being incapable of exerting any counteracting power against forces manipulating her life. She is always portrayed as seeking a voice and feeling like to cry out and scream. She complains:

> I am at my wits' end, and am annoyed with myself and hate myself because I stay silent. When will my soul cry out like a woman surrendering to a redeeming love?[40]

Zahra's verbal failure also develops into spatial dissociation and withdrawal. She retreats into her 'shell' perpetuating the standardized image the others enforced on her. Such dissociation is also revealed though the enclosure and isolation she seeks in the bathroom. Whenever she is under stress, either in Beirut or in Africa, she escapes to the bathroom. It represents her harbor, a haven where she can cut herself off from the world outside. She reflects: '[l]eave me alone in this bathroom! It allows me to disappear in time and space; it cuts me off from all human relations.'[41] The bathroom becomes Zahra's own space or territory that nobody can conquer. Thus, war trauma featured in both narratives is an extension of the pre-war trauma presented in the form of childhood and sexual trauma.

3. Defining Agency in *Story of Zahra* and *Half of a Yellow Sun*

Cross-cultural trauma studies reveal that the manifestation of distress varies according to cultural differences. For instance, critics George F. Rhoades and Vedat Sar present an international investigation of the similarities and differences of long-lasting trauma. They suggest that the reaction to trauma can be 'unique according to a person's culture and similar in aspects to the experiences of others around the world.'[42] In light of this cultural perspective, examining trauma in both narratives reveals that while haunting memories, silence, and dissociation are common traumatic reactions, adaptation to trauma is different. However, such difference is not culturally motivated as will be demonstrated throughout this reading.

'Acting out'[43] and 'working through'[44] are the two strategies of agency that define female resistance and healing from the reoccurrence of such traumatic memories in al-Shaykh's and Adichie's narratives respectively. These two strategies are identified in Freudian psychoanalysis and developed by Dominick LaCapra for the purpose of historical studies. For LaCapra, the emotional response of the historian to events involves one of two extremes: the 'full identification'[45] that leads to the 'acting out,' or the 'pure objectification'[46] that leads to the 'working through.' Applying such understanding of these two strategies to al-Shaykh's and Adichie's narratives articulates a subversive reading that contests all previous interpretations of al-Shaykh's narrative. The scholarship of *The Story of Zahra* has contributed to the construction of a passive definition of victimhood by projecting Zahra's helplessness as an utter obstacle to initiating agency. Accentuating the direness of Zahra's traumatized past, critics have discerned no potential for a possible development of victimhood into agency. Such scholarship has constructed a paratext that controls the reception of al-Shaykh's narrative as an account of traumatic submissiveness. However, identifying the responses of the traumatized females in Adichie's narrative invites a different understanding of Zahra's victimhood, as will be demonstrated later.

In *Half of a Yellow Sun*, survival from trauma is initiated by verbally breaking the victim's traumatic dissociation. Such break involves establishing an alternative dissociation from trauma itself. In this context, LaCapra contends that it is the 'working through' strategy that enables the victim 'to gain critical distance on a problem,'[47] and 'to distinguish between past, present and future.'[48] In Adichie's narrative, dissociation from trauma develops from the reverse articulation of verbal or written testimony to an empathetic listener or reader, which has a therapeutic function. In Freudian terminology, such kind of testimony or storytelling is called 'talking cure.'[49] For psychiatrist and author Judith Herman, the talking cure offers 'relief of many of the major symptoms of post-traumatic stress disorder.'[50] Testimony helps the victim release unconscious emotions and tensions after recalling and reliving the traumatic experience. Such emotional release is therapeutic as it integrates all fragmented images and enables the individual to recover lost details and have a full understanding of his/her experience. In Adichie's narrative, Olanna, upon returning home from Kano, tells Odenigbo about the horror she has witnessed. She describes 'the vaguely familiar clothes on the headless bodies in the yard, the still-twitchy fingers on Uncle Mbaezi's hand, the rolled-back eyes of the child's head in the calabash.'[51] Using Dori Laub's terms, Odenigbo functions here as the 'addressable other' who 'can hear the anguish of one's memories and thus affirm and recognize their realness.'[52] For the traumatic narrative to be effective, communication with the 'other' should involve empathy. Through the empathetic communication, the 'other' who effectively listens to the unfolded traumatic memory shares the painful feelings of the traumatized subject in a loving and supportive way. In *Half of a Yellow Sun*, both Richard and Olanna serve as empathetic listeners to Kainene. Kainene recounts to Richard the crucifixion of Colonel Udodi Ekechi: '[n]orthern soldiers put him in a cell in the barracks and fed him his own shit.'[53] She describes how the soldiers beat and 'tied him to an iron cross and threw him back in his cell'[54] to die on the iron cross. After reconciling with Olanna, Kainene recounts to her about the hideous killing of Ikejide: how a 'piece of shrapnel cut off his head, completely beheaded him, and his body kept running. His body kept running and it didn't have a head.'[55] Scriptotherapy is an equally important written mode of dissociative re-enactment, which initiates Olanna's agency and survival. Scriptotherapy is defined by Suzette Henke as the 'process of writing out and writing through traumatic experience in the mode of therapeutic reenactment.'[56] Such kind of process relies on 'the artistic replication of a coherent subject-position'[57] to generate 'a healing narrative that temporarily restores the fragmented self to an empowered position of psychological agency.'[58] In Adichie's narrative, Olanna powerfully detaches herself from trauma through recounting her victimization to Ugwu, Odenigbo's houseboy, who functions as the male scriptwriter:

> Ugwu was writing as she spoke, and his writing, the earnestness of his interest, suddenly made her story important, made it serve a larger purpose that even she was not sure of, and so she told him all she remembered about the train full of people who had cried and shouted and urinated on themselves.[59]

On the contrary, in al-Shaykh's narrative, Zahra seeks survival through silence and isolation that further extend traumatic dissociation. Psychoanalyst Laub highlights the necessity of testimony for survival. She demonstrates that the survivors 'did not only need to survive so that they could tell their story; they also needed to tell their stories in order to survive.'[60] In al-Shaykh's narrative, had Zahra sought therapeutic connection through verbal communication, she would have found it. While contending that the development of victimhood into healing and agency on Zahra's part is possible, I am not ignoring the socio-cultural constraints on the individual. In fact, the limitation of healing mechanisms in a conservative Islamic environment is fully recognizable. Nonetheless, Zahra's major flaw is that she does not follow the possible social mechanisms presented by another culture. Arguably, she could have profited from being in Africa, where narration to a compassionate listener like her uncle Hashem is a possible choice. She could undergo a cathartic release through confessing to Hashem for he proves to be a reliable person. But she gets him wrong and suspects all his motives. Because he views her as the only remaining link to his home country, Hashem feels the desire 'to touch her hands and face and the hem of her dress,'[61] to feel and smell Lebanon through her. He seems willing to support her and be the desired empathetic listener even when he realizes that she is not a virgin. Hashem tries to know the truth to help Zahra marry the man she is supposed to be in love with and solve the problem, whatever it is. Ironically, fear from Hashem's scorn, anger, or silence is not the barrier to Zahra's confession. She remains silent simply because she does not want to let go of her traumatic past. Zahra could even have narrated her story to the sniper, especially that he has initiated verbal communication through his reverie about the past. Yet, silence was Zahra's only and typical response.

In *Half of a Yellow Sun*, survival from trauma is initiated through strategies other than oral or written confession. Therapists working with trauma survivors recommend body-based strategies to help traumatized individuals transcend suffering and complete their healing. Psychophysical therapist Sylvia Karcher, for instance, suggests that painful experiences can be internalized and integrated into the self through body work. In this context, Karcher introduces the Concentrative Movement Therapy, defined as a body-based psychotherapy that 'proceeds from the assumption that both mental experience and events experienced physically are stored in the body.' [62] Such healing strategy is pertinently represented in Troshikhina Evgeniia's 'Sandplay Therapy for the Healing of Trauma,' (appearing in part III of this volume). Evgeniia suggests Sandplay as an alternative healing mechanism when the 'talk therapy is not effective as a treatment method.' [63] Sandplay therapy, developed by psychotherapist Dora Kalff, helps the traumatized individual create a complete three-dimensional picture in a sand box with toy miniatures. The effect of Sandplay therapy, Evgeniia explains, is that it 'provides space for silent work and clients have opportunity to express themselves without speaking.' [64] Thus, the verbally blocked trauma is symbolically articulated and reduced or healed visually. This psychophysical mechanism of healing helps understand the peculiar strategy of psychotherapy presented in Adichie's narrative. In particular, Olanna's initiative of soap-making can be read as a tactic of survival from war trauma. Olanna is first fearful that she might lose her beloved ones after Umuahia's fierce bombings. Then she decides to 'no longer exist limply, waiting to die. Until Biafra won, the vandals would no longer dictate the terms of her life.' [65] So, she transforms her rage into a challenging energy and exerts herself to the utmost till the soap is made:

> She pours some palm oil into the cooled mixture and stirred and stirred until her arms stiffened from fatigue. There was something delicious in the sweat that trickled under her arms, in the surge of vigor that made her heart thump, in the odd-smelling mash that emerged after cooling. It lathered. She had made soap. [66]

Through the soap-making labor, Olanna manages to reconnect her body and mind. Olanna also integrates the body in order to work through her sexual trauma. In particular, she uses body contact or touch as a strategy of healing. Olanna's sexual intercourse with Richard after Odenigbo's sleeping with Amala has such therapeutic dimension. It is evident that she does not regret the act itself, though she regrets betraying Kainene and Odenigbo. For Olanna, it is not 'a crude revenge, or a scorekeep-ing,' as she reflects. Rather, it is an act of 'redemptive significance.'[67] This redemption process is evident in Olanna's description of the sexual act:

> [I]t was as if she was throwing shackles off her wrists, extracting pins from her skin, freeing herself with the loud, loud cries that burst out of her mouth. Afterward, she felt filled with a sense of well-being, with something close to grace.[68]

Thus, Olanna's body becomes a primary vehicle to transcend her traumatic memories and initiate her healing.

The attempt to counteract traumatic dissociation is also presented in al-Shaykh's narrative. However, such counteraction is developed through the tactic of 'acting out' that features behavioral re-enactment based on physical inscription. Critic Kolk demonstrates how trauma is usually repeated on 'behavioral, emotional, physiologic, and neuroendocrinologic levels.'[69] As such, people who undergo trauma 'have a tendency to relive the past, to exist in the present as if they were still fully in the past, with no distance from it.'[70] LaCapra directly relates such repetition compulsion to the process of 'acting out.' In al-Shaykh's narrative, Zahra attempts to transform this repetition into a tactic of resistance to trauma. She practices behavioral re-enactment by playing with her pimples. Such act represents a physical re-inscription of the painful past on her face. So, Zahra's behavioral re-enactment of her childhood's trauma develops into bodily disfigurement and self-mutilation. On the other hand, Zahra continuously relives iconic memories of her mother's affair by maintaining sexual intercourse with the disgusting Malek. Her body 'never once responded to his or experienced ecstasy.'[71] Still, she never rejects his invitations and keeps seeing him even after her painful abortion. In psychoanalysis, this kind of reaction is an example of the turning-against-the-self defense mechanism. Such tactic is defined as 'the turning back upon the self of an impulse directed against an object' and as 'displacement onto one's self.'[72] This displacement becomes Zahra's alternative and subversive target. But she harms herself instead of harming the others. Consequently, destructive rather than therapeutic reenactment is established.

Though Zahra attempts to use the same healing strategy of body contact as Olanna, her choice of the wrong person leads instead to self- annihilation. Zahra tries to seek healing through sexual intercourse with the sniper. This relationship suspends all memories of a painful past. She feels security and peace amidst war. When she is under the sniper, she remembers times when her need for safety and protection makes her crave returning to her mother's womb. She describes the love-making scene of her and the sniper:

> My cries as I lay in the dust, responding to the sniper's exploring
> fingers, contained all the pain and sickness from my past, when I
> had curled up in my shell in some corner somewhere, or in a
> bathroom, hugging myself and holding my breath as if always
> trying to return to the state of being a foetus in its mother's
> womb.[73]

However, Zahra's final attempt at agency fails as she chooses the wrong person.
She clings to the lord of death for survival.

　　Reading both narratives suggests that it is the 'working through' strategy that
transforms the female victims into fully powerful 'ethical agent[s]'[74] and exposes
the limitation of the 'acting out.' In Adichie's narrative, both Olanna and Kainene
manage to generate a 'countervailing force'[75] that helps them survive and be
engaged in the external world again. Seeking to win the war and help their
community, the two females play complementary roles each from her own
experience and career. While Olanna, as a professor, works on the pedagogical
aspect, Kainene works on the economic side. After Akwakuma Primary School is
turned into a refugee camp, Olanna organizes classes in the yard. With the help of
a friend, Professor Achara, she manages to get some books, benches, and
blackboards. Olanna starts to teach mathematics, English, civics as well as ideals
of the Biafran cause. In Abba, Olanna also joins the villagers who sew 'singlets
and towels for the soldiers,'[76] as part of the win-the-war effort. Believing that they
can make a difference, Kainene decides that they have to make their own income.
She works as a food supplier for the refugee camp and starts a farm to grow the
camp's own protein, soya beans, and akidi. She decides to bring a man from Enugu
who has a fantastic talent for making baskets and lamps to teach the others. She
also asks the Red Cross to send them a doctor every week. Richard describes how
Kainene's work at the refugee camp enhances her healing:

> There was a manic vibrancy about her, about the way she left for
> the refugee camp each day, about the exhaustion that shadowed
> her eyes when she returned in the evenings. She no longer spoke
> of Ikejide. Instead, she spoke about twenty people living in a
> space meant for one and about the little boys who played War
> and the women who nursed babies and the selfless Holy Ghost
> priests Father Marcel and Father Jude.[77]

In al-Shaykh's narrative, Zahra also adopts a win-the-war strategy. She decides to
devote herself toward ending the war. She defiantly proclaims:

This war shall end! I shall finish it! No cause can be won until
the war is stopped. No cause comes before the cause of
humanity, and safety. The war ends here and now.[78]

Thus, Zahra attempts to convince warriors to release their captives.[79] She also
undertakes a voluntary work at a hospital.[80] She even works on diverting the sniper
from using his rifle.[81] Her attempt at agency is revealed through the psychological
transformation she undergoes in the midst of war. Such transformation
progressively enables her to communicate with the others. As a translation of such
transformation, Zahra challenges the haunting fear of her father by her sexual
intercourse with the sniper. She wishes that her father could hear her cries of
pleasure and watch the love-making scene of her and the sniper:

Oh, sniper, let me cry out in pleasure so that my father hears me
and comes to find me sprawled out so. I am one with the dust in
this building of death. Let my father see my legs spread wide in
submission.[82]

Her fear of people 'evaporated with the war' to a point where she 'was able to look
the pharmacist in face and ask for ten packs of contraceptive tablets.'[83] She is
depicted as having a resurrection of the soul. For the first time she is whole, in
body and soul. As her body is emancipated, her soul is set free:

Back at home, as if the war had ended for me already, I watered
the plants I had been neglecting. I cleaned the mirrors with the
newspapers I no longer read. I washed and ironed the cushion
covers from the couch. I spread out winter clothes on chairs to
get rid of their smell of mothballs. I began to build up stores of
provisions, just like my mother before me.[84]

However, all her attempts at peace and agency prove to be futile. Her cause
particularly ends at the hands of the sniper with whom she falls in love.

4. Conclusion

As war narratives, both *Story of Zahra* and *Half of a Yellow Sun* readdress
female non-combatants' victimization and articulate their varied attempts at
healing and agency in the Middle Eastern and African contexts. The paratexts of
al-Shaykh's narrative renounce the possibility of any active role for traumatized
female victims in collective change. However, reading al-Shaykh's narrative in
light of Adichie's reveals Zahra's attempted but limited agency compared with
Olanna's productive agency. As such, Adichie's narrative revises the definition of

victimhood, opening up a space for potential involvement of the traumatized victim in social change.

Notes

[1] Joshua S. Goldstein, *War and Gender: How Gender Shapes the War System and Vice Versa* (Cambridge: Cambridge University Press, 2003), 9.
[2] Ibid.
[3] Miriam Cooke, *Women and the War Story* (Berkeley: University of California, 1996), 123.
[4] Elise Salem, *Constructing Lebanon: A Century of Literary Narratives* (Gainesville: University Press of Florida, 2003), 9.
[5] Miriam Cooke, *War's Other Voices: Women Writers on the Lebanese Civil War* (New York: Syracuse University Press, 1996), 3.
[6] Kai Erikson, 'Notes on Trauma and Community,' in *Trauma: Explorations in Memory*, ed. Cathy Caruth (Baltimore: Johns Hopkins University Press, 1995), 153.
[7] Ibid.
[8] Hanan al-Shaykh, *The Story of Zahra*, trans. Peter Ford (New York: Anchor, 1995), 11.
[9] Ibid., 24.
[10] Ibid., 136.
[11] Chimamanda Ngozi Adichie, *Half of a Yellow Sun* (New York: Knopf, 2006), 145.
[12] Ibid.
[13] Ibid., 147.
[14] Ibid., 312.
[15] Al-Shaykh, *Story of Zahra*, 34.
[16] Ibid., 108-109.
[17] Adichie, *Half of a Yellow Sun*, 221.
[18] Al-Shaykh, *Story of Zahra*, 8.
[19] Ibid.
[20] Ibid., 153-154.
[21] Ibid., 15.
[22] Adichie, *Half of a Yellow Sun*, 34.
[23] Ibid., 39.
[24] Ibid.
[25] Ibid., 30.
[26] Avigdor Klingman and Esther Cohen, *School-Based Multisystemic Interventions for Mass Trauma* (New York: Plenum Publishers, 2004), 161.
[27] Al-Shaykh, *Story of Zahra*, 3.

[28] Cathy Caruth, *Unclaimed Experience: Trauma, Narrative, and History* (Baltimore: Johns Hopkins University Press, 1996), 92.

[29] Caruth, 'Trauma and Experience: Introduction,' in *Trauma: Explorations in Memory*, ed. Cathy Caruth (Baltimore: Johns Hopkins University Press, 1995), 7.

[30] Caruth, *Unclaimed Experience*, 61.

[31] Caruth, 'Trauma and Experience,' 4.

[32] Caruth, *Unclaimed Experience*, 4.

[33] Ibid.

[34] Dori Laub and Shoshana Felman, *Testimony: Crisis of Witnessing in Literature, Psychoanalysis, and History* (New York: Routledge, 1992), 63.

[35] American Psychiatric Association, *Diagnostic and Statistical Manual of Mental Disorders*, 4th edition, text revised (Washington DC: American Psychiatric Association, 2000), 486.

[36] Ibid.

[37] Adichie, *Half of a Yellow Sun*, 154.

[38] Ibid., 154.

[39] Ibid., 155.

[40] Al-Shaykh, *Story of Zahra*, 34-35.

[41] Ibid., 79.

[42] George F. Rhoades and Vedat Sar, ed., *Trauma and Dissociation in a Cross-Cultural Perspective: Not Just a North American Phenomenon* (Binghamton: Haworth Press, 2005), 22.

[43] Dominick LaCapra, *Writing History, Writing Trauma* (Baltimore: Johns Hopkins University Press, 2000), 141.

[44] Ibid.

[45] Ibid., 147.

[46] Ibid.

[47] Ibid., 143.

[48] Ibid.

[49] Sigmund Freud, *Five Lectures on Psycho-Analysis* (London: Penguin, 1995), 8-9.

[50] Judith Lewis Herman, *Trauma and Recovery* (New York: Basic Books, 1992), 183.

[51] Adichie, *Half of a Yellow Sun*, 154.

[52] Laub and Felman, *Testimony*, 68.

[53] Adichie, *Half of a Yellow Sun*, 136.

[54] Ibid.

[55] Ibid., 339.

[56] Suzette Henke, *Shattered Subjects: Trauma and Testimony in Women's Life Writing* (New York: St. Martin's, 2000), xxi.

[57] Ibid., xvi.

[58] Ibid.
[59] Adichie, *Half of a Yellow Sun*, 405.
[60] Dori Laub, 'Truth and Testimony: The Process and the Struggle,' in *Trauma: Explorations in Memory*, ed. Cathy Caruth (Baltimore: John Hopkins University Press, 1995), 63.
[61] Al-Shaykh, *Story of Zahra*, 69.
[62] Sylvia Karcher, '"In My Fingertips I Don't Have a Soul Anymore": Body Psychology with Survivors of Torture—Insights into Work with Concentrative Movement Therapy,' in *At the Side of Torture Survivors: Treating a Terrible Assault on Human Dignity*, ed. Sepp Graessner, Norbert Gurris and Christian Pross, trans. Jeremiah Michael Reimer (Baltimore: Johns Hopkins UP, 2001), 79.
[63] Troshikhina Evgeniia, in this volume.
[64] Ibid.
[65] Adichie, *Half of a Yellow Sun*, 275.
[66] Ibid.
[67] Ibid., 240.
[68] Ibid., 230.
[69] Bessel van der Kolk, 'The Compulsion to Repeat the Trauma: Re-Enactment, Revictimization, and Masochism,' *Psychiatric Clinics of North America* 12 (1989), 389.
[70] Ibid., 2.
[71] Al-Shaykh, *Story of Zahra*, 30.
[72] Grete L. Bibring, et al., 'A Study of the Psychological Processes in Pregnancy and of the Earliest Mother-Child Relationship-II. Methodological Considerations,' *Psychoanalytic Study of the Child* 16 (1961), 65.
[73] Al-Shaykh, *Story of Zahra*, 153.
[74] LaCapra, *Trauma*, 3.
[75] Ibid., 6.
[76] Adichie, *Half of a Yellow Sun*, 183.
[77] Ibid., 314.
[78] Al-Shaykh, *Story of Zahra*, 135.
[79] Ibid., 133.
[80] Ibid., 134.
[81] Ibid., 15.
[82] Ibid., 161.
[83] Ibid., 185.
[84] Ibid., 163.

Bibliography

Adichie, Chimamanda Ngozi. *Half of a Yellow Sun*. New York: Knopf, 2006.

Al-Shaykh, Hanan. *The Story of Zahra*. Translated by Peter Ford. New York: Anchor, 1995.

American Psychiatric Association. *Diagnostic and Statistical Manual of Mental Disorders*, 4th edition, text revised. Washington, DC: American Psychiatric Association, 2000.

Bibring, Grete L., Thomas F. Dwyer, Dorothy S. Huntington and Arthur Valenstein. 'A Study of the Psychological Processes in Pregnancy and of the Earliest Mother-Child Relationship-II: Methodological Considerations.' *Psychoanalytic Study of the Child* 16 (1961): 25-72.

Caruth, Cathy. *Unclaimed Experience: Trauma, Narrative, and History*. Baltimore: Johns Hopkins University Press, 1996.

———. 'Trauma and Experience: Introduction.' *Trauma: Explorations in Memory*, edited by Cathy Caruth, 3-12. Baltimore: Johns Hopkins University Press, 1995.

Cooke, Miriam. *Women and the War Story*. Berkeley: University of California, 1996.

———. *War's Other Voices: Women Writers on the Lebanese Civil War*. New York: Syracuse University Press, 1996.

Erikson, Kai. 'Notes on Trauma and Community.' *Trauma: Explorations in Memory*, edited by Cathy Caruth, 183-199. Baltimore: Johns Hopkins University Press, 1995.

Freud, Sigmund. *Five Lectures on Psycho-Analysis*. London: Penguin, 1995.

Goldstein, Joshua S. *War and Gender: How Gender Shapes the War System and Vice Versa*. Cambridge: Cambridge University Press, 2003.

Henke, Suzette. *Shattered Subjects: Trauma and Testimony in Women's Life Writing*. New York: St. Martin's, 2000.

Herman, Judith Lewis. *Trauma and Recovery*. New York: Basic Books, 1992.

Karcher, Sylvia. "'In My Fingertips I Don't Have a Soul Anymore": Body Psychology with Survivors of Torture, Insights into Work with Concentrative Movement Therapy.' *At the Side of Torture Survivors: Treating a Terrible Assault on Human Dignity.* Translated by Jeremiah Michael Reimer, edited by Sepp Graessner, Norbert Gurris and Christian Pross, 70-94. Baltimore: Johns Hopkins University Press, 2001.

Klingman, Avigdor and Esther Cohen. *School-Based Multisystemic Interventions for Mass Trauma.* New York: Plenum Publishers, 2004.

LaCapra, Dominick. *Writing History, Writing Trauma.* Baltimore and London: Johns Hopkins University Press, 2000.

Laub, Dori. 'Truth and Testimony: The Process and the Struggle.' In *Trauma: Explorations in Memory*, edited by Cathy Caruth, 61-75. Baltimore: John Hopkins University Press, 1995.

Laub, Dori and Shoshana Felman. *Testimony: Crisis of Witnessing in Literature, Psychoanalysis, and History.* New York: Routledge, 1992.

Rhoades, George F. and Vedat Sar, ed. *Trauma and Dissociation in a Cross-Cultural Perspective: Not Just a North American Phenomenon.* Binghamton: Haworth Press, 2005.

Salem, Elise. *Constructing Lebanon: A Century of Literary Narratives.* Gainesville: University Press of Florida, 2003.

Van der Kolk, Bessel. 'The Compulsion to Repeat the Trauma: Re-Enactment, Revictimization, and Masochism.' *Psychiatric Clinics of North America* 12 (1989): 389-411.

Majda R. Atieh is a lecturer at Damascus University (Syria) and a Fulbright scholar affiliated with Howard University (USA). Her current research and teaching interests focus on postcolonial studies, women's writings of the black diaspora, and food pathology studies. Atieh has published on the celebratory resistance writings of Toni Morrison and other African American women writers in refereed journals and edited collections, including *MELUS* (2011), *Tishreen University Journal* (2011, 2012), and *Contemporary African American Fiction: New Critical Essays* (2009).

Ghada Mohammad is a Master's candidate at Damascus University (Syria). Her research interest is focused on the cultural construction of the war narrative.

Re-Living Motherhood: Vocalising Grief, Trauma and Loss in Butler's *Lilith's Brood*

Aparajita Nanda

Abstract
Kai Erikson, the noted sociologist and authority on the social consequences of catastrophic events, defines individual trauma as 'a blow to the psyche that breaks through one's defences...with such brutal force that one cannot react to it effectively...[one] with [draws] into [oneself], feeling numbed, afraid, vulnerable, and very alone.' In Octavia Butler's science fiction trilogy *Lilith's Brood*, Lilith Iyapo is a traumatised victim who awakens 'feeling numbed, afraid, vulnerable, and very alone,' devastated by the loss of her son in a car accident. This chapter looks at the haunting of this loss as it resonates in Lilith's psyche as itinerant intrusions of an inescapable, relentless memory. Flashbacks of Lilith's memory come and go, begging a vocalisation of her grief and demanding a release through language, through Lilith's telling of her story. Lilith, barricaded from dealing directly with her past, takes recourse to different forms of storytelling, where retrieval of the past becomes an act of re-memory. When every remembering becomes an act of forgetting, in the words of Mahmoud Darwish, access to the past requires a resituating of the primary loss in different milieus that calls for a creative listening and understanding by readers. In Lilith's case, the traumatic loss of her child requires her to be reincarnated as a mother figure a number of times. The loss also calls for her motherhood to be split into two related entities, the surrogate and the biological – both incidentally seminal to the narrative of slavery – that compete and later converge to valorise the trope of motherhood that not only forms the core of the different stories but becomes the only way to survive the trauma.

Key Words: Loss, flashbacks, multiple story-telling, re-memory, elision, creative listening, re-living motherhood, surrogate and biological motherhood, grief, trauma.

*****

Hugo and Nebula award winner Octavia E. Butler is one of the best known women science fiction writers. African American by birth, Butler is the first science fiction writer to receive the MacArthur Foundation Genius Grant. Butler, who describes herself as 'comfortably asocial – a hermit in the middle of Seattle – a pessimist...a feminist, a Black...an oil-and-water combination of ambition, laziness, insecurity, certainty, and drive,'[1] was drawn very early on in life to the fantasy world of science fiction. Within the space of science fiction though, all her twelve novels, remain metaphorical renderings of racial discrimination, power struggles, war and its aftermath as they address issues of race, gender, and sexuality. *Lilith's Brood*, a trilogy that comprises of three books *Dawn*, *Adulthood Rites* and *Imago* deals with future human transformation. Butler's text opens in the wake of an apocalypse where the human race nearly brings about its own demise by means of a nuclear warfare. The Oankali, a nomadic, gene-trading alien species, rescue the few surviving humans – but at a price. Any human who opts to be saved must forgo the right to reproduce with other humans. The Oankali plan to interbreed with humans and create a superior breed of human-Oankali constructs and thereby eliminate the 'Human Contradiction,' humanity's toxically flawed 'mismatched pair of genetic characteristics' – intelligence and hierarchical reasoning.[2] To implement their plans, the Oankali abduct Lilith Iyapo, an African American woman, set her up as a figurative mother figure, and make her responsible for convincing human survivors to join the Oankali fold. Lilith, as per the Oankali agenda, will also be the progenitor of the first human-Oankali child, Akin. The Oankali claim the new breed of constructs, rid of their Contradiction, will not repeat the genetically fated history of their human ancestors when they return to Earth. Lilith is clearly a key player in the success of the Oankali plan. However, Lilith has a history – a traumatised history of having lost her son, Ayre, in a car accident – that has left her a victim in the throes of what Linda Hogan calls 'phantom pain': a memory that refuses a material marker of its presence but in its very invisibility engulfs one's being as 'a memory unforgotten.'[3] Lilith seems to slowly adjust to her new reality and yet retain (by way of flashes of memory) a connection with her deceased son. Her 'adjustment' to the reality she has been awakened to moves away from Freud's definition of 'adjustment' and towards a bereavement that embraces a giving up of one's attachment to the deceased.[4] A clear psychic splitting can be noticed in her: in order to survive Lilith often appears nonchalant – apparently oblivious to the trauma that defines her and at other times gives voice to the deep seated trauma in the stories that surface. Her journey toward healing requires that she relive and remake her trauma narrative. And the Oankali both the instigators and the colonists of her trauma provide the necessary traumatic conditions but unwittingly initiate her healing process; a process that will ultimately defeat them.

Motherhood, loss of child, and the resultant trauma has a long history in the African American psyche. In it, motherhood, stifled within the parameters laid out and enforced by the patriarchy, is further fraught with the ravages of slavery. Works of literary criticism focused on African American motherhood have mostly remained confined to issues arising out of slavery. Toni Morrison's *Beloved,* with its heart-rending story of a mother's killing of her child to save it from slavery, has garnered a lot of attention. Morrison deals primarily with themes of grief, trauma, and loss.[5] A more interesting read – one related to my argument of vocalising grief, trauma, and loss as part of a narrative of healing – is Colleen Cullinan's 'A Maternal Discourse of Redemption,' in which she argues that the voice of the mother has regularly been ignored, even in feminist writings, and other voices, like those of the daughters, have been used to articulate that of the mother instead.[6] Cullinan's article focuses on the voice of the mother; she examines 'how women's experiences *as mothers* enter into their experiences of brokenness, sin, healing, and wholeness,' which complements my exploration of the maternal voice as it struggles through the grieving and healing process – what Bill Flatt divides into shock, lamentation, withdrawal, frustration, panic, depression, detachment, adaptation, reinvestment, and growth.[7] On the topic of motherhood, Shirley Stave's 'Toni Morrison's *Beloved* and the Vindication of Lilith' discusses the novel's use of the legend of Lilith as a challenge to that of Eve, drawing on maternity as a trope of extraordinary empowerment and simultaneously foregrounding the 'mother's darker side, the loss of the self to the all-consuming child.'[8] Stave argues that Lilith defies patriarchal sanctions, and argues for 'an unsentimentalised view of motherhood and the psychological complexities that accompany it.'[9] In Butler Lilith's motherhood is ambiguous – a complexity that easily denies and defies more simplistic readings of her other feminist heroines as Dorothy Allison argues. For Butler, I feel, Lilith challenges the traditional meanings and expectations attached to motherhood. The most interesting part of this discourse is that although empowered mothers redefined motherhood, they were still influenced by society's discourses on mothering. Lilith's status draws on both theories, making her an example of Andrea O'Reilly's 'mother outlaws' while simultaneously making her vulnerable to readings such as Allison's.[10] Moreover Lilith's motherhood is complicated by the Oankali/Human four parent (male and female) along with the ooloi, a subadult Oankali, forming a fifth integral part of the relationship she will have with the hybrid child to be born. In the process Lilith demonstrates quintessential motherhood in all its ambiguity, as she mourns for the loss of her biological son, deals with the complicated process of grieving to finally transcend it.

Dawn opens with Lilith, a captive of the Oankali, clearly in a victimised position, 'helpless, alone, and ignorant.'[11] Trapped in what John Bowlby calls a 'numbed' condition, Lilith 'sway[s] dizzily' and virtually gropes her way back to reality, where she becomes the target of questions earmarked to recycle her past – pointed questions that target the phantom pain and bring back memories of trauma:

> *Had she had children?*
> Oh god. One child, long gone with his father. One son. Gone. If there were an afterworld, what a crowded place it would be now.[12]

The reminders open up Lilith's traumatic wounds, making her more vulnerable, a pliable victim of her lost motherhood. Her captors then introduce a five-year-old child to her, Sharad ('autumn' in Sanskrit).[13] Introduced to Lilith in almost the autumn of her life, Sharad reminds her of Ayre, her own son. The 'small boy with

long, straight black hair and smoky brown skin, paler than her own' could not
speak English and is terrified at finding himself stranded with an unfamiliar
woman. He shies away from her and hides in a corner farthest from her. By shying
away from Lilith, the boy only encourages her maternal feelings to surface. She
puts in regulated, patient effort to convince him that, despite the unfamiliarity, she
was not dangerous. And slowly the relationship grows into a two-way contributory
one as 'she began teaching him English – and he began teaching her whatever
language he spoke.'[14] Lilith sings songs to him – almost motherly lullabies,
grateful 'she could touch him,' happy 'even when he wet the bed they shared or
became impatient because she failed to understand him quickly enough.'[15] Sharad
seems to encompass Lilith's entire existence, both physical and mental. She never
complains about the physical discomfort when the child wets the bed nor does she
react to his impatience over her not understanding him quickly enough. In fact, she
starts worrying about him and ponders as to how best protect him from the
Oankali, realising almost instantly that they are both helpless in the hands of their
captors. At this juncture, the child is taken away from her. The text reads
'Experiment completed.'[16] Introducing a human child to Lilith was a ploy to revive
her maternal instincts – a necessary experiment as part of the Oankali agenda to
assure themselves of the successful completion of their plan. It was a test to verify
the viability of their programme, which depended primarily on Lilith becoming a
successful surrogate mother, a maternal accomplice in the Oankali 'captive
breeding program.'[17]

     In the process of completing their experiment, the Oankali revive the phantom
pain, and Lilith is left to deal with revived trauma that refuses to be sealed back
into memory. It keeps making itinerant intrusions with the least excuse. A stray
remark on human isolation by the Oankali Jdahya 'touche[s] a memory in' Lilith –
her motherly instinct roused once more by a memory, she eagerly enquires about
Sharad's well-being.[18] She embarks on a journey of yearning and searching for
Sharad. Her initial queries are snuffed out with a disclaimer: 'The boy has parents
and a sister. He's asleep with them, and he's still very young.'[19] The rejoinder
seeks to eliminate any familiarity or desire on Lilith's part to be protective about
Sharad, as he already has a family to look out for him. But Lilith's maternal
affection leads her to persist in her request to see Sharad. And the Oankali are
quick to take advantage of the situation. They grant permission to her only if she
can acclimate herself with the Oankali and 'walk among [them] without panic.'[20]
Lilith is virtually being blackmailed by the Oankali at this point – her acclimation
to them a definite step in the success of their genetic mutation programme. Later, a
cursory glance at Sharad, sleeping in the womb of the genetically mutated
carnivorous plant that now protects and nurtures the child and waiting to be
awakened by an Oankali-trained human, once again acts as a reminder to Lilith of
her primary role in the Oankali agenda. She compromises and abides by the
Oankali plan only to relive and 'revise' her traumatic memories in an attempt to

'heal a wounded past.'[21] In fact, via Lilith, Octavia Butler, as an African American woman and writer of speculative fiction, keeps alive the tradition of mothers and grandmothers who by 'bringing to light hidden histories...[and] literally re-view[ing]' them, seek to 'envision empowering and nurturing versions of the future.'[22]

As these flashes of a haunting loss keep coming back, they take on different manifestations. Lilith recalls her initial denial of the Oankali offer of motherhood, appalled by what she visualises as her offspring: 'Medusa children. Snakes for hair. Nests of night crawlers for eyes and ears'; her revulsion towards the construct children is further consolidated by what Eric White sums up 'as a figure for everything abject and abominable.'[23] Repelled by the vision of demonic children, Lilith openly accuses the Oankali of manipulating her: 'You're going to set me up as their *mother*? Then put me back to sleep, dammit...I never wanted this job!'[24] Despite these violent rejections, Lilith remains captive to her traumatic memories, which the Oankali exploit to their own advantage. Caught in the throes of an emotional trauma and a physically captive situation, Lilith resigns herself to her lot, and, on a milder note, wistfully regrets her role as a mother to an ooloi – a gender-neutral Oankali – child, Nikanj, wishing that it 'were not a child at all.'[25] The duality recalls the 'Good Mother/Terrible Mother' situation cited by Stave as she references the mythic Lilith in Raphael Patai's *The Hebrew Goddess*.[26]

The repetitive variations of the memory of the traumatic moment of loss – the car accident in which she lost both her son and her husband, Sam – keep coming back to Lilith in recurrent dreams or momentary thought processes. Her detailed reconstruction of that traumatic moment is a vivid instance of reconstruction, what Toni Morrison calls 'literary archaeology,' access to which is provided by imagination that revolves around images: 'the remains, so to speak, at the archaeological site...as [the] route to a reconstruction of a world, to an exploration of an interior life that was not written.'[27] Thus, a blissful world of 'an ordinary Saturday on a broad, dry street in bright sunshine' is ripped apart when a 'young girl, just learning to drive, had rammed head-on into Sam's car.'[28] The phonetic impact of the guttural 'r' and the double onslaught of 'mm' in 'rammed' leads to a detailed imaginative regeneration of the fatal day:

> She had swerved to the wrong side of the road, had perhaps somehow lost control of the car she was driving. She'd had only a learner's permit and was not supposed to drive alone. She died for her mistake.[29]

The juxtaposition of the next image – 'Ayre died – was dead when the ambulance arrived' – simultaneously builds on the pathos even as it highlights the irrationality of the situation: the girl deserved punishment for her transgression, whereas Ayre had fallen victim to the irrationality of fate.[30] A parallel story, where Sam's parents visit their dying son, introduces a primary attempt to deal with the trauma: where Lilith's loss is instantaneous, her in-laws' loss is prolonged, for Sam 'took [t]hree months to die...three months to finish what the accident had begun.'[31] But Sam was virtually dead, for 'he stared through them as he stared through Lilith, his eyes empty of recognition, empty of him...the man himself had already gone.'[32] Later on in the narrative, Lilith recontextualises this memory – this time a displacement in place and time occurs when she links her current life with Sam's brain damage and death, a fate that Lilith fears will be imminent at the hands of the Oankali.

The horror of the resituated trauma, however, does not provide any escape from the core experience; it remains an opaque prelude to what follows. The opacity of the moment resides in what Roberta Culbertson calls manifestations of trauma that inhabit various levels of the victim's body and mind where 'this sort of memory is without language, perhaps without image [that] in circumstances of extremity...tend to actualise [as] symbols.'[33] Lilith's interaction with Paul Titus, the human consort handpicked by the Oankali for her, begins with a simple remark by Titus to deter her going back with the Oankali to a 'Stone age' earth:

> 'You said you had a baby.'
> 'My son. Dead.'
> 'Yeah. Well, I'll bet when he was born, you were in a hospital with doctors and nurses all around helping you and giving you shots for the pain. How would you like to do it in a jungle with nothing around but bugs and rats and people who feel sorry for you but can't do shit to help you?'[34]

Unconscious of the identification formulating in her mind, Lilith stares at Titus, recalling the way her mother had looked at her:

> She had caught herself giving her son the same look when she thought he was doing something he knew was wrong. ... 'How much,' she thought, 'of Titus was still fourteen, still the boy the Oankali had awakened and impressed and enticed and inducted into their own ranks,'

and now were using him to serve their own end.[35] Lilith, caught at this moment of facing up to her sense of loss over her son, is torn by the dormant desire in her to respond to the 'kiss by an eager boy,' meaning Titus.[36] The symbolic quality of the situation wavers between a son and a lover, recalling the essential Oedipal complex and collapsing the two even as it defies a simple answer. And yet, when faced with Titus's animal-like aggression, Lilith foils his attempt to rape her by citing the exact instance that had trapped her a moment ago:

'How many times have they made you do this before?' she asked desperately. ... He caught her arm, jerked her to him. 'Maybe they've made you do it with your mother!' she shouted. He froze and she prayed she had hit a nerve. 'Your mother,' she repeated. 'You haven't seen her since you were fourteen. How would you know if they brought her to you and you –' He kicked her hard. The last sound she heard before she lost consciousness was his ragged, shouted curse.[37]

As she slowly regains consciousness she is coaxed back to reality by the soothing voice of her Oankali child-mate, Nikanj, and healed of the injuries inflicted by Titus. During her convalescing sleep, Lilith's brain chemistry is altered to acquire Oankali traits. 'With altered body chemistry...as strong and as fast as her nearest animal ancestors,' Lilith is made ready to fulfil the Oankali role tailor-made for her. She is accorded the power to choose her wards, provided she can eliminate their individual resistance and create a homogenous 'cohesive unit,' that would abide by the Oankali agenda.[38] As Lilith meticulously scrutinizes dossiers containing personal biographies of her wards' backgrounds, she looks towards the successful completion and execution of the Oankali agenda, towards grooming her wards to become more like the alien race. As a result of Lilith's increased strength and power (she now controls the food and environment for her wards), the humans are incredibly reliant on her and thus rendered powerless, increasing the likelihood that they would follow the Oankalis' (and Lilith's) wishes.

Lilith's surrogate motherhood also contends with her allegiance to Nikanj. Her initial wistful reaction to the child is replaced by a growing sense of reciprocity that transforms into a strong bond complicated by sexual overtones. Lilith develops intrinsic sexual ties with Nikanj that defy the simple dualities of a mother-child relationship. She risks being branded a traitor by the humans as she strips naked to save Nikanj after his sensory organ is severed. Humans were expected to have sex with an ooloi, a gender-neutral alien seducer:

> Human beings liked to touch one another – needed to. But once they mated through an ooloi, they could not mate with each other in the Human way – could not even stroke or handle one another in the Human way.[39]

However, Lilith is the first human to have sex with an ooloi without being drugged into a submissive state. Lilith 'did not pretend outwardly or to herself that she would resist Nikanj's invitation – or that she wanted to resist it.'[40] The relationship grows in nuanced cadences, from an 'eagerness that suddenly blossomed in her...so intense [that] it was suspicious,' to where, she lay down, perversely eager for what it could give her. She positioned herself against it, and was not content until she felt the deceptively light touch of the sensory hand and felt the ooloi body tremble against her.[41]

In fact, she concludes, 'Nikanj could give her an intimacy with Joseph [her human mate] that was beyond ordinary experience.'[42] Her maternal relationship with Nikanj – her maternal status in general – is thus complicated, as she desires this contact which underscores the fact that she is no longer totally human, given that she can no longer desire Joseph without her ooloi's presence. Lilith and her partner stand radically changed through their contact with the ooloi/Oankali validating the point that as Lilith is changed by trauma – trauma can also be changed by and in a closer relationship with the other.

Nominated as the mother figure and groomed to fulfil her surrogacy role, Lilith's enhanced role in Oankali society opens up a space of possibilities, what Bridget Haylock, in this volume, calls 'an autonomous place for feminine expression, for *ecriture feminine*, in the symbolic world.'[43] It allows Lilith to re-live her loss and deal with the haunting trauma of her lost son. In her role of surrogate mother, Lilith now has several children to love and nurture, to groom and shape. As the possibility for multiple stories emerge with each of Lilith's wards, each story becomes an act of re-memory, a resituating of the primary loss in different milieus, what Toni Morrison in *Beloved* calls a 'told story that lay before [Denver's] eyes' – stories that Lilith, like Denver, had to step into.[44] As Lilith reads through the dossiers, she steps into these 'told stories,' which virtually open up spaces, conflating the interpersonal and intrapersonal experiences, crucial components in creating positive outcomes from negative experience.[45] Lilith remembers her traumatic history by 'incorporat[ing] the future, past, and contemporary timelines within the same or complementary literary framework.'[46] She 'lives' through and participates in the lives of the people she awakens, creating an external interpersonal space, understanding and augmenting her own feelings through an intrapersonal process occurring within each ward's psyche. Thus in Victor Dominic, a lawyer who survived a childhood accident, Lilith awakens a potential ally, who is suspicious of the Oankali and 'very creative at lying to them'.[47] Where Lilith's son had succumbed to his accident instantaneously, Victor, an accident survivor with a calm, resilient mind, could have been Ayre if he had lived.

Different stories open up different possibilities, and call for imaginative readings, as they bring forth lived realities. Gabriel Rinaldi, an actor *par excellence*, had the Oankali stumped as to his true identity, and came 'near defeating the Oankali.'[48] He could be potentially valuable to Lilith for his improvising abilities. Another candidate was Joseph Li-Chin Shing, a widower, an intelligent and steady man, one who had once contemplated suicide but had put his life "'on hold' until he found out what had happened in the world and who was running things now.'[49] His curiosity, which got the better of him and prevented him from taking his life, could be an asset for Lilith. She also awakens one she sees as an errant child, the diabolic Conrad Loehr – with his a seven-year run with the New York police, he is accustomed to ordering people around, but his volatile nature is combined with a sense of protectiveness. She ultimately lives to regret her choice though, as Loehr axes Joseph to death. These stories, of different people in a different time and place, enable her to literally 're-member' her present life with lived histories, histories that provide her with the hope of enabling possibilities in the future as well as unanticipated disasters.

As Lilith reads the personal dossiers of her wards in a somewhat despair-ridden, disorganised state, she re-lives her own past, in some cases drawing literal parallels, as with Victor Dominic, while in others, such as with her 'errant child' Conrad, indulging in prospect-seeking as she judges, nurtures, and even sometimes rejects the vicarious motherhood thrust on her. But in doing so, she is able to deal with her traumatic memories. So when Tate, a woman Lilith awakens, asks her 'You didn't have kids, did you?' and pushes her point home by egging Lilith on, saying 'It's really hard for you to talk about your life before, isn't it?' Lilith's almost nonchalant answer is,

> I lived those memories for my two years of solitary. By the time the Oankali showed up in my room, I was ready to move into the present and stay there....And, as for kids, I had a son. He was killed in an auto accident before the war.[50]

This therapeutic space of release also allows Lilith to empower herself as she determines to undermine the Oankali plan and reorganise her life. Faced with divided loyalties – to her saviours and healers, particularly Nikanj, and her human wards – Lilith propagates and justifies the Oankali gene trade with the humans even as she charts out her own plans within the parameters of the Oankali narrative. In her search for likely people to awaken, she looks for a few potential allies who would trust her, play along with her, and understand that 'unless they could escape the Oankali, their children would not be human' and so 'accept anything until they were sent to Earth.'[51] Moreover, her human allies would have to be 'thoughtful people who would...learn all she could teach them, all the Oankali could teach them, then use what they had learned to escape and keep themselves alive,' and thereby successfully commission her subversive plan of undermining the Oankali tenets by abiding by the letter of the law.[52] As she symbolically acquiesces to the Oankali agenda of genetic trade, her actions belie her independent and courageous stance as a mother figure who has the welfare of her human wards at heart.

But her dual allegiance makes her walk a very thin line. The fact that Lilith remains the primary spokesperson for the Oankali cause situates her as a traitor to the humans. The trope of the traitor seems to be an appendage that the rabbinic Lilith carries with her as she changes her loyalties from Adam and God to Satan; it is handed down to the Butlerian Lilith with all its treacherous connotations.[53] Eva Federmayer points out that Lilith in her role of a mother, despite being abhorred as a traitor by humans, seeks to help both the humans and the Oankali so that they can survive by adaptation, an adaptation that means not to merely comply with existing patriarchal laws but to survive through continued renegotiations. This theme further resonates with the stigma of black slave women being the 'traitor of the race' given their status in the white slavemaster's household.[54] Naturally, some humans 'believe [her] for a little while. Then some of them…decide [she is] lying to them,' which Lilith reconciles within herself, thinking, 'It was inevitable that some of the people she Awakened would disbelieve her…distrust her.'[55]

And yet, as *Dawn* draws to a close, Lilith virtually sacrifices herself for the human cause as she lets Nikanj lead her into 'the dark forest,' where she is impregnated her against her will, becoming the mother of the first male human-Oankali construct child, as she hopefully awaits the return of the humans.[56] This child, Akin, gives Lilith another opportunity to re-live her motherhood. As Akin is born, Lilith watches over him wistfully, knowing deep down within herself that he is only half human. She is thankful to Nikanj for making Akin 'look completely Human,' but the mother in her worries whether 'his senses are all right,' as she says,

> 'That's all I can expect, I guess.' A sigh. 'Shall I thank you for making him look this way – for making him seem Human so I can love him…for a while.' … 'And I think you go on loving them even when they change.'[57]

Akin is a born-and-bred Oankali and is totally disconnected from his human self. Akin's other name, Eka, means 'lonely' in Sanskrit. Akin's saga is a story of a desire to bond with the 'other,' to alleviate his loneliness, to create familial bonding through knowledge of the human part of his identity as well as the Oankali part. Lilith fascinates him, although

> there was something wrong with her [flesh] – something he did not understand. It was both…deadly and compelling. … In fact, though he had clearly been Human and native to this place, this *Earth*, like Lilith, he had not been Lilith's relative.[58]

Clearly a lack of connection with Lilith haunts Akin's mind. His mother seems to exist as a remote presence, a presence Akin is fascinated by but which frustrates his understanding of her.

Lilith seems to move into a phase of mourning, Bowlby's 'reorganisation[al],' phase, which finds the mourner integrating new sets of social behaviour even as she weans herself away from the haunting, primary loss of her biological child.[59] Lilith emerges as a perceptive, caring mother whose intuitive knowledge tells her that her biological son, Jodahs in *Imago*, is the first human-construct ooloi, an accidental mishap who is otherwise perfect. Unlike Jodahs's human father, Tino, one of Lilith's human suitors, Lilith does not explode with anger and push for an exile of the child as per Oankali law. She supports Nikanj's desire to make an exception for the child and let him be with them, even though if Nikanj was unable to convince the other Oankali and reach a consensus in her favour, Lilith would be exiled. In fact, Jodahs experiences the last vestiges of his humanity as he wistfully muses,

> Lilith came to share my platform, though she could have raised her own. My scent must have disturbed her, but she sat near me and looked at me. ... I could remember being inside her. I could remember when there was nothing in my universe except her.[60]

In her reconstructive phase, Lilith emerges as an integral part of her Oankali family; she admits a 'literal, physical addiction' built on the reciprocity of pleasure and pain between herself and Nikanj, her 'grotesque lover...[and] child.'[61] Lilith seems to come a full circle as she realises that humans will always regard her as a traitor. She fascinates the reader in all her complexity as, despite this damning knowledge, she defends the human resistors, telling the Oankali, 'Do nothing unless they come after us. ... If they do come, run.'[62] Only as a last resort, she says, 'If they catch you, kill.'[63] Her cryptic advice to kill the humans brings to the fore her changed status – one that is 'weighted with guilt...[a] betrayal of her own Human kind for people who were not Human, or not altogether Human'; one that admits her allegiance to a new family, a replacement for the one she has lost.[64] She re-memories the journey of her re-born life: her initial abhorrent dismissal of Nikanj impregnating her with Joseph's seeds as the ooloi had envisaged the need for Lilith to have children; and her growing love for Nikanj and her closeness to her 'reconstructed' family, something she 'didn't have with the family [she] was born into or with [her] husband and son.'[65] Her conversation with Jesusa, a human she convinces to mate with Jodahs, leads her to an honest admission of her sexual liaison with Nikanj. A story is re-told, maybe for the last time – a story to be passed on to another human, to give up her 'human' life and become the consort of an Oankali to create a construct family. This final re-telling brings a sense of peace to Lilith and creates the last and lasting image of her as Jodahs looks on:

She was drawing with black ink or dye on bark cloth...scenes of Earth before the war. ... She was drawing an outdoor family meal with all of us gathered and eating from gourd dishes and Lo bowls. All. My parents, my siblings – and Jesusa and Tomas.[66]

Lilith's re-living of motherhood – both the surrogate and the biological – progresses through wistfulness, regret, and loss as she moves through stages of grief. *Dawn* opens in the initial phase of grief – a numbed Lilith in shock goes through deep frustration and even panic as, given the Oankali agenda to fulfil, she yearns and searches for filial substitutes for her deceased son. Haunted by moments of disorganisation and despair, Lilith slowly reaches a sense of calm before beginning to reorganise her life. Thus *Dawn* ends with Lilith awaiting the return of her human wards, and *Adulthood Rites* begins with her knowing that her biological son is like her only in looks – looks that are temporary and that will change. All she can do is love him 'for a while.'[67] Despite this sense of loss, Lilith seems more reconciled to her loss in *Adulthood Rites*, more at peace with herself, advising Akin only when he needs her. She is no longer the vulnerable victim, a residue of a trauma that has left her broken in mind and spirit. The devastating loss of Ayre, the grief that throttled her, has now been somewhat released through the 'told stories' that she has lived through – sometimes first-hand, as with Akin, and sometimes vicariously through her human wards and Nikanj. However, it is only in *Imago* that Lilith reorganises her life, playing a seminal role in the life of her human-ooloi construct son, Jodahs, as she stands integrated with her new family, represented in the drawings she creates. Often, as with narratives of trauma, connections are elusive – they are there and not there. The connections, however, need to be sought, need to be conjectured by a creative listening and understanding by the invested reader.

Notes

[1] See https://sites.google.com/a/depauw.edu/the-parable-of-the-sower/octavia-e-butler-1.

[2] Octavia Butler, *Lilith's Brood* (New York: Grand Central Publishing, 2000), 38.

[3] Linda Hogan, *The Woman Who Watches over the World: A Native Memoir* (New York: W. W. Norton, 2001), as quoted in Marissa Parham, 'Saying 'Yes': Textual Trauma in Octavia Butler's *Kindred*,' *Callaloo* 32 (2009): 1315-1331, 1315.

[4] Regarding trauma, survival and memory, see the 'continuing bond' theory discussed in George A. Bonanno and Stacey Kaltman, 'Toward an Integrative Perspective on Bereavement,' *Psychological Bulletin* 125 (1999): 760-776; Dennis Klass, 'The Deceased Child in the Psychic and Social Worlds of Bereaved Parents

during the Resolution of Grief,' *Continuing Bonds: New Understanding of Grief*, ed. Dennis Klass, et al. (Philadelphia: Taylor and Francis, 1996), 199-215; Ruth Malkinson, *Cognitive Grief Therapy: Constructing A Rational Meaning To Life Following Loss* (New York: W.W. Norton, 2007); and Rama Ronen, et al., 'The Relationship between Grief Adjustment and Continuing Bonds for Parents Who Have Lost a Child,' *Omega* 60 (2009-2010): 1-31. See also Veena Das, *Life and Words: Violence and the Descent Into the Ordinary* (Berkeley: University of California Press, 2007). Das talks about women in India who had undergone the trauma of partition when the country was divided into India and Pakistan. In their everyday lives, these women continued as if nothing had happened but gave voice to the deep seated trauma in communal gatherings – in the stories they told. Das emphasizes this psychic splitting to be an imperative for everyday life to go on.

[5] See Terry Paul Caesar, 'Slavery and Motherhood in Toni Morrison's *Beloved*,' *Revista de Letras* 34 (1994): 111-120; Inderjit Grewal, 'The Monstrous and Maternal in Toni Morrison's *Beloved*,' *Hosting the Monster*, eds. Holly L. Baumgartner, et al. (Amsterdam: Rodopi, 2008), 63-80; Deborah Horvitz, 'Nameless Ghosts: Possession and Dispossession in *Beloved*,' *Studies in American Fiction* 18 (1990): 157-167; Elizabeth House, 'Toni Morrison's Ghost: The Beloved who is not Beloved,' *Studies in American Fiction* 18 (1990): 17-26; and Jean Wyatt, 'Giving Body to the Word: The Maternal Symbolic in Toni Morrison's *Beloved*,' *Publications of the Modern Language Association of America* 108 (1993): 474-488.

[6] Colleen Cullinan, 'A Maternal Discourse of Redemption: Speech and Suffering in Morrison's *Beloved*,' *Religion and Literature* 34 (2002): 77-104. For feminist writings that ignore the mother's voice, see, in particular, Marianne Hirsch, 'Maternity and Rememory,' *Representations of Motherhood*, eds. Donna Bassin, et al. (New Haven: Yale University Press, 1994), 92-110.

[7] Cullinan, 'A Maternal Discourse of Redemption,' 78. And Bill Flatt, 'Some Stages of Grief,' *Journal of Religion and Health* 26 (1987): 143-148.

[8] Shirley A. Stave, 'Toni Morrison's *Beloved* and the Vindication of Lilith,' *South Atlantic Review* 58 (1993): 49-66, 50.

[9] Ibid., 65.

[10] See Dorothy Allison, 'The Future of Female: Octavia Butler's Mother Lode,' in *Reading Black, Reading Feminist*, ed. Henry Louis Gates, Jr. (New York: Meridian, 1990), 471-78, 471; Erika Horwitz, 'Resistance as a Site of Empowerment: The Journey away from Maternal Sacrifice,' in *Mother Outlaws: Theories and Practices of Empowered Mothering*, ed. Andrea O'Reilly (Toronto: Women's Press, 2004), 43-58, 54; Larry McCaffery, *Across the Wounded Galaxies: Interviews with Contemporary American Science Fiction Writers* (Urbana: University of Illinois Press, 1990), 67; and Andrea O'Reilly, 'Maternal

Conceptions in Toni Morrison's The Bluest Eye and Tar Baby: 'A Woman Has to Be a Daughter before She Can Be Any Kind of Woman,'' in *This Giving Birth: Pregnancy and Childbirth in American Women's Writing*, ed. Julie Tharp and Susan MacCallum-Whitcomb (Bowling Green, OH: Popular, 2000), 83-102.

[11] Butler, *Lilith's Brood*, 5.

[12] John Bowlby, *Attachment and Loss*, Vol. 3 (New York: Basic Books, 1980), 116. Butler, *Lilith's Brood*, 7.

[13] Butler herself traces Sharad's genealogy through Lilith, who says, 'I think he must have been East Indian.' Butler, *Lilith's Brood*, 19.

[14] Ibid., 10.

[15] Ibid.

[16] Ibid., 11.

[17] Ibid., 60.

[18] Ibid., 18.

[19] Ibid., 19.

[20] Ibid., 20.

[21] Andrea Hairston, 'Octavia Butler: Praise Song to a Prophetic Artist,' *Daughters of Earth: Feminist Science Fiction in the Twentieth Century*, ed. Justine Larbalestier (Connecticut: Wesleyan University Press, 2006), 287-304, 298.

[22] Gina Wisker, 'Your Buried Ghosts Have a Way of Tripping You Up: Revisioning and Mothering in African-American and Afro-Caribbean Women's Speculative Horror,' *Femspec* 6 (2005): 71-86, 73, 85.

[23] Butler, *Lilith's Brood*, 43. Eric White, 'The Erotics of Becoming: *Xenogenesis* and 'The Thing,'' *Science Fiction Studies* 20 (1993): 394-408, 402.

[24] Butler, *Lilith's Brood*, 111-112.

[25] Stave, 'Toni Morrison's *Beloved* and the Vindication of Lilith,' 57. See also Raphael Patai, *The Hebrew Goddess* (Detroit: Wayne State University Press, 1967).

[26] Stave, 'Toni Morrison's *Beloved* and the Vindication of Lilith,' 57. See also Raphael Patai, *The Hebrew Goddess* (Detroit: Wayne State University Press, 1967).

[27] Toni Morrison, 'Site of Memory,' in *Inventing the Truth*, ed. William Zinsser (Boston: Houghton Mifflin, 1987), 101-124, 112, 115.

[28] Butler, *Lilith's Brood*, 77.

[29] Ibid.

[30] Ibid.

[31] Ibid.

[32] Ibid., 77-78.

[33] Roberta Culbertson, 'Embodied Memory, Transcendence, and Telling: Recounting Trauma, Re-Establishing the Self,' *New Literary History* 26 (1995): 169-95, as quoted in Parham, 'Saying Yes,' 1324.
[34] Butler, *Lilith's Brood*, 91.
[35] Ibid., 93.
[36] Ibid., 94.
[37] Ibid., 96.
[38] Ibid., 153.
[39] Ibid., 305.
[40] Ibid., 161.
[41] Ibid., 187, 191.
[42] Ibid., 161.
[43] Bridget Haylock, 'The Trauma of the Colonised: Writing Female in Baynton's *Human Toll*' in this volume.
[44] Morrison, *Beloved*, 36.
[45] Richard Tedeschi and Lawrence Calhoun, *Trauma and Transformation: Growing in the Aftermath of Suffering* (London: Sage, 1995), 131.
[46] K. Denea Stewart-Shaheed, 'Re-membering Blackness in the Neo-Slave Writings of Octavia Butler and Zora Neale Hurston,' *Reclaiming Home, Remembering Motherhood, Rewriting History: African American and Afro-Caribbean Women's Literature in the Twentieth Century,* eds. Verena Theile and Marie Drews (Newcastle upon Tyne: Cambridge Scholars Publishing, 2009), 233-251, 234.
[47] Butler, *Lilith's Brood*, 118.
[48] Ibid., 122.
[49] Ibid., 120-121.
[50] Ibid., 134-135.
[51] Ibid., 117.
[52] Ibid., 117.
[53] See Michelle Osherow, 'The Dawn of a New Lilith: Revisionary Mythmaking in Women's Science Fiction,' *NWSA Journal* 12 (2000): 68-83; and Sarah Wood, 'Subversion through Inclusion: Octavia Butler's Interrogation of Religion in *Xenogenesis* and *Wild Seed*,' *Femspec* 6 (2005): 87-99; and Barbara Koltuv, *The Book of Lilith* (York Beach, Me.: Nicholas-Hayes, 1986).
[54] Eva Federmayer, 'Octavia Butler's Maternal Cyborgs: The Black Female World of the *Xenogenesis* Trilogy' *Hungarian Journal of English and American Studies* 6 (2000): 103-118, 113. In addition to Federmayer, see also Angela Davis, 'Reflections on the Black Woman's Role in the Community of Slaves,' in *The Massachusetts Review* 13 (1972): 81-100.
[55] Butler, *Lilith's Brood*, 167.

[56] Ibid., 248.
[57] Ibid., 254.
[58] Ibid., 257.
[59] Bowlby, *Attachment and Loss*, 120-22.
[60] Butler, *Lilith's Brood*, 541.
[61] Ibid., 679, 79 .
[62] Ibid., 572.
[63] Ibid.
[64] Ibid., 670.
[65] Ibid., 671.
[66] Ibid., 690.
[67] Ibid., 254.

Bibliography

Allison, Dorothy. 'The Future of Female: Octavia Butler's Mother Lode'. In *Reading Black, Reading Feminist*, edited by Henry Louis Gates, Jr., 471-78. New York: Meridian, 1990.

Anatol, Giselle Liza. 'Maternal Discourses in Nalo Hopkinson's Midnight Robber'. *African American Review* 40 (2006): 111-124.

Bonanno, George A. and S. Kaltman. 'Toward an Integrative Perspective on Bereavement'. *Psychological Bulletin* 125 (1999): 760-776.

Bowlby, John. *Attachment and Loss*. Vol. 3. New York: Basic Books, 1980.

Butler, Octavia. *Lilith's Brood*. New York: Grand Central Publishing, 2000.

Caesar, Terry Paul. 'Slavery and Motherhood in Toni Morrison's *Beloved*'. *Revista de Letras* 34 (1994): 111-120.

Caruth, Cathy, ed. *Trauma: Explorations in Memory*. Baltimore: John Hopkins Press, 1995.

Culbertson, Roberta. 'Embodied Memory, Transcendence, and Telling: Recounting Trauma, Re-Establishing the Self'. *New Literary History* 26 (1995): 169-95.

Cullinan, Colleen. 'A Maternal Discourse of Redemption: Speech and Suffering in Morrison's *Beloved*'. *Religion and Literature* 34 (2002): 77-104.

Darwish, Mahmoud. *Memory for Forgetfulness: August, Beirut, 1982*. Translated by Ibrahim Muhawi. Berkeley: University of California Press, 1995.

Das, Veena. *Life and Words: Violence and the Descent into the Ordinary*. Berkeley: University of California Press, 2007.

Davis, Angela. 'Reflections on the Black Woman's Role in the Community of Slaves'. *The Massachusetts Review* 13 (1972): 81-100.

Federmayer, Eva. 'Octavia Butler's Maternal Cyborgs: The Black Female World of the *Xenogenesis* Trilogy'. *Hungarian Journal of English and American Studies* 6 (2000): 103-118.

Flatt, Bill. 'Some Stages of Grief'. *Journal of Religion and Health* 26 (1987): 143-148.

Freud, Sigmund. 'Mourning and Melancholia'. In *The Standard Edition of the Complete Psychological Works of Sigmund Freud*, Vol. 14, edited and translated by James Strachey, 239-260. London: Hogarth Press, 1917.

Grewal, Inderjit. 'The Monstrous and Maternal in Toni Morrison's *Beloved*'. In *Hosting the Monster*, edited by Holly L. Baumgartner and Roger Davis, 63-80. Amsterdam: Rodopi, 2008.

Hairston, Andrea. 'Octavia Butler: Praise Song to a Prophetic Artist'. In *Daughters of Earth: Feminist Science Fiction in the Twentieth Century*, edited by Justine Larbalestier, 287-304. Middletown, Ct.: Wesleyan University Press, 2006.

Hirsch, Marianne. 'Maternity and Rememory: Toni Morrison's *Beloved*'. In *Representations of Motherhood*, edited by Donna Bassin, Margaret Honey, and Meryle Mahrer Kaplan, 92-110. New Haven: Yale University Press, 1994.

Hogan, Linda. *The Woman Who Watches Over the World: A Native Memoir*. New York: W. W. Norton, 2001.

Horvitz, Deborah. 'Nameless Ghosts: Possession and Dispossession in *Beloved*'. *Studies in American Fiction* 18 (1990): 157-167.

Horwitz, Erika. 'Resistance as a Site of Empowerment: The Journey Away from Maternal Sacrifice'. In *Mother Outlaws: Theories and Practices of Empowered Mothering,* edited by Andrea O'Reilly. Toronto: Women's Press, 2004. 43-58.

House, Elizabeth. 'Toni Morrison's Ghost: The Beloved who is not Beloved'. *Studies in American Fiction* 18 (1990): 17-26.

Klass, Dennis. 'Continuing Conversation about Continuing Bonds'. *Death Studies* 30 (2006), 843-858.

————. 'The Deceased Child in the Psychic and Social Worlds of Bereaved Parents during the Resolution of Grief'. In *Continuing Bonds: New Understanding of Grief,* edited by Dennis Klass, Phyliss R. Silverman, and Steve L. Nickman, 199-215. Philadelphia: Taylor and Francis, 1996.

Koltuv, Barbara. *The Book of Lilith.* York Beach, Me.: Nicholas-Hayes, 1986.

Malkinson, Ruth. *Cognitive Grief Therapy: Constructing a Rational Meaning to Life Following Loss.* New York: W.W. Norton, 2007.

McCaffery, Larry. *Across the Wounded Galaxies: Interviews with Contemporary American Science Fiction Writers.* Urbana: University of Illinois Press, 1990.

Morrison. Toni. *Beloved.* New York: Vintage International, 1987.

————. 'Site of Memory'. In *Inventing the Truth,* edited by William Zinsser, 103-24. New York: Houghton Mifflin, 1995.

O'Reilly, Andrea. 'Maternal Conceptions in Toni Morrison's The Bluest Eye and Tar Baby: 'A Woman Has to Be a Daughter before She Can Be Any Kind of Woman''. In *This Giving Birth: Pregnancy and Childbirth in American Women's Writing,* edited by Julie Tharp and Susan MacCallum-Whitcomb, 83-102. Bowling Green, OH: Popular, 2000.

Osherow, Michelle. 'The Dawn of a New Lilith: Revisionary Mythmaking in Women's Science Fiction'. *NWSA Journal* 12 (2000): 68-83.

Parham, Marissa. 'Saying Yes: Textual Trauma in Octavia Butler's *Kindred*'. *Callaloo* 32 (2009): 1315-1331.

Patai, Raphael. *The Hebrew Goddess*. Detroit: Wayne State University Press, 1967.

Ronen, Rama, Wendy Packman, Nigel Field, Betty Davis, Robin Kramer, and Janet Long. 'The Relationship between Grief Adjustment and Continuing Bonds for Parents Who Have Lost a Child'. *Omega* 60 (2009-2010): 1-31.

Stave, Shirley A. 'Toni Morrison's *Beloved* and the Vindication of Lilith'. *South Atlantic Review* 58 (1993): 49-66.

Stewart-Shaheed, K. Denea. 'Re-Membering Blackness in the Neo-Slave Writings of Octavia Butler and Zora Neale Hurston'. In *Reclaiming Home, Remembering Motherhood, Rewriting History: African American and Afro-Caribbean Women's Literature in the Twentieth Century*, edited by Verena Theile and Marie Drews, 233-251. Newcastle upon Tyne: Cambridge Scholars Publishing, 2009.

Tedeschi, Richard and Lawrence Calhoun. *Trauma and Transformation: Growing in the Aftermath of Suffering*. London: Sage, 1995.

White, Eric. 'The Erotics of Becoming: *Xenogenesis* and *The Thing*'. *Science Fiction Studies* 20 (1993): 394-408.

Wisker, Gina. 'Your Buried Ghosts Have a Way of Tripping You Up: Revisioning and Mothering in African-American and Afro-Caribbean Women's Speculative Horror'. *Femspec* 6 (2005): 71-86.

Wood, Sarah. 'Subversion through Inclusion: Octavia Butler's Interrogation of Religion in *Xenogenesis* and *Wild Seed*'. *Femspec* 6 (2005): 87-99.

Wyatt, Jean. 'Giving Body to the Word: The Maternal Symbolic in Toni Morrison's *Beloved*'. *Publications of the Modern Language Association of America* 108 (1993): 474-488.

Aparajita Nanda, Visiting Associate Professor to the departments of English and African American Studies, UC Berkeley, has taught for over 15 years at Jadavpur University, India. Fulbright faculty teaching scholarship awardee, she now teaches both at UC Berkeley and Santa Clara University. She has been widely published in scholarly peer-reviewed journals and is the editor of *Romancing the Strange: The Fiction of Kunal Basu* (2004) and *Black California* (2010). Her forthcoming publications include a chapter in *Critical Anthology of California Literature* edited Blake Allmendinger, Cambridge UP (2014).

The Trauma of the Colonised: Writing Female in Barbara Baynton's *Human Toll*

Bridget Haylock

Abstract

In this chapter I argue that the radical textual practice in Barbara Baynton's (1857-1929) novel, *Human Toll* (1907), foreshadows contemporary feminine appropriation and subversion of the Bildungsroman genre which testifies to traumatic experience; specifically the creative emergence from the traumatic inheritance of feminine embodiment, demonstrated by concern with feminine subjectivity and signified by the colonised female (body). What Baynton argues for in *Human Toll* is an autonomous place for feminine expression, for *écriture féminine*, in the symbolic world. In a perturbation of genres, Baynton combines melodrama—the *genre par excellence* in which women have agency by default; romance; and the Bildungsroman, to create an impression of how fraught access to creative agency is for women in the context of trauma, and the cultural constraints on women at the cusp of Federation in the Australian Bush. As her heroine emerges from the feminine traumatic paradigm, her encounters with many aspects of the phallocentric world provoke traumatic repetition. For Baynton no masculine edifice is sacrosanct: Catholicism, property law, marriage, sex, education, wealth, and class are all found to be wanting in relation to the feminine. Experiences of opposition and denial serve to spur the protagonist into a fervent conviction of her desire for agency, and to find creative and cathartic expression in writing. In doing so, as Suzette Henke contends, the female author initiates an enabling discourse of testimony and self-revelation. In audaciously reinscribing the claims of feminine desire into the texts of a traditionally patriarchal culture, this *écriture féminine* attempts to reframe embodied experience through experimentation of assumptions around signifying practices, interrogating the outcome for its relation to power and feminine subjectivity.

Key Words: Barbara Baynton, *Human Toll*, trauma, feminine desire, creative emergence, *écriture féminine*, genre.

*****

1. Introduction

In this chapter I argue that the textual practice in Barbara Baynton's (1857-1929) novel, *Human Toll,* foreshadows contemporary Australian female-authored writings that testify to traumatic experience.[1] I specifically focus on the traumatic inheritance of feminine embodiment, demonstrated by the work's thematic concern with feminine subjectivity and signified by the colonised female (body), and argue that *Human Toll* represents an example of female resistance through creative emergence.

In the novel Baynton has created an articulate argument for the paramount challenge of her time: feminine subjectivity, or 'the woman question' as it was then known, which addressed issues such as the denial of financial autonomy, 'control of their sexuality and childbearing, and access to social power' for women.[2] Gender roles as constructed at the beginning of the twentieth century in Australia were polarised and harshly prescriptive. Baynton was a radical voice, who nevertheless wrote and found publishers for her work in an era when women had limited influence outside the domestic sphere. Her first collection of short stories, *Bush Studies,*[3] was published in England, because the subject matter 'was considered too difficult and uncomfortable for an Australian audience.'[4] The same company, Duckworth, in England, for its Greenback Colonial Library imprint, published her short novel, *Human Toll*, in 1907. It is noteworthy that she was published at a time when women were particularly politically active, the first wave of feminism. The narrative works as a testimonial: it performs 'the historical and contradictory double task of the breaking of the silence and of the simultaneous shattering of any given discourse,' the radical nature of which, partially explains the reason for its lack of commercial success.[5] Her work was not recognised again until the second wave of feminism in the 1970s, when Australian scholars rediscovered the voices of earlier female writers. *Human Toll* was reprinted in 1980 when it appeared in a series, *Portable Australian Authors,* one of which featured Baynton's collected works.

Human Toll depicts the painful experience of a young woman's coming of age into a symbolic world that refuses to recognise her agency. Luce Irigaray argues that 'from a feminine locus nothing can be articulated without a questioning of the symbolic itself.'[6] Here, Baynton contests woman's status and argues for the feminist cause in the Australian context, and her contention continues to be relevant more than one hundred years later. While many themes are dealt with in the novel, and as Irigaray states, 'there are centuries of sociocultural values to be rethought, to be transformed' if women are to find a value in being women and not just identified as mothers, the focus of my argument centres upon Baynton's call for the necessity of a place in the symbolic for the creative emergence from trauma by women.[7]

A close reading of *Human Toll* brings to light the many gaps and silences, which direct the reader to consider the author's textual practice in the light of theories of trauma and creativity. What such an analysis reveals is that the symbolic world as constructed represses what it deems dangerous—embodied feminine desire; this then can only mean traumatic experience for women. As Gayle Rubin contends, 'according to Freudian orthodoxy, the attainment of 'normal' femininity extracts severe costs from women.'[8] Then as Karen Horney asserts, 'women's whole reaction to life would be based on a strong subterranean resentment.'[9]

Baynton combines, manipulates and subverts several literary modes: the gothic romance, melodrama and, most especially, the Bildungsroman, written in a modernist style focalised through a central female character. The melodramatic genre as practised in women's narratives, with its heightened domestic and emotional *mise en scène*, offers a cogent screen for prevalent trauma and abuse. E. Ann Kaplan argues that melodrama ''corrects' the misogynist bias of male-dominated culture' and offers images of suppressed women; she notes that feminist critics of melodrama and gender argue 'that melodrama exposed female suffering if it was unable to oppose it.'[10] In a concerted effort to claim agency Baynton also uses carnivalesque elements, to create a richly oppositional text.

She thus writes back to the masculine culture of the traumatic inheritance of female embodiment as constructed in the Australia of early Federation, where the female body is a cultural creation 'inscribed and reinscribed by social norms, practices, and values' and which can be read as a system of signs that denotes a consequently problematised subjectivity.[11] In this chapter I will consider *Human Toll* in the light of trauma theory, female embodiment, and creative emergence—which is defined as the appearance of an autonomous subjectivity from a traumatic paradigm via artistic practice—as demonstrated in the novel.

2. Trauma, Silence, Witnessing

To read a literary text in the context of trauma theory is to perceive trauma as a threat to existence; one for which causal events are not fully encoded and of which the memories are thus often foreclosed. It is sometimes possible however to discover in a text traces of an originary trauma by looking for recurrent symbols. As this applies to *Human Toll,* the originary trauma is the fact of Ursula (or Ursie)'s mother's death, which, as Ursula is then an infant, presents a direct threat to her survival. For Elizabeth Grosz, the 'corporeal connection to the mother that women in patriarchy are required to abandon' results in traumatic experience.[12] For Ursula, 'her mother she could not remember.'[13] This affirms Julia Kristeva's position that 'matricide is our vital necessity' so women might successfully enter the symbolic world, and which assumes that the gendered position 'woman' holds an abject status.[14] This inaccessibility to memory of the mother's death is also a signifier for the power-less female. Being born female, she represents the dis-empowered maternal line; her birth is the death of the possibility of the child carrying forward a paternal line in the symbolic because she cannot 'kill' the mother if she is already dead; but her birth is an act of resistance, where resistance is the response to the traumatic realisation of female embodiment in a patriarchally symbolised world. Kay Shaffer rightly acknowledges that in reading Baynton's work:

> . . . from a post-structuralist position, woman is an empty
> signifier whose place is filled by the codes which name woman
> in the discourses of mythology, religion and politics in which
> woman is denied her difference outside of the patriarchal order.[15]

However, Shaffer does not discuss its traumatic affects, nor any possibility of creative emergence. Suzette Henke asserts that 'every novel incorporates shards of social, psychological and cultural history into the texture of its ostensibly mimetic world.'[16] Baynton narrates how women's trauma builds resistance and opposition and gradually creates a picture of what life is for women in *fin de siècle* Australia, where the proportion of males to females was seven to one. Early on, for example, women comprised twenty per cent of transported convicts and, beginning in 1851, the colonial gold rushes brought a huge influx of male diggers to the goldfields. For a century from 1793, a bounty was offered to encourage single women to migrate from Europe in a concerted effort to balance the gender ratio, which, by 1907, in newly federated Australia remained disproportionately weighted in favour of males.

Common among bush stories, according to Caroline M. Pascoe, is the trope of the strong independent and motherless, even sisterless, young woman, the Australian Girl or Bush Girl, more associated with an accomplished squatter's daughter, than identified with the maternal.[17] However, in presenting Ursula as having no female relatives, no female genealogy, Baynton shows women as vulnerable and consistently depicts a world wherein the female is reliant on male relationships for her survival, even if they all fail her. Ursula's entry into the socio-symbolic world from whence she might gain education and then ironically use that knowledge to create a different role for herself must always be mediated through a male, which, when this expectation is disappointed, necessitates that traumatic repetition becomes a fact of survival. As Cathy Caruth argues, trauma becomes not only an effect of destruction, but also 'an enigma of survival,' which drives creative emergence.[18]

Characteristic of trauma survivors is 'emotional detachment', 'withdrawal from engagement with others', and often 'protracted depression'; 'since the Sunday of the storm she had met all dangers silently' wherein non-engagement serves as a protective mechanism against perceived further threats.[19] [20] In the encounter with traumatic repetition, survival for Ursula means that she must constantly repress the affect of disturbing circumstances. Firstly when her mother dies; then, when her father expires, her conscious knowledge of these events is denied by those around her, so again she cannot grieve. Boshy, assumes a protective role, but is then usurped by the paternalistic Cameron, who arrives to remove Ursula from all she has known and appropriate her inheritance for himself 'We must take the child . . . she must be schooled.'[21] He will not leave her in the bush to grow up as 'a wild animal.'[22] As the local arbiter of symbolic law, he cannot allow Ursula to grow into herself; she must be silenced, confined and educated just enough, so she may make a good marriage and take her rightful woman's place in the symbolic. For the young female, separated from the semiotic (dead) mother and taken out into the symbolic world, and into sexual service for men, the semiotic continues to work; it is at the thetic, that borderline of instantiation between the symbolic and the semiotic that the subject both comes into being and is under threat. 'The child met them outside, her eyes unnaturally open, her mouth unusually indrawn, and unnaturally and unusually silent.'[23] In order to survive, Ursula, the traumatised subject, disassociates as she cannot be present to witness another threat to her existence.

In the character of the barren and loveless Widow Irvine, Baynton appears to be parodying the woman's status as devout Wesleyan Christian and widow, both states of disempowerment for a woman, as both describe her relationship to male hierarchy, not her own subjectivity. In this relationship, Baynton offers a potential alternative for women: the widow and this girl child have a chance to learn how to grow strong together and become uncompromising females. However, Mr Civil vies for power over them and overshadows their relationship. Baynton here uses a melodramatic plot to confront the inequity within the traditional colonial domestic environment: deviation from prescribed roles is disallowed, and Ursula and her 'Aunt' are forced to succumb to the will of the socially dominant man. After being locked up for her audacity at church when she pokes out her tongue at Civil, Ursula is described as 'a representative of the cruel sex' when she tortures a hornet and a fly.[24] Indifferent to their suffering 'she slowly pulled off their wings.'[25] This highlights the desensitised state of a trauma survivor as Ursula unconsciously acts out her trauma. Judith Herman contends that 'the study of trauma in sexual and domestic life becomes legitimate only in a context that challenges the subordination of women and children.'[26]

In the opening chapter Boshy, who, while alive, facilitates a maternal function for her, describes Ursula as 'the innercentest liddle lamb,' an image that recurs with the neglected lambs of the selection's flock needing watering, that also contains anagrammatically 'incest'—innocence always already threatened by incest.[27] It is bookended by images of crow-pecked, eyeless sheep bogged in muddy waterholes and the grown Ursula's 'poddy lamb', being accidentally crushed to death by sly, drunken Hugh Palmer as he flees with Ursula's inheritance.[28] This image is a recurrence of the mother in *The Chosen Vessel*, and of the misapprehension of the raped and slaughtered, white-robed mother and child for a dead 'sheep.' Thus these lambs and sheep might be seen as standing in for feminine experience in the symbolic where they are viewed with the masculine gaze as vulnerable and needing tending, only to be abandoned and disregarded at a whim, once (ab)used, and quickly dismissed and discarded as carcass, and/or vessel empty of signification. Boshy says 'It seems t' me, Lovey, that these lambs ov Gord in this towen must play putty well ther same games as ther lambs in ther

Bush.'[29] The lamb image also connects with Baynton's religious theme; she devotes the whole of the third chapter to Sunday: the preparation for, the going to and the returning from a church service. She describes the visiting minister variously as, 'waresman', 'showman', 'spiritual cuckoo', 'spiritual physician', 'preacher', and 'parson.'[30] Ursula experiences the stultifying and oppressive effects of church, tyrannical Civil's hypocrisy and the threat of a vengeful God, which causes subsequent confusion for her about religion. The eyeless Christ on the cross in the bush cannot save her, cannot slake her thirst. This again is the sociosymbolic order mediated through the masculine, failing to provide.

When Aunt/Mrs Civil dies:

> As ever an unreality girt and governed the girl's normal senses – surely this bed-scene must be familiar. An indefinable impulse seized her to go outside, find, then softly sigh through a crack, but low down – she wanted it almost level with the bed.[31]

Thus for Ursula the trauma of death is repeated. This urge is a repetition of the death of her father when she was small, and:

> she went noiselessly round to the widest crack in the bedroom and looked through . . . but neither motion nor sound answered her . . . the sense of the mysterious fell upon her, and her mouth set maturely as she turned away.[32]

Little Ursula represses what she cannot bear to know, for it would threaten her existence 'neither has she any fixed idea of her father's death.'[33] The unconscious memory returns as an uncanny image when confronted by another traumatic situation or trigger event. 'Traumatic memories lack verbal narrative and context; rather they are encoded in the form of vivid sensations and images.'[34] When Mrs Civil's funeral procession passes the waiting Ursula 'she sank on her knees, then she fell face downward, blind with tears and grief for an undefinable sorrow . . . A waiting quiet possessed her, but she felt alone.'[35] Although this appears to be an overreaction to her Aunt's death, here, Ursula is involuntarily grieving the death of her mother. This is the return of the repressed, 'her surprised tears deluged and embarrassed her,' which arises unbidden from the unconscious.[36] Another repressed traumatic memory surfaces when, after the dance, she awakes to spring birdsong, however:

> A vivid sense of past and coming trouble gripped her, blended with a far-away, but subtle feeling of familiarity. Before, somewhere and time ungraspable, blurred and beset with bewildering details, she had lain alone in bed, listening to

gladsome bird voices, mingled with a sense of distressed humanity.[37]

The birdsong triggers the sense memories of her father's death, which itself is a screen for the originary trauma of her mother's passing. But the memory is not a complete narrative; traumatic memories are often foreclosed, 'fractured, partial, fading into an oblivion' as is access to early childhood memory.[38] A shrieking grandmother and a fierce thunderstorm herald the drowning death of Henry, the Indigenous boy, and trigger a traumatic episode for Ursula, who fears *she* is about to die, especially, as Mr Civil claims, that an angry God is after her. Ursula implores Andrew to 'plant me in the brick oven' she crawls back into the warm, comforting womb, into a safely confined space 'till the violence of the deluging rain silenced heaven's flash and fire' that her traumatised feelings might subside.[39]

Ursula witnesses her own trauma even as she experiences it. The narrative, focalised through the girl, stands as her testimony to traumatic experience in the symbolic. As Shoshana Felman argues, testimony is the positioning of that which is witnessed by the witness and which 'cannot be carried out by anybody else.'[40] *Human Toll* is a chronologically structured Bildungsroman; Baynton allows the reader more information only as Ursula's understanding of her emotional responses and desire increases in direct proportion to her age. Through its bush opening, the reader can only see as far as the child can, to the 'breath-misted' cows and the shack across the river.[41] Eventually, after living in town and seeing the circus, the girl can imagine 'that great world beyond these hills and near the sea.'[42] However, as a female, Ursula's access to the greater phallocentric world is foreclosed; her mind is free to conjure, but since her material inheritance has been denied, unless she marries and travels with a husband, Ursula has no means of financial support, and lacking an education, she is in effect rendered a prisoner in her own life.

Human Toll describes this witnessing through the many references to eyes and sight, which also draws attention to the masculine gaze or western society's privileging of the masculine scopic over the female sensual experience. What Baynton shows is the conflict between the more powerful subject of the masculine gaze and its object, the female, and the feminine witnessing of the traumatic experience of being that object. Boshy implores Ursula to keep her eyes open, 'her sleepless eyes with their strange lonely expression.'[43] Boshy translates the symbolic for Ursula. However, he is also marginalised and abject; he has sacrificed an eye to be able to partially access both the semiotic and symbolic worlds. Anticipating Irigaray's critique of photocentricity as a key aspect of phallocentric culture Baynton applies the trope of vision strategically throughout the novel. She describes Sigmund Freud's analysis of 'the omnipotence of gazing, knowing' where the 'eye-penis' is the source of the 'phallic gaze'; thus does the threat of castration present the fear of loss of sight, knowledge, and therefore power.[44]

Baynton uses the gaze to show how the economy of desire plays out in the relationships to power of each of her characters. Who can see and what they can see, for example, Nungi chastises Boshy 'Fat lot you can see, ole Bungy-Blinkey-eye, ole one-eye!'[45] Ursula goes with Nungi to the well to ensure no debbil-debbils come up in the bucket. In this racially unequal society, she, as a white child, has more power, than the dual heritage adult male, Nungi, 'The little girl's eye-service had been thorough and earnest. Long before he could sight the filled bucket . . . she would strain her eyes then announce.'[46] Baynton uses this theme to show the defiant independence possible of the feminine 'yur gut yur mother's eyes' Boshy gasps to Ursula;[47] that woman's different desire is equally valid when questions of agency arise around her body and her sexuality. Civil attempts to enter Ursula's room in the night 'his eyes. These smouldering lasciviously under his raised, dye-clogged eyebrows, were set as though fed by those of the girl, blazing with a tigerish hate into his.'[48] Ursula responds to his advances by aiming 'a heavy blow at his leering face with the candlestick' associated with the projection of light and thus the facilitation of the male gaze, this action disables the unwanted scrutiny.[49] Palmer, observing Ursula, sees 'her face was a puzzle' and her 'terrible little face.'[50] He is confronted by her recalcitrance, and does not know where to place his desire as a man when she refuses his 'woman'-as-constructed category; she challenges his envisioned world. 'The wide, child-like eyes looking up at him. He looked away from them, for their sincerity challenged his insincerity into silence.'[51] Seeing deeper into Ursula:

> Andrew, intently watching the girl, saw no understood sign of sorrow. Her mouth had set into a straight line, but her eyes were dry and staring. So she had left them all years ago . . . dry eyed and almost silent. A sullen, laboured grief against her seized him.[52]

Baynton envisaged the possibility of a different language of perception for masculinity, based on empathy rather than difference. However, she does not believe this is possible, Andrew 'felt without analyzing [sic] that not years but the world had rolled between him and her.'[53] Ursula has matured in his absence. Her traumatic experience makes it impossible for her to conduct a normal relationship as pre-scripted in post-colonial Australia, let alone consider the concept of a modern one. Mina's baleful green eyes see with a masculine gaze and are taken by crows: her feminine vision is colonised and compromised; whereas Ursula preserves her own 'precious eyes' with a hand, she uses her will to protect her feminine (in)sight, which is the keenest of all her 'unnaturally acute' senses.[54]

The females who die in *Human Toll* are many: Ursula's mother, presumably of childbirth; Widow Irvine/Mrs Civil is subtly poisoned by her husband; Margaret Cameron also dies in childbirth; Mina dies lost in the bush from hysterical postnatal psychosis, precipitated by sexual abuse; and Mina's female baby dies of abuse and neglect. The toll to which the title of the novel refers is, as stated in the story, 'the toll of motherhood' which Margaret Cameron pays, as so many women have done and continue to do, with her life.[55] [56] However, the human toll of the title is not only the tragedy of maternal mortality; it is also the suppression of the feminine which is the price exacted from women to ensure the stability of the symbolic. Feminine will and subjectivity are constructed around servicing masculine desire, at the expense of her unutterable and disallowed desire. The sociosymbolic position of women in newly federated Australia was a place of absence, and women valued only in relation to men. As Baynton writes, 'Subdued and magnetized (sic) into submission, Ursula sat turning her tearful eyes from one uncompromising face to the other.'[57] The very fact of being born female was, and I would argue still can be, a place of lack and this is further secured for male domination by the requirement that the female subject be rendered mute as unrepresentable in the symbolic order, and only partially and unpredictably accessible in the semiotic. Herman writes that 'in order to escape accountability for his crimes . . . secrecy and silence are the perpetrator's first line of defence,'[58] to which Baynton draws attention in the ironically named character of Mr Civil, and the 'Lord and master's attempts to silence her.'[59] Herman attests that the more power held by the perpetrator of abuse 'the greater is his prerogative to name and define reality' hence Civil's insistence that everyone bend to his will, including his wife whom he impels to drink herself to death.[60] 'The subordinate condition of women is maintained and enforced by the hidden violence of men.'[61] Civil's authority and injustice towards Ursula is highlighted as a signifier for the patriarchal symbolic, and the behaviour meted out to his wife is merely suggested on the periphery of the story, hidden from view. After Mrs Civil's death when Ursie is left living with Mr Civil alone 'Ursula felt like a trapped animal forced to feed from her hated captor's hand.'[62] A woman's experience becomes unspeakable when, being 'already devalued (a woman, a child), she may find that the most traumatic events of her life take place outside the realm of socially validated reality.'[63]

By introducing Ursula waking to birdsong and, unbeknownst to her, her father's death and her own disinheritance, Baynton paints a day redolent with promise. However, she reveals that the psychological truth is a lie: Boshy and Queeby do their utmost to hide the truth from the child, knowing that, for them, this means the loss of Ursula. Instead, the little girl is left to read the clues around her and reach her own experiential conclusion. Boshy eventually responds to the child's entreaties with 'arsk no questions, Lovey, an' I'll tell yer no lies.'[64] Cultural inculcation stipulates that as a female, Ursula must learn to accept the symbolic version of the world, even at the expense of her own desire remaining unknowable to her. Although still a child, Boshy charges her with 'a-ketchin' an' a-snarin' an' a-trippin' him. Already she is deemed treacherous; he tells her God won't love her if she continues in tricking him.[65] This shows patriarchal duplicity: the controlling originates with him; the deception comes from Boshy, from him whose façade is friend. Lying to her also amounts to silencing her words, upholding the inherited 'tradition of female silence' to which Ursula is heir and Boshy, proxy maternal, bound to edify.[66] Ursula has no provenance, no female genealogy:

> His 'my dear' gave her a convulsive shiver; still, she made no spoken sign of aversion, for already she was experiencing the inequality of her struggle to alter the thing that is.[67]

There are myriad examples in the novel where Baynton's female characters do not voice their truth. One of the common affects of trauma is the inability to access any memory of the originary traumatic experience, and to allow it to exist in conscious thought. In traumatic silence there is denial and inequity: woman is compelled to deny that she witnesses her own subjectivity. Silence can conversely be interpreted as defiant feminine opposition, however as this behaviour is expected, it only serves to strengthen patriarchal practice.

3. Female Embodiment

Human Toll is a study in the binary of male/female subjectivity based upon gender constructed on sexual difference, but characterised by mutual imbrication. Gender differences, which are social constructs, are projected onto 'sexual difference,' which in turn 'naturalises' the binary division of sexual difference, itself a cultural construct in the sense of a continuum with much distortion in between.

Within this framework, Baynton writes of the gendered body constructed in a society with a robust masculinist heritage and patriarchal power structure. The body is the target of, and 'the vehicle of expression' for, cultural inscription and gender discourse.[68] Driven by the traumatic experience of an impossibly prescriptive gender role for women, Baynton resists this definition and explores whether and how it might be feasible for woman to be empowered, for society to embrace sexual difference and for the female to have an autonomous place within that phallocentric order. However *Human Toll* chronicles repeated failed attempts due to intervention by symbolic law and illustrates prevention of the construction of a successful alternative, based on the premise that woman's difference cannot be assimilated into that order. 'Women have been objectified and alienated as social subjects . . . through the denigration and containment of the female body.'[69] Woman as body is the abjected other, which cannot be signified in patriarchal practice.

Although situated at the beginning of a century when the New Woman was a significant feature of the contemporary culture of First Wave Feminism, and especially manifest in fiction, there is evidence in *Human Toll* of a decided cynicism with regard to the possibility of political change between the sexes, especially in regional Australia. As Grosz contends 'the body may be seen as the crucial term, the site of contestation, in a series of economic, political, sexual and intellectual struggles.'[70] At this time in Australia the few choices women had to lead respectable lives usually involved marriage or religious service. The right to own property, for example, was only granted to married women, who were not expected to take paid work outside the domestic sphere.

When Ursula asks Boshy whether her parents were married, the lag cannot answer, he does reply 'did yer daddy never tell yer, you he's own flesh an' blood, w'ether 'e was married or nut?'[71] Ursula tries to find her legitimate place in the world, as a girl, she wonders if her inheritance would be any different, more legitimate, if matrimony had been involved in her parentage. Baynton makes it clear that as a female Ursula has no legal right to claim land which her father owned, whether her parents were married or not. For as a chattel herself, it is incongruous for her to own property. When Boshy informs Ursula that she cannot touch Merrigulandri because she's a girl; she defiantly retorts 'Who can stop me?' and 'I can touch everythin' I want t'.'[72] Baynton challenges an orthodoxy that denies her the right to enact agency in the world.

In the novel the white male body is constituted as all powerful, however, it is noteworthy that *Human Toll* begins and ends with the image of a dead patriarch: in the beginning it is Ursula's father, at the end Christ on the cross. In contrast, many other characters are made distinctive by their grotesque physical abjection. Marginalised men such as ex-convicts, Chinamen, Indigenous Australians, and women from all classes are depicted from a white androcentric viewpoint with compromised bodies: one hand missing, only one eye, half of one race and half of another, or not of the white race at all, disabled, hungry and mutilated. They are uneducated, inarticulate and unsophisticated. These are characters with challenging corporeality who do not have equal access to power. The insubstantial huts stand in for woman's bodies, leaky vessels with easily transgressible boundaries. 'Ursula, weird of face, her diminutive body dressed in misfitting clothes, was from the onset a target.'[73] In this world, the only women who transgress the boundary of respectability are never accorded it in the first place. Ursula encounters 'old Granny McGrath . . . her feet and head were bare, and her grey hair was straggling in unusual disorder.'[74] In this case, Granny and her two companions were of 'sympathetic bond of race and creed' that is, Indigenous.[75] Fanny, the maidservant, walks out on Sunday afternoons 'with lady friends of like occupation' discussing 'the various 'shes' they served.'[76] This description of 'lady friends of like occupation' implies that the women are not ladies, as ladies have no occupation except that of being a lady. The 'like occupation' referred to is so obliquely referenced that it could be one of prostitution. Any woman not of the white upper or middle-classes, was disregarded by men of power as being a probable target of easy sex, especially maidservants who were often young girls and frequently Indigenous, who also significantly, serve women.

In patriarchal society, female sexuality, a potential source of much strength for women, is 'experienced in the setting of a sexually based power hierarchy' and controlled by symbolic law.[77] The coming of the circus heralds Ursula's sexual awakening: 'it stirred her strangely'; she is devastated when the circus folk leave without her, and feels that 'all seasons would now be alike to her widowed heart.'[78] When Mr Civil sexually threatens Ursula, she runs to the Steins', then both Hugh Palmer and Gus Stein unsuccessfully proposition her. From Palmer's perspective 'no particular beauty distinguished her face, but the dainty harmony of it, and her body, appealed irresistibly to him.'[79] Now that she is of age, the threat to her existence has become more focussed on her female body; her value as a sexual woman comes to the fore, as she has no father there is no one to mediate for her in the symbolic, and no inheritance with which to trade. Ursula is defined by her body; as female body she is accorded a certain status and expected to conform to the prevalent 'social practices, such as marriage . . . and validate the power relations between men and women.'[80]

Ursula resists the symbolic inscription that genders her body and retains an oppositional subjectivity. However, as much as Ursula rejects having to become woman, the expectations of those around her would see otherwise as her body betrays her to the male gaze. Patriarchy classifies women and their bodies as paradoxes, the masculinist virgin/whore dialectic making intrinsic sexuality for women an improbable prospect. As Barbara Creed notes, there is conflict between notions of female sexuality, by which 'she is defined' and then described, as monstrous/abject, and femininity which is understood as passive.[81]

Baynton shows Ursula denying her own desire, repeatedly repressing her craving for Andrew, or 'Mina's husband' as he does towards her, because this would transgress symbolic law: he is married, albeit unhappily. This is confusing for Ursula, who, to make the transition from nature to culture must deny her potentially 'dangerous' appetites.[82] When he is preparing to leave Merrigulandri to head north, Ursula follows an 'uncontrollable impulse' to find Andrew, fearful that he will go in the night without a word.[83] Ursula and he stand a shadow-length apart, motionless and voiceless, in the moonlight—often a trope of passion in a romance novel. However, here Baynton writes that instead of presaging new life, this is 'Death's moment.'[84] This parody of the romantic plot highlights Irigaray's hypothesis that 'without a transformation in language and culture there can be no space for their intersubjective relations as a couple.'[85] The only way that Ursula and Andrew can respectably unite is in death.

Death is juxtaposed with food, the giver of life:

> with disconcerting wonder Ursula watched the food pass through the lips that had so lately kissed the dead woman's, for even to Ursula, even here the cold presence of death seemed to penetrate.[86]

While the physical fact of her Aunt's death conjures the traumatic repetition of Ursula's separation from her mother, this scene also highlights how her body masks trauma even from herself; traumatic experience, which cannot be accessed via language or the conscious mind is encoded physically in her every gendered gesture. The connection of death with food signifies the trauma held within the body, which explains the feeling of 'disconcerting wonder'; something is awry, the presence of food in this context is uncanny.

The text is replete with images of blood, which signifies the maternal and life, but which Baynton appends to images of abjection and death, revealing its place as aligned with the feminine in the symbolic order. When Boshy dies, Ursula 'wiped the blood from his nose and mouth. Drops had fallen on her hands and wrists, but they were left.'[87] She is entreated to stir the pig's blood by Mina; undeterred by Andrew's misgivings Ursula, defiant, steps towards the strung up pig and the vat of blood. She recoils in horror, instead captivated by watching Mina as life drains from her; she has 'white lips' her 'bloodless lips tremble' and her face is 'colourless'. Ursula resolves to take over and she soon becomes mesmerised, 'her nostrils, filled with the steaming odour, dilated ominously' and she faints from the revulsion.[88] Baynton pre-empts Kristeva's thesis that menstrual blood must be disavowed according to symbolic law; indeed any evidence of femininity must be abjected. 'I expel *myself*, I spit *myself* out, I abject *myself*, within the same motion through which I claim to establish myself . . . turns me inside out, guts sprawling.'[89]

Baynton creates this oppositional account of feminine subjectivity, so that as Grosz argues, 'developing alternative accounts of the body may create upheavals in the structure of existing knowledges, not to mention in the relations of power governing the interactions of the two sexes.'[90] Baynton attempts to galvanise sympathy for the desire of this young woman to have agency within her own life so that she might enjoy being female.

Judith Butler's thesis of performative gender can be useful to decipher Baynton's argument for attention to sexual difference in her narrative detailing the great effort required by women to realise and oppose limitation. Gender is 'a corporeal style . . . a repetition and ritual which achieves its effects through its naturalization (sic) in the context of a body.'[91] This, in the framework of Baynton's work, reveals itself as the repetitive traumatic experience of the female subject living a feminine gendered life in a female-signified body. Ursula is traumatised by a restricting gender role, but equally traumatic is the attempt to step outside of that role. Her position is paradoxical, emphasising the manipulative method of the phallocentric world that denies the practice of overt coercion, and which the confused feminine subject has difficulty effectively comprehending, answering or defying. This is illustrated in the last chapter, wherein Ursula is 'bushed'—at a loss as to know what to do, a pun that links directly to the opening trope of entrapment in the unreadable labyrinth of the bush. Although she returns repeatedly to the spider:

> Had she without knowing turned back, or was it another web? Calmly, and again undismayed, the spider was industriously respinning in repair. It was the same. Yet she thought she had gone forward; she must mind, for never had she been good at locality.[92]

Ariadne's thread cannot lead Ursula from this labyrinth, at the heart of which lies the originary trauma, the fact of her feminine subjectivity and the question of agency.

4. Writing Female: Creative Emergence

Human Toll foreshadows the late twentieth-century feminine appropriation and subversion of the Bildungsroman genre to describe feminine experience: wherein as Henke contends, the female author is creating 'an enabling discourse of testimony and self-revelation, to establish a sense of agency, and to unearth a panoply of mythemes that valorise a protean model of female subjectivity.'[93] In the novel, Baynton interrogates the opportunities available to the emergent female in the symbolic world and discovers them to be limited and restrictive. As her protagonist emerges from the feminine traumatic paradigm, her encounters with many aspects of the phallocentric world provoke traumatic repetition. For Baynton no masculine edifice is sacrosanct: the Catholicism, property law, marriage, sex, education, wealth, and class are all found to be wanting in terms of their failure to accommodate, except negatively, the feminine. Experiences of opposition and denial serve to spur Baynton's protagonist into a fervent conviction of her desire for agency, and to find creative and cathartic expression in writing.

Ursula has no female antecedents from whom to learn; like all women, she has 'no tradition behind [her], or one so short and partial that it [is] of little help. For we think back to our mothers if we are women.'[94] Virginia Woolf argues that the reason for the erratic history of women's writing is 'the value that men set upon women's chastity and its effect upon their education.'[95] This means that, historically, there was no appreciation of a significant female literary genealogy in the symbolic world until women endeavoured to create their own, to work against prevailing attitudes and fashion a unique feminine heritage. Baynton contributes to the feminine literary canon for herself, and especially her female readers, through Ursula, who, in the absence of a tangible maternal connection, learns about relationships through her 'precocious reading.'[96] While this work has similarities with the romance novel, Baynton derides that genre as introducing 'high-flown love scenes' that 'grafted into her mind certain ideals of both sexes, fortunately lifeless in law.'[97] Her heroine, expecting that life might be like it is in the stories, is thwarted in love, the wily machinations of her peers ensuring that their selfish desires are achieved at the expense of her own. Novels thus provide a necessary female-centred culture for Ursula, even though they reinforce masculine values and 'acquiesce in the dominant ideology's endorsement of the primacy of an alliance with a man' in contrast to the heroine's own desire for uninhibited artistic and self-expression.[98]

The little formal education Ursula receives equips her with revolutionary potential, 'Omnipotent knowledge sent illuminating shafts through the child's active brain, and rapidly she ripened into a reader.'[99] The oppressors' own tool, literacy, can be used for liberating ends, for it is in writing, the very narrativisation of experience of thwarted hopes and gagged expression, that the unspeakable emerges, releases its repressive energy, and traumatic experience finds expression, and is transformed into creative potential: trauma is allowed to speak. Rosi Braidotti argues that 'creativity . . . entails the active displacement of dominant formations of identity, memory and identification.'[100] Creativity arises from within the subject: it subverts unconscious repressive drives and wilfully expresses desire. Shoshana Felman argues the case for looking for the 'the feminine resistance in the text' which I contend is signified by the desire for the act of creative expression.[101] When Ursula repeats 'I will write [myself in]' she is saying, 'I will not forget (myself).' In audaciously reinscribing 'the claims of feminine desire onto the texts of a traditionally patriarchal culture' Baynton celebrates the feminine and introduces semiotic discourse into the canon.[102] Henke notes that narratives written by marginalised subjects, both male and female, often challenge hegemonic discourse. Ironically, the very process of the writing in permits the writer to emerge 'as the semifictive protagonist of an enabling counternarrative . . . free to rebel against the values and practices of a dominant culture,' but able to do so in the guise of a writer of fiction.[103]

While masculine literary heritage speaks of the experience of war, adventure, political intrigue and desire, feminine literature is replete with the traumatic experience of female embodiment in a masculine symbolised world. *Écriture féminine* is the 'inscription of woman's difference in language . . . or writing (the) body.'[104] What *écriture féminine* attempts is a reframing of embodied experience, through experimentation of assumptions around signifying practices, interrogating the outcome for its relation to power and feminine subjectivity.

Whilst Herman argues that traumatic reactions occur when 'neither resistance nor escape is possible', and reflects upon the choiceless and entrapping nature of trauma, I suggest that the experience of trauma can create opportunities to rewrite life narratives, and that the very fact of the existence of *écriture féminine* is proof of resistance and therefore of the kind triggered by trauma.[105] Many narratological methods are found in *écriture féminine*: devices such as polysemy, a non-linear narrative structure, shifting temporality, an interiority of perspective, repetitious language, psychological fragmentation and multiple points of view, all of which can denote texts that represent the unrepresentable—trauma.

As Felman argues, the challenge is to 'reinvent' language:

> to re-learn how to speak: to speak not only against, but outside of the specular phallocentric structure, to establish a discourse the status of which would no longer be defined by the phallacy of masculine meaning.[106]

Power relationships are revealed in lexicon, syntax and the mode of communication. Irigaray asserts that 'my use of writing . . . signifies an attempt to create a new cultural era: that of sexual difference.'[107] In *Human Toll* Baynton does not go so far as to literally illustrate a woman doing a 'man's' job, as she does in her earlier work, but she does show Ursula growing into the symbolic world and rejecting the prescribed maternal role at every turn, which in 1907, was a radical position.

One of the key themes that Baynton tackles in the novel is the young woman's emergent psyche. Henke's analysis of the Bildungsroman as having an inherent heteroglossic structure wherein she conceives of:

> at least three different subject-positions emerge in the coming of age text: first, the authorial consciousness . . . second, the early, fragmented (and often traumatised) version of the self; and finally, the ostensibly coherent subject of utterance evinced through the process of narrative disclosure.[108]

Baynton achieves this in the novel through Ursula's maturation: she is initially a child, and the narration, while focalised through the girl, is omniscient: the reader is subject to the injustices and everyday traumas that Ursula silently witnesses.

In the middle section, as Ursula steps into her early womanhood and rejects repeated sexual advances, repressed trauma surfaces and serves to stimulate her to consider her future possibilities: after seeing the circus, Baynton writes that nothing 'could take the ambitious taste from Ursula's unsatiated mouth.'[109] This is a life-changing event for her in that she is introduced to a different and expressive way of life. 'Never would the girl forget that night, with its tinselled and spangled glories' and the reality saddened her, 'she sighed heavily, for, alas! Her wonderful potentialities were known only to herself.'[110] At the time of publication of *Human Toll*, few careers were open to women. At the dance:

> the music had sent her mentally triumphing over a glorious future, if not conceived, then quickened by Ashton's circus. She saw neither room nor dancers, but a vast theatre filled with

homage tributers, and for her, though for what rare attribute was not clear.[111]

When Ursula considers 'That's twice to-night I've been asked to marry' she admits that even though neither man was her ideal, 'later, when she had done some great thing, there would be a possibility even of her ideals.'[112]

> 'What are you goin' to do, Ursie?'
> 'Write a book,' she said shortly.   .
> It was a statement that took her by surprise, for till she spoke, her
> future plans had not been within her mental focus.[113]

Ursula tells Hugh that she wants 'to work for my living: tell me how?'[114] He eventually asks her to marry him, 'She was quite unembarrassed. 'No, oh no; if I can't be an actress, I'm going to write a book'.'[115] Andrew, exemplifying a new ethics of sexual difference, or the possibilities of the new century, is supportive of Ursula; he later urges Ursula, 'You must have money, plenty of money, then you can go where you like. Go to London, Ursie, and write your book.'[116]

This foreshadows Virginia Woolf's argument that, 'a woman must have money and a room of her own if she is to write fiction,'[117] although Ursula, like Woolf, has 'no model in my mind.'

In the final section, Ursula grasps the reality of her situation: as a woman alone in her society, she is powerless unless aligned with a man, married. In attempting to imagine a different way of life, to be able to follow her desire, Ursula admits that, 'she really had never meant to go'; it is too unknown, too far from Andrew and the acceptable feminine ideal, for her to conceive of it as possible. Compelled back to Merrigulandri by the result of Mina's rape, and her own unspoken love for Andrew, Palmer taunts her, 'Have you begun your book yet, Ursula?' continuing that she will have to marry first.[118] To which she replies, 'How could I here?' In the bush Ursula struggles:

> against her nature, and in the end conquer[s] herself. It was a
> mental feat that kept all introspection and retrospection, if not at
> bay, quiescent. A quiet sadness settled on her; she scarcely spoke
> [until] unrestrained mentally, she faced the reality—instead of
> world-wide fame—'Mina's keeper'.[119]

Baynton's contemporaries, Rosa Praed and Miles Franklin also document 'a female perspective on the Australian bush' in their novels, and echo the conviction that, there, women could not achieve 'a decent life.' [120] Franklin's *My Brilliant Career* centres on 'the particular problem of being a woman and a writer (or a creative artist of any kind)' and was an enabling precedent that opened a discursive space within which Baynton could also contend.[121][122] Franklin's Bildungsroman describes the plight of a young woman growing up into a rural community that attempts to impede her socially challenging aspirations. Franklin and Baynton presage Woolf's thesis:

> For it needs little skill in psychology to be sure that a highly gifted girl who had tried to use her gift for poetry would have been so thwarted and hindered by other people, so tortured and pulled asunder by her own contrary instincts, that she must have lost her health and sanity to a certainty.[123]

Woolf contends that in order to be able to write, the state of mind of the writer is vital, indeed it 'must be incandescent.'[124] This would then appear to preclude Ursula from an artistic practice, her being constrained by the depression to which the narrator admits, and that hails from the more profound trauma to which she is heir. She struggles and succeeds in maintaining her dignity, but in returning to the bush, Baynton emphasises that women cannot escape their gendered role in the symbolic world. She never shows Ursula writing: it is always part of a nebulous future that never arrives.

Human Toll demonstrates an alliance with the *écriture feminine* writing style in its thematic focus on feminine experience, its focalisation, and is evident in the last chapter with Ursula's circuitous confusion shown as she repeatedly encounters the spider, and finally with the ambiguous ending. In being aligned with feminine sexuality, as expected in *écriture feminine*, there is no dramatic climax, no easy dénouement; Ursula either sinks into mother earth and her death, or perhaps she really is rescued to the possibility of romance with Andrew. To endure suffering to the extent that Ursula has, presumably for a man, 'opens' for critical examination Baynton's project and reinforces the inherent parody. Ursula struggles with her love for Andrew, desperate to honour her own subjectivity and creativity and unconsciously cognisant of what desire for a man would mean for a chance of a different feminine life, she denies acknowledging her feelings for him until her will is broken by the confrontation with death at the end of the narrative.

Foreshadowing later feminist theorists, what Baynton argues for in *Human Toll* is an autonomous place for feminine expression in the symbolic world. A place where female embodiment is respected, women are educated, and are free to write if they wish.

5. Conclusion

Human Toll is an important early feminist work, in which Baynton interrogates the discourse of the feminine in Australian society. In this respect, the narrative as a whole can be said to be emblematic of the newly federated country, itself emerging from a traumatic beginning, the legacy of which still prevails.

Analogous with traditional romance novels of the time, the narrative centres on the development of a young woman:

> negotiating a future for herself through an often complex network of choices and distinctions to do not only with love and relationships but with social conventions, financial security and career destinations.[125]

However, Baynton prefers to challenge social customs, highlighting the 'uncompromising assertion of female exploitation' evident in patriarchal culture.[126] She refuses an anodyne account of Australian femininity as she parodies the Australian Girl, Bush Girl or New Woman of popular romance and melodrama genres, revealing them as upholding the masculine status quo rather than creating a new place for the feminine in the symbolic order. In *Human Toll,* feminine experience is exposed to be one of traumatic encounter with the masculine-symbolised world.

The opposition that Ursula attempts brings her to face death; it is only through the death of the feminine role as imposed, that the 'newly born woman' can arise unfettered, as creative expression from the semiotic realm.[127]

Notes

[1] *Human Toll* was published in 1907.

[2] Patricia Grimshaw, *Creating a Nation* (Ringwood: McPhee Gribble, 2007), 155.

[3] *Bush Studies* was published in 1902.

[4] Nina Philadelphoff-Puren, 'Reading Rape in Colonial Australia: Barbara Baynton's 'The Tramp', The *Bulletin* and Cultural Criticism, *JASAL* (2010): 1-14.

[5] Shoshana Felman and Dori Laub, *Testimony : Crises of Witnessing in Literature, Psychoanalysis, and History* (New York: Routledge, 1992), 224.

[6] Luce Irigaray, *This Sex Which Is Not One,* trans. Catherine Porter with Carolyn Burke (Ithaca: Cornell University Press, 1985), 162.

[7] Luce Irigaray, *Je Tu Nous: toward a culture of difference,* trans. Alison Martin (New York: Routledge Classics, 2007), 11.

[8] Gayle Rubin, 'The Traffic in Women,' in *Toward an Anthropology of Women,* ed. Rayna R. Reiter (New York: Monthly Review Press, 1975), 184.

[9] Karen Horney, *Feminine psychology,* ed. Harold Kelman (New York: WW Norton, 1967), TBA.?

[10] E. Ann Kaplan, *Trauma Culture: the Politics of Terror and loss in media and literature* (New Brunswick: Rutgers University Press, 2005), 72.

[11] Elizabeth A. Grosz, *Volatile Bodies: Towards a Corporeal Feminism* (St. Leonards: Allen and Unwin, 1994), 138.
[12] Ibid., 40.
[13] Barbara Baynton, *Portable Barbara Baynton,* ed. Sally Krimmer and Alan Lawson (St. Lucia: University of Queensland Press, 1980), 158.
[14] Julia Kristeva, *Black Sun: Depression and Melancholia* (New York: Columbia University Press, 1989)3.
[15] Kay Schaffer, *Women and the Bush: Forces of Desire in the Australian Cultural Tradition* (Cambridge: Cambridge University Press, 1988), 158.
[16] Suzette Henke, *Shattered Subjects: Trauma and Testimony in Women's Life-Writing* (New York: St. Martin's Press, 1998), xiv.
[17] Caroline M. Pascoe, 'Screening Mothers: Representations of motherhood in Australian films from 1900 to 1988.' (Unpublished Doctoral thesis, University of Sydney, 1998), 33.
[18] Cathy Caruth, 'Violence and Time: Traumatic Survivals,' *Assemblage* 20 Apr (1993): 24.
[19] Judith Herman, *Trauma and Recovery* (New York: BasicBooks, 1992), 43, 42, 94.
[20] Baynton, *Portable Barbara Baynton,* 182.
[21] Ibid., 143.
[22] Ibid., 142.
[23] Ibid., 145.
[24] Ibid., 169.
[25] Ibid., 46.
[26] Herman, *Trauma and Recovery,* 9.
[27] Baynton, *Portable Barbara Baynton,* 133; Selection: in the Australian colonial context, 'selection' refers to a parcel of land acquired under a system of free selection.
[28] Poddy lamb – a lamb that is required to be handfed.
[29] Ibid., 71.
[30] Ibid., 158.
[31] Ibid., 209.
[32] Ibid., 138.
[33] Ibid., 158.
[34] Herman, *Trauma and Recovery,* 38.
[35] Baynton, *Portable Barbara Baynton,* 210.
[36] Ibid.
[37] Ibid., 250.
[38] Judith Butler, Foreword to *Matrixial Borderspace,* by Bracha L. Ettinger (Minneapolis: University of Minneapolis Press, 2006), viii.

[39] Baynton, *Portable Barbara Baynton*, 172.
[40] Felman, *Testimony*, 206.
[41] Baynton, *Portable Barbara Baynton*, 4.
[42] Ibid., 186.
[43] Ibid., 134.
[44] Irigaray, *This Sex,* 47.
[45] Baynton, *Portable Barbara Baynton*, 9.
[46] Ibid., 127.
[47] Ibid., 194.
[48] Ibid., 233.
[49] Ibid.
[50] Ibid., 249.
[51] Ibid., 240.
[52] Ibid., 75.
[53] Ibid., 206.
[54] Ibid., 298.
[55] It is estimated that in 1921 the maternal mortality rate in Australia was 45 in 10,000 births, or about one in two hundred.
[56] Ibid., 211.
[57] Baynton, *Portable Barbara Baynton*, 159.
[58] Ibid., 8.
[59] Ibid., 193.
[60] Herman, *Trauma and Recovery*, 32.
[61] Ibid.
[62] Baynton, *Portable Barbara Baynton*, 211.
[63] Herman, *Trauma and Recovery*, 8.
[64] Baynton, *Portable Barbara Baynton*, 129.
[65] Ibid.
[66] Rosi Braidotti, 'Mothers, Monsters and Machines,' in *Writing on the Body: Female Embodiment and Feminist Theory*, eds. Katie Conboy, Nadia Medina and Sarah Stanbury (New York: Columbia University Press, 1997), 60.
[67] Baynton, *Portable Barbara Baynton*, 225.
[68] Moira Gatens, 'Power, Bodies and Difference,' in *Feminist Theory and the Body: a Reader,* ed. Janet Price and Margrit Shildrick (Edinburgh: Edinburgh University Press, 1999), 231.
[69] Elizabeth A. Grosz, *Volatile Bodies: Towards a Corporeal Feminism.* (St. Leonards: Allen and Unwin, 1994), xiv.
[70] Ibid., 19.
[71] Baynton, *Portable Barbara Baynton*, 133.
[72] Ibid.

[73] Ibid., 174.
[74] Ibid., 171.
[75] Ibid.
[76] Ibid., 170.
[77] Miriam Dixson, *The Real Matilda: Woman and Identity in Australia 1788 to the Present* (Sydney: UNSW Press, 1999), 23.
[78] Baynton, *Portable Barbara Baynton*, 184.
[79] Ibid., 235.
[80] Gatens, 'Power, Bodies and Difference', 231.
[81] Barbara Creed, *The Monstrous-Feminine: Film, Feminism, Psychoanalysis* (London: Routledge, 1993), 3.
[82] Conboy, *Writing on the Body,* 3.(If this isn't Braidotti should this be a new full note?)
[83] Baynton, *Portable Barbara Baynton*, 261.
[84] Ibid., 262.
[85] Irigaray, *Je, Tu, Nous,* 19.
[86] Baynton, *Portable Barbara Baynton*, 210.
[87] Ibid., 231.
[88] Ibid., 180.
[89] Julia Kristeva, *Powers of Horror: an Essay on Abjection* (New York, Columbia University Press, 1982), 3.
[90] Grosz, *Volatile Bodies,* 20.
[91] Judith Butler, *The Judith Butler Reader,* ed. Sara Salih (Malden, Blackwell Publishers, 2004), 93.
[92] Baynton, *Portable Barbara Baynton*, 142.
[93] Henke, *Shattered subjects* xvi.
[94] Virginia Woolf, *A Room of One's Own* (London: Penguin, 2002), 114.
[95] Ibid., 41.
[96] Baynton, *Portable Barbara Baynton*, 228.
[97] Ibid.
[98] Carole Ferrier, ed., *Gender, Politics and Fiction: Twentieth Century Australian Women's Novels* (St Lucia: University of Queensland Press, 1985), 9.
[99] Baynton, *Portable Barbara Baynton*, 174.
[100] Rosi Braidotti, 'Intensive Genre and the Demise of Gender', *Angelaki Journal of The Theoretical Humanities,* 13 2 (2008): 45.
[101] Shoshana, Felman, *What Does a Woman Want? : Reading and Sexual Difference* (Baltimore: Johns Hopkins University Press, 1993), 9.
[102] Henke, *Shattered Subjects* xvi.
[103] Ibid., xvi.

[104] Arleen B. Dallery, 'The Politics of Writing the (Body): *Écriture Feminine,*' in *Gender/Body/Knowledge: Feminist reconstructions of being and knowing,* eds. Alison M. Jaggar and Susan R. Bordo (New Brunswick: Rutgers University Press, 1989) 52.

[105] Herman, *Trauma and Recovery,* 34.

[106] Felman, *What Does a Woman want?* 40.

[107] Irigaray, *Je, Tu, Nous,* 52.

[108] Henke, *Shattered Subjects* xv.

[109] Baynton, *Portable Barbara Baynton,* 185.

[110] Ibid.

[111] Ibid., 242.

[112] Ibid., 246.

[113] Ibid., 215.

[114] Ibid., 236.

[115] Ibid., 241.

[116] Ibid., 260.

[117] Woolf, *A Room of One's Own,* 1.

[118] Baynton, *Portable Barbara Baynton,* 267.

[119] Ibid.

[120] Dale Spender, *The Penguin Anthology of Australian Women's Writing,* (Ringwood: Penguin Books, 1988), 205.

[121] *My Brilliant Career* was published in 1901.

[122] Julieanne Lamond, 'Stella vs Miles: Women Writers and Literary Value in Australia,' *Meanjin* 70.3 Spring (2011): 32-39.

[123] Woolf, *A Room of One's Own,* 75.

[124] Ibid., 36.

[125] Ken Gelder and RachaelWeaver, eds., *The Anthology of Colonial Australian Romance Fiction* (Carlton: Melbourne University Press, 2010), 1.

[126] Dale Spender, *Writing a New World: Two Centuries of Australian women Writers* (London: Pandora, 1988), 192.

[127] Hélène Cixous and Catherine Clément, *The Newly Born Woman,* trans. Betsy Wing, introduction by Sandra M. Gilbert. (Minneapolis: University of Minnesota Press, 1986), x.

Bibliography

Books:
Baynton, Barbara. *Portable Barbara Baynton,* edited by Sally Krimmer and Alan Lawson. St. Lucia: University of Queensland Press, 1980.

Braidotti, Rosi. 'Mothers, Monsters and Machines.' In *Writing on the Body: Female Embodiment and Feminist Theory*, edited by Katie Conboy, Nadia Medina and Sarah Stanbury. New York: Columbia University Press, 1997.

Butler, Judith. Foreword to *Matrixial Borderspace*, by Bracha L. Ettinger Minneapolis: University of Minneapolis Press, 2006.

Caruth, Cathy, ed. *Trauma: Explorations in Memory*. Baltimore: Johns Hopkins University Press, 1995.

Cixous, Hélène and Catherine Clément. The Newly Born Woman. Translated by Betsy Wing. Minneapolis: University of Minnesota Press, 1986.

Creed, Barbara. *The Monstrous-Feminine: Film, Feminism, Psychoanalysis.* London: Routledge, 1993.

Dallery, Arleen B. 'The Politics of Writing (the) Body: Écriture Feminine.' In *Gender/Body/Knowledge: Feminist Reconstructions of Geing and Knowing.* Edited by Alison M. Jaggar and Susan R. Bordo, 52-67. New Brunswick: Rutgers University Press, 1989.

Dixson, Miriam. *The Real Matilda: Woman and Identity in Australia 1788 to the Present.* Sydney: UNSW Press, 1999.

Ettinger, Bracha. *The Matrixial Borderspace.* Minneapolis: University of Minnesota Press, 2006.

Felman, Shoshana. *What Does a Woman Want? Reading and Sexual Difference.* Baltimore: Johns Hopkins University Press, 1993.

Felman, Shoshana and Dori Laub. *Testimony: Crises of Witnessing in Literature, Psychoanalysis, and History.* New York: Routledge, 1992.

Ferrier Carole, ed. *Gender, Politics and Fiction: Twentieth Century Australian Women's Novels.* St Lucia: University of Queensland Press, 1985.

Gatens, Moira. 'Power, Bodies and Difference.' In *Feminist Theory and the Body: a Reader*, edited by Janet Price and Margrit Shildrick. Edinburgh: Edinburgh University Press, 1999.

Gelder, Ken, and Rachael Weaver, eds. *The Anthology of Colonial Australian Romance Fiction.* Carlton: Melbourne University Press, 2010.

Grimshaw, Patricia. *Creating a Nation.* Ringwood: Mcphee Gribble, 2007.

Grosz, Elizabeth. *Volatile Bodies: Towards a Corporeal Feminism.* St. Leonards: Allen and Unwin, 1994.

Henke, Suzette A. *Shattered Subjects: Trauma and Testimony in Women's Life-Writing.* New York: St. Martin's Press, 1998.

Herman, Judith. *Trauma and Recovery.* New York: Basic Books, 1992.

Horney, Karen. *Feminine Psychology,* edited by Harold Kelman. New York: WW Norton, 1967.

Irigaray, Luce. *Je Tu Nous: Toward a Culture of Difference.* Translated by Alison Martin. New York: Routledge Classics, 2007.

———. *Speculum of the (Other) Woman.* Translated by Gillian C. Gill. Ithaca: Cornell University Press, 1985.

———. *This Sex Which Is Not One.* Translated by Catherine Porter with Carolyn Burke. Ithaca: Cornell University Press, 1985.

Jaggar, Alison M. and Susan R Bordo eds. *Gender, Body, Knowledge, Feminist Reconstructions of Being and Knowing.* Rutgers: The State University, 1989.

Kaplan, E. Ann. *Trauma Culture: The Politics of Terror and Loss in Media and Literature.* New Brunswick: Rutgers University Press, 2005.

Kristeva, Julia. *Black Sun: Depression and Melancholia.* New York: Columbia University Press, 1989.

———. *Powers of Horror: an Essay on Abjection.* New York: Columbia University Press, 1982.

Pascoe, Caroline M. *Screening Mothers: Representations of Motherhood in Australian films from 1900 to 1988.* Unpublished Doctoral thesis, University of Sydney, 1998.

Rubin, Gayle. 'The Traffic in Women.' In *Toward an Anthropology of Women*, edited by Rayna R. Reiter. New York: Monthly Review Press, 1975.

Salih, Sarah and Judith Butler, eds. *The Judith Butler Reader*. Malden: Blackwell, 2004.

Schaffer, Kay. *Women and the Bush: Forces of Desire in the Australian Cultural Tradition*. Melbourne: Cambridge University Press, 1988.

Spender, Dale. *Writing a New World: Two Centuries of Australian Women Writers*. London: Pandora, 1988

Woolf, Virginia. *A Room of One's Own*. London: Penguin, 2002.

Articles:
Braidotti, Rosi. 'Intensive Genre and the Demise of Gender.' *Angelaki Journal of the Theoretical Humanities* 13 2 (2008).

Caruth, Cathy. 'Violence and Time: Traumatic Survivals. *Assemblage* 20 Apr (1993): 24.

Lamond, Julieanne. 'Stella vs Miles: Women Writers and Literary Value in Australia.' *Meanjin* 70.3 (2011): 32-39.

Philadelphoff-Puren, Nina. 'Reading Rape in Colonial Australia: Barbara Baynton's *The Tramp*, The *Bulletin* and Cultural Criticism.' *JASAL* (2010): 1-14.

Bridget Haylock is a tutor and PhD of Creative Writing Candidate at the University of Melbourne. Her current research and writing interests focus on the expression of the creative emergence from trauma in contemporary Australian female-authored texts.

Intergenerational Transmission of Trauma: The Case of the Dersim Massacre of 1937-1938

Filiz Celik

Abstract

Destruction, loss of life and shelter are the consequences of all kinds of disasters yet human-made disasters seem to leave more indelible marks on the affected societies.[1] Today, acts of collective violence such as genocide, ethnocide, and massacres have become hot topics of debates regarding International Law and Human Rights violations.[2] Survivors continue to suffer from the consequences of oppression and stereotyping for decades afterwards. Further, there is strong evidence to suggest that trauma can be transmitted to later generations.[3] This chapter examines the intergenerational transmission and effects of trauma due to collective violence, specifically, the 1937-1938 Dersim Massacre. The genocidal massacre of Dersim resulted in tens of thousands of deaths and thousands of people internally displaced by the government forces, and also a lost generation of children. This chapter is informed by ten semi-structured interviews that were conducted with second and third generation survivors from Tunceli (formerly known as Dersim). In order to identify how the Massacre-induced trauma is transmitted to later generations, participants were asked questions about a) how they first learned about the Massacre; b) what did the Massacre mean for them at the time they learned about it; c) what it means for them now, and; d) did they believe that the Massacre influences their lives and, if so, how? Following preliminary bottom-up analysis, a consistent pattern emerged that there was both a silence regarding the trauma of Massacre within the families, and an overexposure to it.[4]

Key Words: Massacre, intergenerational trauma, collective violence, overexposure to parental/grandparental trauma, conspiracy of silence.

*****

1. Introduction

00:23 seconds

Old man: If this is not going to be broadcast then I will speak. But, if you are going to get yourself in trouble...we shouldn't talk.

Interviewer: No, no, we are going to keep this to ourselves.

Old man: You will keep it to yourself.

Interviewer: Yes.

Old man: What if it is confiscated; what will happen?

Interviewer: No, nothing will happen. This is only words. What can happen because of words?

Old man: Anyhow, leave it, leave it.

Interviewer: Come on, tell us...

Old man: No, no.

Interviewer: Really, there is no broadcasting of this. You know me and I know you.

Old man: You never know. You turn that off, and then I will tell you. If you don't turn that off, I will not speak. Dangerous business is a bad thing.

Interviewer: Let's turn it off then.

Old man: Now then, this Kemal Pasha, [angry] but I told you to turn that off!

01.10 seconds[5]

In the opening scene of a documentary movie called 'Dersim 38', an aged survivor, 62 years after the events, was still more than reluctant to have his testimony recorded. The transcriptions from this documentary movie is used for this chapter because it captures rare recorded examples of how the silence of trauma operates within this society. The documentary movie is amongst the numerous films since the late 1990s and like others, this movie heavily rely upon oral history collection. The transcribed excerpt, also gives way to a debate regarding ethics of data collection. I do not consider this to be the matter of discussion for this chapter . Hence, my intention here is not to highlight any ethical or unethical conduct of the interviews, but what I believe to be the goal of the director, is to convey the message to the reader.

The destruction of life, livelihood and shelter are the most obvious consequences of disasters – regardless of the natural or human-made in nature.

Beneath physical and superficial loss and hurt lie psychological wounding, and the terrors waiting to resurface to haunt the victims as they attempt to recover from their physical traumas. Cathy Caruth draws on the term 'latency' used by Freud to refer to the delay between the occurrence of the traumatic event and its effects on the individual.[6] In spite of the commonness of this delay, for both types of disasters, Intergenerational Transmission of Trauma, hereafter referred to as ITT, is a more expected outcome of human-made disasters. Today human-made disasters (e.g. collective violence, genocide and ethnocide) are interdisciplinary subjects (history, psychology, sociology, philosophy, anthropology, politics, medicine), as well as the hot topics of debates regarding International Law and Human Right's violations.[7] Yet, all around the world, victims of such violence continue to be unseen victims of such atrocities and they both as individuals and as collectives largely continue to suffer in silence.

Today, wars between and within countries, terrorism, genocidal killings and ethnic cleansing are items of everyday media coverage.[8] Although human history has been filled with unimaginable killings, wars and conflicts, the beginnings of the most marked genocidal atrocities are linked to the modern times. More specifically, the genocidal killings began by perceiving the indigenous population as inhuman, savage, and primitive, thus justifying the genocidal acts. Following this 'justification', the annihilation of tens of millions tended to be embedded in social engineering projects that suited the perpetrating nation, and this went hand-in-hand with the rise of the nation-state. The modernist ideas and ideologies associated with such acts transformed the 20th century into a century of genocide.[9] Mark Mazower postulates that ethnic cleansing is one of the by-products of modernism[10] and it remains a global issue in our post-modern times. Therefore, the 20th century, tainted with the annihilation of non-combatants, is marked with the massacres of human societies i.e. from the Massacre of Armenians in 1894 to the Sudanese in Darfur in 2003. In all of these unspeakable atrocities, much of the attention is not focused on the suffering of humans, but on the violence.[11]

An individual is embedded in a society, and their psychological state is shaped by the multiple social forces, and yet responses of trauma in general are studied as an individual phenomenon.[12] It is only through research into the Holocaust that extreme trauma of persecution paved the way for the development of further trauma theories,[13] for example, the investigation of trauma as affecting the collectivity. Experiences of massive trauma can produce collective traumatic memory. This is the starting point to consider the notion of ITT. ITT purports that trauma will be transmitted down the generations, that is, to those who do not have first-hand experience of the traumatic events. The effects, then, are residual in nature.

ITT is defined as the cumulative psychological trauma passed down from one generation to the next was first introduced to the research community by the Canadian clinicians.[14] They were concerned with the number of children of

Holocaust survivors who sought clinical treatment.[15] When trauma is sudden and unexpected yet shared by a collective, although the responses are unique to individual, they are likewise shared. Through this notion, the way was paved for the development of further trauma theories in the field, that is, the intergenerational or multigenerational transmission of trauma.[16] Hence, it continued to be vigorously studied via the application of Western models. However, following the research into the effects of the Holocaust on subsequent generations, other populations also started to research trauma their collectives endured; to name a few Native Americans, African Americans, South Africans, and Aboriginals.

For example, the term used to refer to trauma endured by the Native Americans due to Colonialism of the Europeans (white people) is 'historical trauma'. Here the suffering of indigenous people resulted in cultural genocide that is linked to physical, emotional, and spiritual devastation in subsequent generations. This perspective views the trauma and loss across time and place.[17] Loss of identity, a sense of cultural shame, and feelings of self-hatred are the result of this devastation and these are the intergenerational effects of what is conceptualised as the historical trauma. In this group, intergenerational effects of the trauma are linked to high rates of depression, anger and aggression, in turn resulting in social problems such as alcoholism, family and interpersonal violence, and child abuse. These are regarded as Native American's unconscious expressions of the trauma they endured.[18]

Another group identified to be effected by ITT are African Americans, their trauma is conceptualized as 'cultural trauma'. This concept is used in relation to slavery, beginning with selling of Africans as property till the end of this practice. Ron Eyerman says that: 'Whether or not they directly experienced slavery or even had ancestors who did, Blacks in the United States were identified with and came to identify themselves through the memory and representation slavery.'[19]

In the case of slavery, what is gathered is that historical racism is combined with the current oppression. Ron Eyerman further suggests that the current situation enables the reinterpretation and representation of their collective identity. The impact of the cultural trauma seems to be socio-political disenfranchisement of the African Americans who have high homicide rates particularly among males, difficulty in sharing emotion, substance abuse, and poverty.[20]

Such variety in understanding the intergenerational effects of the trauma brings us to topic of multi-disciplinary approach in understanding ITT. For example, Antonius C. G. M. Robben and Marcelo M. Suarez-Orozco suggest that the effects of collective violence should be studied in collaboration with Psychology and Anthropology. These disciplines are involved directly in the study of violence and its consequences. By merging the knowledge-base of both disciplines, we can better understand both individual human suffering and how this is represented in various cultural formations and societal norms. They exemplify their suggestion, that an anthropologist is not trained to deliver any kind of therapeutic help to survivors and thus often avoided the subject of human-made violence and collective trauma. However, their roles in uncovering the socio-cultural processes following such events are invaluable to the field of collective violence and trauma studies.[21] As Yael Danieli suggest such trauma result in the rapture of the many of the spheres of the lives ranging from economy to theology.[22]

Thus, ITT and trauma studies are discovering that time and place are the embodiments of the lives of people. Where and when, are the key determinants of how great traumas are experienced and more importantly what the effects are on the subsequent generations. This chapter is largely based on the preliminary findings of an on-going research. The aim of this chapter is firstly, to investigate trauma as a collective experience, and secondly, the responses to traumatic events in the descendants of the survivors of the Dersim Massacre 1937-1938 in a remote province in Eastern Anatolia, Turkey.

In doing so, this chapter will first give a brief historical background of Dersim so that the empirical data can be associated with the geographical location, the massacre, and its aftermath. Furthermore, the empirical research findings due to the transmission of trauma and because of silence and denial associated with this silence, the overexposure to trauma will be highlighted as they have emerged as the main facilitators of the ITT in the Dersim Massacre of 1937-1938.

2. Dersim Massacre 1937-1938

Dersim is a region with no clear-cut boundaries that existed in the Eastern Anatolia of today's Turkey from the time of Ottomans until the Republic of Turkey in 1938. Due to its remote mountainous and geographical positioning Dersim largely remained inaccessible and impenetrable to outside influences for centuries. However, this has come to an absolute end after the genocidal massacres during 1937-1938.[23] Part of the Dersim province was named as the city of Tunceli.[24] The other parts of the districts were merged into neighbouring administrative districts by the end of the massacres, and forced resettlements of the large portion of its surviving population. Today, the city of Tunceli, as well as the surrounding areas that were once part of Dersim refers to their origin as from Dersim. In the context of this chapter those who are resident in the city of Tunceli and those who associate their belonging to the district of Dersim will hereafter be referred to as Dersimi.

Dersim accommodates a multi-ethnic, multi-lingual, multi-faith, and multi-tribal society. Due to diversity of its population and the culture, Dersim was a target of centuries of ongoing violence. Dersim lost presence of Armenian population in the process of violent expulsion of the Armenians by 1922. The violence towards Dersim in order to subdue the region reached its peak between March 1937 and September 1938 through heavy military campaigns aimed at its physical and cultural destruction.

Dersimis have also been targets of violence due to their religious differences. Religiously they adhere to the Alevi faith. Alevi, a minority faith adhered by both Turks and Kurds alike, is not homogeneous and the differences are intensified regionally. Moreover, in Dersim practice of Alevi faith shows differences to those Turks living in the Kurdish part of Turkey. In Dersim people traditionally associated their identity through the membership of tribes. Tribes of Dersim are linked to one another through the socio-religious order of the Kizilbas/Alevi faith. In this order some of the tribes are from priestly casts called 'ocak', where their chieftains are revered by the members of the other tribes.

Alevi people act on the belief that their religious life is governed internally. Therefore, the basic commandments such as not to kill, speak the truth, and be fair to others are acknowledged and observed by the Alevi similar to the members of the other faiths. However, Alevi people assume that people are essentially good beings and they should continue to be so, and that this is non-negotiable. They profess that they are Muslims, and they largely to follow the formal religious practices of Islam,[25] namely the five pillars.[26] Therefore, they are often in the middle of a debate whether their beliefs are their continuation of Islam or amalgamation of the pre-Islamic beliefs and Gregorian Armenian traditions with the Islamic assimilation, particularly since the second half of the first millennium. Due to Alevi's reverence of Caliph it is stipulated that they share common history with the Shia School of Islam and Sufism in Anatolia under the pressure of Islamisation of Ottoman Empire.[27]

Sultan Selim I, the 9th Sultan of the House of Osman, was the head of Sunni Islam and he was utterly disturbed with his subjects' support of the Shah Ismail of Safavids. In the 1514 Battle of Caldiran the Ottomans defeated Shah Ismail, and carried out mass executions of the Kizilbas people. The term Kizilbas has since then been replaced by Alevi.[28] Sunni theologians declared Kizilbas/Alevis as heretics and infidels and the rumours regarding their alleged immorality continues to this day. It is such rumours, or more precisely, the centuries long influence of such rumours that Dersimis are also discriminated against by those with whom they share membership to the same ethnic groups such as Kurds and Zazas.

Dersim was predominantly populated by Zaza and Kurds who adhered to Alevi faith and was also home to Christian Armenians and received a minority influx of Sunni Turks amongst others. Until the 19th century the ethnic diversity of Dersim does not appear as a major issue. The subjects of the Ottoman Empire were categorized based on a 'millet system'. In this system Sunni Muslims were 'ummet' and Christian and Jewish communities were 'millet'. Kizilbas/Alevi people, with respect to administrative aspects treated as millet, were in fact not given any rights or privileges of either millet or ummet.[29] One of the consequences of the Great War had been the end of diversely populated empires for nation-states. Nation-states assumed 'the people' to be definable and homogenous unit to the countries they belonged to. The ethnic diversity of the people in the territories that was bordered as the state was not only ignored but measures were taken to subdue them into desired national identities.

The modern Republic of Turkey was formed through such discourses as the forefathers of the modern republic decided upon a Turkish and liberal Sunni Muslim identity for 'the people' of the state. In the process of this social constructionism, the 1934 Law of Resettlement was ratified to 'create a country speaking with one language, thinking in the same way, and sharing the same sentiment'.[30] This law is considered to have paved the way for the 1935 Tunceli Law which details the annihilation of Dersimis.[31] Part of this province was renamed as the City of Tunceli with a special legislation that was ratified in the Grand National Assembly of Turkey on December 25, 1935, which came into force, following its publication in the gazette on January 2, 1936. The law detailed the annihilation of Dersimis and the parliamentary debates leading to the ratification of the law is quoted in Ismail Besikci's book called 'the Genocide of Dersim-Dersim Jenosidi'. The book was published in 1977, but was banned in Turkey for decades and the author imprisoned for its publication.[32]

Dersimis, unfortunately similar to victims of other atrocities, have endured the most undignified methods of death and survival. Some were executed by shooting after being collected in village squares, and others were made to walk to places for their mass execution. Some were killed by bayonets so that the bullets would not be wasted. Those who managed to escape the armed forces often died when hiding under treacherous circumstances. Many babies had to be smothered so their cries would not give away their whereabouts. Some children survived only because they were mistaken as dead underneath their mothers' dead bodies. At the end of the two year-long military campaign, 13,806 were dead and 11,683 were forced into exile to different parts of Turkey.[33] Girls were targeted in particular, they were sent away to live with the Turkish families in different parts of the country, their contacts severed with their families. Daughters of those who remained in Dersim were also taken away and placed in boarding schools. However, all this remained a taboo subject in Turkey until the late 1990's.

Martin van Bruinessen wrote in his article regarding Dersim Massacres, 'The events represent one of the blackest pages in the history of Republican Turkey, gracefully passed over in silence or deliberately misrepresented by most historians, foreign as well as Turkish.'[34] He then calls attention to the fact that the two most popular international scholarly books about the emergence of Turkey do not even mention the Massacre.

In massive traumas the target population is not massacred overnight, but subjugated by the dominant group over a period of time. Silence here is an invisible, intangible entity induced by the perpetrators. Silence, in a conventional sense, is a lack of sound or in communication, an absence of words. Nevertheless, in the absence of words, much can be communicated or miscommunicated, thus leaving children with curiosity as to what happened and why it happened. Silence creates a victimhood that brings with it the transmission of trauma. ITT would occur regardless of whether the later generations are exposed to trauma or not. There is a vast body of research that suggests that attempting to keep silent about the trauma is a major mechanism of its transmission.[35]

It is only towards the end of the 1990s that publications about the massacre started to appear. Since then, people have become more at ease to talk about it. The real progress in loosening the taboo of silence about the Dersim Massacre began following the comments of the MP Onur Oymen during a parliamentary debate on November 12, 2009. He responded to suggestion of the ruling party with regards to allowing certain concessions for political rights of the Kurds. In his speech he proclaimed that allowing certain cultural rights to Kurds were losing the battle with terrorism. He also opposed the ruling party's suggestion of ending the mutual bloodshed to 'no longer let the mothers cry for their martyred sons', stating it was unreasonable, and gave examples of the Dersim Massacre, as he termed it, the 'Dersim Rebellion'. He talked about how the military operations were conducted with no consideration for the cries of the mothers because 'they did what had to be done'.[36]

CHP[37] Tunceli MP Huseyin Aygun talked to Zaman Newspaper holding his own party responsible for what had happened in Dersim during 1937-1938.[38] Huseyin Aygun's comments caused a huge uproar in and amongst the supporters of his party, the majority demanding his suspension from the party. Following this, Turkey's Prime Minister Recep Tayyip Erdogan spoke at a televised meeting calling the events a massacre carried out by a series of pre-planned atrocities, and holding the opposition party CHP responsible for the events.[39] Although there is no place for redress and retribution, the current state of affairs in relation to the discussions, debates, and public presence of the Dersim Massacre is the least oppressed.

3. The Trauma of the Dersim Massacre and Its Legacy

Today the term trauma is employed in various contexts from medical sciences to literary studies. The use of the term is no longer restricted to labelling of extremely stressful events, sexual, or emotional abuse. It is used to understand the effects of the events such as experiences of concentration camps and other atrocities on people both at the individual and collective levels.[40] Trauma is when an individual specific occurrence is known to affect not only individuals but others around them like their family and other close ones.[41] Therefore, trauma could be transmitted to others, which may be within or between generations. In the literature, this *interpersonal* transmission of trauma is termed as secondary traumatisation,[42] or as vicarious traumatisation.[43]

Extreme traumatisation, experienced by a group of people is also referred to as massive psychic trauma.[44] Because it is experienced by the group, it is automatically inferred that the trauma is perhaps not shared, but does fall on the collective to various degrees (e.g. all the surviving members of the family will be influenced by it). Trauma in the context of human-made disasters, the transmission of trauma is often passed onto later generations, as all the members of the current generations would fall victim to it. Changing of the natural life course of people through human-made disasters and creating a collective experience of trauma would result in the permanent changes of the fabric of the society.[45] It is not a part of one's natural course of psychosocial development to come to terms with massacred family backgrounds, particularly something that was too destructive and wide-spread to comprehend.

Here the question is how the trauma experienced by parents and even grandparents is transmitted to children and grandchildren. The research into ITT was at first focused on trauma transmission to the second generation. The second generation began seeking psychological help with the symptomatology of survivors. However, research was soon extended to third generations and then conducted by other survivors of the massive traumatic events.[46] Today there is a large and growing volume of literature of ITT from both clinical and non-clinical perspectives, to name a few, involving but not exclusive to, Native American genocide,[47] African American Slavery,[48] Aboriginals of Australia,[49] Gulag of Stalin's Russia,[50] and oppressive military regime of Argentine.[51]

Despite being a widely researched the topic of ITT has not yet found its way into the Diagnostic and Statistical Manual of Mental Disorders. The closest entry to the ITT was the 'survivor syndrome' in 1980 into DSM-III.[52] This was later removed and replaced with Post Traumatic Stress Disorder (PTSD) with DSM-IV.[53]

ITT's delayed entry to DSM could be due to non-reconciliation amongst researchers and clinicians regarding the prevalence of it. According to a review of the literature conducted by Irit Felsen[54] and Nathan Kellerman[55] when compared with the control group children of the Holocaust did not show any psychopathology. Nonetheless, this does not indicate that trauma of the parents, grandparents and even great-grandparents did not have an impact on the later generations. This impact may be some trauma response other than corresponding to psychopathological diagnostic. Perhaps here what is transmitted is not necessarily the original trauma itself but the effects of the trauma endured by earlier generations. The notion ITT in the 1960s clinical work[56] focused on how children exhibited the trauma of their parents. A loose categorisation of intergenerational trauma is that transmission may occur directly or indirectly. The former refers to survivors' children who show the signs of psychological distress that are expected to be seen in a survivor's population. The latter refers to survivors' children who experience a stressful upbringing, where parent-child relationships are impaired due to parents' diminished ability for successful emotional functioning.[57]

Bessel van der Kolk postulates that trauma is an end result of events or occurrences that are outside the range of everyday experiences.[58] He suggests that because of the sudden, unexpected and overwhelming nature of the events, it is the unpreparedness that makes overcoming these events problematic. A great emphasis is placed on the integration of these events into one's life in a meaningful way otherwise the individual might fixate on the trauma. The inability to overcome the trauma, i.e. disturbing nature of the involuntary and intrusive traumatic memories, the inability to assign meaning to what had happened, are some symptoms of the Post-Traumatic Stress Disorder or psychological pathology. Similarly, Ronnie Janoff-Bulman compares the circumstances of pre and post-traumatic worlds in order to make sense of trauma.[59] In the pre-traumatic world we have assumptions about the world we live in and we know more or less what to expect during the course of our daily lives. Everyday events although may be stressful at times are not necessarily traumatic. Yet, following the sudden and unexpected events our assumptions are shattered and we may lose the ability to continue, because we no longer know what we should expect. The trauma of an event that is outside the range of everyday experiences and unfamiliar to a degree that people cannot operate with what they previously assumed about the functioning of the world around them. Then non-integration of the event into one's everyday life, and failing to establishing new set of assumptions to operate on, could lead to traumatic stress, associated psychopathology and post-traumatic stress.

The more unexpected and the more sudden the trauma, the more challenging the post-traumatic adaptation becomes. Research reveals that human-made, intentional and unexpected traumas result in greater traumatic responses compared to natural disasters.[60] Natural disasters, however destructive in its nature are often regarded as an 'act of God' and the disaster is unpreventable. To some it came from a deity and that it was meant to happen, and to others it is our vulnerability against the forces of Mother Nature. For example, following disasters, there is physical and the psychological damage ranging from poverty, hunger, increased susceptibility to disease, infant mortality, deteriorating mental health, PTSD, painful memories, loss, grief and desensitization. Disrupted communal ties, the loss of predictable social networks, continued violence and dislocated populations can increase and prolong the problems.[61] Although the loss may be insufferable in many levels, natural disasters do not target a specific group or groups because of their shared characteristic that are deemed as undesirable and to be eradicated. The nature of the human-made disasters are essentially dehumanizing elements which involve robbing people of their dignity while physically annihilating the masses in order to destroy their socio-historical existence.[62]

Furthermore, the experiences of the survivors of the human-made disasters are more isolating compared to those of the victims of natural disasters. Events on domestic level are often perpetrated by contemporaries of the people that fallen victim to it. Victims and survivors are not supported often due to fear of others to be associated with the group that were victim to such disasters. It is generally acknowledged that support is a key protective factor in the aftermath of the massive traumatic events. Moreover, following traumatic events, survivors would turn to their closest friends or family for support. This support is important in order to recreate a sense of a meaningful world and it is important that those who provide social support are able to assist on such a quest.[63] The lack of support and restorative justice, in the case of human-made disasters, are risk factors that are linked to a prolonged traumatic response in affected societies.[64] Through the provision of support, sympathy, and assistance both at the individual and institutional levels people may feel more equipped to deal with what had happened to them. Traumatised people are likely to continue to live the remainder of their lives as trauma survivors,[65] and the support they receive is extremely paramount to not only the survivor's quality of life but to their children's too. Therefore, instead of trying to understand why such events befell them, people may just acknowledge the inhumanity of their perpetrators and manage to move on and have meaningful lives where they can move forward.

Compared to the first half of the 20th century the provision of psychological help by the Non-Governmental Organizations has become common place, both in cases of natural and human-made disasters. However, how much of this aid is sufficient, effective and/or culturally appropriate is debatable. Often such provisions are based on the Western models and are not communicable to the local people in the non-Western worlds. The provision of aid almost always comes to an end as soon as the immediate danger to the physical existence of a population is considered to be over.

The Dersim Massacre 1937-1938 was experienced at a time when there were no preventive measures for crimes against humanity in place. In the process of nation building Dersim was declared as an abscess on the Republic of Turkey by the Interior Minister of the time.[66] The oppressive nature of the behaviour of the Turkish authorities continued to dominate the discourses describing the events. In local press, Dersimis were attacked brutally, there were no mention of the gravity of the indiscriminate attacks on civilians, and moreover, the eradication of the Dersimis was received with gratification. Internationally, the Dersim Massacre was left unrecorded in the years preceding the second Great War. Furthermore, when considering the case of Dersim, although the immediate physical threat was largely removed when the military operations came to an end, it cannot be said for the actual threat. Later generation Dersimis expressed that they have been living under military control, they feel the ongoing and overwhelming presence of the military in their lives, they faced with arbitrary detentions, false imprisonments, torture or ill treatment in custody, and a life in constant fear of what atrocity might befall them next.

Dersimis denied of the victim/survivor status had to come to terms with their losses and began to re-build their lives in the ruins of their previous lives. Their losses and the lack of support were further intensified with the discrimination against surviving Dersimis. The impact of the Dersim Massacre, both on the victims and subsequent generations, remained as an isolating experience for the survivors. In time, the survivors' chose to remain silent, not being able to make sense of the atrocities they suffered. Later generations were not only left to deal with the stigma attached to them because of their place of origin, but also had to make sense of both the silence of their parents/grandparents in the aftermath of such injustices that indelibly marked their past and present. The coping mechanisms the survivors' chose was to remain silent. Whereas, for the later generations it included being involved with the left-wing groups that opposed the system where they could take pride in their differences that were considered a threat by the ruling elite and their supporters.

4. Dersim Massacre, Trauma and Later Generations

Risk factors that have been identified as the precursors of trauma transmission range from behavioural, genetic pre-disposition, to family dynamics.[67] There is no one certain universal conditions to identify at play for the transmission. However, there are factors identified that might mitigate and/or aggravate the effects of the trauma suffered by the survivors onto the later generations. These factors range from the age of the survivors at the time of trauma, family members' exposure to trauma i.e. closeness and number of the loss or injured members of family, and the families' ability to cope and adapt.[68] Yet in the ITT literature, silence appears to be a marker of the post-trauma period in terms of transmission. Yael Danieli referred to this as the 'conspiracy of silence' and further stipulated that lack of expressing the trauma left reactions of people to stimulus associated with trauma unexplained. Therefore, it played a great role in the transmission of trauma.[69]

Findings indicate consistency with the existing data in the literature regarding ITT. Both second and third generation participants often expressed feelings and circumstances associated with the Massacre that would be expected to be survivors' reactions. Furthermore, participants articulated feelings and behaviours that could be associated with victims of trauma but not with the second and third generation descendants of survivors – some of whom had no knowledge of the events until adulthood. Such statements included: 'I can smell the bodies burning'; 'I can't help hearing the cries of the babies left alone to die' and 'I could hear people crying whenever we drove past that junction even before I knew about the Massacre'. Participants also expressed affective states such as feeling very angry, not knowing how to deal with the anger inside them, and not being able to sleep because of the nightmares associated with the Massacre.

A. Dersim Massacre in the Lives of the Later Generations

Findings of this research that informed the writing of this chapter indicate that heightened awareness of the Dersim Massacre is a major occurrence amongst later generation Dersimis. In some cases, participants' heightened awareness of the parental/grandparental trauma was explicit to the degree of participants' constant preoccupation with the trauma in their everyday lives. The events and feelings associated with the past events were presented as if they themselves were the survivors of the events who could not have come to terms with their experiences. All participants eagerly described their current lives in relation to the Massacre and its effects on themselves and their families. Dersimis' heightened awareness were particularly related to areas of the parental/grandparental trauma, loss of the lives of the relatives during the Massacre, constant attempts to evaluate their past, current, and future lives in relation to the massacre. Despite their distrust in authorities and security forces their desire to state their identity as Dersimis. In particular, it was their perception of their own identity as Dersimi in the eyes of the others, and how others' perception of them as Dersimi influenced almost all aspects of their lives from social to professional.[70]

Certain patterns emerged from the interviews with second and third generation Dersimis that shed light onto how they have come to have this heightened awareness of the events that occurred before their lives began, and how they were afflicted with such trauma-related feelings and behaviours. The Massacre was still an everyday subject and therefore difficult avoid. Adults spoke in front of children amongst themselves, but never directly to the children. It was often the aged relatives who talked about their memories to the younger generation. Yet, many children as well as some grandchildren had never heard of it until they became teenagers or adults. Hearing about the Massacre in passing, they would start to read and research about it in their teenage and adult years. Through personal efforts they would learn, and then they could begin to make sense of what it was that they heard as a child.[71]

B. After the Massacre: in Silence and Overexposed

Findings of the present study indicate that the trauma suffered from Dersim Massacre of 1937-1938 were transmitted to later generations both through over-exposure to parental/grandparental trauma and through silence regarding the past. The majority of the participants of this study talked about the existence of the Massacre as central to their lives from early childhood. These individuals were not only overhearing the people narrating their memories of the Massacre but they were also subjected to the prolonged mourning of their parents/grandparents about the loss of loved ones, loss of life style, and the space where they could be themselves. Such participants grew up in the families where the Massacre was an everyday topic of conversation, for instance a 25 year old, second generation female said:

> ...I know this very well, my father's place in our life, their story starts after the 38, we have always been told from there, I mean they would not tell us anything about before the 38 because there is no place, it is only for bad things, things that were lived during

the 38 and for us, for me at least my father's story, my father's and others stories starts after 38... As I said before, here 1938 is the first number we learn, I don't remember how old I was but as I said, for it was being talked about around me and it was the big pain of people, I thus learned about it...

A 28 year old, third generation, male spoke of not knowing about the Massacre and therefore not being able to consciously receive anything regarding the trauma suffered by his parents as well as other people in the region where he grew up:

...don't remember how I heard about it first but I learned eventually by reading about it and by looking around, when I went to university...

Yet, the most frequent narrative was that participants had heard of the Massacre in their childhood, but could not make sense of it, or they could not make sense of what they heard until after they started to read and learn about it during adolescence. For example, a 33 year old, third generation, female spoke of the existence of the Massacre and related trauma in her life since childhood, but not being able to make sense of it:

...when I first learned, for me, you are a kid, there are books around... and 38 is always talked about, but you are just a kid and you cannot understand what is it but later when you start understanding, when you are being told then you say, hah, this 38 is that 38 they were talking about...

Regardless of what age they learned about the Massacre and how they first learned and made connection between the Massacre and their lives, all of the participants spoke of it as the single most important event that has affected their lives. They all expressed grief and sadness regarding the atrocities. They were disappointed and angry that even after seven decades it was a still being denied to learn why Dersimis were massacred. The most recurring question was: What could have been the wrongdoing of the non-combatants who were children, women and the aged who were killed so brutally? In such questioning, participants expressed their frustration at both knowing and not knowing what had happened. In knowing what had happened there arose the need for acknowledgement from the witnesses and bystanders and more importantly from the authorities.

Although the participants did speak about their grief and sadness as part of the mass trauma ranging from unburied relatives to the loss of cultural heritage at length. They nevertheless seemed more focused upon the post-trauma period than the Massacre itself. Specifically, they focused on the silence regarding the

Massacre, and the experiences of their families in relation to the Massacre. Kaethe Weingarten refers to the role of silence and victimhood in political violence and says that because parents' assumptions about the world are shattered, and its safety, in an attempt to protect their children they may remain silent.[72] However, although the silence regarding the trauma endured, they may become extremely aware of any stimulus that reminds them of the trauma. In this enmeshed communicative world it is possible that children would grow up trying to discover what is hidden and would be traumatised as a result of this knowing or not knowing.

In the context of the Dersim Massacre learning about the Massacre is observed to occur rather passively. Children would often be ignored when adults conversed about the Massacre, and in turn children would be unable to make sensible connections with what they were hearing and how it affects them. Repetitions of these instances indicate that children were largely ignored as individuals capable of feelings in relation to adult matters. However, such attitude may also be the consequence of the trauma suffered by survivors, as the magnitude of the events and the trauma caused by these events may have impaired their ability in more sensible parenting. Once the children were old enough to ask questions, they were often denied their family's history, and instead given very general and brief responses regarding the events. Furthermore, grief, although always present through sadness, unexplained tears, and the topic in local music it was not properly communicated. For example, children grew up with parents murmuring requiems, they could often neither understand their meanings nor their presence in their lives. For example, a 31 year old, third generation, female said:

> ...As I said it was talked about when I was 6-7 years old but I wasn't aware of it. I started reading about this when I was 15-16. That is when I learned about the Dersim Massacre. What was being told were more like stories, tales. I mean we didn't know what it meant, at that time. But when you are 15-16 then you become seriously curious about it and start reading, listening. Then you start listening to what is being told differently...

It may indeed be an aggravating factor for the trauma transmission because later generations often feel frustrated about finding out what had happened, and as they come closer to the historical truth. The term 'conspiracy of silence' was coined by Yael Danieli to understand the effects of those traumatic events that did not offer any medium of communication between the survivors and their children, significant others, families and the wider world around them.[73] Similarly, despite the lack of communication, in the case of the Holocaust, the children of survivors seemed to have been influenced by the experiences of their parents often to a degree that exerts very similar psychological responses. In regards to Dersim, in response to this silence some would express their feelings of resentment towards their parents because they were never told about it, whereas others would justify their behaviour as their parents' protective parenting. Regardless, now as adults, they articulated feelings of anger and despair that the magnitude of the events were so sheer that it did not only silence the very victims of the events but also the bystanders and witnesses alike. Therefore, conclusions can be drawn that silence regarding the trauma did not prevent the transmission of the trauma but aggravated it.

C. The Lack of Vocabulary

Whether the later generations were burdened with trauma of the Dersim Massacre of 1937-1938 through over-exposure or silence, or both, the lack of vocabulary seems to be one of the underlying reasons for both circumstances. The silence is imposed in different but often intersecting conditions, and is still continuing to pervade the trauma. The atrocities are acknowledged by the current Prime Minister, and the discussions regarding the Massacre are taking place publicly, but these discussions are limited to Dersimis defence that the events were inhumane methods of annihilation against the overwhelming majority defending the events as the repression of the rebels who had to be disciplined. As long as the victimhood status is not given to Dersimis in relation to the Massacre aimed at their annihilation, it cannot be possible to remove the silencing caused at this level. Furthermore, silence emerged from the terror of the traumatic experiences in a 'top to bottom' fashion, from the state to the citizens that restricted the existing vocabulary to the defence of their innocence. People reserved their opinions of the events in order to protect themselves from further harm.

At the individual level, by not having the vocabulary to speak of their experiences, the trauma has resulted in survivors unable to communicate their loss and grief. The magnitude of destruction the Massacre caused feelings of shame, guilt, and helplessness. These conditions were further deepened through the isolation of the survivors. Without any support systems in place, they could neither meaningfully comprehend what had happened nor respond to it in a manner that they could place their experiences behind them. Such attempts in keeping silent may also be associated with the survivors' attempt to dissociate themselves from the terror of what they were subjected to. Eric Lindermann considers this type of silence to be helpful as long as the trauma is present but not once the actual trauma is removed.[74] David Bathory also points out that 'dissociation has been largely removed from the diagnosis of trauma but remains as a coping mechanism for many traumatized people.'[75] Perhaps this was helpful for the survivors during and in the immediate aftermath of the trauma, however, as the time passed not dealing with the trauma could present itself as something to be addressed. Therefore, it is essential to break the silence at national and institutional levels so the remaining survivors and their descendant could speak of the sufferings and the trauma it brought.

5. Concluding Remarks

Silence, as a result, could often leave the later generations with a legacy where they discovered their family history sometimes through the society's collective memory. Once they found out what happened, they had the task of integrating this into their identity dimensions. In the case of Dersim, the only medium for them to vocalize themselves was through involvement with political groups – including those that carried out clandestine missions. For example, the radical leftist movement in Turkey is known to look for and recruit ground support from Dersim, and also to intensify their guerrilla fights in this region.[76] In addition to that, Dersimis' support for the leftist movements in the 1970s and the Kurdish movement beginning with the 1990s resulted in an intensification of the military control. The year 1994 marked another period of complete insecurity for the residences as thousands were homeless through forced village evacuations and government initiated forest fires.[77] It can be inferred that the trauma of the Dersim Massacre is still continuing and further complicated through the violence targeting them in the region. In addition to this, the discrimination that they suffer both as the unruly citizens of Turkey in the region, and as Dersimis outside region contribute to further rippling of the existing trauma, and effecting the later generation as something beyond the realms of ITT. As long as the Dersim Massacre is not recognized and Dersimis are not returned their dignity, the trauma can be said to be continuing to pervade the consciousness not only survivors but their descendant. It may only be in the future when Dersimis can speak of the trauma, loss, and the pain they suffered without concerns and fear that we may began to understand the effect of the massacre on the psyche of Dersimis and in the post-traumatic period.

The participants whose accounts informed the writing of this chapter were at the time residents in Dersim. All of the participants had spent some of their lives outside of Dersim for numerous reasons ranging from education, military services, to work commitment of the members of the family. They came from different families in Dersim who were affected by the Massacre to different degrees in terms of losses incurred by their families. Regardless of how the trauma was communicated to them they have placed a great emphasis of the trauma in their lives. Yet, both second and third generation participants are affected by the trauma of the Dersim Massacre through both overexposure to the traumatic past and/or deliberate or non-deliberate attempts of keeping the silence of their families. They were unable to share the sheer magnitude of the trauma with later generations and/or felt compelled in order to protect later generations from harm that could come from demanding the historical truth.

In the case of the Dersimis, there is not much information as to how survivors managed to cope with the trauma. Survivors were left alone as they had to come to terms with their losses and were faced with the immediate rebuilding of their lives. Dehumanizing treatment of the population common to human-made disasters must have brought a range of feelings such as fear, helplessness, guilt and even shame, depression and anxiety for them to overcome. Authorities did not provide the survivors with any material or psychological support, but continue to defensively repudiate the events and marginalize Dersimis to this day. In this chaos, survivors had neither the opportunity nor the skills to mourn their losses. The immediate task was to rebuild their lives, such as finding shelter and food, and creating families. Perhaps in such an environment dissociation served as the best possible coping mechanism, and therefore by remaining silent about their experiences survivors both protected themselves from talking about their horrific experiences as well as from the dangers of persecution by the authorities. Furthermore, it seems to be a double jeopardy pushing the survivors and often their children to a degree to create fertile environment for denial. In denying what had happened Dersimis could have existed without an immediate threat of further annihilation. Any discourses that were charged with the notion of ethno-religious loyalties were dangerous, illegal, and banned. Therefore, the historical truth of the traumatic events of the Dersim Massacre could not be discussed until very recently. An apology for the Dersim Massacre did come 74 years later on November 23, 2011, the Turkish Prime Minister made a formal apology for the killing of people in Dersim. A public apology from a Prime Minister was a huge step in the loosening of the conspiracy of silence at a national level, but they are still awaiting further actions, such as the opening of archives, and restoring the dignity of those who perished.

Nonetheless, all of the participants, regardless of how they have come into contact with the trauma suffered, their collective demand is to know why their people were made to endure such atrocities. The younger the participants the higher were the demands for an apology, irrespective of their generational belonging. It is generally acknowledged that a supportive post-traumatic environment could contribute greatly to the healing process. When trauma is inflicted on an individual, it is mostly the support of those close to the individual that can comfort them. However, when it is a community exposed to trauma, then the wider society – that is national and/or international agencies must assume a duty of care, help repair the damage, and establish a sense of order and justice to the affected communities. Failing to do so could render generations to come vulnerable to the world into which they are born.

Majda R. Atieh and Ghada Mohammad discuss the victimization of non-combatants through examples from literary works and criticize the lack of focus on the issue from African and Middle Eastern scholarly texts. These authors signify the importance of making the survivors of trauma part of the social change that would bring the recovery.[78] In the context of this chapter, it has been discussed that victims of genocidal atrocities are largely left to mend their own wounds. Victimhood is overlooked not only by national agencies but also global ones such as NGOs and International Criminal Courts. Perhaps in breaking the silence, victims can be compensated by being given material allowances to rebuild their lives, and by returning of their dignities. Although there would be no going back to physical and emotive states prior to traumatic times, they may be helped to integrate the terrors of what they have endured to their lives. Thus, they could become empowered and focus on the healing of the existing trauma. It is essential to remove their marginalization, in doing so the healing process may begin, which could then save further generations from the transmission of legacies of trauma. Therefore, the healing process, in relation to the legacies of the inter-generational trauma, should be sought within the restorative justice system, and with the trauma-endured societies in mind. By addressing the issues they may create a world in which such societies could develop a trust between themselves and their world is an essential step.

A quotation below from a 63 year old, second generation, male is prototypical of other participants' interviews. It shows that, despite more than seven decades after the event, we may not even have started the beginnings of the healing process.

...we heard from them, and we tell you but they lived it for real. I cannot help, it is not possible to get rid of the fear, and you think that any time, if you make something solid here, an investment, something for the future, it might be 38 again, and everything is gone but I wish it won't happen again, I really do wish...

Notes

[1] Fran H. Norris, 'Psychological Consequences of Disasters', *PTSD Research Quarterly* 13 (2002): 1-7.
[2] Alexander Laban Hinton, 'The Dark Side of Modernity: Toward an Anthropology of Genocide', in *Annihilating Difference: The Anthropology of Genocide*, ed. Alexander Laban Hinton (London: University of California Press, 2002), 1-42.
[3] Yael Danieli, ed., *International Handbook of Multigenerational Legacies of Trauma* (London: Plenum Press, 1988).
[4] Participants of this research were five second generation, and five third generation adults, aged between the ages of 22 and 63, all at the time of the study residents in Dersim. One to one, semi-structured, in-depth interviews were conducted with each participant. Dedicated to the participants of this research, who in the end were pleased that they were able to voice their experience and break the silence. Filiz Celik, 'Intergenerational Transmission of Trauma of Human-made Disasters: Case of Dersim Massacre 1937-38' (PhD Dissertation, on-going, Birkbeck, University College London.)
[5] Documentary movie: *Dersim 38* directed by Cayan Demirel, (2000), [Translated from Turkish by this author].

[6] Cathy Caruth, ed., *Trauma: Explorations in Memory* (London: The John Hopkins University Press, 1995), 3-13.

[7] Hinton, *Dark Side of Modernity*, 1-42.

[8] John M. Ingham, *Psychological Anthropology Reconsidered* (New York: Cambridge University Press), 1996.

[9] Paul Bartrop, 'The Relationship Between War and Genocide in the Twentieth Century: A Consideration', *Journal of Genocide Research* (2002): 519-532. Hinton, *Dark Side of Modernity*.

[10] Mark Mazower, 'Violence and the State in the Twentieth Century,' *The American Historical Review* (Chicago: The University of Chicago Press on behalf of the American Historical Association) 107 (2002): 1158-1178, Viewed 04 May 2011, http://www.jstor.org/stable/10.1086/532667.

[11] Ronnie Janoff-Bulman, 'Victims of Violence', in *Psychotraumatology: Key Papers and Concepts in Post-Traumatic Stress*, ed. George S. Everly, Jr. and Jeffrey M. Lating (London: Plenum Press, 1995), 73-86.

[12] Bessel van der Kolk, 'The Psychological Consequences of Overwhelming Life Experiences,' in *Psychological Trauma*, ed. Bessel van der Kolk (Washington: American Psychiatric Press, 1987), 1-31.

[13] Werner Bohleber, *Destructiveness, Intersubjectivity and Trauma: The Identity Crisis of Modern Psychoanalysis* (London: Karnac Books, 2010)

[14] Vivian Rakoff, John J Sigaland and Norman B Epstain, 'Children and families of concentration camp survivors'. *Canada's Mental Health* 14, (1966): 24-26.

[15] Yael Danielli, Introduction to *International Handbook of Multigenerational Legacies of Trauma*, ed. Yael Danielli (London and New York: Plenum Series, 1998), 1-27.

[16] Werner Bohleber, *Destructiveness, Intersubjectivity, and Trauma: The Identity Crisis of Modern Psychonalysis* (London: Karnac, 2010).

[17] Eduardo Duran and Bonnie Duran, *Native American Post-colonial Psychology*, (Albany, NY: State University of New York Press, 1995); Beth Hudnall Stamm and Henry E Stamm, IV, 'Trauma and Loss in Native North America: An Ethnocultural Perspective', *Honoring Differences: Cultural Issues in the Treatment of Trauma and Loss*, eds. Kathleen Nader, Nancy Dubrow and Beth Hudnall Stamm (Philedelphia, USA: Brunner/Mazel, 1999), 49-69.

[18] Maria Yellow Horse Brave Heart, 'The Historical Trauma Response among Natives and Its Relationship with Substance Abuse: A Lakota Illustration'. *Journal of Psychoactive Drugs* 35 (2003): 7-14; Duran And Duran, *Native American Post-colonial Psychology*.

[19] Ron Eyerman, *Cultural Trauma: Slavery and the Formation of the African American Identity* (Cambridge, UK: Cambridge University Press, 2001), 14.

[20] Ibid.

[21] Antonius C. G. M. Robben and Marcelo M. Suarez-Orozco, 'Interdisciplinary Perspectives on Violence and Trauma', in *Cultures under Siege: Collective Violence and Trauma*, eds. Antonious C. G. M. Robben and Marcelo M. Suarez-Orozco (Cambridge: Cabridge university Press, (2000), 1-43.

[22] Danieli, *Multigenerational Legacies of Trauma.*

[23] Martin van Bruinessen, 'Genocide in Kurdistan? The Suppression of the Dersim Rebellion in Turkey (1937-1938) and the Chemical War against the Iraqi Kurds', *Conceptual and Historical Dimensions of Genocide*, ed. George J. Andreopoulos (USA: University of Pennsylvania Press, 1988), 141-70.

[24] Ismail Besikci, *Tunceli Kanunu (1935) ve Dersim Jenosidi.* [The 1935 Law Regarding Tunceli and the Genocide of Dersim] in Turkish. (Bonn: Wesenan Rewsen, first published in 1977, reprinted in 1991).

[25] Kai Hafez, *The Islamic World and the West: An introduction to Political Cultures and International Relations* (The Netherlands: Brill, 2000, Translated from German by Mary Ann Kenny).

[26] Five obligatory acts of Islam, ignored by Alevi 1-Islamic creed, 2- daily prayers, 3- almsgiving, 4- fasting during Ramadan and 5- pilgrimage to Mecca at least once in a lifetime.

[27] Paul J. White and Joost Jongerden, eds., *Turkey's Alevi Enigma: A Comprehensive Overview* (The Netherlands: Brill, 2003). L. Molyneux-Seel. 'A Journey in Dersim.' *The Geographical Journal* (1944): 49-68; Henry H. Riggs, *Days of Tragedy in Armenia: Personal Experiences in Harpoot, 1915-1917* (London: Gomidas Ins, 1977).

[28] Martin van Bruinessen, 'The Kurds and Islam' (Working Paper no. 13, Islamic Area studies project, Tokyo, Japan, 1999), Viewed 5 May 2011, http://www.let.uu.nl/~martinj.vanbruinessen/personal/publications/Kurds_andIsl.

[29] Krisztina Kehl-Bodrogi, 'Ataturk and the Alevis: A Holly Alliance?' in *Turkey's Alevi Enigma: A Comprehensive Overview*, eds. Paul White and Joost Jangerden (The Netherlands: Brill, 2003), 53-71; Karin Vorhoff, 'The Past in the Future: Discourses on the Alevis in Contemporary Turkey', *Turkey's Alevi Enigma: A Comprehensive Overview*, ed. Paul White and Joost Jangerden (The Netherlands: Brill, 2003), 93-110.

[30] The Law Regarding the Administration of the City of Tunceli, no: 2884, 25th of December 1935, TBMM Zabit Ceridesi (National Assembly Minutes Journal).

[31] Besikci, Genocide of Dersim.

[32] Ibid.

[33] Yonca Poyraz Dogan, 'PM Erdogan Apologizes over Dersim Massacre on Behalf of Turkish State', *Today's Zaman*, 23.11.2011, Viewed 01 August 2012, http://www.todayszaman.com/news-263658-pm-apologizes-over-dersim-massacre-on-behalf-of-turkish-state.html.

[42] Van Bruinessen, *Genocide in Kurdistan?* 144.

[35] Danieli, Multigenerational Legacies of Trauma.

[36] Hurriyet Daily News, 'Alevis Continue to demand justice for Dersim', *Hurriyet Daily News*, 14 December 2009, Viewed 10 December 2011, http://www.hurriyetdailynews.com/n.php?n=alevis-continue-to-demand-justice-for-8216dersim8217-2009-12-14.

[37] CHP (Cumhuriyet Halk Partisi - Republican People's Party) renamed from People's Party in 1924 is the first political party of the Republic of Turkey and was in power until Turkey's transition to multi-party system in 1950.

[38] Habib Guler, 'State, CHP responsible for Dersim Massacre, says CHP Deputy Aygün', *Today's Zaman*, 10 November 2011, Viewed 13 November 2011, http://www.todayszaman.com/newsDetail_getNewsById.action?load=detayandnewsId=262241andlink=262241.

[39] BBC News, 'Turkey PM Erdogan Apologises for 1930s Kurdish Killings', *BBC News*, 23 November 2011, Viewed 25, 11, 2011, http://www.bbc.co.uk/news/world-europe-15857429.

[40] Melvin Konner, 'Trauma, Adaptation and Resilience: A Cross Cultural and Evolutionary Perspectives' in *Understanding Trauma: Biological, Psychological and Cultural Perspectives*, eds. Laurence J. Kirmayer, Robert Lemelson and Mark Barad (Cambridge University Press, New York, 2007), 300-338.

[41] Charles R. Figley, *Compassion Fatigue: Coping with Secondary Traumatization Stress Disorder in Those Who Treat the Traumatized* (Philadelphia, PA: Brunner/Mazel, 1995).

[42] Ibid.; Stamm and Stamm, *Trauma and Loss in Native North.*

[43] Lisa McCann and Laurie Anne Pearlman, 'Vicarious Traumatization: A Framework for Understanding the Psychological Effects of Working with Victims', *Journal of Traumatic Stress* 3 (1990): 131-149; Laurie Anne Pearlman and Karen W. Saakvitne, *Trauma and the Therapist: Countertransference and Vicarious Traumatization in Psychotherapy with Incest Survivors* (New York: Norton, 1995).

[44] Henry Krystal, 'Studies of Concentration-Camp Survivors', *In Massive Psychic Trauma*, ed. Henry Krystal (New York: International Universities Press, 1968), 23-46.

[45] Michelle M. Sotero, 'A Conceptual Model of Historical Trauma: Implications for Public Health Practice and Research', *Journal of Health Disparities Research and Practice* 1 (2006): 93-108.

[46] Yael Danieli, ed., *International Handbook of Multigenerational Legacies.*

[47] Maria Yellow Horse Brave Heart, *Historical Trauma Response.*

[48] Ron Eyerman, *Cultural Trauma.*

[49] Judy Atkinson, *Trauma trails, Recreating Song Lines : The Transgenerational Effects of Trauma in Indigenous Australia* (Spinifex Press, North Melbourne, 2002)

[50] Katharine G. Baker and Julia B. Gippenreiter, 'Stalin's Purge and Its Impact on Russian Families', *International Handbook of Multigenerational Legacies of Trauma*, ed. Yael Danieli (London, UK: Plenum Press, 1998), 403-434.

[51] Lucila Edelman, Diana Kordon and Dario Lagos, 'Transmission of Trauma: The Argentine Case', in *International Handbook of Multigenerational Legacies of Trauma*, ed. Yael Danieli (London, UK: Plenum Press,1998), 403-434.

[52] Yael Danieli, *Multigenerational Legacies of Trauma*, 1-17.

[53] American Psychiatric Association, *Diagnostic and Statistical Manual of Mental Disorders*, 4th ed. (Washington DC: American Psychiatric Association, 1994).

[54] Irit Felsen, 'Transgenerational Transmission of Effects of the Holocaust: The North American Research Perspective', Danielli, *International Handbook of Multigenerational Legacies of Trauma*, 43-68.

[55] Natan Kellermann 'Psychopathology in Children of Holocaust Survivors: A Review of the Research Literature', *Israel Journal of Psychiatry and Related Sciences* 38.1 (2001): 36-46.

[56] Rakoff, et al., *Children and Families of Concentration Camp.*

[57] Felsen, 'Transgenerational Transmission of Effects of the Holocaust'; Danieli, *Multigenerational Legacies of Trauma*, 1-17.

[58] van der Kolk, *Psychological Consequences of Overwhelming.*

[59] Janoff-Bulman, *Victims of Violence.*

[60] Norris, *Psychological Consequences of Disasters.*

[61] Hinton, *Dark Side of the Modernity.*

[62] Steven K. Baum, *The Psychology of Genocide: Perpetrators, Bystanders, and Rescuers* (Cambridge: Cambridge University Press, 2008), 1-8.

[63] Judith L. Herman, 'Complex PTSD: A Syndrome in Survivors of Prolonged and Repeated Trauma', *Psychotraumatology: Key Papers and Concepts in Post-Traumatic Stress*, ed. George S. Everly, Jr. and Jeffrey M. Lating (London: Plenum Press, 1995), 87-97.

[64] Danieli, *Multigenerational Legacies of Trauma*, 669-689.

[65] Bessel Van der Kolk, 'The Compulsion to Repeat the Trauma: Re-Enactment, Revictimization and Masochism', *Psychiatric Clinics of North America* 12 (1989): 389-411.

[66] Besikci, Genocide of Dersim.

[67] Ibid.

[68] Besikci, Genocide of Dersim.

[68] Natan P. F. Kellermann, 'Psychopathology in Children of Holocaust Survivors: A Review of the Research Literature', *Israel Journal of Psychiatry and Related Sciences* 38.1 (2001): 36-46.
[69] Yael Danielli, 'Families of Survivors of the Nazi Holocaust: Some Short and Some Long Term Effects', *Stress and Anxiety*, eds. Charles D. Speilberger, Irwin G. Sarason, and Norman Milgrim (New York: McGrawHill Hemisphere), 405-421.
[70] Filiz Celik, *Intergenerational Transmission of Trauma*.
[71] Ibid.
[72] Kaethe Weingarten, 'Witnessing the Effects of Political Violence in Families: Mechanisms of Intergenerational Transmission and Clinical Interventions', *Journal of Martial and Family Theraphy* 30 (2004): 45-59.
[73] Danieli, *Multigenerational Legacies*, 4-6.
[74] Eric Lindemann, 'Symptomology and Management of Acute Grief', *American Journal of Psychiatry* 101 (1944): 141-148.
[75] David S. Bathory, 'Healing Worldwide Wounds- Applied Trauma Theory', Bathory International LLC Somerville New Jersey USA, 2. Global Conference: Trauma Theory and Practice, Viewed 13 May 2012, http://www.inter-disciplinary.net/wp-content/uploads/2012/02/bathorytpaper.pdf.
[76] Martin van Bruinessen, 'Forced Evacuations and Destruction of Villages in Dersim (Tunceli) and Western Bingöl, Turkish Kurdistan', September-November 1994, Viewed 05 March 2009, http://www.let.uu.nl/~martin.vanbruinessen/personal/publications/index-text.html#articles#2.
[77] Ibid.
[78] Majda R. Atieh and Ghada Mohammad, 'Post-Traumatic Responses in the War Narratives of Hanan alShaykh's *The Story of Zahra* and Chimamanda Ngozi Adichie's *Half of a Yellow Sun*', in this volume.

Bibliography

Alexander, Jeffrey C., Ron Eyerman, Bernhard Giesen, Neil J. Smelser and Piotr Sztompka, eds. *Cultural Trauma and Collective Identity*. London: University of California Press, 2004.

American Psychiatric Association. *Diagnostic and Statistical Manual of Mental Disorders*, 4th ed. Washington DC: American Psychiatric Association, 1994.

Atkinson, Judy. *Trauma Trails, Recreating Song Lines: The Transgenerational Effects of Trauma in Indigenous Australia*. Spinifex Press, North Melbourne, 2002.

Bartrop, Paul. 'The Relationship Between War and Genocide in the Twentieth Century: A Consideretion'. *Journal of Genocide Research* (2002): 519-532.

Baum, Steven K. *The Psychology of Genocide: Perpetrators, Bystanders, and Rescuers.* Cambridge: Cambridge University Press, 2008.

BBC News, 'Turkey PM Erdogan apologises for 1930s Kurdish killings'. *BBC News*, 23 November 2011. Viewed 25 November 2011. http://www.bbc.co.uk/news/world-europe-15857429.

Baker, G. Katharine and Julia B. Gippenreiter. 'Stalin's Purge and Its Impact on Russian Families'. In *International Handbook of Multigenerational Legacies of Trauma*, edited by Yael Danieli, 403-434. London, UK: Plenum Press, 1998.

Besikci, Ismail. *Tunceli Kanunu (1935) ve Dersim Jenosidi.* [The 1935 Law Regarding Tunceli and the genocide of Dersim] in Turkish. Bonn: Wesenan Rewsen, reprinted in 1991.

Bohleber, Werner. *Destructiveness, Intersubjectivity, and Trauma: The Identity Crisis of Modern Psychonalysis.* London: Karnac, 2010.

Caruth, Cathy, ed. *Trauma: Explorations in Memory.* London: The John Hopkins University Press, 1995.

Celik, Filiz. 'Intergenerational Transmission of Trauma of Human-made Disasters: Case of Dersim Massacre 1937-38'. PhD Dissertation, Birkbeck, University College London.

Danieli, Yael. ed. *International Handbook of Multigenerational Legacies of Trauma.* London: Plenum Press, 1988.

———. 'Families of Survivors of the Nazi Holocaust: Some Short and Some Long Term Effects'. *Stress and Anxiety*, Vol. 8, edited by Charles D. Speilberger, Irwin G Sarason, N Milgrim, 405-421. New York: McGrawHill Hemisphere, 2000.

Figley, Charles R. *Compassion Fatigue: Coping with Secondary Traumatization Stress Disorder in Those Who Treat the Traumatized.* Philedelphia, PA: Brunner/Mazel, 1995.

Gellately, Robert, and Ben Kiernan, eds. *The Specter of Genocide: Mass Murder in Historical Perspective.* Cambridge: Cambridege University Press, 2003.

Hinton, Alexander L., ed. *Annihilating Difference: The Anthropology of Genocide.* London: University of California Press, 2002.

Hurriyet Daily News, 'Alevis Continue to demand justice for Dersim'. *Hurriyet Daily News*, 14 December 2009. Viewed 10 December 2011. http://www.hurriyetdailynews.com/n.php?n=alevis-continue-to-demand-justice-for-8216dersim8217-2009-12-14.

Ingham, John M. *Psychological Anthropology Reconsidered.* New York: Cambridge University Press, 1996.

Keiser, Hans-Lukas, ed. *Turkey Beyond Nationalism: Towards Post-Nationalist Identities.* London: I.B. Tauris, 2006.

Kirmayer, Laurence J., Robert Lemelson, and M. Barad, eds. *Integrating Biological, Clinical and Cultural Perspectives.* New York: Cambridge University Press, 2007.

Konner, Melvin. 'Trauma, Adaptation and Resilience: A Cross Cultural and Evolutionary Perspectives'. *Understanding Trauma: Biological, Psychological and Cultural Perspectives*, edited by Laurence J. Kirmayer, Robert Lemelson and Mark Barad, 300-338. Cambridge University Press, New York, 2007.

La Capra, Dominick. *History in Transit: Experience, Identity, Critical Theory.* London: Cornell University Press, 2004.

Mazower, Mark. 'Violence and the State in the Twentieth Century.' *The American Historical Review* 107.4 (2002): 1158-1178.

Norris, N Fran. 'Psychological Consequences of Disasters'. *PTSD Research Quarterly* 13.2 (2002): 1-7.

Oktem, Kerem. *Angry Nation: Turkey since 1989.* London: Zed Books, 2011.

Rakoff, Vivian, John Sigal and Norman Epstein. 'Children and Families of Concentration Camp Survivors'. *Canada's Mental Health* 14 (1966): 24-26.

Riggs, Henry. *Days of Tragedy in Armenia: Personal Experiences in Harpoot, 1915-1917.* London: Gomidas Ins, 1977.

Semelin, Jacques. *Purify and Destroy: The Political uses of Massacre and Genocide.* Translated from the French by Cynthia Schoch. London: Hurstand Company, 2007.

Shalev, Arieh Y., Rachel Yehuda and Alexander C. Macfalane, eds. *International Handbook of Human Responses to Trauma.* London: Kluwer Academic/ Plenum Publishers, 2000.

Sotero, Michelle. 'A Conceptual Model of Historical Trauma: Implications for Public Health Practice and Research'. *Journal of Health Disparities Research and Practice* 1.1 (2006): 93-108.

Van Bruinessen, Martin. 'Kurds, Turks, and the Alevi revival in Turkey'. *Middle East Report* (1996): 7-10.

―――. 'Genocide in Kurdistan? The Suppression of the Dersim Rebellion in Turkey (1937-1938) and the Chemical War Against the Iraqi Kurds'. *Conceptual and Historical Dimensions of Genocide*, edited by George J. Andreopoulos, 141-170. USA: University of Pennsylvania Press, 1988.

Van der Kolk, Bessel A., ed. *Psychological Trauma.* Washington: American Psychiatric Press, 1987.

―――. 'The Psychological Consequences of Overwhelming Life Experiences'. *Psychological Trauma*, edited by Bessel A. Van der Kolk, 1-31. Washington: American Psychiatric Press, 1987.

Werner, Bohleber. *Destructivenenss, Intersubjectivity, and Trauma: The Identity Crisis of Modern Psychoanalysis.* London: Karnac Books Limited, 2010.

White, Paul J. 'The Debate on the Identity of Alevi Kurds'. *Turkey's Alevi Enigma: A Comprehensive Overview*, edited by Paul J. White and Joost Jongerden. Leiden: Brill, 2003.

Filiz Celik is a PhD candidate at Birkbeck, University of London, researching Intergenerational Transmission of Trauma (ITT). Her research is focused on the traumatic effects of the Dersim Massacre (1937-1938) on second and third generations. In doing, so she considers the survivors and their descendants as agents in their particular socio-political and historical contexts, rather than as mere actors assigned to the role of victimhood.

Narrating Trauma, From *Testimonio* to Memoir: The Case of Rigoberta Menchú

Patricia Varas

Abstract
Trauma can find expression in different narrative strategies that may even seem at odds. This is the case of the Guatemalan indigenous activist and Nobel Peace Prize winner Rigoberta Menchú Tum, who preferred *testimonio* to narrate her community and her personal ordeal during the civil war; and afterwards shifted to the memoir to collect her experiences following the war and the Nobel Prize. Menchú adopts different genres to articulate collective and personal memory and trauma. The Quiché are the product of the rape by the white people; that is the legacy of their collective memory. Consequences of this rape are the poverty of the Mayans, the loss of their customs, the theft of their lands, and their extermination. Postmemory as a form of collective memory in indigenous cultures in Latin America can have a ritualistic connection with deep roots in the form of life and teachings of the ancestors with implications not envisioned in Marianne Hirsch's definition of this type of memory. I propose to discuss how Menchú chooses different narratives to give shape to her personal and collective memories and how narrating intergenerational trauma has the potential to help the victim of painful memories, regardless of cultural differences and philosophical conceptions of the individual and the community.

Key Words: Autobiography, Guatemala, intergenerational memory, magic, Maya, memoir, postmemory, Rigoberta Menchú, *testimonio*, trauma.

*****

1. Introduction

Rigoberta Menchú Tum, the Guatemalan indigenous leader, became famous before she was awarded the Nobel Peace Prize (1992) for her struggle and denunciation of the plight of the Mayan peoples in Guatemala during the period called *La Violencia* (1978-1985) in the civil war in that country (1960-1996). She chose to tell her story to the anthropologist Elizabeth Burgos in what would become her famous *testimonio I, Rigoberta Menchú: An Indian Woman in Guatemala* (1983).[1] Many years later she would adopt the memoir, *Crossing Borders* (1998),[2] to narrate her life after the Prize and world recognition.

I propose in this chapter to discuss how the selection of narrative structure or genre undertaken by Menchú informs us on how trauma can be narrated, how memory can be recovered and given meaning, and the concomitant social and aesthetic consequences of these choices. I am not suggesting that Menchú's decisions are completely conscious, after all she was in exile running for her life when she met Burgos, yet she shows a determination to work through her recollections, to present her pain and triumphs and those of her people in the most appropriate manner. Thus, the *testimonio* seems to be the best narrative to give coherence to the on-going troubles her community, family, and person are suffering under the unleashed repression against peasants and indigenous peoples during the civil war. In contrast, the memoir offers her narrative strategies that express other facets of her identity and growing experiences after the war and once the Peace Accords were negotiated in 1996.

    Testimonio is a specific Latin American genre, which especially marked cultural and literary studies of the region during the 1980s and 1990s.[3] This narrative has a series of characteristics that have been thoroughly discussed by the critics. I use George Yúdice's succinct yet comprehensive definition:

> Testimonial writing may be defined as an authentic narrative, told by a witness who is moved to narrate by the urgency of a situation (e.g. war, oppression, revolution, etc.). Emphasizing popular, oral discourse, the witness portrays his or her own experience as an agent (rather than a representative) of a collective memory and identity. Truth is summoned in the cause of denouncing a present situation of exploitation and oppression or in exorcising and setting aright official history.[4]

Leigh Gilmore and Gayatri Spivak treat the testimonial as a form of autobiographical text in their studies on autobiographical narratives. Both critics discuss the limitations of each genre in treating the female or post-colonial *I*. For Gilmore, Menchú's testimonial text is an example of how this literature tests the limits of autobiography with 'its compulsory inflation of the self to stand for others.'[5] While for Spivak, 'this deliberate and powerful play of the individual and representativity is the impossible signature of the ghostly witness in all autobiography.'[6] I make a distinction between *testimonio* and autobiography or memoir, which I use interchangeably. I analyze Menchú's *testimonio* primarily as a narrative that emphasizes the 'collective memory and identity' and the political urgency of denouncing a situation of oppression to set 'aright official history' and which perhaps has, as we shall see, a political agenda of sorts.[7] Instead I treat her memoir as directed by a strong personal desire to consciously compose a story that communicates the recollections of the vicissitudes and triumphs of a life. Menchú is still setting things right, but the incentive is dictated less by the political conditions of her country and more by her personal and familial ones.

    The immediacy of *testimonio* permits Menchú to articulate the trauma resulting from the suffering of poverty and oppression to which the indigenous peoples of Latin American have been subjected for centuries. The connection with this pain is linked not only to an ancient past told by the ancestors, but also to the repressive and racist policies of the modern Guatemalan government. Menchú by choosing to articulate collective trauma by bearing witness in *I Rigoberta Menchú*, develops a fitting frame to give coherence to two memories that coalesce: social memory (distinguished by clear political undertones) and postmemory (passed on for generations) and seeks justice through the ethical need to tell her story.

After years have passed, Menchú embraces the memoir/autobiography to once again tell us about her community and herself. It is well-known that to be able to organize recollections of an event it is best to have some chronological distantiation from it, even perhaps to have conducted some forgetting. Without the same urgency as during the war and physical and psychological repression, Menchú in her memoir has the time to select events, to organize them in a narrative in which magic, metaphors, and humour appear. The impulse to tell is more symbolically centred on the figure of the Maya activist who has won a Nobel Price, walks the halls of the United Nations, and travels around the world than on the suffering community. Postmemory is also an important way to remember in the memoir, as it puts Menchú in touch with magical motifs that encourage a symbolic act of remembering. If in the *testimonio* there was an urgent need to tell the *truth*, in the memoir the aesthetic envisioning of the past takes place and there is less concern with intermingling imagination and creativity in the act of remembering and telling. As Sturken sustains, forgetting is necessary for remembering, 'a desire for coherence and continuity produces forgetting.'[8]

In *Crossing Borders*, Menchú does not disassociate from the idea of a collective voice or orality, however; she still thanks her collaborators Gianni Minà and Dante Liano and the presence of her family and Chimel – her village – are vital for processing her memories, for example. I do not want to fall into polarizations which neatly divide the autobiographical as recalling states of consciousness such as thoughts, feelings, experiences and the public memory as grounded in shared learning, social repetition, and/or rearticulation because they will not do when studying the process that Menchú undertakes in the texts to remember and recover from trauma.[9] Menchú's *testimonio* and memoir confirm the strong interconnection between private/individual and collective/social memory and the feelings awakened by memorable events on the actor or actors.

In both narratives we are able to see the role of postmemory in indigenous culture and confirm that memory is a construction that can be shaped in different manners, with different objectives, and audiences in mind. This should not throw a negative judgment over its veracity, legitimacy or validity. No memory is a reproduction nor is it meant to be unique. Contestation, doubts, versions, multiplicity are all characteristics of the labours of memory.[10]

2. *Testimonio* and Memoir: Two Sides of the Same Coin

James E. Young argues the importance of 'the poetics of a witness's testimony' in his study on writing about the Holocaust.[11] He proposes convincingly that there are many interpretative filters in the writing and reading of a testimonial narrative and that how the events are created tells us how they were understood by the witness. Thus, Menchú's *testimonio* and memoir present hermeneutical issues on how to read her processing of trauma, on how to understand her use of narrative strategies to convey her experiences, and on what role we as readers must play within each text.

The transference of intergenerational memory is acquired through the stories told through generations and, especially in indigenous societies, can have more of a ritualistic connection and less than an *imaginary* one that has implications not envisioned in Marianne Hirsch's definition:

> [Postmemory] is a powerful and very particular form of memory precisely because its connection to its object or source is mediated not through recollection but through an imaginative investment and creation.[12]

In the case of the Quiché postmemory has deep roots in the form of life and teachings of the ancestors: 'our parents were raped by the white men, the sinners, the assassins.'[13] The Guatemalan indigenous activist writes in her *testimonio* that the Quiché communal identity is based on the stories told by their *abuelos* (elders) as well as on the ritualistic repetition of actions or customs that are passed on from one generation to the other. The Quiché have an obligation to keep 'the customs, the secrets of our ancestors' because this is 'a commitment with the whole community. All is done in memory of the community.'[14] She states the same idea in her memoir: 'the grandfather and the grandmother are equal to wisdom, hope, culture, transmitters of traditions, of everything, as well as they possess all the experiences.'[15] This is legacy of their collective memory, which is passed on as postmemory or intergenerational memory.

This form of memory is of great importance in native communities where white/colonial/Christian hegemony has subjected the indigenous people, marginalizing them into poverty through the systemic use of violence, and where a space of terror, which Taussig refers to as 'the landscape of death', is the legacy.[16] The intergenerational transmission of accounts and experiences can become an instrument of struggle and recovery from the 'memory of pain.'[17] As a collective memory it refers to important events that shape the community and as a traumatic memory it leaves an indelible mark on the group that has suffered a horrendous event which has 'harmfully, affected collective identity'[18] to the extent of destabilizing it.

Postmemory as a memory that is passed on from generation to generation is a form of collective memory that roots the receivers of this memory, in this case Menchú, in a community. Even though it is a memory of pain, the filiation necessary to bequeath it ensures and strengthens a sense of belonging and identity.

This filiation has to be tremendously powerful as it breaks the boundaries of the genetic; it is not limited to the family, it extends to the community as a whole.[19] This belonging is made clear in her *testimonio*; it defines the narrative and gives meaning to the genre. Menchú in the first page consistently repeats and emphasizes that her story is not unique; that her experiences do not belong to her alone, becoming a spokesperson and agent for her collective: 'I want to focus on the fact that I am not alone...' and that 'my personal situation includes the reality of a whole people.'[20] Menchú from the beginning frames a *we* that is going to be remembering and reliving a past that is painful and full of 'very dark times.'[21] This collective identity building is emphasized in the Spanish title, whereas in the English translation the first person pronoun and the name dominate, making the critics and readers think of the autobiographic *I*.[22] Rigoberta becomes herself, acquires an identity, the moment when as a child she becomes aware of the poverty her family and community live in and above all when she realises her powerlessness to help her mother take care of the family, 'and that is how my conscience was born.'[23] Towards the end of her narrative she further reaffirms her communally-centred identity, 'I am not the owner of my own life, I have decided to give it to a cause.'[24]

This same filiation and stress on the communal appear in the memoir, although more emphasis is given to some personal experiences. Menchú undertakes in her memoir, as the possessor of the 'grandparents' memory,'[25] the telling of the many privations her family lived, as well as the recollection of what her grandparents told them: 'Those feelings [of pain] will never leave one's life. I remember my grandfather, who never ceased from telling us beautiful stories, revelations, and mysteries.'[26] The title of her memoir in Spanish reflects an ambiguity that captures the fluidity of Menchú's autobiography and reminds us of how the subaltern must struggle to construct an identity. Her mother could never quite pronounce her Hispanicised name; her father obtained with enormous difficulty her birth certificate, and only after several fines she acquired her 'legal identity.'[27] Rigoberta is named the granddaughter of the Maya. Throughout the text she presents the idea that she is the recipient of the collective knowledge of the ancestors or elders (the *abuelos*) of her community in the form of postmemory, as well as she refers to her individual parents and grandparents and the information they have transmitted to her. In this manner she encompasses many forms of knowledge, some that are shared by all the Quiché and some that pertain only to her. As is the case when she protests the way she is treated in Guatemala in the public sphere after her exile, pointing out that political interests dominate over friendship:

> If I am unconditionally on their side I am treated as an excellent *compañera*, an exemplary woman, a national hero, but if I make my own decisions they say I am undisciplined, that I am their

enemy, that I am no longer their hero. How hard is Guatemala!
How difficult it is to live in this my country![28]

In the memoir she now has a new standing that is the result of the notoriety and
recognition of her *testimonio* and the Nobel Peace prize, 'I wrote many books [and]
I created a memory and in real life a legend of the Guatemalan people.'[29] If the
testimonio anchored her firmly as part of a community, it is as if in her memoir she
can embrace the fact that she has constructed a legitimate and authoritative place as
a subaltern that is not common among indigenous women in Western society. A
fact that Spivak had noted from the start: Rigoberta Menchú as 'an organic
intellectual taken for the true subaltern, represents herself as representative even as
she points out she is not representative.'[30]

Even the *unique* qualities that mark Menchú's personality and decisions stem
from familial/communal choices. In *I Rigoberta Menchú* she explains that her
family was different, non-conformist, and often times broke away from tradition.
Menchú recalls how her father encouraged her to be independent and work for the
good of their people, disregarding if this meant not following the rules of the
ancestors.[31] While in *Crossing Borders*, several chapters are devoted to explaining
the bonds that tie her to her family, which had been dismembered and
reconstructed because of the political activism of its members and the terrible
repression against the Maya in Guatemala. She identifies her family as one in
which all children were given the 'same opportunities,' regardless of their sex and
confesses that 'my family didn't follow some of the rules set by tradition.'[32]

Both parents play a key role in Menchú's narratives, where the political and
historical converge with the private. However, I want to concentrate on the role of
the mother, as Menchú's remembering is marked by continuity with this figure.[33]
The mother, Juana Tum, was a conservative woman, tied to her traditions, and
together with her husband an elected elder of her community; yet she was a leader
who risked her life for her community, a loving mother who suffered immensely
seeing her children work at a tender age and go to bed hungry, who embodied the
double tasks of a working woman in and outside the home, and who died a horrible
and violent death. Her wisdom is a legacy that Menchú remembers, 'my mother
would say to me: I do not force you to stop being a woman, but your participation
in the struggle must be the same as your brothers,'[34] although she doesn't truly
comprehend her as she will confess in her memoir. This woman who was a shaman
and midwife, who could interpret signs, and who extended her love to all escaped
Menchú's total understanding in her *testimonio*. Only in her memoir does she
finally grasp the meaning of her mother's complex and multiple self:

> When my mother was alive I didn't understand her and couldn't
> discover her. Maybe I admired many things in her, but I didn't
> truly understand her, or wanted to imitate her.[35]

Menchú through her narratives struggles to grasp the construction of her individual and collective identity as a Mayan organizer, woman, and as an international leader. Postmemory is a driving force in both texts to heal and achieve this construction. Studies on the healing of trauma emphasize the importance of the community and the restoration of social bonds. Judith Lewis Herman also tells us that 'a narrative that does not include the traumatic imagery and bodily sensations is barren and incomplete.'[36] In both narratives Menchú establishes strong bonds with her community and/or family – 'we, the indigenous families, the Mayan families, would be unhappy living without people or children,'[37] – as well as tries to describe the unimaginable, putting into words what she and the Quiché have lived. In the *testimonio* the narrative originates from a collective voice, at times even obliterating the individual's pain to allow the community's to take over. In the memoir, Menchú has the ability to revisit her pain by creating an emotional narrative that allows her to deal with the trauma more openly, while developing strong familial bonds with the family she has recovered.

Elizabeth Burgos, the anthropologist who transcribed the *testimonio*, has confirmed the state of trauma in which Menchú was immersed when she told her story; she was in full mourning. Burgos explains that through her witnessing and recollection Menchú created a mythology of the dead and a 'genealogy of pain'[38] to remember them. Thus she becomes a sort of Antigone, commemorating the dead and mourning by articulating the reality of death.[39] In her traumatized state, Menchú repeats the imagined scenes of torture and death of her family and friends, regretting not being able to bury them. She accepts that the only way to lay them to rest is through a ritualistic and symbolic collective act. To conduct a funeral in a home is meaningless because the torture and death did not take place in a house, 'they didn't die in a house, therefore they deserve that this place [where they were burned alive] becomes sacred.'[40] She comes across the same feeling of powerlessness when mourning her father and finds solace in the community, 'it does not matter that I have not been to where my father is buried… There will be many *compañeros* that we will need to bury, and then our love will be for everyone, not only for my father.'[41] Victor D. Montejo, echoing Lewis Herman findings, explains that this act of imagining is not only a psychological individual effort by Menchú, but also 'in this process of forcing the self to relive those moments of desperation, pain, and death, the mind tries to recall the strongest images of death and destruction experienced collectively.'[42]

The *unimaginable* violence to which Menchú and her people are subjected takes away from them their subjectivity and ability to respond, short of risking death. Thus in the collective voice of the *testimonio*, through solidarity she is able to express her and her people's suffering, and question and attack the system that consistently exploits and subjugates them. This is corroborated when we read,

> I would like to give this testimony, which I have not learned in a
> book and that I have not learned alone, all of this I have learned
> with my people.[43]

In her memoir, Menchú creatively recaptures the postmemory of pain that is the ancestral legacy which is embedded socially, culturally, economically, and historically and destroys any semblance of human dimension. She can finally deal with the trauma of the death of her family, neighbours, and friends and can now reconstruct an alternative world away from the 'space of death.'[44] Menchú has been awarded the Peace Prize, has wandered the halls of the United Nations, has become famous, and can return home to Chimel. She tells us: 'I have had to live a tragic life and tell about it in a book so that people would open their eyes about the indigenous people of Guatemala.'[45] In the autobiography she is able to avail herself of narrative recourses that are more expressive than in her testimony: she prefers metaphors over metonymy; she is candid and reveals herself (she still keeps some secrets, though); there are moments of humour and changes of perspective that allow us to understand that there is a conscious narrative voice telling her story.[46]

In both texts Menchú carries a double heavy burden: she needs to tell what she knows, she has the ethical responsibility of bearing witness, and seeking justice; and she also has to keep silent as a guardian of the secrets of her community. The readers can only approach her texts as empathetic listeners, but not seek identification with her and the Quiché, an effort that is truly impossible.[47] Menchú makes decisions actively about what should be told and what should be silenced. She must decide what she incorporates of her Quiché and family legacies and further transmits to future generations and to the *other*/readers. Silences and secrets, after all, are necessary for the processing of memory as well, since revisiting it doesn't mean reliving exactly the past and events, but following a balancing act of going and not going back. Otherwise the pain might be too great and the act of recollecting becomes impossible.

In the *testimonio* there is an effort to remember correctly, even if it is unverifiable. This desire to share with the reader the reality that the indigenous peoples of Guatemala were living during the war is urgent and puts a high stake on Menchú's recollection, impelling her to talk to Burgos. Yet the labour of memory is still present in the reconstruction of trauma and maybe the naïve reader will interpret each event and description as representing the real. But since Menchú in her *testimonio* opens up to the public the configuration of her memory in which she undertakes the condensation of various events into one, the substitution of herself as eyewitness in events to which she was not present, and depicts someone else's death as her brothers' she becomes open to 'unsympathetic scrutiny'[48] as the one conducted in David Stoll's book.[49]

Judith Zur, in her work on remembering and mourning among Guatemalan war widows, finds that these *faulty* representations of reality can be the product of many things. Among them forced repression or amnesia imposed by the authorities and not less the traumatic state that compresses events in order to obliterate them, the protective mechanism of dissociation, and the 'obsessional review'[50] of events as a product of the guilt and/or shame for not having done enough to protect the dead or disappeared victims. What is of particular interest to understand about Menchú's *flawed* accounts in her *testimonio* is that Zur discusses the provisionality of memory; how the women in their 're-working' of memory are constantly recreating their narratives to make sense of the traumatic events within their present needs. These narratives are in constant change reflecting 'a specific moment in the process of history.'[51] Furthermore, the incorporation of 'other people's memory into one's own' is encouraged 'in order to create narratives which make sense to the group.'[52] These narratives break with one of the most insidious effects of political repression, 'repression of the psychoanalytic kind.'[53]

The narrow focus that is applied when reading a *testimonio* is no longer relevant in *Crossing Borders*. The singularity and representativity of the testimonial experience that is encouraged by the legalistic frame imposed on it is suspended in the memoir. Menchú is able to use different tropes and aesthetic tools to conduct the processing of her trauma into a narrative that will articulate her memory so that it can then, once again, reside in the realm of social experience but this time not as a disconnected set of images that inspire fear, but as part of a past that has shaped her identity and which will mark her for the rest of her life.

There are some pivotal moments in her memoir in which Menchú uses magic to construct her traumatic narrative. This magic, like postmemory, is part of a mnemonic effort deeply rooted in ancestral beliefs. Real and surreal seamlessly merge; the division between the realms is porous among trauma victims, but also in certain cultures. The first instance is to explain death in 'the space of death,' owing to the rape by the white people and resulting in the poverty of the Mayas, the loss of their customs, the theft of their lands, and their extermination. Menchú thus recreates the past to recover the dead in her family and community. She has an enormous responsibility, as one of the few survivors she must tell her story, similar to the Holocaust survivors. Menchú makes of the unthinkable a narrative that although painful articulates memory, preventing forgetting. In her *testimonio* the deaths of her mother and brother were told in horrible detail, 'a form of figuration that gives these episodes a hallucinatory and symbolic intensity different from the matter-of-fact narration one expects from testimonio.'[54] In her memoir these terrible episodes acquire an almost mythic dimension, as she reconnects with her mother's dreams and foreboding. Juana Tum's suffering is grounded in her ability to interpret signs, which is part of her Maya inheritance and is passed on by her to the next generations. Thus she can foretell that together with her son's death and the bees disappearing from her village the family will disintegrate as well.[55] Menchú's brother Patrocinio's death was preceded by the song of a bat and of an owl omen's foreboding that 'perhaps his destiny was foretold.'[56] Furthermore, other omens surround Patrocinio's death, 'the dogs were crying, and they cried of sadness, the bees disappeared and other things happened' anticipating the 'hard times to come.'[57] Between her mother's secrets and premonitions Menchú can tell her story within a context that is not only determined by the torture and torment Patrocinio suffered in 'the space of death,' but is also part of a narrative in which Patrocinio comes alive as a young man on his way to visit his girlfriend and a mother caring and waiting for him. His death means the end of a way of life that can only be partially recovered through postmemory; through the remembrance of the ancestors' ways.

The desire to return to a space of harmony and peace and to move away from death and horror is sometimes a utopian dream or an imperative to not dwell on the negative and try to recover and restore a past that once existed and that one hopes will come again. This reelaboration in fact goes beyond Freud's displacement of painful memories by 'screen memories,' which is a defensive mechanism to substitute them. I believe that the creative and magical recovery of ancestral postmemory plays an important part in reestablishing this space. Magic is not dissociation, but re-imagination; by reliving through the images of others other possibilities that may comfort the person in the act of remembering and assuage her grief may take place.

A second instance of the use of magic is when Menchú arrives at and describes Chimel. Memory is ritualistic in *Crossing Borders* and it is awakened through the oral stories told by the ancestors, and traditional mediated images – postmemory – and the unconscious world of dreams. In the autobiography memory is a remarkable symbolic construction, a discourse of truth and identity which heavily relies both on the imagined and the lived. In her memoir Menchú can envision a utopian world, 'a more just and human world,'[58] thanks to the fact that she is being able to give coherence to the past, creating a narrative of healing. In effect, she is overcoming the pain and the melancholia resulting from her losses. Menchú conducts a dream-like act through which she establishes Chimel as a promised land. In Chimel, as *lieux de mémoire*, memory crystallizes because it is a place where 'a sense of historical continuity persists'[59] and where magic and affect find expression. This is a 'bewitching' and naturally beautiful place were the spirits of so many dead villagers and *guerrilleros* dwell. Menchú says, 'Chimel is a place with much magic, very deep.'[60] When visiting this magical place Menchú mixes times; present and past become one. The place seems changed: 'the biggest surprise was that I found the place very small. It was like a miniature of Chimel… The mysterious stones were very small.'[61]

Menchú expresses her strong emotions at going back home and her fears of the many memories that will be awakened, yet she collapses time and moves with fluidity in a totalizing effort to recover past/present/life/death:

Some days before leaving for Laj Chimel I dreamed of mother, I
dreamed of the house I grew up, they were the same as before.
Since that moment sadness wouldn't leave me... I didn't feel
hatred against the people who destroyed my community,
destroyed my house, my family. I only wanted to cry. I only
missed a past that seemed so near, when I was a little girl, young,
when I had a home that I will not be able to recover. The heart
always keeps great feelings of pain. It was the week we most
talked of mother, of father, of so many things I thought time had
taken care of erasing.[62]

Menchú recognizes the impossibility of resolving the trauma, since 'resolution of
the trauma is never final; recovery is never complete.'[63] In spite of the pain, her
recovery is such that she is able to move on, to not fall in an infinite *aporia*, and to
organize politically to protest Chimel's environmental devastation. This activism is
the best way to transcend the atrocities her community and Menchú experienced.

3. Conclusion
Menchú has assumed her responsibility to recover the collective memory of her
people and to articulate it in narratives that will make sense, act as memorials, and
inform others of the plight of her community. As she says in her *testimonio*:

As I told a man who was asking me, who wanted specific data
that I tell exactly what happened in the Spanish embassy [where
36 people died, mainly indigenous peasants and among them
Vicente Menchú, Rigoberta's father]: I cannot have a personal
version by imagining what happened since none of our
compañeros has survived and can tell the truth.[64]

She has found the words, the tone, and aesthetic generic representation to render an
account of the unimaginable. Each 'landscape of memory' requires specific
narratives of trauma to remember effectively because 'narratives of trauma may be
understood then as cultural construction of personal and historical memory.'[65] She
has 'worked through' her trauma, sometimes getting stuck in painful reliving that
has translated in repetitions and fragmentations in the narrative. Menchú,
nevertheless, in her narratives assumes her loss, as painful as it may be, and
through active transmission accepts that the past cannot be recovered as it was and
that changes will continue to occur as stories pass from one to another and from
one generation to another. I believe that this forward-looking attitude is illustrated
in her decision to become a mother herself. In the *testimonio* she had expressed
that because of her fear and trauma she would remain childless and that there

would be time for that later, when the context would allow for child-bearing.[66] The moment is ripe in her memoir where she now has a child.

Memory is a moral space, where continuity and moral practices are established, as Lambek suggests.[67] Menchú, through postmemory, magic, dreams, secrets, and generic strategies, develops narratives that allow for the articulation of trauma. This creative recreation responds to the magical and mythical thought patterns of her community, which cannot be completely understood by Western criticism. The cultures which live under a legacy of the suffering of poverty deserve a careful look through instruments that develop from their reality. After all, indigenous postmemory as a form of collective memory turns upside down the values of history, reality, and facts.

Notes

[1] Rigoberta Menchú, *Me llamo Rigoberta Menchú y así me nació la conciencia*, ed. Elizabeth Burgos (Mexico: Siglo Veintiuno Editores, 1999). All translations from the Spanish version are mine.

[2] Rigoberta Menchú, *Rigoberta: La nieta de los mayas* (Mexico: Aguilar, 1998). All translations from the Spanish version are mine.

[3] See the *Latin American Perspectives* issue devoted to testimonio: 'Voices of the Voiceless in Testimonial Literature. Part I', 8.3 (1991).

[4]George Yúdice, 'Testimonio and Postmodernism', in *The Real Thing: Testimonial Discourse in Latin America*, ed. Georg M. Gugelberger (Durham: Duke University Press, 1996), 44.

[5] Leigh Gilmore, *The Limits of Autobiography: Trauma and Testimony* (Ithaca: Cornell University Press, 2001), 5.

[6] Gayatri Spivak, 'Three Women's Texts and Circumfession', in *Postcolonialism and Autobiography*, eds. Alfred Hornung and Ernstpeter Ruhe (Amsterdam: Rodopi, 1998), 9.

[7] George Yúdice, 'Testimonio and Postmodernism', 44.

[8] Marita Sturken, *Tangled Memories: The Vietnam War, the AIDS Epidemic, and the Politics of Remembering* (Berkeley: University of California Press, 1997), 8.

[9] See Roger I. Simon, *The Touch of the Past: Remembrance, Learning, and Ethics* (New York: Palgrave Macmillan, 2005), 88.

[10] I borrow the term from Elizabeth Jelin's book, *State Repression and the Labors of Memory*, trans. Judy Rein and Marcial Godoy-Anativia (Minneapolis: University of Minnesota Press, 2003).

[11] James E. Young, *Writing and Rewriting the Holocaust. Narrative and the Consequences of Interpretation* (Bloomington: Indiana University Press, 1988), 3.

[12] Marianne Hirsch, *Family Frames. Photography, Narrative and Postmemory* (Cambridge: Harvard University Press, 1997), 22.

[13] Rigoberta Menchú, *Me llamo Rigoberta Menchú*, 92.

[14] Ibid., 38.

[15] Rigoberta Menchú, *Rigoberta: La nieta*, 145.

[16] Michael Taussig, 'Culture of Terror–Space of Death. Roger Casenet's Putumayo Report and the Explanation of Torture', *Comparative Studies in Society and History* 26.3 (1984): 468.

[17] Allan Young, 'Bodily Memory and Traumatic Memory', in *Tense Past. Cultural Essays in Trauma and Memory*, eds. Paul Antze and Michael Lambek (New York: Routledge, 1996), 91.

[18] Jeffrey C. Alexander, *Trauma. A Social Theory* (Cambridge: Polity Press, 2012), 14.

[19] This sense of community gives postmemory another dimension from the one established by critics who see intergenerational transmission as based mainly on familial ties. Thus, issues such as the saturation of second generation receivers or the pedagogical difficulties of teaching traumatic events and memorializing them for future generations are non-debatable among the Quiché and other indigenous communities, for example.

[20] Rigoberta Menchú, *Me llamo Rigoberta Menchú*, 21.

[21] Ibid.

[22] The English translation features the first person pronoun, *I Rigoberta Menchú*.

[23] Rigoberta Menchú, *Me llamo Rigoberta Menchú*, 55.

[24] Ibid., 270.

[25] Rigoberta Menchú, *Rigoberta: La nieta*, 115.

[26] Ibid., 118.

[27] Ibid., 114,

[28] Ibid., 73.

[29] Ibid., 314.

[30] Gayatri Spivak, 'Three Women's Texts and Circumfession', 9.

[31] Rigoberta Menchú, *Me llamo Rigoberta Menchú*, 167.

[32] Rigoberta Menchú, *Rigoberta: La nieta*, 115.

[33] Memory and trauma are gendered. Pain marks the body in how threats, violence, and events are remembered and emphasized. Gender difference is a site of resistance, witnessing, and identity while still part of universal humanity. See Anne Cubilié, *Women Witnessing Terror. Testimony and the Cultural Politics of Human Rights* (New York: Fordham University Press, 2005), 12.

[34] Rigoberta Menchú, *Me llamo Rigoberta Menchú*, 235.

[35] Rigoberta Menchú, *Rigoberta: La nieta*, 127.

[36] Judith Lewis Herman, *Trauma and Recovery. From Domestic Abuse to Political Terror* (London: Pandora, 2001), 177.

[37] Rigoberta Menchú, *Rigoberta: La nieta*, 29.

[38] Elizabeth Burgos, 'Memoria, transmisión e imagen del cuerpo: variaciones y recreaciones en el relato de un escenario de guerra insurgente', in *Stoll-Menchú: la*

invención de la memoria, ed. Mario Roberto Morales (Guatemala: Consucultura, 2001), 29. My translation.

[39] Ibid., 46.

[40] Rigoberta Menchú, *Me llamo Rigoberta Menchú*, 206.

[41] Ibid., 211.

[42] Victor D. Montejo, 'Truth, Human Rights, and Representation. The Case of Rigoberta Menchú', in *The Rigoberta Menchú Controversy*, ed. Arturo Arias (Minneapolis: University of Minnesota Press, 2001), 372-3.

[43] Rigoberta Menchú, *Me llamo Rigoberta Menchú*, 21.

[44] Michael Taussig, 'Culture of Terror–Space of Death', 468.

[45] Rigoberta Menchú, *Rigoberta: La nieta*, 208.

[46] See my essay where I discuss in more detail the tropes in Menchú's memoir, 'Memoria y postmemoria en *Rigoberta: La nieta de los mayas*', *Revista de Crítica Literaria Latinoamericana* 37.74 (2011): 329-50.

[47] See Doris Sommer, 'Resisting the Heat: Menchú, Morrison, and Incompetent Readers', in *Cultures of United States Imperialism*, eds. Amy Kaplan and Donald E. Pease (Durham, Duke University Press, 1993), 407-32.

[48] Leigh Gilmore, *Limits of Autobiography*, 4.

[49] David Stoll, *Rigoberta Menchú and the Story of All Poor Guatemalans* (Boulder: Westview Press,1999).

[50] Judith Zur, 'Remembering, and Forgetting. Guatemalan War-Widows' Forbidden Memories', in *Trauma: Life Stories of Survivors*, eds. Kim Lacy Rogers, Selma Leydesdorff, and Graham Dawson (New Brunswick: Transaction Publishers, 2004), 50-51.

[51] Ibid., 51.

[52] Ibid.

[53] Gavin Smith, 'Pandora's History: Central Peruvian Peasants and the Re-covering of the Past', in *Between History and Histories: The Making of Silences and Commemorations*, eds. Gerald Sider and Gavin Smith (Toronto: University of Toronto Press, 1997), 81.

[54] John Beverley, *Against Literature* (Minneapolis: University of Minnesota Press, 1993), 81.

[55] Rigoberta Menchú, *Rigoberta: La nieta*, 121.

[56] Ibid.

[57] Ibid., 122.

[58] Ibid., 108.

[59] Pierre Nora, 'Between Memory and History: *Les Lieux de Mémoire*', *Representations* 26 (1989): 7.

[60] Rigoberta Menchú, *Rigoberta: La nieta*, 75.

[61] Ibid., 76.

[62] Ibid., 76.

[63] Judith Lewis Herman, *Trauma and Recovery*, 211.
[64] Rigoberta Menchú, *Me llamo Rigoberta Menchú*, 212.
[65] Laurence Kirmayer, Laurence. 'Landscapes of Memory. Trauma, Narrative, and Dissociation', in *Tense Past. Cultural Essays in Trauma and Memory*, eds. Paul Antze and Michael Lambek (New York: Routledge, 1996), 175.
[66] Rigoberta Menchú, *Me llamo Rigoberta Menchú*, 250.
[67] Michael Lambek, 'The Past Imperfect. Remembering as Moral Practice', in *Tense Past*, 248.

Bibliography

Alexander, Jeffrey C. *Trauma. A Social Theory*. Cambridge: Polity Press, 2012.

Beverley, John. *Against Literature*. Minneapolis: University of Minnesota Press, 1993.

Burgos, Elizabeth. 'Memoria, transmisión e imagen del cuerpo: variaciones y recreaciones en el relato de un escenario de guerra insurgente'. In *Stoll-Menchú: la invención de la memoria*, edited by Mario Roberto Morales, 18-95. Guatemala: Consucultura, 2001.

Cubilié, Anne. *Women Witnessing Terror. Testimony and the Cultural Politics of Human Rights*. New York: Fordham University Press, 2005.

Gilmore, Leigh. *The Limits of Autobiography. Trauma and Testimony*. Ithaca: Cornell University Press, 2001.

Hirsch, Marianne. *Family Frames. Photography, Narrative and Postmemory*. Cambridge: Harvard University Press, 1997.

Jelin, Elizabeth. *State Repression and the Labors of Memory*. Translated by Judy Rein and Marcial Godoy-Anativia. Minneapolis: University of Minnesota Press, 2003.

Kirmayer, Laurence. 'Landscapes of Memory. Trauma, Narrative, and Dissociation'. In *Tense Past. Cultural Essays in Trauma and Memory*, edited by Paul Antze and Michael Lambek, 173-98. New York: Routledge, 1996.

Lambek, Michael. 'The Past Imperfect. Remembering as Moral Practice'. In *Tense Past. Cultural Essays in Trauma and Memory*, edited by Paul Antze and Michael Lambek, 235-54. New York: Routledge, 1996.

Latin American Perspectives 'Voices of the Voiceless in Testimonial Literature. Part I' 8.3 (1991).

Lewis Herman, Judith. *Trauma and Recovery. From Domestic Abuse to Political Terror.* London: Pandora, 2001.

Menchú, Rigoberta. *Rigoberta: La nieta de los mayas.* Mexico: Aguilar, 1998.

————. *Me llamo Rigoberta Menchú y así me nació la conciencia.* Edited by Elizabeth Burgos. Mexico: Siglo Veintiuno Editores, 1999.

Montejo, Victor D. 'Truth, Human Rights, and Representation. The Case of Rigoberta Menchú'. In *The Rigoberta Menchú Controversy,* edited by Arturo Arias, 372-91. Minneapolis: University of Minnesota Press, 2001.

Nora, Pierre. 'Between Memory and History: *Les Lieux de Mémoire'. Representations* 26 (1989): 7-24.

Simon, Roger I. *The Touch of the Past: Remembrance, Learning, and Ethics.* New York: Palgrave Macmillan, 2005.

Smith, Gavin. 'Pandora's History: Central Peruvian Peasants and the Re-covering of the Past'. In *Between History and Histories: The Making of Silences and Commemorations,* edited by Gerald Sider and Gavin Smith, 80-97. Toronto: University of Toronto Press, 1997.

Sommer, Doris. 'Resisting the Heat: Menchú, Morrison, and Incompetent Readers'. In *Cultures of United States Imperialism,* edited by Amy Kaplan and Donald E. Pease, 407-32. Durham: Duke University Press, 1993.

Spivak, Gayatri. 'Three Women's Texts and Circumfession'. In *Postcolonialism and Autobiography,* edited by Alfred Hornung and Ernstpeter Ruhe, 7-22. Amsterdam: Rodopi, 1998.

Stoll, David. *Rigoberta Menchú and the Story of All Poor Guatemalans.* Boulder: Westview Press,1999.

Sturken, Marita. *Tangled Memories. The Vietnam War, the AIDS Epidemic, and the Politics of Remembering.* Berkeley: University of California Press, 1997.

Taussig, Michael. 'Culture of Terror–Space of Death. Roger Casenet's Putumayo Report and the Explanation of Torture'. *Comparative Studies in Society and History* 26.3 (1984): 467-97.

Varas, Patricia. 'Memoria y postmemoria en *Rigoberta: La nieta de los mayas*'. *Revista de Crítica Literaria Latinoamericana* 37.74 (2011): 329-50.

Young, Allan. 'Bodily Memory and Traumatic Memory'. In *Tense Past. Cultural Essays in Trauma and Memory*, edited by Paul Antze and Michael Lambek, 89-102. New York: Routledge, 1996.

Young, James E. *Writing and Rewriting the Holocaust. Narrative and the Consequences of Interpretation*. Bloomington: Indiana University Press, 1988.

Yúdice, George. 'Testimonio and Postmodernism'. In *The Real Thing: Testimonial Discourse in Latin America*, edited by Georg M. Gugelberger, 42-57. Durham: Duke University Press, 1996.

Zur, Judith. 'Remembering, and Forgetting. Guatemalan War-Widows' Forbidden Memories'. In *Trauma: Life Stories of Survivors*, edited by Kim Lacy Rogers, Selma Leydesdorff, and Graham Dawson, 45-58. New Brunswick: Transaction Publishers, 2004.

Patricia Varas is a professor of Spanish and Latin American Studies at Willamette University. She has published extensively on Latin American modernity, film, culture, and women's writing.

Part III

Prevention and Reconciliation

Bereaved Mothers' Mental Health after the Sichuan Earthquake

Yao Xu, Helen Herrman, Atsuro Tsutsumi and Jane Fisher

Abstract
There are long-term health consequences of direct exposure to natural disasters including an increased prevalence of mental health morbidities, such as depression, anxiety and post-traumatic stress disorder (PTSD). Bereavement of a child is also a severe adverse life event that carries an increased risk of long term mental health problems including prolonged grief disorder (PGD). People who have faced these circumstances simultaneously through losing a child in a disaster therefore may have high vulnerability to chronic mental health morbidity. However, no systematic investigations have been reported examining it. This study investigated the prevalence of symptoms of anxiety, depression, PTSD, and PGD in women 30 months after they had experienced the death of a child in the May 2008 earthquake in Sichuan, China. Of the 226 participants, over eighty per cent of the women had clinically significant symptoms of depression, PTSD, or PGD and one third of the women had clinically significant symptoms of anxiety. Majority of the women were experiencing symptoms of more than one psychological disorder. The most prevalent co-morbidity was co-occurring symptoms of depression, PTSD and PGD. Overall, depression, PTSD and PGD were the major psychological problems among the bereaved mothers after the earthquake. Further studies are needed in order to understand the best advice and provide enhanced mental health care of such bereaved populations and suggest effective interventions for relevant organizations to improve health care services for them.

Key Words: Mental health, bereavement, disaster, mothers, child loss.

*****

I could not believe what I saw through my eyes. Everywhere, you know, everywhere is the reality you just could not believe ... There were no other sounds, only the sound of crying from all the people in here ... The only thing I could tell myself is here is not Wenchuan; here is a hell above ground ... At 5:57, it was daybreak, we rescued eighty-two people from ruins, and the voice of all the people has changed. Our tools were not enough for everyone, so some soldiers dug with their hands and lift up with their shoulders. We were all very excited for every rescued life, also felt deep sadness for each corpse we dug up. Many of us could not stop crying when digging and searching living lives. Liu Xiaoyi's hands were bleeding. When he used his hands excavated the sixth bodies, he cried and kept saying to himself:

'He is alive, he must be alive!' ... At noon we were ready to dine with the food we brought. A lot of people watched at us. We decided to give our food to them ... A girl about ten-year-old refused food no matter how we persuaded her. I asked her why not, she said because she could not find her mother and she wanted her mother.[1]
- *A soldier from a rescue team of May 12th, 2008 Sichuan earthquake in China - cited in a local newspaper, translated by YX.*

On Monday, 12 May 2008, Wenchuan was hit by an earthquake that registered 8.0 on the Richter scale at 13:09 (local time) in Sichuan province of China. Hence, this earthquake is also known as the Wenchuan earthquake (Chinese: 汶川大地震; pinyin: *Wènchuān dà dìzhèn*). Wenchuan as the earthquake's epicentre was eighty kilometres, fifty miles west-northwest of Chengdu, the capital of Sichuan, with a focal depth of nineteen kilometres.[2] Approximately fifteen million people lived in the affected areas, and people also felt the earthquake as far away as in Beijing, 1,500 kilometres away, and Shanghai, 1,700 kilometres away.[3] Office buildings were shaken with the quake, whilst strong aftershocks, some exceeding magnitudes of 6.0, continued to hit the area, even months after the main quake, causing new damage.[4]

One year later, the State Council of China pronounced that 69,277 people had died, 17,923 were missing, 361,822 people were seriously injured, and 6,900 schoolrooms had collapsed.[5] Of these, 68,636 people died in Sichuan province. The earthquake left about 4.8 million people homeless, though the number could be as high as 11 million.[6] Because the earthquake struck in the early afternoon when most students were at their desks and young students were taking a nap, 5,335 school children from Sichuan died or went missing.[7] Due to the one-child policy in China, majority of bereaved parents had lost their only child. On November 6, 2008, the Central Government announced that it would spend 1 trillion yuan, about 146.5 billion U.S. dollars, over the next three years to rebuild areas ravaged by the earthquake.[8]

In this chapter, we firstly briefly described disasters. Then we discussed health consequences after the disasters, in particular, post-disaster mental health problems among people who had lost the loved ones. Finally, we used our study as representative study to get further understanding of the issue.

Image 1: Dujiangyan, after the 2008 Sichuan earthquake, photo taken by YX

1. Disasters
The World Health Organization (WHO) defines a disaster as,

> ...any occurrence that causes damage, ecological disruption, loss of human life for deterioration of health and health services on a scale sufficient to warrant an extraordinary response from outside the affected community area.[9]

Based on the primary causes, disasters are generally classified into two types: natural and human-made or non-natural. A natural disaster is a consequence when a natural hazard affects and/or the built environment. It is a major adverse event resulting from natural processes of effecting the Earth, such as earthquakes, floods, wild fires, tsunami, tornadoes, hurricanes and cyclones, tropical storms, ice storms, droughts and volcanic eruptions.[10] A natural disaster can include loss of life, injury, economic loss and environmental loss. The severity of the losses depends on the ability of the affected population to resist the hazard: their resilience.[11] This understanding is concentrated in the formulation: 'disasters occur when hazards meet vulnerability'. Thus an event will not constitute a natural disaster if it occurs in an area without vulnerability, for example, an earthquake in an uninhabited area.[12] Traditionally these disasters are seen as unavoidable. Although early warning systems are developed to various degrees, the impact can be extremely powerful and may cause substantial destruction, social disruption and many other consequences.[13]

On the other hand, human-made disasters are caused by hardware failure, human error and intentional human acts resulting in technological accidents such as explosions, transport accidents, water and soil pollution, food contamination, terrorism and wars.[14] Because such human-made disasters are seldom preceded by warnings they may have a sudden onset or occur after prolonged political instability. While the impact is extremely powerful, the destruction is often concentrated and causes less social disintegration. These disasters may result in a sense of loss of personal control, for which someone or some agency may be seen as responsible.

Table 1: Deaths associated to natural disasters and development status

Sources: Adapted from United Nations Development Programme (2004)[15] with data from the International Emergency Disasters Database

During 2000 to 2011, 8,459 disasters occurred which affected billions of people around world. This number represents a sixty-eight per cent increase compared to 5,030 in the 1990s, and more than forty per cent of them happened in Asia.[16] Only in 2010, there were nearly 300,000 people lost their lives in more than 370 natural disasters around the world.[17] Importantly, in the past decade, over two million children have been killed in war and six million permanently disabled or injured.[18] In general, human-made disasters occur more frequently, but natural disasters affect much larger numbers of people and cause more simultaneous losses.[19] In the 1990s, almost 600,000 fatalities were due to disasters around the world. Of these, more than eighty-six per cent of the deaths occurred after natural, rather than human-made, events.[20] Losses due to natural disasters are twenty times greater (as a percentage of Gross Domestic Product) in developing settings than in industrialized countries.[21] Figure 1 shows the relationship between the number of natural disasters deaths from 1980 to 2000 and countries' development status. It is clear that low and medium human development countries have greater mortality from natural disasters than high development countries even when population density is controlled.[22]

Earthquakes illustrate the burden of natural disasters.[23] Globally, there are over 20,000 earthquakes a year, and over half are magnitude five or greater. Earthquakes can result in significant loss of human life: an earthquake in Iran in 1990 killed 50,000 people; in the American earthquake of 1988 over 25,000 died, and the 1976 earthquake in Tangshan, China, resulted in at least 255,000 deaths and perhaps as many as 655,000.[24]

This kind of words like 'perhaps' are often used in reporting disaster loss, it is because the real impact of a disaster may far more worsen than these official numbers. Measuring disaster loss is itself a major conceptual and methodological challenge.[25] A major barrier to describing and analysing disaster loss and its impact is the lack of reliable data and information on all levels. Disaster losses occur on all levels, from individual household losses to losses due to exceptional catastrophic events, such as major earthquakes and cyclones that can affect entire regions. The ways in which people are identified as being affected is partial. Estimates are based on assessments of the number of people experiencing damage to livelihoods or to a residence, or interruption of basic services. But these are difficult data to collect in a post-disaster period, particularly if there is not an accurate pre-disaster baseline. More difficult thing to measure is longer-term impacts, such as the consequences of the death, or income reducing on a household or extended family, or the consequences of migration or resettlement.[26]

Human deaths are the most reliable measure and indicator of disaster loss. But sometimes, the reporting numbers reveal only the tip of the iceberg in terms of real number of deaths.[27] People's bodies can be damaged, buried in ruins, or even swept out to seas in disasters that make the death toll calculation hard and unsure. Take Japan as an example, the final death toll of the 1995 Kobe earthquake was logged as 6,434 until December 2005, a decade after the quake hit. Even though most of bodies were found within a year as Kobe's population was compact and most bodies buried under their houses when they collapsed. Nevertheless, the final mortality figure from the 2011 Tohoku earthquake and tsunami could be much slower to confirm. Because the tsunami had swept many victims out to sea and even destroyed entire neighbourhoods and families, in many cases no one was survival to report the names of missing persons. The uncountable are so many and so hard to find. The final number will be counted until they wash ashore.[28]

However, the major and widespread adverse impacts of disasters are not only taking people's lives, but also can result survival individuals in a threat to personal safety, disruption of community and family structures, personal and societal losses, and most importantly poor health status.[29]

2. Stressors of Disasters

The majority of people exposed to disasters can perform and recover well in a short period; however, some individuals have long-term health problems including injury, distress, or changes in health behaviours such as an increase in alcohol or tobacco use after disasters.[30] The probability of having these conditions and changes varies according to the time and experiences since the disaster onset. Physical conditions and emotional responses often co-exist. In some instances, physical conditions may increase the probability of emotional changes. For example, a disaster may result in a chronic physical health condition such as injuries and disabilities, which have the potential to contribute to worsen mental health status. The reverse direction of causality is possible, with mental health problems resulting in poorer health maintenance efforts in chronic physical health conditions.[31]

Stressors are conditions or events that cause physical or psychological reactions to individuals under specific conditions.[32] Natural disasters usually include multiple stressors that can have differential effects on survivors.[33] Examples include personal physical harm and injury, loss of loved ones and other bereavement, threat of death and injury of other people, loss of property and dislocation and relocation.[34]

A. Physical Harm or Injury

Natural disasters can cause bad injuries, burns, illnesses, disabilities and other physical problems. In countries with poorly developed infrastructure and few health resources or services, the effects of natural disasters on people with the problems described above are particularly devastating. Untreated or inadequately treated broken bones and infected wounds can lead to unnecessary deaths, severe and long lasting disabilities.[35]

B. Loss of Loved Ones and Other Losses

The death of a family member or friend is a powerful stressor. Other bereavements and losses may also have a significant impact such as the loss of pets, work, community connections, personal identity and property. It is especially difficult for survivors to deal with deaths or losses when they have happened unexpectedly from a natural disaster.[36]

C. Threat of Death and Injury of Others

In a natural disaster, people have to face either the personal threat of the possibility of death, massive shock, or the mass deaths and injury of others. Exposure to, or seeing other people's deaths or injury, especially the deaths of children, may increases the risk of adverse reactions in the general population, as well as in trained rescue personnel and hospital workers even though they may have had training to prepare and protect them psychologically.[37]

D. Dislocation and Relocation

Loss of home, family or community usually happens after a natural disaster. People often have to move to makeshift houses and/or then may remove to new permanent houses continue their lives in a new location. This kind of change may disrupt their original community and its structure in some way. The larger the impact of a disaster, the greater potential disruption will affect the community. For example, a train crash survivor can return home to family and friends, because her community may remain the same. However, the recovery environment for an earthquake survivor is totally different: both the home and work site may have been destroyed, and relatives, friends and colleagues may be dead or injured.[38]

3. Physical Health after Disasters

Many health problems that may occur in the acute phase: injuries, burns, fractures, cuts and lacerations, and specific disaster-related symptoms, such as crush syndrome and acute renal failure during and immediately after earthquakes, eye-problems during and after the sarin attack in Tokyo, hearing-problems directly after the explosion in Toulouse, burns after a discotheque fire in Volendam, and a cough during and after the World Trade Center attacks in New York.[39] However, the majority of disaster survivors do not have long-term health problems. A minority of survivors develops chronic symptoms (like fatigue, back pain) and diseases (like hypertension, diabetes); often they attribute their deteriorated health to disaster exposure.

In the aftermath of disasters, survivors experience physical symptoms, whether related or unrelated to distress and/or psychological problems. Some of these symptoms may be presented to a physician, who decides whether the symptom experienced is 'medically explained' or 'medically unexplained'. The term medically unexplained symptoms describe physical symptoms that need seek help from professionals but have no clinically determined pathogenesis after an appropriate diagnostic evaluation. 'Unexplained' means that no consensual scientific explanation has been advanced that meets with universal acceptance.[40]

In particular, as one of the primary aspects of women's health, reproductive and sexual health is beginning to be recognized as key components of disaster relief efforts. In particular, disasters may also affect women's reproductive outcomes in an adverse way including early pregnancy loss, premature delivery, miscarriage, stillbirths and low birth weight.[41] For example, a study from Israel reported an increase in delivery rates during the 48 hours following an earthquake and a significant increase in the premature delivery rate.[42]

Menstruation is another 'problem' for women after disasters in a short time period. During the 1998 floods in Bangladesh, adolescent girls reported perineal rashes and urinary tract infections because they were not able to wash out menstrual rags properly in private, often had no place to hang the rags to dry, or access to clean water. They reported wearing the still damp cloths, as they did not have a place to dry them.[43]

4. Health Behaviors Changes after Disasters

Behavioral responses to disasters include changes in sleep, eating patterns, and use of addictive substances, including smoking and drugs. In general, there is a tendency of increasing alcohol consumption among persons who experienced stressful events.[44] Following a 1987 ferry accident near Belgium, forty-nine percent of survivors reported that their alcohol consumption increased 'a lot' in the six months after the accident.[45] But other studies found that only a part of pre-disaster alcohol or drug use disorders were still abusing it and few new disorders were detected.[46] There were no significant differences have been found between women and men in these studies.

Less apparent to disaster survivors are the signs of disaster-related long-term behavioral signs that may include decreased job performance, marital problems, and recurring nightmares.[47] In particular, following the Buffalo Creek disaster, Robert Lifton and Eric Olson found that psychic numbing and the impairment of post-disaster relationships.[48] In addition, survivor guilt is a phenomenon that may lead to serious reactions such as suicide among survivors.[49]

For some people symptoms of distress may persist for months. Individuals exposed to disasters have been found to increase their use of alcohol, tobacco, and other drugs, especially those with pre-existing alcohol abuse or other psychiatric difficulties. One to two months after September 11, residents in a suburb of Manhattan reported an increase of substance use (alcohol, cigarettes or marijuana): 24.6% reported increased alcohol use; 9.7% showed increased cigarette smoking; and 3.2% increased use of marijuana.[50]

5. Mental Reactions During Disasters

'Disaster mental health' is relatively new field and not regularly found in scholarly databases until the 1990s. This field is a result of the confluence of a number of different studies focusing on reactions and response to the consequences of natural and human-made disasters.[51] People usually have a normal to an abnormal event. Disasters survivors initially show some signs of emotional distress as an immediate or acute-phase reaction to the disaster, but the great majority of them can manage this reaction by themselves through some suggested existing coping strategies, support networks and material resources.[52] Mild to moderate stress reactions in the early post-phases of a disaster are highly prevalent among survivors and their families, community members and rescue workers in the disaster.[53] Although stress reactions may be thought of as 'extreme' and cause psychological symptoms, they generally do not become chronic problems. Most people recover fully from even moderate stress reactions within six to sixteen months.[54] But for major stress reactions, they may develop to severe long lasting mental disorders if people do not have any effective interventions or treatments in the early stage of post-disaster.[55]

In fact, the effects of traumatic events may not always negative. Experienced survivors may learn from previous disasters experiences that they can handle crises effectively, and feel that they are better off for having met this type of challenge. A disaster may also bring a community closer together or reorient an individual to new priorities, goals or value. This concept has been referred to as 'posttraumatic growth' by some authors,[56] and is similar to the 'benefited response' reported in the combat trauma literature.[57]

A. Individuals

Disasters often result in specific responses in survivors and those affected by the events. These stress reactions seem to follow common patterns that are defined by feelings, thoughts and behaviors. As previously described, the majority of these are transient and people recover with time.

The symptoms most often seen include emotional effects such as shock, anger, irritability, helplessness and loss of control; physical effects such as fatigue, sleep disturbances, hyperarousal, and somatic complaints; cognitive effects such as concentration difficulties, confusion, intrusive thoughts and worry; and interpersonal effects such as social withdrawal, relationship difficulties and impairment in functioning.[58]

Although many of the above reactions seem negative, people also have a number of positive responses in the aftermath of disaster. These include resilience and coping, altruism such as helping save or comfort others, relief at surviving disaster, sense of excitement and greater self-worth, changes in the way they view the future, and feelings of 'learning about strengths' and 'growing ' from experiences.[59]

In general, early after disasters occur, psychological defenses are activated. An alarm is sometimes followed by this stage that usually increases fear and anxiety, resulting in various psychophysiological reactions. At the moment of impact there is frequently a relatively short stun reaction. After this, there is usually an inventory and rescue stage. Joy, relief, fear grief, and other very individualized responses are typically seen at this time. Many emotional extremes people may experience are based on their experience and loss. At this point, communities and individuals frequently enter a 'honeymoon' period that fills with strong community cohesion and expressions of appreciation, relief, and gratitude.[60]

However, there is almost always a period of anger and disillusionment after 'Honeymoon': people start to be fully aware of their losses; recovery does not occur as rapidity as expected; angry with insurance companies or relief agencies. Finally, there is typically a reconstruction stage in which people incorporate the disaster experience and loss, and then move ahead with their lives. Some are left with the psychological scars of the experience; some change little from the way they were before the disaster; and some appear to become stronger and better able to cope in the future. Figure 2 is a graphic description of the stages of psychological response.[61]

Figure 2: Phases of psychological response to disasters

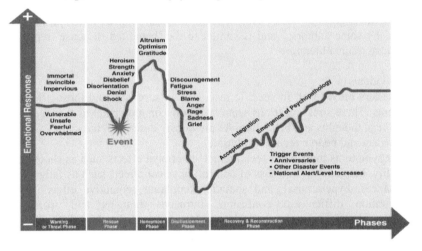

People's mental health responses to disasters have three key time points: 1-3 days, within 3 months and 1-3 years, and these time points are also important for their future psychological recovery.[62]

B. Families

Family as a unit has particular significant interactive impacts among family members in a disaster. The stress from disasters can strengthen the bonds between family members.[63] At the time of the crisis, most families attempt to come together and confront the disaster as one unit with joint protection and planned actions. For keeping the maximum number of survival family members, this kind of unit usually behaves and moves together toward the same direction for the same purpose. In the immediate post-disaster phase, families are usually primarily concerned with the rescue and safety of their own members, and then help friends and even strangers. Protection of the youngest and most vulnerable members seems to be the top goal. If family members know someone within their family is still trapped or injured, or if the family member's body is still missing, other members will desperately search for absent members, even their bodies. For the terms of long-term recovery, family tends to be an important source of support for each other.[64]

Factors influencing the recovery of families include bereavement, material losses and extended stress.[65] Larger families are more vulnerable as they may have more chances to face different stressors from the experiences. However, the older and better educated family members seemed less vulnerable and positive support networks helped reducing these stresses.[66] Higher income affected families also seemed to be in a better situation, as is not surprised that such families usually have more resources to deal with the crisis.

In addition, the interactive impact of the distress between family members has considerable implications for family stability and should never be neglected. Parents' distress seems to be a source of upset for their children. Because parents' emotions have directly effect on children's, and children's capability to deal with disaster is mostly learned from parents as how the parents cope with their own distress and whether the parents have ability to support their child. Marital relationship is another interactive factor may influence the recovery process of couples. The quality of marriage, especially aspects of care and support between couples are an important resource to deal with the distress of a disaster. Health behaviors like self-medication or drinking alcohol may further impact on the functioning of the whole family. Stresses from dislocation and relocation are also likely to take further effect on the recovery of the individual members and the family as a unit.

C. Communities

As individuals and families are the components of a community, accompany with individuals' interpersonal changes and families' interactive structure changes, the roles and rules of a community will be changed following a disaster. This kind of change may lead to a second personal disaster for everyone in the communities. Trauma related to this process often occurs with the displacement, relocation, property loss, and unemployment that may increase the risks and rates of social problems such as increased divorce rates, child abuse, disruptive behavior, and antisocial behavior.[67]

Communities may successfully go through a disaster and be strengthened by the ways in which they have 'pulled together' to deal with the impact and aftermath. Community services, networks of support, and post-disaster organization may contribute to such outcomes, but lack of these in the community may be associated with more negative outcomes.[68]

6. Risk Factors for Post-Disaster Mental Health

While disasters often impact on human beings very broadly, people are not equal at risk of loss and harm. There are some factors indicate the differences.

A. Gender

Evidence shows that women and men may suffer differently following a disaster.[69] Take a Western Ethiopian refugee camp report as an example, it found that, with continuing food aid, young Sudanese men were still undernourished because as men they had never learned how to cook.[70] Not only within households, men's role as protectors may place a greater responsibility on them for taking risk during and after a disaster as volunteers and rescue workers. The large majority of the 800,000 soldiers and civilians who helped clean up the Chernobyl site over several years and were most exposed to the radiation were men.[71] Women, on the other hand, are increasingly vulnerable to disasters due to socially determined differences in roles and responsibilities of women and men, and gender inequalities in access to resources and decision-making power.[72] Excess deaths among females following an earthquake in Maharashtra, India were attributed to women being in homes damaged by the earthquake and men being in open areas working farms. Boys were at school away from the village, and girls were at home helping mothers with household works. Similarly, in the 1991 cyclone in Bangladesh, many women died at home as they had to wait for their husbands to return and make an evacuation decision.[73]

It is obvious that gender-specific effects are factors in post-disaster outcomes, particularly after natural disasters, whether it is a difference of biological, social, or an interaction of both. Nevertheless, women tend to be more vulnerable than men in a number of areas influenced by this gender effect:

- *Post-disaster mortality, injury, and illness rates* which are often reported higher for girls and women:
  Data from 141 countries over the period 1981 to 2002 indicated higher female disaster mortality and morbidity rates compared to men in natural disasters.[74] This may because of the differences in social roles and responsibilities discussed above;
- *Economic loss*es which hugely impact economically insecure women:
  In low-income and lower-middle-income countries, women mainly work in agriculture, self-employed or working in the informal economy. These jobs are usually the most impacted by natural disasters, thus women become over represented among the unemployed in post-disaster contexts. Besides, unlike men, women are primarily responsible for household duties such as childcare and care for the elderly or disabled, hence they have less liberty and mobility to look for jobs or alternative sources of income after a disaster.[75]

- *Increased rates of sexual and domestic violence* against girls and women in disaster contexts:

Many families are forced to relocate to shelters after their houses are destroyed in natural disasters. Inadequate facilities, such as cooking resources, mean that a woman's domestic burden increases at the same time as her economic burdens. When women's economic resources are taken away, their bargaining position in the household is adversely affected. As men often migrate for jobs, a rise of female-headed households may put women in a dangerous position facing increasing risk of sexual and domestic violence following a disaster.[76]

B. Age

A study about the effects of a hurricane in the US on an adult population found that younger adults showed more psychological symptoms than middle-aged people.[77] Martie Thompson and colleagues also investigated the health burden by age. They found that these burdens peaked in middle age, because besides the stress of the disaster, middle-age people also need to face parental stress, family stress, financial stress, occupational stress, and also the stress of providing support to others.[78]

Moreover, children are also at particular risk during times of a disaster. Because they are less prepared to deal with stress due to their particular physical and psychological characteristics. The severity of children's reactions will depend on their specific risk factors. These include exposure to the actual event, personal injury or loss of a loved one, level of parental support, dislocation from their home or community, the level of physical destruction, and pre-existing risks, such as a previous traumatic experience or mental illness.[79]

C. Social Support

Social support has been most widely assumed as a factor related to disaster exposure groups, which can have either a positive or negative effect.[80] Effective support from professionals can help adjustment to traumatic experiences significantly and thereby improve their physical and mental health.[81] Spouses, parents, friends and colleagues are the main sources of support for bereaved parents. Women value support from their families most highly, whereas men seek help from friends and colleagues.[82] Importantly, marital relationship status is essential for understanding couples' recovery.[83] Marital stress or divorce may lead to adjustment problems and delay the process of recovery. Also, married women or single parents may be more vulnerable to disaster effects, possibly because they are relied upon to support others, which creates additional burdens.[84]

D. Relationship Status

Research on factors associated with the recovery environment indicates that relationship status is important in understanding recovery.[85] Marital stress has been found to increase after disasters and husbands' mental health status usually predicts wives' and vice versa.[86] This stress or even divorce may lead to adjustment problems and delay the process of recovery. Besides, married women or single parents may be more vulnerable to disaster effects, possibly because they are relied upon to support others, creating additional burden.[87]

E. Psychological Intervention

Receiving a psychological intervention can also be regarded as an important factor in disaster research.[88] After the Sydney rail disaster, Bruce Singh and Beverley Raphael found that there was a tendency for those who had counselling to do better than those who had no such intervention.[89] Better psychological outcomes have been reported among post-disaster population who participated in a professional intervention after Sichuan earthquake in China than those who did not.[90]

F. Previous Disaster or other Traumatic Events Experiences

Disaster workers are one group that this factor is particularly relevant. A long-term study about psychiatric morbidity in firefighters exposed to the Ash Wednesday bushfires in South Australia in 1983 showed that 29 months after the bushfires, twenty-one percent of the 459 firefighters were still experiencing recurrent images that interfered with their lives.[91] Repeated exposure to disaster trauma may put these people, such as firefighters and police officers, at a particular increased risk of developing psychiatric morbidity.

However, while increased vulnerability may be one outcome of previous exposure to traumatic events, prior exposure experiences could also be a protective factor to strengthen their ability to respond to the similar events.[92]

G. Pre-Existing Psychopathology and Family Psychiatric History

Pre-existing psychological problems and family psychiatric history have been shown to predict disaster-related distress in a number of studies.[93] However, they are not necessary or sufficient indicators to generate mental health conditions after disasters. Trauma related symptoms, for example, might occur in people with no prior psychiatric difficulties; conversely, many people with previous psychiatric illness remain free from psychopathology after disasters.[94]

7. Specific Psychological Problems after Disasters

According to Antony Taylor and A. Frazer's model,[95] people may be classified into six levels according to their relationship to the disaster impact zone and the psychological consequences of their disaster experience:

- *Primary victims*: Persons in the front line who have experienced maximum exposure to disasters.
- *Secondary victims:* Grieving relatives and friends of the primary victims.
- *Third-level victims:* Rescue and recovery personnel.
- *Fourth-level victims:* The community involved in the disaster as support groups.
- *Fifth-level victims:* People who are not directly involved in the disaster but experience distress or disruption.
- *Sixth-level victims:* Those who are in some way indirectly involved.[96]

Obviously, those who are directly exposed to a disaster and have experienced the loss of loved ones in the disaster are the most vulnerable population. They may have a high risk of developing psychological problems in both short- or long-term periods.[97] The most common post-disaster psychological problems appear to be depression, posttraumatic stress disorder (PTSD), other anxiety disorders and bereavement complications.[98]

A. Depression

Depression is an illness that involves the body, mood, and thoughts. As an invisible disease, it affects a person's eating and sleeping, and how she feels about herself. Symptoms include a persistent sad mood; loss of interest or pleasure in activities that were once enjoyed; significant change in appetite; inadequate sleeping or oversleeping; loss of energy; feelings of worthlessness or inappropriate guilt; difficulty thinking or concentrating; recurrent thoughts of death or suicide. Without any treatment, depression symptoms can last for weeks, months, or even years. Individuals with symptoms of depression need to seek help and support from professionals.[99]

B. Anxiety and Posttraumatic Stress Disorder (PTSD)

Anxiety is a natural and necessary warning response for humans. However, when it becomes extreme and uncontrollable, people will have a wide range of physical and affective symptoms as well as changes in behaviour and cognition such as disturbances of sleep, concentration, and social or occupational functioning. This process does not require any specific external stimulus. As listed in the Diagnostic and Statistical Manual of Mental Disorders (DSM IV-TR),[100] anxiety disorders include generalized anxiety disorder, social anxiety disorder, specific phobia, panic disorder with and without agoraphobia, obsessive-compulsive disorder, posttraumatic stress disorder (PTSD), anxiety secondary to medical condition, acute stress disorder, and substance-induced anxiety disorder.

Of these, PTSD has been widely studied following both natural and human-made disasters.[101]

PTSD is not the only trauma related disorder, nor perhaps the most common, but it is probably the most commonly studied diagnosis after a disaster. Diagnostic symptoms for PTSD include re-experiencing the original trauma(s) through flashbacks or nightmares, avoidance of stimuli associated with the trauma, and increased arousal such as difficulty falling or staying asleep, anger, and hyper vigilance. Formal diagnostic criteria require that the symptoms last more than one month and cause significant impairment in social, occupational, or other important areas of functioning.[102] The most frequent symptoms are intrusive thoughts and then exaggerated startle responses.[103]

C. Prolonged Grief Disorder (PGD)

As bereavement is a powerful stressor in disasters, the reaction to the loss of a loved one by death have been most described and researched than the other types of disaster bereavement.[104] Usually, there may be an initial brief period of shock, numbness and disbelief, and denial. After this period, bereaved persons will experience intense separation distress or anxiety. There also may be searching behaviours, particularly if it is not certain that the person is dead, or the body has not been identified. A sense of anger may be recognized by the bereaved person as angering towards the deceased for not being there and for being amongst those who died. Then the bereaved person moves to focus more on the psychological bonds with the dead person, the memories of the relationship, painful reminders of the absence of the person, and progressively accepting the death, although with on-going feelings of sadness or loss.[105] These complicated emotions of anxiety, distress, sadness and anger are usually referred to as prolonged grief disorder (PGD). PGD (also known as complicated or traumatic grief) is a form of trauma-related disorder that occurs after the death of a significant other. It is characterised by symptoms such as intense yearning for the deceased, difficulties accepting the loss and related bitterness or anger persisting for at least 6 months after the death.[106]

Numerous community studies support findings of high rates of symptoms of these disorders in exposed communities.[107] Six months after the 1989 earthquake in Newcastle, Australia, PTSD rates were forty per cent in the group who had direct exposure, were older aged females with lower social support, whose rate decreased to nineteen per cent two years later.[108] Following the 1999 Turkey earthquake, after some three years, the rates of PTSD and comorbid depression were forty per cent and eighteen per cent, respectively. PTSD was strongly related to fear during the earthquake, while depression related to loss of family members.[109] In 2002, the U.S. Centre for Disease Control and Prevention (CDC) conducted a national population-based mental health survey in Afghanistan more than two decades after the Soviet war in Afghanistan, 1979-1989. The prevalence of symptoms of depression was seventy-three per cent and fifty-nine per cent, of symptoms of anxiety was eighty-four per cent and fifty-nine per cent, and of PTSD was forty-eight per cent and thirty-two per cent for female and male Afghan residents respectively.[110]

Few studies have explored the long-term mental health consequences of bereavement in disasters. Pal Kristensen et al. examined the prevalence of mental health problems in bereaved people who had been either directly or not directly exposed to the 2004 Asian tsunami disaster.[111] Among the directly exposed group, thirty-four per cent had PTSD, twenty-five per cent depression, and twenty-three per cent PGD, whereas the prevalence among those not directly exposed was five per cent PTSD, ten per cent depression, and fourteen per cent PGD. Six months after the 2008 Sichuan earthquake, forty-four per cent of the bereaved group (losses including any family members or friends) had anxiety, eighty per cent had depression and sixty-three per cent had PTSD, whereas seventeen per cent of the non-bereaved group had anxiety, sixty-seven per cent had depression and forty-three per cent had PTSD.[112] While disaster-related bereavement has a profoundly adverse effect on mental health, risk was differed by the relationship to the person who has died.

People who have lost a child are the group most vulnerable to having mental disorders post-disaster compared to the losses of a spouse, a parent, another relative or a friend.[113] This also pertains to the non-disaster context.[114] Seven to eight months after the 2008 Sichuan earthquake, eighty per cent of bereaved parents had PTSD symptoms and eighty-two per cent had depression symptoms, compared to sixty-two per cent and sixty-nine per cent respectively for bereaved spouses, fifty-three per cent and forty-seven per cent for bereaved offspring/siblings, and twenty-seven per cent and thirty-eight per cent for non-bereaved group.[115] Loss of children also increases the risk for developing symptoms of complicated grief and higher levels of psychological impairment than loss of parents/siblings.[116] In particular, parents who had lost young children (<19 years) seem to have a higher risk for mental disorders than for those who have lost adult children.[117] Parents' narratives describe feeling that they would never fully recover from such a loss as they were 'still having a terrible time and there are certain bad days even now seven years later'.[118] Importantly, Singh and Raphael found that bereaved mothers were even more vulnerable to psychological problems than bereaved fathers after their child died in the Sydney railway disaster.[119] Almost all bereaved mothers were affected with chronic depression, whereas only half of the fathers experienced it. The majority of the bereaved mothers had needed to see a psychiatrist and two of them had needed psychiatric hospitalization.[120]

8. Representative Research

In order to further the understanding of bereaved mothers' mental health status after a disaster, I shall refer to a study that I have conducted for my PhD project.[121]

One aim of this project was about investigating the prevalence of and co-morbidities of psychological problems including symptoms of anxiety, depression, PTSD, and PGD among bereaved mothers after disasters. This was a community-based cross-sectional study conducted in China. By using structured interviews, women were interviewed 30 months after they had lost their child to the May 12th, 2008, Sichuan earthquake.

Questions included four instruments. Anxiety symptoms were assessed with Zung's 20-item Self-Rating Anxiety Scale (SAS), which measures the presence and severity of anxiety-related symptoms.[122] Based upon DSM-IV[123] criteria, the SAS contains both physiological symptoms such as muscle tremors, physical pain, urinary frequency, sweating, face flushing, insomnia, and psychological symptoms that include nervousness, fear, mental disintegration, panic, apprehension, restlessness, nightmares and those commonly associated with anxiety. Responses to statements were scored on a Likert-type scale of 1-4 to indicate how much of the time they describe the participant's experience: 'a little of the time', 'some of the time', 'good part of the time', 'most of the time'.

Depression symptoms were assessed by the 20-item Centre for Epidemiological Studies Depression Scale (CES-D), reflecting the characteristic symptoms of depression: depressed mood, feelings of guilt and worthlessness, feelings of helplessness and hopelessness, psychomotor retardation, loss of appetite, and sleep disturbance.[124] It has a similar form to the Zung Anxiety Scale with responses to statements being scored on a 0-4 Likert scale.

PTSD was evaluated with the 17-item PTSD Checklist-Civilian (PCL-C),[125] which assesses each of the 17 DSM-IV[126] symptoms of PTSD. It assesses the symptoms in relation to traumatic events. The symptoms endorsed may not be specific to just one event, which can be helpful when assessing survivors who have symptoms due to multiple events. Each question is scored on a 1-5 Likert-type scale from 'Not at all' to 'Extremely'.

Prolonged grief disorders (PGD) was evaluated with the 19-item Inventory of Complicated Grief (ICG),[127] which describes emotional, cognitive, and behavioural states associated with prolonged grief. Each item is on a 5-point scale (0-4): 'never' 'rarely sometimes', 'often' and 'always'.

Data collection was carried out from October 2010 to March 2011 in a town called Dujiangyan, in Sichuan, China, one of the two main towns and large population centres that experienced major destruction. Dujiangyan was only fifty kilometres southwest of the epicentre of the earthquake. More than ten per cent of the buildings in Dujiangyan, including three middle schools where students were attending mid-afternoon classes, were destroyed and nearly 1,000 children died.[128] The population of women in this town is 0.303 million and 73.1% women aged from 15-64 years old. The average education years and illiteracy rate for women is 7.5 years and 9.9%.[129] Before the earthquake, there was no mental health service in the town, however after the earthquake, fourteen town-level hospitals set up mental health division, twenty-three public health centres established mental health departments and 157 village-level health care stations provided a mental health service.[130]

In total, 244 bereaved mothers participated but 18 did not complete the survey. The results showed that the mean age of the women was 39.85 years old. The majority of the women had finished at least primary education, were married with unpaid job, and had lived in Dujiangyan for more than ten years. Only one woman had more than one child and did not lose both children in the earthquake, the others all had lost their only children. The average age at which the children had died was 14 years old.

Over half the participants thought their health was just fair, seventy women reported poor or very poor health. The results from the instruments of anxiety (the SAS[131]), depression (the CES-D[132]), PTSD (the PCL-C[133]), and PGD (the ICG[134]) showed that most of the mean scores on these psychometric measures were higher than the clinical cut-off points. These women had a very high prevalence of psychological problems even thirty months after the earthquake. Of the 226 participants, over eighty per cent of them had clinically significant symptoms of depression or PTSD, nearly ninety per cent had PGD symptoms and about one third of the women had anxiety symptoms. Depression, PTSD, and PGD tended to be the major psychological problems. Notably, over eighty per cent of the women had more than one psychological problem when we calculated the percentage of co-morbidity among them. The co-morbidity that was most prevalent among these post-disaster bereaved mothers was comorbid conditions co-occurring with depression, PTSD and PGD.

Compared to previous studies, the prevalence of psychological problems was much higher in women thirty months after the earthquake in this study than in the bereaved population of the same area six months after the disaster[135] and non-bereaved post-disaster population in other studies.[136] The depression prevalence in this study was higher than the prevalence reported in a study conducted six months after the same earthquake.[137] The rate of PTSD was also much larger in this study than that of another 2008 Sichuan earthquake study[138] and the 2004 Asian tsunami study.[139] By using the same instrument, the Inventory of Complicated Grief, more participants in this study had PGD symptoms compared to the bereaved population two years after the 2004 Asian tsunami[140] and after an earthquake in Iran.[141]

Obviously, women experiencing a disaster and also the loss of their only child need a longer time to recover than other post-disaster populations. It is also possible that their recovery has unintentionally been hampered by national and international supports and donations. Before the earthquake, these women's role was helping farming and caregiving, which was their main source of income. After the earthquake, governments supplied living resources and funds for them, which were more than they would have earned before the earthquake. Each surviving family was given a free apartment. For many Chinese families, buying an apartment is a major undertaking or life task that may take their whole working life to accomplish. In addition, Dujiangyan is a tourist town; leasing apartments to tourists is one part of earning for local people. Hence, many women in these families, including bereaved mothers, usually stayed at home instead of looking for jobs. This may have possibly led to non-intentional social isolation, which may have worsened the women's mental health.

There is increased mental health services set up in Dujiangyan and forty per cent of the participants had received psychological intervention after the earthquake. Nevertheless the prevalence reported in our study was still high. Possible reasons for it might be some women did not know about these services; they did know but did not seek help from them; or they did go but the intervention they had may not have been effective. Meanwhile, because everyone in the town may have some mental health problems, they may not be aware of their problems and think they were 'OK' as everyone the same. Hence, they never thought about seeking help from professionals

In conclusion, the robust evidence of this study indicated that the dual burden of direct exposure to natural disasters and the loss of a child, particularly the only child, have long-term and severe effects on women's mental health. Depression, PTSD, and PGD were the main problems and the prevalence was much higher among bereaved mothers than both bereaved and non-bereaved populations after the earthquake. The results suggested that there is an urgent need for outreach and a re-evaluation of post-disaster interventions in this population. Further studies are needed in order to frame suitable psychological interventions and services that might consider the level and complexity of symptoms of depression, PTSD and PGD to offer this group of women and similar bereaved populations.

Notes

[1] Ming Hai Zhu and Hua Feng He, 'A Soldier's Dairy of Wenchuan Experience,' *Fujian Daily*, May 26th, 2008.
[2] GOV.cn (Chinese Government's Official Web Portal), 'Magnitude of SW China Earthquake Revised to 8.0,' *Xinhua News Agency*, http://english.gov.cn/2008-05/18/content_981724.htm; U.S. Geological Survey (USGS), 'Magnitude 7.9 - Eastern Sichuan, China,' USGS. http://web.archive.org/web/20080517023123/http://earthquake.usgs.gov/eqcenter/e qinthenews/2008/us2008ryan/.
[3] BBC, 'Hundres Buried by China Quake,' BBC, http://news.bbc.co.uk/2/hi/asia-pacific/7395496.stm; State Council of China, 'Anniversary of the Wenchuan Earthquake,' *China Daily*, 12 May 2009.
[4] Ibid.

[5] Ibid.

[6] Jake Hooker, 'Toll Rises in China Quake,' *New York Times*, Viewed 27 May 2008, http://www.nytimes.com/2008/05/26/world/asia/26quake.html; Relief Web, 'More than 4.8 Million Homeless in Sichuan Quake: Official,' *Agence France-Press*, Viewed, 27 May 2008, http://reliefweb.int/node/266249.

[7] State Council of China, 'Anniversary of the Wenchuan Earthquake.'

[8] Alibaba.com, 'FACTBOX-China's Recent Measures to Spur Growth,' Viewed 27 May 2011, http://news.alibaba.com/article/detail/economy/100020445-1-factbox-china%2527s-recent-measures-spur-growth.html.

[9] Department of Gender Women and Health, World Health Organization, 'Gender and Health in Natural Disaster,' in *Gender and Health* (Geneva: World Health Organization, 2005).

[10] Ibid.

[11] B. Wisner et al., *At Risk: Natural Hazards, People's Vulnerability and Disasters* (Wiltshire: Routledge, 2004).

[12] Ibid.

[13] Department of Gender Women and Health, 'Gender and Health in Natural Disaster.'

[14] Ibid.

[15] United Nations Development Programme (UNDP), *Reducing Disaster Risk: A Challenge for Devlopment* (New York: Bureau for Crisis Prevention and Recovery, UNDP, 2004).

[16] Centre for Research on the Epidemiology of Disasters, 'Disaster List,' SuperAdminEMDAT, Viewed 20 May 2011, http://www.emdat.be/disaster-list.

[17] Ibid.

[18] Robert J. Ursano and Jon A. Shaw, 'Children of War and Opportunities for Peace,' *JAMA: The Journal of the American Medical Association* 298.5 (2007).

[19] R. J. Ursano et al., eds., *Textbook of Disaster Psychiatry* (Cambridge: Cambridge University Press, 2007).

[20] Department of Gender Women and Health, 'Gender and Health in Natural Disaster.'

[21] Wisner et al., *At Risk*.

[22] Wisner et al., 'Reducing Disaster Risk: A Challenge for Devlopment.'

[23] U.S. Geological Survey (USGS), 'National Earthquake Information Center,' http://earthquake.usgs.gov/earthquakes/.

[24] Ibid.

[25] Wisner et al., *At Ris'*

[26] Ibid.

[27] Ibid.

[28] Juro Osawa et al., 'A Long, Painful Reckoning,' *The Wall Street Journal*, March 17, 2011 2011.

[29] Department of Gender Women and Health, 'Gender and Health in Natural Disaster.'

[30] Craig L. Katz et al., 'Research on Psychiatric Outcomes and Interventions Subsequent to Disasters: A Review of the Literature,' *Psychiatry Research* 110.3 (2002).

[31] Center for Disease Control and Prevention, 'Surveillance for Illness and Injury after Hurricane Katrina-New Orleans, Louisiana,' in *MMWR Morbility Mortality Weekly Report*, ed. Center for Disease Control and Prevention (2005a).

[32] R. E. Cohen, *Disaster Mental Health Services: Manual for Workers* (Miami: US Library of Congress, 1998).

[33] Ursano et al., *Textbook of Disaster Psychiatry*.

[34] V. Raphael, 'Disaster Mental Health Response Handbook,' in *Disaster Mental Health Response Handbook B2: Disaster Mental Health Response Handbook* (Sydney, NSW: New South Wales Health, 2000).

[35] Ibid.

[36] Ibid.

[37] Ibid.

[38] Ibid.

[39] C. J. Yzermans, B. Van der Berg, and A. J. E. Dirkzwager, 'Physical Health Problems after Disasters,' in *Mental Health & Disasters*, ed. Yuval Neria, Sandro Galea, and Fran H. Norris (New York: Cambridge University Press, 2009).

[40] Ibid.

[41] Department of Gender Women and Health, 'Gender and Health in Natural Disaster'; Xu Xiong et al., 'Exposure to Hurricane Katrina, Post-Traumatic Stress Disorder and Birth Outcomes,' *Am J Med Sci* 336.2 (2008).

[42] Department of Gender Women and Health, 'Gender and Health in Natural Disaster.'

[43] Ibid.

[44] Selby C. Jacobs, *Traumatic Grief: Diagnosis, treatment, and prevention* (Philadelphia: Taylor & Francis Group, 1999); Katz et al., 'Research on Psychiatric Outcomes and Interventions Subsequent to Disasters: A Review of the Literature.'

[45] S. Joseph et al., 'Increased Substance Use in Survivors of the Herald of Free Enterprise Disaster,' *British Journal of Medical Psychology* 66(1993).

[46] Katz et al., 'Research on Psychiatric Outcomes.'

[47] B. W. Flynn, 'Disaster Mental Health: The U.S. Experience and Beyond,' in *Humanitarian Crises, The Medical and Public Health Response*, ed. J. Leaning, S. M. Briggs, and L. C. Chen (Cambridge: Harvard University Press, 1999).

[48] R. J. Lifton and E. Olson, 'The Human Meaning of Total Disaster: The Buffalo Creek Experience,' *Psychiatry* 39 (1976).

[49] Flynn, 'Disaster Mental Health.'

[50] Katz et al.,'

[51] Joshua L. Miller, *Psychosocial Capacity Building in Response to Disasters* (New York: Columbia University Press, 2012).

[52] B. H. Young et al., *Disaster Mental Health Services: A Guidebook for Clinicians and Admininstrators* (St Louis, M0: National Center for PTSD, Department of Veteran Affairs Employee Education System, 1998).

[53] Ursano et al., *Textbook of Disaster Psychiatry.*

[54] Ibid.

[55] Ibid.

[56] R. G. Tedeshi and L. G. Calhoun, *Posttraumatic Growth: Conceptual Foundation and Empirical Evidence* (Philadelphia, PA: Lawrence Erlbaum Associates, 2004).

[57] Ursano et al., *Textbook of Disaster Psychiatry.*

[58] Raphael, 'Disaster Mental Health Response Handbook.'; Young et al., *Disaster Mental Health Services: A Guidebook for Clinicians and Admininstrators.*

[59] Ibid.

[60] Flynn, 'Disaster Mental Health.

[61] Ibid.

[62] Katz et al., 'Research on Psychiatric Outcomes.

[63] Raphael, 'Disaster Mental Health Response Handbook'.

[64] Ibid.

[65] Beverley Raphael, Julie Dunsmore, and Sally Wooding, 'Tenor and Trauma in Bali: Australia's Mental Health Disaster Response,' *Journal of Aggression, Maltreatment & Trauma* 9.1/2 (2004).

[66] Raphael, 'Disaster Mental Health Response Handbook.'

[67] Ibid.

[68] Ibid..

[69] Department of Gender Women and Health, 'Gender and Health in Natural Disaster.'

[70] Ibid.

[71] Ibid.

[72] Ibid.

[73] Ibid.

[74] E. Neumayer and T. Plumper, 'The Gendered Nature of Natural Disasters: The Impact of Catastrophic Events on the Gender Gap in Life Expectancy, 1981-2002,' *Annals of the Association of American Geographers* 97.3 (2007).

[75] Department of Gender Women and Health, 'Gender and Health in Natural Disaster.'

[76] Raphael, 'Disaster Mental Health Response Handbook.'

[77] M. Thompson, F. H. Norris, and B. Hanacek, 'Age Differences in the Psychological Consequences of Hurricane Hugo,' *Psychology and Aging* 8 (1993).

[78] Ibid.

[79] Raphael, 'Disaster Mental Health Response Handbook.'

[80] W. Stroebe, H. Schut, and M. Stroebe, 'Grief Work, Disclosure and Counseling: Do they Help the Bereaved?,' *Clinical Psychology Review* 25 (2005).

[81] H. Laakso and M. Paunonen-Ilmonen, 'Mothers' Experience of Social Support Following the Death of a Child,' *Journal of Clinical Nursing* 11.2 (2002); Babette G. Levin, 'Coping with Traumatic Loss: An Interview with the Parents of TWA 800 Crash Victims and Implications for Disaster Mental Health Professionals,' *International Journal of Emergency Mental Health* 6.1 (2004).

[82] Laakso and Paunonen-Ilmonen, 'Mothers' Experience.'

[83] Raphael, 'Disaster Mental Health Response Handbook.'

[84] Ibid.

[85] Ibid.

[86] Fran H. Norris and Carrie L. Elrod, 'Pschosocial Consequences of Disaster: A Review of Past Research,' in *Methods for Disaster Mental Health Research*, ed. Fran H. Norris, et al. (New York: The Guilford Press, 2006).

[87] Raphael, 'Disaster Mental Health Response Handbook.'

[88] M. S. Stroebe et al., 'The Prediction of Bereavement Outcome: Development of an Integrative Risk Factor Framework,' *Social Science & Medicine* 63.9 (2006).

[89] B. Singh and B. Raphael, 'Postdisaster Morbidity of the Bereaved: A Possible Role for Preventive Psychiatry?,' *Journal of Nervous and Mental Disease* 169.4 (1981).

[90] Yin Yuan et al., 'Comparison of PTSD Symptoms, Depression and Anxiety between Bereaved and Non-Bereaved Survivors after the Wenchuan earthquake (汶川地震丧亲与非丧亲者 PTSD、焦虑和抑郁的对比研究),' *Chinese Journal of Behavioral Medicine and Brain Science* 18.12 (2009).

[91] Raphael, 'Disaster Mental Health Response Handbook.'

[92] Ibid.; Ursano et al., *Textbook of Disaster Psychiatry*.

[93] C. C. Chen, T. L. Yeh, and Y. K. Yang, 'Psychiatric Morbidity and Post-Traumatic Symptoms among Survivors in the Early Stage following the 1999 Earthquake in Taiwan,' *Psychiatric Research* 105 (2001); ShihCheng Liao et al., 'Acute Stress Syndromes of Rescue Workers within One Month after Major Earthquake (震災後一個月內救難人員之急性壓力症候群),' *臺灣醫學* 6.1 (2002); A. C. McFarlane, 'Helping the Victims of Disaster,' in *Traumatic Stress: From Theory to Practice*, ed. J. R. Freedy and S. E. Hobfoll (New York: Plenum Press, 1995).

[94] Ibid.

[95] A. J. W. Taylor and A. G. Frazer, *Psychological Sequelae of Operation Overdue following the DC10 Aircrash in Antarctica* (Wellington, New Zealand: Victoria University of Wellington, 1981).

[96] Ibid.

[97] Raphael, 'Disaster Mental Health Response Handbook.'

[98] Janice L. Genevro, Tracy Marshall, and Tess Miller, 'Report on Bereavement and Grief Research,' *Death Studies* 28.6 (2004); Katz et al., 'Research on Psychiatric Outcomes'; Pal Kristensen, Lars Weisæth, and Trond Heir, 'Psychiatric Disorders among Disaster Bereaved: An Interview Study of Individuals Directly or not Directly Exposed to the 2004 Tsunami,' *Depression & Anxiety (1091-4269)* 26.12 (2009).

[99] Katz et al., 'Research on Psychiatric Outcomes.'

[100] American Psychiatric Association, *Diagnostic and Statistical Manual of Mental Disorders.*

[101] C. S. Fullerton et al., 'Disaster-Related Bereavement: Acute Symptoms and Subsequent Depression,' *Aviation, Space, And Environmental Medicine* 70.9 (1999).

[102] American Psychiatric Association, *Diagnostic and Statistical Manual of Mental Disorders.*

[103] Ursano et al., *Textbook of Disaster Psychiatry.*

[104] Jacobs, *Traumatic Grief: Diagnosis, Treatment, and Prevention.*

[105] Ibid.

[106] Ibid.

[107] Raphael, 'Disaster Mental Health Response Handbook.'

[108] V. J. Carr et al., 'Psychosocial Sequelae of the 1989 Newcastle Earthquake: II. Exposure and Morbidity Profiles during the First 2 Years Post-Disaster,' *Psychological Medicine* 27.1 (1997).

[109] E. Salcioglu, M. Basoglu, and M. Livanou, 'Post-Traumatic Stress Disorder and Comorbid Depression among Survivors of the 1999 Earthquake in Turkey,' *Disasters* 31.2 (2007).

[110] B. Lopes Cardozo et al., 'Mental Health of Women in Postwar Afghanistan,' *Journal of Women's Health* 14.4 (2005).

[111] Kristensen, Weisæth, and Heir, 'Psychiatric Disorders among Disaster Bereaved.'

[112] Yuan et al., 'Comparison of PTSD Symptoms, Depression and Anxiety between Bereaved and Non-Bereaved Survivors after the Wenchuan Earthquake (汶川地震丧亲与非丧亲者PTSD、焦虑和抑郁的对比研究).'

[113] C. L. W. Chan et al., 'Posttraumatic Stress Disorder Symptoms Among Adult Survivors of the 2008 Sichuan Earthquake in China,' *Journal of Traumatic Stress* 24.3 (2011).

[114] Middleton et al., 'A Longitudinal Study'.

[115] Cecilia L. W. Chan et al., 'Symptoms of Posttraumatic Stress Disorder and Depression among Bereaved and Non-Bereaved Survivors following the 2008 Sichuan Earthquake,' *Journal of Anxiety Disorders* 26.6 (2012).

[116] Ibid.

[117] Chan et al., 'Symptoms of Posttraumatic Stress Disorder.'

[118] Levin, 'Coping with Traumatic Loss'.

[119] Singh and Raphael, 'Postdisaster Morbidity.'

[120] Ibid.

[121] Xu, Yao, Herrman, Helen, Bentley, Recebcca, Tsutsumi, Asturo, and Fisher, Jane. *PhD Project: Women's Mental Health after they had Lost a Child in the 2008 Sichuan Earthquake.* Unpublished work. University of Melbourne, Melbourne, Australia.

[122] W. W. K. Zung, 'A Rating Instrument for Anxiety Disorders,' *Psychosomatics* 12.6 (1971).

[123] American Psychiatric Association, *Diagnostic and statistical Manual of Mental Disorders.*

[124] L. S. Radloff, 'The CES-D Scale: A Self-Rport Depression Scale for Research in the General Population,' *Applied Psychological Measurement* 1(1977).

[125] K. J. Ruggiero et al., 'Psychometric Properties of the PTSD Checklist: Civilian Version,' *Journal of Traumatic Stress* 16.5 (2003).

[126] American Psychiatric Association, *Diagnostic and Statistical Manual of Mental Disorders.*

[127] Holly G. Prigerson et al., 'Inventory of Complicated Grief.

[128] Jeffrey Hays, 'Sichuan Earthquake in 2008: Geology, Damage, Survivors and the Dead,' http://factsanddetails.com/china.php? 407&catid=10&subcatid=65#00.

[129] Chang De (郑长德) Zheng, 'Si Chuan Wen Chuan Te Da DI Zhen Shou Zai Di Qu Ren Kou Tong Ji Te Zheng Yan Jiu (四川汶川特大地震受灾地区人口统计特征研究),' *Journal of Southwest University for Nationalities* 205 (2008).

[130] Wenjun (毛文君) Mao et al., 'Analysis of the mental health status of the victims after earthquake in Dujiang Yan (都江堰地震灾后安置点人群心理健康状态分析),' *Sichuan Medical Journal* 30.6 (2009).

[131] Zung, 'A Rating Instrument for Anxiety Disorders.'

[132] Radloff, 'The CES-D Scale.'

[133] Ruggiero et al., 'Psychometric Properties of the PTSD Checklist.'

[134] Prigerson et al., 'Inventory of Complicated Grief.'

[135] Chan et al., 'Symptoms of Posttraumatic Stress Disorder.'

[136] Alireza Ghaffari-Nejad et al., 'The Prevalence of Complicated Grief among Bam Earthquake Survivors in Iran,' *Archives of Iranian Medicine* 10.4 (2007).'
[137] Yuan et al., 'Comparison of PTSD Symptoms, Depression and Anxiety.'
[138] Ibid.
[139] Kristensen, Weisæth, and Heir, 'Psychiatric Disorders among Disaster Bereaved.'
[140] Ibid.
[141] Ghaffari-Nejad et al., 'The Prevalence of Complicated Grief'.

Bibliography

Alibaba.com. 'Factbox-China's Recent Measures to Spur Growth.' http://news.alibaba.com/article/detail/economy/100020445-1-factbox-china%27s-recent-measures-spur-growth.html.

American Psychiatric Association. *Diagnostic and Statistical Manual of Mental Disorders: Dsm-Iv-Tr*. 4th ed., text revision ed. Washington, D. C.: American Psychiatric Association, 2000.

BBC. 'Hundres Buried by China Quake.' *BBC*, http://news.bbc.co.uk/2/hi/asia-pacific/7395496.stm.

Carr, V. J., T. J. Lewin, R. A. Webster, J. A. Kenardy, P. L. Hazell, and G. L. Carter. 'Psychosocial Sequelae of the 1989 Newcastle Earthquake: II: Exposure and Morbidity Profiles During the First 2 Years Post-Disaster.' *Psychological Medicine* 27.1 (1997): 167-78.

Center for Disease Control and Prevention. 'Surveillance for Illness and Injury after Hurricane Katrina-New Orleans, Louisiana.' In *MMWR Morbidity Mortality Weekly Report*, edited by Center for Disease Control and Prevention, 1018-21, 2005a.

Centre for Research on the Epidemiology of Disasters. 'Disaster List.' SuperAdminEMDAT, http://www.emdat.be/disaster-list.

Chan, CLW, CW Wang, ZY Qu, BQB Lu, MS Ran, AHY Ho, Y Yuan, *et al.* 'Posttraumatic Stress Disorder Symptoms among Adult Survivors of the 2008 Sichuan Earthquake in China.' *Journal of Traumatic Stress* 24, no. 3 (2011): 295-302.

Chen, C. C., T. L. Yeh, and Y. K. Yang. 'Psychiatric Morbidity and Post-Traumatic Symptoms among Survivors in the Early Stage Following the 1999 Earthquake in Taiwan.' *Psychiatric Research* 105 (2001): 13-22.

Christ, G., G. Bonanno, R. Malkinson, and S. Rubin. 'Bereavement Experiences after the Death of a Child.' In *When Children Die: Improving Palliative and End-of-Life Care for Children and Their Families*, edited by M. Field and R. Berhman. 553-79. Washington, DC: National Academy Press, 2003.

Cohen, R. E. *Disaster Mental Health Services: Manual for Workers.* Miami: US Library of Congress, 1998.

Davies, D.E. 'Parental Suicide after the Expected Death of a Child at Home.' *British Medical Jounral* 332. 7542 (2006): 647-48.

Department of Gender Women and Health, World Health Organization. 'Gender and Health in Natural Disaster.' In *Gender and Health.* Geneva: World Health Organization, 2005.

Flynn, B. W. 'Disaster Mental Health: The U.S. Experience and Beyond.' Chap. 2 In *Humanitarian Crises, the Medical and Public Health Response*, edited by J. Leaning, S M. Briggs and L. C. Chen. 97-124. Cambridge: Harvard University Press, 1999.

Fullerton, C. S., R. J. Ursano, T. C. Kao, and V. R. Bharitya. 'Disaster-Related Bereavement: Acute Symptoms and Subsequent Depression.' *Aviation, Space, And Environmental Medicine* 70.9 (1999): 902-09.

Genevro, Janice L., Tracy Marshall, and Tess Miller. 'Report on Bereavement and Grief Research.' *Death Studies* 28.6 (2004 2004): 491-575.

Ghaffari-Nejad, Alireza, Mohammadreza Ahmadi-Mousavi, Mohsen Gandomkar, and Hamed Reihani-Kermani. 'The Prevalence of Complicated Grief among Bam Earthquake Survivors in Iran.' *Archives of Iranian Medicine* 10.4 (2007): 525-8.

GOV.cn (Chinese Government's Official Web Portal). 'Magnitude of Sw China Earthquake Revised Ti 8.0.' Xinhua News Agency, http://english.gov.cn/2008-05/18/content_981724.htm.

Hays, Jeffrey. 'Sichuan Earthquake in 2008: Geology, Damage, Survivors and the Dead.' http://factsanddetails.com/china.php? 407&catid=10&subcatid=65- 00.

Hooker, Jake. 'Toll Rises in China Quake.' *New York Times*, http://www.nytimes.com/2008/05/26/world/asia/26quake.html.

Jacobs, Selby C. *Traumatic Grief: Diagnosis, Treatment, and Prevention*. Philadelphia: Taylor & Francis Group, 1999.

Johannesson, K. B., T. Lundin, C. M. Hultman, T. Frojd, and P. O. Michel. 'Prolonged Grief among Traumatically Bereaved Relatives Exposed and Not Exposed to a Tsunami.' *Journal of Traumatic Stress* 24.4 (2011): 456-64.

Joseph, S., William Yule, R. Williams, and P. Hodginkson. 'Increased Substance Use in Survivors of the Herald of Free Enterprise Disaster.' *British Journal of Medical Psychology* 66 (1993): 185-91.

Katz, Craig L., Lori Pellegrino, Anand Pandya, Anthony Ng, and Lynn E. DeLisi. 'Research on Psychiatric Outcomes and Interventions Subsequent to Disasters: A Review of the Literature.' *Psychiatry Research* 110.3 (2002): 201-17.

Kristensen, P., L. Weisaeth, and T. Heir. 'Predictors of Complicated Grief after a Natural Disaster: A Population Study Two Years after the 2004 South-East Asian Tsunami.' *Death Studies* 34.2 (2010): 137-50.

Kristensen, Pal, Lars Weisæth, and Trond Heir. 'Psychiatric Disorders among Disaster Bereaved: An Interview Study of Individuals Directly or Not Directly Exposed to the 2004 Tsunami.' *Depression & Anxiety (1091-4269)* 26.12 (2009): 1127-33.

Laakso, H., and M. Paunonen-Ilmonen. 'Mothers' Experience of Social Support Following the Death of a Child.' *Journal of Clinical Nursing* 11.2 (Mar 2002): 176-85.

Levin, Babette G. 'Coping with Traumatic Loss: An Interview with the Parents of Twa 800 Crash Victims and Implications for Disaster Mental Health Professionals.' *International Journal of Emergency Mental Health* 6.1 (2004 2004): 25-31.

Li, Jiong, Dorthe Hansen Precht, Preben Bo Mortensen, and Jorn Olsen. 'Mortality in Parents after Death of a Child in Denmark: A Nationwide Follow-up Study.' [In English]. *Lancet* 361.9355 (2003 Feb 2003): 363-7.

Liao, ShihCheng, YueJoe Lee, ShiKay Liu, MingBeen Lee, ShengChung Wang, JiaShin Chen, and ChihTao Cheng. 'Acute Stress Syndromes of Rescue Workers within One Month after Major Earthquake (震災後一個月內救難人員之急性壓力症候群).' 臺灣醫學 6, no. 1 (2002): 1-9.

Lifton, R. J., and E. Olson. 'The Human Meaning of Total Disaster: The Buffalo Creek Experience.' *Psychiatry* 39 (1976): 1-18.

Lopes Cardozo, B., O. O. Bilukha, C. A. Gotway, M. I. Wolfe, M. L. Gerber, and M. Anderson. 'Mental Health of Women in Postwar Afghanistan.' *Journal of Women's Health* 14.4 (2005): 285-93.

Mao, Wenjun (毛文君), Yin (袁茵) Yuan, Maosheng (冉茂盛) Ran, Di (孔娣) Kong, Tao (张涛) Zhang, Weiqun (楼玮群) Lou, Xiaolu (王筱璐) Wang, Xiao'en (何孝恩) He, and Liyun (陈丽云) Chen. 'Analysis of the Mental Health Status of the Victims after Earthquake in Dujiang Yan (都江堰地震灾后安置点人群心理健康状态分析).' *Sichuan Medical Journal* 30.6 (2009): 970-73.

McFarlane, AC. 'Helping the Victims of Disaster.' In *Traumatic Stress: From Theory to Practice*, edited by JR Freedy and SE Hobfoll. 287-314. New York: Plenum Press, 1995.

Middleton, W., B. Raphael, P. Burnett, and N. Martinek. 'A Longitudinal Study Comparing Bereavement Phenomena in Recently Bereaved Spouses, Adult Children and Parents.' *The Australian and New Zealand Journal of Psychiatry* 32.2 (1998): 235-41.

Miller, Joshua L. *Psychosocial Capacity Building in Response to Disasters*. New York : Columbia University Press, c2012., 2012. Bibliographies.

Murphy, S. A., L. C. Johnson, L. Wu, J. J. Fan, and J. Lohan. 'Bereaved Parents Outcomes 4 to 60 Months after Their Children's Deaths by Accident, Suicide, or Homicide: A Comparative Study Demonstrating Differences.' [In English]. *Death Studies* 27.1 (Jan 2003): 39-61.

Neumayer, E., and T. Plumper. 'The Gendered Nature of Natural Disasters: The Impact of Catastrophic Events on the Gender Gap in Life Expectancy, 1981-2002.' [In English]. *Annals of the Association of American Geographers* 97.3 (Sep 2007): 551-66.

Norris, Fran H., and Carrie L. Elrod. 'Pschosocial Consequences of Disaster: A Review of Past Research.' Chap. 2 In *Methods for Disaster Mental Health Research*, edited by Fran H. Norris, S. Galea, Matthew J. Friedman and Patricia J. Watson. 20-42. New York: The Guilford Press, 2006.

North, C. S., E. M. Smith, and E. L. Spitznagel. 'Posttraumatic Stress Disorder in Survivors of a Mass Shooting.' *Am J Psychiatry* 151.1 (1994 1994): 82-8.

Osawa, Juro, Phred Dvorak, Daisuke Wakabayashi, and Toko Sekiguchi. 'A Long, Painful Reckoning.' *The Wall Street Journal*, March 17, 2011 2011.

Prigerson, Holly G., Mardi J. Horowitz, Selby C. Jacobs, Colin M. Parkes, Mihaela Aslan, Karl Goodkin, Beverley Raphael, *et al.* 'Prolonged Grief Disorder: Psychometric Validation of Criteria Proposed for Dsm-V and Icd-11.' *PLoS Medicine* 6. 8 (2009): e1000121.

Prigerson, Holly G., Paul K. Maciejewski, Charles F. Reynolds, Andrew J. Bierhals, Jason T. Newsom, Amy Fasiczka, Ellen Frank, Jack Doman, and Mark Miller. 'Inventory of Complicated Grief: A Scale to Measure Maladaptive Symptoms of Loss.' *Psychiatry Research* 59.1-2 (1995): 65-79.

Radloff, L. S. 'The Ces-D Scale: A Self-Report Depression Scale for Research in the General Population.' *Applied Psychological Measurement* 1 (1977): 385-401.

Raphael, Beverley, Julie Dunsmore, and Sally Wooding. 'Tenor and Trauma in Bali: Australia's Mental Health Disaster Response.' *Journal of Aggression, Maltreatment & Trauma* 9.1/2 (2004): 245.

Raphael, V. 'Disaster Mental Health Response Handbook.' In *Disaster Mental Health Response Handbook B2: Disaster Mental Health Response Handbook*. Sydney, NSW: New South Wales Health, 2000.

Relief Web. 'More Than 4.8 Million Homeless in Sichuan Quake: Official.' Agence France-Press, http://reliefweb.int/node/266249.

Reyes, G. 'International Disaster Psychology: Purposes, Principles, and Practices.' Chap. 1 In *Handbook of Inernational Disaster Psychology: Fundamentals and Overview*, edited by G. Reyes and G. A. Jacobs. 1-14. Westport: Praeger Publishers, 2006.

Ruggiero, K. J., K. Del Ben, J. R. Scotti, and A. E. Rabalais. 'Psychometric Properties of the Ptsd Checklist - Civilian Version.' [In English]. *Journal of Traumatic Stress* 16.5 (Oct 2003): 495-502.

Salcioglu, E., M. Basoglu, and M. Livanou. 'Post-Traumatic Stress Disorder and Comorbid Depression among Survivors of the 1999 Earthquake in Turkey.' *Disasters* 31.2 (2007): 115-29.

Sanders, Catherine M. 'A Comparison of Adult Bereavement in the Death of a Spouse, Child, and Parent.' *Omega: Journal of Death and Dying* 10.4 (1979): 303-20.

Singh, B., and B. Raphael. 'Postdisaster Morbidity of the Bereaved. A Possible Role for Preventive Psychiatry?'. *Journal of Nervous and Mental Disease* 169.4 (1981 1981): 203-12.

State Council of China. 'Anniversary of the Wenchuan Earthquake.' *China Daily*, 2009. 5.12 2009.

Stroebe, M. S., S. Folkman, R. O. Hansson, and H. Schut. 'The Prediction of Bereavement Outcome: Development of an Integrative Risk Factor Framework.' *Social Science & Medicine* 63.9 (Nov 2006): 2440-51.

Stroebe, W., H. Schut, and M. Stroebe. 'Grief Work, Disclosure and Counseling: Do They Help the Bereaved?'. *Clinical Psychology Review* 25 (2005): 395-414.

Taylor, A. J. W., and A. G. Frazer. *Psychological Sequelae of Operation Overdue Following the Dc10 Aircrash in Antarctica*. Vol. 27, Wellington, New Zealand: Victoria University of Wellington, 1981.

Tedeshi, R. G., and L. G. Calhoun. *Posttraumatic Growth: Conceptual Foundation and Empirical Evidence*. Philadelphia, PA: Lawrence Erlbaum Associates, 2004.

Thompson, M., F. H. Norris, and B. Hanacek. 'Age Differences in the Psychological Consequences of Hurricane Hugo.' *Psychology and Aging* 8 (1993): 606-16.

U.S. Geological Survey (USGS). 'Magnitude 7.9: Eastern Sichuan, China.' USGS, http://web.archive.org/web/20080517023123/http://earthquake.usgs.gov/eqcenter/e qinthenews/2008/us2008ryan/.

———. 'National Earthquake Information Center.' http://earthquake.usgs.gov/earthquakes/.

United Nations Development Programme (UNDP). 'Reducing Disaster Risk: A Challenge for Devlopment.' New York: Bureau for Crisis Prevention and Recovery, UNDP, 2004.

Ursano, R. J., Carol S. Fullerton, Lars Weisaeth, and B. Raphael, eds. *Textbook of Disaster Psychiatry*. Cambridge: Cambridge University Press, 2007.

Ursano, Robert J., and Jon A. Shaw. 'Children of War and Opportunities for Peace.' *JAMA: The Journal of the American Medical Association* 298.5 (2007): 567-68.

Wisner, B., P. Blaikie, T. Cannon, and I. Davis. *At Risk - Natural Hazards, People's Vulnerability and Disasters*. Wiltshire: Routledge, 2004.

Xiong, Xu, Emily W. Harville, Donald R. Mattison, Karen Elkind-Hirsch, Gabriella Pridjian, and Pierre Buekens. 'Exposure to Hurricane Katrina, Post-Traumatic Stress Disorder and Birth Outcomes.' *Am J Med Sci* 336.2 (2008): 111-5.

Xu, Yao, Herrman, Helen, Bentley, Recebcca, Tsutsumi, Asturo, and Fisher, Jane. *PhD project: Women's mental health after they had lost a child in the 2008 Sichuan earthquake.* Unpublished work. University of Melbourne, Melbourne, Australia.

Young, B. H., J. D. Ford, J. I. Ruzek, Matthew J. Friedman, and F. D. Gusman. *Disaster Mental Health Services: A Guidebook for Clinicians and Admininstrators.* St Louis, Mo.: National Center for PTSD, Department of Veteran Affairs Employee Education System, 1998.

Yuan, Yin, Wen Jun Mao, De Hua Yang, Mao Sheng Ran, Di Kong, Tao Zhang, Wei Qun Lou, *et al.* 'Comparison of Ptsd Symptoms, Depression and Anxiety between Bereaved and Non-Bereaved Survivors after the Wenchuan Earthquake (汶川地震丧亲与非丧亲者 ptsd、焦虑和抑郁的对比研究).' *Chinese Journal of Behavioral Medicine and Brain Science* 18.12 (2009): 1109-11.

Yzermans, C. J., B Van der Berg, and A. J. E. Dirkzwager. 'Physical Health Problems after Disasters.' Chap. 5 In *Mental Health & Disasters*, edited by Yuval Neria, Sandro Galea and Fran H. Norris. 67-93. New York: Cambridge University Press, 2009.

Zheng, Chang De (郑长德). 'Si Chuan Wen Chuan Te Da Di Zhen Shou Zai Di Qu Ren Kou Tong Ji Te Zheng Yan Jiu (四川汶川特大地震受灾地区人口统计特征研究).' *Journal of Southwest University for Nationalities* 205 (2008): 21-28.

Zhu, Ming Hai, and Hua Feng He. 'A Soldier's Dairy of Wenchuan Experience.' *Fujian Daily*, May 26th, 2008.

Zung, W. W. K. 'A Rating Instrument for Anxiety Disorders.' [In English]. *Psychosomatics* 12.6 (1971): 371-7.

The authors are very grateful to the Dujiangyan Family Planning and Human Development Bureau and the Dujiangyan Mental Health Centre in Sichuan Province, China who facilitated data collection and provided office space and administrative support. The study could not have been completed without their commitment and collaborative assistance. We are especially grateful to the participants who shared their experiences of personal tragedy in the interests of improving international understanding of the mental health consequences of natural disasters.

Yao Xu is a Ph.D student in the Centre of Women's Health, Gender and Society at the University of Melbourne. While interests in women's health, gender equity, mental health and reproductive health, currently her Ph.D research is about women's mental health after disasters.

Helen Herrman is the co-supervisor of YX. She is a Professor of Psychiatry in Orygen Youth Health at University of Melbourne. Her interests are mental health and public health, particularly in low-income countries, depression, quality of life and metal health promotion.

Atsuro Tsutsumi is the fieldwork supervisor of YX. He joined UNU-IIGH as a Research Fellow. He was a former Program Coordinator with JICA China office in Chengdu for Post-disaster Mental health and Psychosocial Support Program.

Jane Fisher is the principle supervisor of YX. She is the director of research in Jean Hailes Research Unit at Monash University. Her interests are women's mental health in fertility, conception, pregnancy and postpartum period.

Recovery in Rwanda: The Traditional Courts for Reconciliation

Moara Crivelente

Abstract
The genocide in Rwanda officially ended almost two decades ago. Every Rwandan family has tragic stories to tell, and there is debate over how to promote peace. Reconciliation is one of the main concerns, and President Paul Kagame's government established many local courts. Traditionally, when seeking reconciliation locally, people gather in small community courts, called Gacaca, where victims confront their offenders and the perpetrators of violent crimes seek forgiveness. The Government intends to keep promoting this method, despite criticism based on the argument that the Gacaca do not deal with the fundamental causes of the genocide – the struggle between Hutus and Tutsis – and that the system does not apply *effective justice*, a concept that will be further discussed ahead. In that sense, it is further argued that the Gacaca system should limit its contribution to reconciliation, in a coordinated effort for accountability, punishment and recovery. On the other hand, those in favour of this system argue that thousands of people were directly or indirectly involved in the genocide. Consequently, the judiciary system is unable to prosecute the thousands of suspects waiting for their trials. However, if the Gacacas do not offer *justice* as a whole, it is still an attempt found by the community to recover and to reintegrate its members. This is the debate from which this chapter departs, also covering the strategies employed by the Government to combine traditional and standard justice systems, the responses given by the local community to these efforts and their consequences, and the processes of post-conflict reconstruction. In this sense, the quest for a positive peace in the process of recovery from collective trauma is, here, the main focus.

Key Words: Reconciliation, trauma recovery, peace-building, transitional justice, community courts.

*****

1. Recovery Concepts

The reconstruction process of social, political and economic structures in a country torn by war involves its people's willingness for reconciliation – defined as an effort based in mechanisms for compromise and in the conflict's actors' involvement as human beings that establish relationships.[1] Reconciliation is also the search for truth and for forgiveness aiming at repairing the relationships between individuals, on an inter-community level.[2] It is one of the foundations for the currently dominant understanding of conflict resolution and peace-building, a fundamental component on the efforts made towards a direct, structural and cultural peace, that is, a *positive peace*, as described by Johan Galtung.[3] This is opposed to a *negative* peace in which only superficial areas of a culture of violence would be addressed. This distinction highlights the importance of more comprehensive efforts.

The ethnic aspect usually defined as a cause for the conflict between Hutus and Tutsi—historically and discursively constructed, instrumentalized by political leaders—has a long history and deep roots that must be addressed. In an effort to initiate this, which would be a process, the Gacaca Courts, local courts based on communitarian values, were recovered from previous traditions by the post-conflict Government, focusing not necessarily on punishment, but first and foremost in forgiveness and reconciliation. This process is important due to Rwanda's reconstruction of economic and, more importantly, social structures.

Nonetheless, a contraposition between peace and justice is constantly made, mostly by critics who do not consider Gacaca's objectives to be *actual justice*, or *effective* enough in facilitating the building of peace in a community. Having in mind its subjectivity, the concept of justice will be referred to in this chapter as an endeavour for accountability and punishment (either to deprive criminals from society or to protect the society from the criminals) for the sake of simplicity and consistency with the critics mentioned ahead.

The chapter will present this issue by comparing the efforts of reconciliation in the quest for justice employed by the United Nations' and Rwanda's standard court system. Additionally, it will broach the debate over the efficacy of these reconstruction and peace-building processes in Rwanda. For that, it will take into account reconciliation versus justice priorities, a contraposition set by some of the current process' critics. Furthermore, it will also take into account the psychological impact of the process of truth telling employed by the Gacaca courts. Still, it is necessary to demonstrate the importance of reconciliation for Rwanda's post-conflict reconstruction.

2. Some Fundamental Issues

To analyse an event so politically complex in terms of its international relations would require a big set of theories on the actors positions, the negotiations and their mediation, the utility of an international system self-promoted as an 'international community' through the United Nations (UN), the *relativisation* and subjectivity inherent to conflict resolution and transformation, and so on. More important to this chapter, still, are the psychological impacts that extreme violence has not only on victims but also on perpetrators, and the impact that trauma has on peace building. The authors cited here are relevant to one part of this complicated issue—the aftermath of the genocide that was mostly prompted by violent discourse throughout history and most recently expanded through the media, especially the radio.

Transmitting ideology and propaganda through mass media is nothing new. Professor Teun Van Dijk dedicates one of his articles to the clarification of the notion of *manipulation*, which is employed by Noam Chomsky in his writings about propaganda and by various theorists who use the *Critical Discourse Analysis* (CDA) in their work. CDA is aimed at studying the power relations through discourse, at putting in evidence the oppression exerted by elites, and also evidencing the 'justification' of violence, which was what happened in Rwanda.

Van Dijk writes about ideology developing arguments on *mental models*, a theoretical construct developed through cognitive psychology. According to Van Dijk, 'in a theory of discourse production and comprehension (…), the notion of a model is especially attractive, since it accounts for the (personal, subjective) interpretation of the discourse by language users.'[4] He relates it to *identity*—either gradually constructed, mainly through discourse and the manipulation of history, or mentally absorbed in specific events, such as wars—by arguing:

> In their representation of self, people construct themselves as being a member of several groups (…). This self-representation (or self-schema) is located in episodic (personal) memory. It is a gradually constructed abstraction from personal experiences (models) of events. Since such models usually feature representations of social interactions, as well as *interpretations of discourse*, both experiences and their inferred self-representations are at the same time socially (and jointly) constructed. Part of our self-representation is inferred from the way others see, define and treat us.[5]

The manipulation of identities and, more specifically, of nationalist sentiments, their escalation and manipulation for political purposes, are not recent observations in critical studies. Applying CDA, this manipulation is analyzed by authors like Noam Chomsky and van Dijk, among many others. Peter Berger, Thomas Luckmann and Josep Fontana argue for the fundamental (though not exclusive) role of the media in the construction of the social reality, particularly when it is conflictive; *framing,* the construction of narrative structures, can be better understood when comparing political and media environments in certain contexts. Wiranjala Neerakody explains frames as 'rhetorical weapons' or when the sender of a message puts 'blinkers' and 'blinders' on the receivers, 'guiding their view or attention in a particular direction and away from alternative viewpoints.'[6] For that, the messenger uses instruments such as adjectives, metaphors, analogies (using or inventing similarities between two things), euphemisms, dysphemisms (exaggerated terms to make something sound more unpleasant than it really is), and 'manufactured hysteria'.[7]

This is also what happened when popular radio stations in Rwanda propagated daily messages of hatred that incited direct violence against Tutsis. This is the case of the station, *Radio Télévision Libre des Mille Collines* (RTLM), which gave a lot of space for the 'Hutu Power' discourses centred on extremist ideology and often called Tutsis 'cockroaches' and a minority of 'traitors and murderous' who came back to steal Hutu land.[8] Some speeches would go further, urging their fellow Hutus to pick up whatever weapons they had, including machetes, and eliminate Tutsis and moderate Hutus who would relate to Tutsis.[9] RTLM was established in 1993, in opposition to the peace talks between the Government of the President Juvenal Habyarimana and the RPF. According to M. Kimani, through her analysis of this radio station's broadcast, the most common inflammatory statements consisted of reports of Tutsi RPF rebel atrocities (33%), allegations that Tutsis in the region were involved in the war or a conspiracy (24%), and allegations that RPF wanted power and control over Hutus (16%).[10]

After the President Habyarimana's airplane was shot down—a crime that Hutus in power, with the connivance of French officials, tried very hard to pin on the RPF—the radio called for the 'final war' to 'exterminate the cockroaches.'[11] [12] The founders of the radio were convicted of genocide by the International Criminal Tribunal for Rwanda (ICTR) later established by the UN. Their role in fuelling violence and hatred was considerably important to the mass engagement in murders. The President was one of the radio's strongest backers. One of the founders, Ferdinand Nahimana, was also the director of the Rwanda Bureau of Information and Broadcasting, the agency that regulates mass media in Rwanda.[13] According to the ICTR:

> The Interahamwe and other militia listened to RTLM and acted on the information that was broadcast by RTLM. RTLM actively encouraged them to kill, relentlessly sending the message that the Tutsi were the enemy and had to be eliminated once and for all.[14]

The complexities of analysing conflicts have been constantly recognized and expanded on in the theoretical field. Until recently, conflicts were framed as motivated either by 'greed' or by 'grievances' when related to political and economic power or to historical traumas and ethnic divides. An example is, in 2002, when Paul Collier, working with the World Bank, and Anke Hoeffler, with the Centre for the Study of African Economies, analysed the different influence the two 'fuels' (greed or grievance) could have on civil wars and concluded that factors which determine financial and military viability of war are more important than objective grounds for grievance.[15] Soon, even this dichotomy became too simplistic for conflict analysis.

Mary Kaldor analyses current conflicts under the light of a 'new wars' theory. She argues that globalization had a great influence on the changes that low intensity conflicts suffered, which include: the finance sustaining war, especially based in international crime; the claims motivating wars, centred on identity and not on territories; and the tactics, now based in guerrilla warfare and in terror.[16] Kaldor's description of current motivations and methodologies in 'new wars' has been criticized as not that different from earlier theories and hence, not that 'new.' Besides the questionable 'newness' of this description, it can be argued that international crime is not the most important 'viability' guarantee for wars; the heavy military-industrial complex maintaining military spending (also known officially as 'Defence spending'), international arms trade are also important factors.

Identity could also be considered a central claim motivating current wars. It is certainly one of the *tools* more commonly used in the process of mobilization. Political and religious leaders, for instance, have a tendency to *instrumentalize* differences and historical constructions or perceptions of the other, as motivation for violence. In that sense, it could be overwhelmingly complex to analyse conflicts, keeping in mind all the questions regarding each general model. Authors like Vicenç Fisas, from the School for Peace Culture, in Barcelona, Spain, suggest different levels of analysis to understand conflicts: their apparent causes, characteristics and classifications; the actors involved in the conflict – those with or without voice in the media – and the third parties directly or indirectly involved; the negotiation and mediation process between the parties; the state of hostilities and the tracks chosen for the conflict transformation or peace process.[17]

Moreover, on a technical level, the retro-alimentation of various factors should also be taken into account: they range from the causes and incentives for violence, the opportunities (or the spark that lead to violence, such as political or economic crisis) and the viability or capacities enabling or favouring collective action.[18] And on an analytical level, on the basis of social realities, the approach suggested by Johan Galtung to three kinds of violence, conforming what he builds as a 'triangle of violence', could be retrieved: cultural violence—myths, glories and traumas that justify violence; structural violence—maintaining injustice, inequality and power relations between groups; and direct violence—either physical or psychological.[19]

In that sense, *conflict resolution* is another theoretic field constantly being revised, suggesting that there is not a static model, or a 'template.' According to Morton Deutsch, for example, a *constructive* conflict resolution could be an effort centred on skills for establishing an effective, open, trusting working relationship between the parties; on establishing a cooperative problem-solving approach to the conflict; on developing effective group processes and decision-making processes; and on substantive knowledge of the relevant issues. This final item is a reminder of the importance of an as accurate as possible conflict analysis.[20] Still, conflict *resolution* and conflict *transformation* are notions sometimes divergent for the capacity that conflicts have to enable changing situations of injustice and social inequality. Therefore, conflicts can be *transformed* into solutions through cooperation, and not *resolved*, as if it would mean *ending* conflicts.

In conflict resolution—or at least in its dominant version involving *liberal peace* values installed by the UN—mediation and negotiation are fundamental steps in bringing parties in conflict to a settlement. From there, another general problem is the 'format' that negotiations usually assume. John Paul Lederach, for example, focuses on the analogy used by conflict resolution theorists and practitioners: 'the table', or the circles where negotiations take place. To Lederach, the problem is that, around the table, only a few political actors can sit, supposedly representing a variety of perceptions, interests and positions.[21] The representation, along with the viability and sustainability of a peace process, hence, will be highly unlikely, especially because the few political actors taking part at the negotiations would not be able – or even inclined – to represent the vastly distinct interests.

In that sense, and for supporting this unsustainable model of negotiations, the liberal peace notions of conflict resolution are questioned by Oliver P. Richmond. He starts with the assumption that 'liberal institutionalism, security sector reform, democratic institutions, liberal notions of civil society and a rule of law, together with market development, offer a silver bullet from the 'new world order'(…).'[22] Furthermore, recalling the frame that the UN and other international institutions, such as the World Bank, have established for conflict resolution, *state building* is also highly questionable as a supposed pre-condition. Building governance institutions, democracy mechanisms, market economies and security sector reforms (just some of the programs on which state-building programs are centred) with the direct intervention of foreign actors, or 'donors', is an experiment that affects 'millions of people's lives often carelessly and in a way that makes little sense to them.'[23]

Having said that, both Lederach and Richmond, along with many other authors, advocate for the importance of *infrapolitics peace building*. These are efforts centred in local actors and practices often unrecognized by international actors who often overlook local agency and capacity to guarantee and sustain conflict transformation. As Richmond puts it, the anchoring of peace building to globalization has failed; a better and more sustainable strategy would be the focusing conflict resolution on localization and infrapolitics, as well as transnationalization, for the emergence of an 'emancipatory discourse' about peace.[24]

3. Post-Genocide Efforts

The international efforts for peace building in Rwanda started mostly with the United Nations' implementation of the International Criminal Tribunal for Rwanda (ICTR), after a request made by the immediate post-conflict Government. The country was in no condition to conduct the suspects' trials, not only for the instability of a society recently affected by a genocide and tending to seek revenge, but also for the lack of resources – mostly human but also structural and financial – to conduct the proceedings fairly; over 90% of judges and prosecutors, mostly moderate Hutus, were murdered during the conflict.[25]

However, the Rwandan Government decided to re-evaluate its request when it came to know the court's statute. The main objections were against the location of the court in foreign soil—Tanzania, against the lack of capital sentences,[26] and against the temporal limit established for trials of crimes committed in 1994. The new Government was convinced that the genocide had begun in 1992. These objections reveal, the complexity of the process and the disagreements between the international actors and local Government. Additionally, the international actors lacked human and financial resources for the ICTR.[27] The unwillingness to cooperate of Kenya and former Zaire – where the majority of the suspects of crimes connected to the genocide had fled to – was also an obstacle for the efficiency of the trials. The inefficiency of the international efforts transmitted a perception of failure, which is considerably harmful in a post-conflict society that needs to begin reconstructing and, for that, needs efficient processes. This issue is introduced in the concept of *peace building,* usually defined as the reconstruction of a variety of structures within a society that permit the establishment of peace, including justice.[28] The ICTR began the analysis of only a few cases, and the psychosocial programs initiated lacked efficacy – mostly for the use of western methods, clearly out of context, for the approach based on western cultures on a very different social reality. These programs are considered essential to the peace building process, for it seeks to deal with and possibly heal traumas, enabling a healthy reconstruction of the social life in a post-conflict context.[29]

The debate about the importance of justice or the preference for reconciliation is still on-going. In 1994, he conflict in Rwanda caused the death of around 850,000 Tutsis and moderate Hutus in few weeks.[30] The numbers vary considerably, mostly because of the difficulty of access to credible information. On its aftermath, accountability and punishment were, above all, psychological needs, but also a structural problem: how is it possible to rebuild the country with thousands of people incarcerated and removed from the process? The crimes were not perpetrated only by people connected to the Hutu Government, but also by ordinary citizens mobilized by a violent nationalist discourse, propagated mostly by popular media, such as the radio, which facilitated the execution of the genocide plan.[31]

The Government established after the conflict is headed by the RPF, an organization that accomplished something the international actors could not: the stopping of the genocide. However, the attainment of the power by the Tutsis, who are both the *winners* and a specific group part in the conflict, in a Government settled as transitory, creates a similar situation to that which existed before the armed conflict: the concentration of power and political institutions by only one identity group, which critics say makes this transition gravely flawed.[32] Joseph

Sebarenzi, former member of the Rwandan Parliament, says it is necessary to create solid democratic institutions to enable power sharing among different groups, preventing events like the genocide, supported by the Hutu Government of the time.[33] However, reconciliation is still an on-going process, and power-sharing initiatives still perceived as problematic for a traumatized population.

Despite efforts made by the present Government – headed by the President Paul Kagame, of the RPF's leadership – in processes dedicated to justice and reconciliation, the latter has been classified as extremely deficient, as a result of the focus given to the former.[34] The issue is deeply important for its connection with the Government's capacity to see expectations, like the thirst for accountability, satisfied. It is a political challenge directly linked with the escalation of violence through vengeance and other conflictive episodes, sparked by the fact that victims share spaces with those who are still seen as their offenders,[35] within a society marked by impunity.

4. The Gacaca Courts: Traditional Justice and Reconciliation

As *communitarian* and *traditional* courts, the Gacacas are said to be the best way found by the Rwandan to deal autonomously with their problem.[36] The courts were introduced as a combination of some sort of truth commission and other programs aiming at promoting forgiveness and reconciliation, essential to the quest for justice and a foundation to the reconstruction of the Rwandan society. Truth commissions are established to investigate evidences and testimonies, aiming at finding a negotiated common truth, building a historic memory and treating the suffering caused by the conflict. The proceedings focus in 'social-healing workshops' – usually mediated by psychologists and local leaders, following the re-education of victims and perpetrators, aiming at managing traumas for the society's reconstruction – and are organized by the Government, with special attention to risk groups, such as children orphaned by the genocide. For scholars dedicated to the debate over peace building, justice and the construction of a memory should serve for prevention and for dismantling mechanisms that allow violence, so the tragedy does not repeat itself.[37]

According to the UN Sub-Commission on the Promotion and the Protection of Human Rights report published in 1997, the number of imprisoned people suspected of grave human rights violation was so high that it was almost impossible to try them fairly, within a reasonable period of time. In that sense, the Rwandan case is exceptional: more than 90,000 people were imprisoned– the majority of them charged with crimes of genocide – and the judiciary system could not deal with the situation in a sufficiently effective manner.[38]

In that sense, establishing the Gacaca Courts' jurisdiction *in* 2001, as the trial and prosecution of crimes against humanity committed between October, 1990 and December, 1994, contributed not only to the efforts of reconciliation and justice employed in a traditional and local manner but also to more efficiency in the process.[39] The Gacacas' goals are: to tell the truth about the genocide, actively engage the local population in its hearings; to speed up the genocide trials, to increase the judiciary system's institutional capacities; to eliminate the culture of impunity; to promote reconciliation and unity between the Rwandan people; and to demonstrate how Rwanda can deal with its own problems through a judiciary system based in its own traditions, despite adaptations made to fit some international standards, mentioned below.[40]

The model implemented today maintains the importance of the general population's role, of the decentralization of justice, of the possibility of commutation of the prison sentences to public service and, fundamentally, of reconciliation. Different from the original tradition, the current model is supposed to apply the criminal law and can impose large prison sentences. In 1996 there were established four *criminalization categories*, the first corresponding to organizing and supervising crimes related to genocide and the last corresponding to crimes against property. In this framework, it is estimated that sixty years would be necessary to try all the suspects in a classical system.[41]

The Gacacas, with different instances organized in a hierarchical logic, have been accelerating the process considerably by bringing cases to a local level, in which the community is actively engaged in establishing the truth.[42] The previous framework for the Gacacas was based in certain common values, in norms of reciprocity and mutual trust, which the armed conflict and the genocide fatally wounded. The different phases of the process, in the current methodology, start with the elaboration of lists of people killed among the region's inhabitants, of victims and damages, and also a list of suspects. Then, the individual case files are prepared for each suspect whose crimes are organized by category and cases sent to the respective Gacaca Court. Lastly, the trials and their verdicts take place, and possibly their punishment.[43]

The proceedings, with incentives on confessions, facilitate the process in regard to the investigation and to evidence gathering, accelerating it and contributing to the reduction of the number of trials in the classical judiciary system. The confessions, in these cases made to the community, guarantee the reduction of the sentences.[44] However, this practice can be questionable in some points, for example, when it establishes a certain power relation between equal citizens – the ones forgiving and the ones hoping to be forgiven. The truth telling through the confession is made in a narrative mode, with factual details.

That is also when, according to psychological studies, the link between truth and reconciliation, established as a truism, should be questioned. There are very few studies on the psychological impact that the truth-telling process has on war victims and on its impact for post-war peace building. Karen Bornéus, for instance, calculates that the Rwandan survivors that have witnessed in the Gacaca sessions have 20% higher risk of suffering from depression and 40% higher risk of having Post-Traumatic Stress Disorder (PTSD) than those who have not witnessed. She argues that it has to do with the short and intensive trauma exposure during the Gacaca sessions. Therefore, the healing objective should not be linked with the truth-telling process in some contexts.[45]

Fuaad M. Freh, also writing for this collection, suggests interesting approaches for 'the exploration of an individual's personal account in order to reveal their underlying understandings and ways of making sense of their experiences.'[46] His work was dedicated to the analysis of the experiences of bomb attacks survivors in Iraq, during the event, and the interpretation they made of the experience, in connection to documented coping strategies. The method he used, Interpretative Phenomenological Analysis, emphasizes 'the uniqueness of how individuals perceive, interpret and make sense of their own experience, social world, and personal dilemma (…).'[47] His method could be very useful for the interpretation of the responses given by victims during the Gacaca sessions, confirming or putting in question their coping strategies for the trauma they have experienced.

Still, another important issue to have in mind is the risk of victimization, which turns the experience of being a victim into one of the collective and mythologized victimhood, as argued by Martina Fischer, who also notes that victimization seems to play a particular role in ethno-political contexts.[48] It also risks a way of denying and arguing for the relativization of crimes. Furthermore, it has been indicated that legal prosecution itself may exacerbate discourses of conflict about who is the victim and who is the perpetrator. Therefore, accountability does not automatically pave the way to reconciliation, conflict transformation or a stable peace.[49]

On the other hand, it is considered essential to a great deal of conflict resolution theories, as a way to demonstrate commitment to justice. Reparations are demanded and the perpetrators are punished publicly, actions that can be therapeutic for victims and exemplary for the society. On the Gacaca system, critics believe that accountability and punishment are not sufficiently or even efficiently provided, at least not in the sense discussed in this chapter. The first pre-trials, for instance – evidence gathering, testimonies and first hearings –started in 1996, being 9,721 cases until 2003, with none complete in 2004, and still 80,000 suspects detained, waiting their own trials.[50] It means that the process is very slow for a country that has to move forward on its peace building strategy.

According to Joseph Sebarenzi, a former member of the Parliament of Rwanda, the Gacacas should deal only with the reconciliation process, and leave the judicial proceedings to the standard courts, so justice can be achieved through international parameters.[51] Contrary to that belief, for instance, in 2003, President Kagame announced a directive for the liberation of all prisoners who would confess their crimes and had served at least half of their sentences under the Gacaca law – though it did not include those sentenced for crimes of genocide. Those who were freed would follow programs of re-education in what were called *solidarity camps*.[52] This is an example of the Government's and other political actors' stance on a different approach to the conflict resolution and the peace building process.

The measures cited are inserted on the group of efforts for dealing with the matter locally, based on what the Government believes is necessary for Rwanda in this phase, and not on international standards of procedures for the realization of *justice*.

5. General Thoughts: Reconciliation, Reconstruction and Development

A variety of outstanding cases are already known. One well-known case is that of the woman who had lunch with her neighbour—who had killed her five children during the genocide—after the neighbour completed seven years in jail. His sentence was reduced for the value given to his confession, at a Gacaca session.[53] These are unintelligible cases in the minds of some and lead others to question the reality of forgiveness. On the other hand, the psychological impact that truth-telling has on the genocide survivors must be taken into account. The aim of healing should not be linked to the truth-commissions element of the reconciliation process in Rwanda. It should be, as Bornéus argues, carefully designed, and not an automatic element of peace building processes in general.

Reconciliation here is maximized 'when the perpetrators recognize their responsibility, repent and are then forgiven by their victims,' as noted by Desmond Tutu, head of the Truth and Reconciliation Commission in South Africa.[54] The Gacacas' proceedings also have a truth commission role, with the goal of healing both individuals and the nation. Exposing the truth is compared to religious confessions, seeking absolution and forgiveness, promoting a balance between too much and insufficient memory in a society's reconciliation.[55]

Rwandan post-genocide reconstruction is considered example/ exemplary in many aspects because of the challenge to include the whole society in the process using justice, recognition, and mostly through reconciliation. As for the State structure, despite criticism regarding the lack of democratic institutions and power sharing,[56] it is important to note the country's on-going progress and development.[57] The Rwandan GDP rose from 7.3% in 2003 to 11.2% in 2008, and the *per capita* gains will be four times higher until 2020. The country is considered the growth engine of its region. There has been a significant rise in women's participation in politics and business – with numbers higher than in European countries – and establishment of education and health programs that include scholarship programs to hutus.[58] This process and these policies were unprecedented and contribute to the efforts of mentality change. The model seems to work, so far, despite reservations as to the real consideration for *justice*. It is worth remembering that this is not a concept clearly established, or part of an absolute framework; it is a concept formed by subjectivity.

The suggestion put forward by intellectuals and politicians like Sebarenzi about the establishment of *democratic institutions* can be the beginning of a solution, though it has to take into account fundamental issues, such as traumas still very alive and rooted not only on the genocide of the early 1990s but in events even before that.

The current concept of justice employed by the Gacacas is based on reconciliation and on the role of the community, focused primarily on reintegration for the reconstruction of a fractured society.[59] However, it is based on what some call the *winner's justice*, which seems obvious taking into account that the Government established by the RPF is, indeed, based on a victory against the violence supported by the former Government. It also seems to lack accountability in a more punitive aspect, according to its critics. The question to be answered is, then, what would be the appropriate balance between reconciliation, accountability and state or peace building in Rwanda's post-conflict recovery, keeping in mind the impact it would have on the very people affected by it.

Notes

[1] John Paul Lederach, *Building Peace: Sustainable Reconciliation in Divided Societies* (Washington, DC: United States Institute of Peace Press, 2002), 27.

[2] Trudy Govier, *Taking Wrongs Seriously: Acknowledgement, Reconciliation and the Politics of Sustainable Peace* (New York: Humanity Books, 2006), 13.

[3] Johan Galtung, *Peace by Peaceful Means* (Oslo: PRIO, 1996).

[4] Teun van Dijk, *Ideology: A Multidisciplinary Approach* (London: Sage Publications, 1998), 188.

[5] Ibid.

[6] Niranjala Weerakody, *Research Methods for Media and Communication* (Sydney: Oxford University Press, 2009).

[7] Ibid.

[8] Russell Smith, 'The Impact of Hate media in Rwanda', *BBC News*, 3 December 2003), viewed January 30, 2012, http://news.bbc.co.uk/2/hi/africa/3257748.

[9] M. Kimani, 'RTLM: the Medium that Became a Tool for Mass Murder', in *The Media and the Rwandan Genocide*, ed. Allan Thompson (London: Pluto Press, 2007).

[10] Ibid.

[11] See, for example: Mark Doyle, 'Ties Frayed by Decades of Tension', *BBC News*, 24 November 2006, viewed 20 February 2012, http://news.bbc.co.uk/2/hi/africa/6181988.stm.

[12] Smith, 'Impact of Hate Media in Rwanda'.

[13] A. Des Forges, 'Call to Genocide: Radio in Rwanda, 1994', in *The Media and the Rwandan Genocide*, ed. Allan Thompson (London: Pluto Press, 2007).

[14] International Criminal Tribunal for Rwanda, ICTR, Case No. ICTR-99-52-T Judgement, 2003, viewed 18 February 2012, http://www.ictr.org/ENGLISH/cases/Barayagwiza/judgement/Summary-Media.pdf.

[15] Paul Collier and Anke Hoeffler, *Greed and Grievance in Civil War* (Oxford: Centre for the Study of African Economies, 2002), viewed 30 January 2012, http://economics.ouls.ox.ac.uk /12055/1/2002-01text.pdf.

[16] Mary Kaldor, *New and Old Wars: Organized Violence in a Global Era* (Oxford: Polity Press, 1999).

[17] See, for example: Vicenç Fisas, *Cultura de Paz y Gestión de Conflictos* (Barcelona: Icaria Editorial y Unesco, 1999).

[18] Ibid.

[19] Galtung, *Peace by Peaceful Means.*

[20] Morton Deutsch, 'Constructive Conflict Resolution: Principles, Training, and Research', in *The Handbook of Interethnic Coexistence,* ed. Eugene Weiner (New York: Continuum Publishing, 1998), 199-216.

[21] John P. Lederach, *Building Peace: Sustainable Reconciliation in Divided Societies,* (Washington, DC: U.S. Institute of Peace Press, 1997).

[22] Oliver P. Richmond, 'Liberal Peace Transitions: a Rethink is Urgent', *Open Democracy,* 19 November 2009, viewed 20 February 2012, http://www.opendemocracy.net/oliver-p-richmond/liberal-peace-transitions-rethink-is-urgent.

[23] Ibid.

[24] Ibid.

[25] Richard J. Goldstone, *For Humanity Reflections of a War Crimes Investigator* (New Haven: Yale University Press, 2000), 109.

[26] Ibid., 112. According to the President Bizimungu at the time, it was not a good moment to suggest the death penalty abolition, even though he himself was against it.

[27] Govier, *Taking Wrongs Seriously,* 136. In fact, financial reports state that 1 billion USD were spent at the trials of only ten suspects, which is considered extremely disproportionate comparing to the court's proceedings.

[28] '[I]nvolving a multiplicity of actors and activities on the search for a variety of overlapped objectives and operating within a variety of time frames.' See: John Prendergast, 'Applying Concepts to Cases: Four African Case Studies', in *Building Peace: Sustainable Reconciliation in Divided Societies,* ed. John Paul Lederach, (Washington: United States Institute of Peace Press, 2002), 173.

[29] Herbert Kelman, 'Transforming the Relationship Between Former Enemies: A Social-Psychological Analysis', in *After the Peace. Resistance & Reconciliation,* ed. Robert Rothstein (Boulder: Lynne Rienner, 1999), 193-221.

[30] Goldstone, *For Humanity Reflections,* 105.

[31] Prendergast, 'Applying Concepts to Cases', 172.

[32] Stef Vandeginste and Filip Reyntjiens, 'Rwanda: An Atypical Transition', in *Roads to Reconciliation,* eds. Elin Skaar et al. (Oxford: Lexington Books, 2005), 101-127.

[33] Joseph Sebarenzi, interviewed by Christianne Amanpour, in *The Story of Post-Genocide Rwanda and its Economic Success* (New York: CNN, 18 November 2009).

[34] Ibid.

[35] Carlos Martín Beristain, 'El Papel de la Memoria Colectiva en la Reconstrucción de Sociedades Fracturadas por la Violencia', in *Guerra y Desarrollo: La Reconstrucción Post-conflicto* (Bilbao: UNESCO ETXEA, 2002).

[36] National Service of Gacaca Jurisdictions. *The Competence of the Gacaca Court*, viewed 18 May 2010, http://www.inkiko-gacaca.gov.rw/En/EnCompetence.htm.

[37] Beristain, 'El papel de la Memoria Colectiva.'

[38] UN Sub-Commission on the Promotion and the Protection of Human Rights, *Question of the Impunity of Perpetrators of Human Rights Violations (Civil and Political)* (New York: UN, 26 June 1997).

[39] In which elders used to hold meetings when necessary, to 'put sanctions to the violation of rules shared by the community, with the sole goal of reconciliation'. See: Vandeginste and Reyntjiens, 'Rwanda: An Atypical Transition'.

[40] National Service of Gacaca Jurisdictions. *The competence of the Gacaca Court*, viewed 18 May 2010, http://www.inkiko-gacaca.gov.rw/En/EnCompetence.htm.

[41] Ibid.

[42] Local, regional or national, guaranteeing the concentration of the worst crimes in the highest levels and the possibility of other suspects to appeal, in a higher instance.

[43] Vandeginste and Reyntjiens, 'Rwanda: An Atypical Transition'.

[44] Ibid.

[45] Karen Bornéus, 'The Trauma of Truth-Telling: Effects of Witnessing in the Rwandan Gacaca Courts on Psychological Health', in *Journal of Conflict Resolution* 54.3 (2010): 408-437.

[46] Fuaad Muhammad Freh, 'An Exploration of PTSD and Coping Strategies: Response to the Experience of Being in a Bomb Attack in Iraq', in *Trauma: Theory and Practice* (Oxford: Inter-Disciplinary Press, 2013).

[47] Ibid., 6.

[48] Martina Fischer, 'Transitional Justice and Reconciliation: Theory and Practice', in *Advancing Conflict Transformation: The Berghof Handbook II*, eds. B. Austin et al. (Opladen/Farmington Hills: Barbara Budrich Publishers, 2011), 405-430.

[49] Ibid.

[50] Vandeginste and Reyntjiens, 'Rwanda: An Atypical Transition'.

[51] Sebarenzi, interviewed by Christiane Ammanpour, 2009.

[52] Vandeginste and Reyntjiens, 'Rwanda: An Atypical Transition'.

[53] Christiane Ammanpour, *The Story of Post-Genocide Rwanda and its Economic Success* (New York: CNN, 18 November 2009).

[54] Martha Minow, *Between Vengeance and Forgiveness: Facing History after Genocide and Mass Violence* (Boston: Beacon Press Books, 1998), 61.
[55] Ibid., 188.
[56] Govier, *Taking Wrongs Seriously,* 264. It is said that only *some* moderate hutus are accepted in a Government structure which implements policies for the elimination of ethnic terms and of the notion of group differentiations.
[57] Ammanpour, *The Story of Post-Genocide Rwanda.*
[58] Philip Gourevitch, interviewed by Christianne Amanpour, in *The Story of Post-Genocide Rwanda and its Economic Success,* (New York: CNN, 18 November 2009).

Bibliography

Amanpour, Christiane. *The Story of Post-Genocide Rwanda and its Economic Success.* New York: CNN, November 18, 2009.

Beristain, Carlos Martín. 'El Papel de la Memoria Colectiva en la Reconstrucción de Sociedades Fracturadas por la Violencia.' In *Guerra y Desarrollo: La Reconstrucción Post-conflicto,* edited by UNESCO. Bilbao: UNESCO ETXEA, 2002.

Bornéus, Karen. 'The Trauma of Truth-Telling: Effects of Witnessing in the Rwandan Gacaca Courts on Psychological Health.' In *Journal of Conflict Resolution,* 408-437. Bilbao: Sage Publications, 2010.

Fischer, Martina. 'Transitional Justice and Reconciliation: Theory and Practice.' In *Advancing Conflict Transformation: The Berghof Handbook II,* ed. B. Austin. 405-430. Opladen/Framington Hills: Barbara Budrich Publishers, 2011.

Galtung, Johan. *Peace by Peaceful Means.* Oslo: PRIO, 1996.

Goldstone, Richard J. *For Humanity Reflections of a War Crimes Investigator.* New Haven: Yale University Press, 2000.

Gourevitch, Philip. Interviewed by Christianne Amanpour. *The Story of Post-Genocide Rwanda and its Economic Success.* New York: CNN, November 18, 2009.

Govier, Trudy. *Taking Wrongs Seriously: Acknowledgement, Reconciliation and the Politics of Sustainable Peace.* New York: Humanity Books, 2006.

Kelman, Herbert. 'Transforming the Relationship Between Former Enemies: A Social-Psychological Analysis.' In *After the Peace. Resistance & Reconciliation,* edited by Robert Rothstein, 193-221. Boulder: Lynne Rienner, 1999.

Lederach, John Paul. *Building Peace: Sustainable Reconciliation in Divided Societies.* Washington: United States Institute of Peace Press, 2002.

Mamdani, Mahmood. 'When Victims Become Killers: Colonialism, Nativism, and the Genocide in Rwanda.' In *Violence in War and Peace: An Anthropology,* edited by Philippe Bourgois and Nancy Scheper-Hughes, 468-474. Oxford: Blackwell Publishing, 2004.

Minow, Martha. *Between Vengeance and Forgiveness: Facing History after Genocide and Mass Violence.* Boston: Beacon Press Books, 1998.

National Service of Gacaca Jurisdictions. *Sentences applicable in the Gacaca Courts.* Accessed May 18, 2010. http://www.inkiko-gacaca.gov.rw/En/EnSentence.htm.

———. *The Competence of the Gacaca Court.* Accessed May 18, 2010. http://www.inkiko-gacaca.gov.rw/En/EnCompetence.htm.

———. *The Objectives of the Gacaca Courts.* Accessed May 18, 2010. http://www.inkiko-gacaca.gov.rw/En/EnObjectives.htm.

Paris, Roland. 'Peacebuilding and the Limits of Liberal Internationalism.' In *International Security,* (1997) 54-89.

Prendergast, John. 'Applying Concepts to Cases: Four African Case Studies.' In *Building Peace: Sustainable Reconciliation in Divided Societies,* edited by John Paul Lederach, 153-180. Washington: United States Institute of Peace Press, 2002.

Sebarenzi, Joseph. Interview with Christianne Amanpour, in *The Story of Post-Genocide Rwanda and its Economic Success.* New York: CNN November 18, 2009.

UN Sub-Commission on the Promotion and the Protection of Human Rights. *Question of the Impunity of Perpetrators of Human Rights Violations (Civil and Political).* New York: UN, June 26, 1997.

Vandeginste, Stef; and Reyntjiens, Filip. 'Rwanda: An Atypical Transition.' In *Roads to Reconciliation*, edited by Elin Skaar et al., 101-127. Oxford: Lexington Books, 2005.

Verdeja, Ernesto. *Unchopping a Tree: Reconciliation in the Aftermath of Political Violence*. Philadelphia: Temple University Press, 2009.

Whittaker, David J. *Conflict and Reconciliation in the Contemporary World*. London: Routledge, 1999.

Moara Crivelente is a political scientist and has an MA degree on the Communication of International Armed and Social Conflicts. Her main academic interests are the peace studies, peace communication, community-based conflict resolution and local resistances.

Cloth, Memory and Mourning

Beverly Ayling-Smith

Abstract
'Cloth holds the sometimes unbearable gift of memory, and its memory is exacting: it does not forget even the benign scars of accident.'[1] Artists have used cloth, whose long association with the body throughout a lifetime and afterwards in death makes it uniquely placed to be used as a metaphor for the trauma of grief, mourning and loss in contemporary art practice. By using textiles to evoke the psychic pain of being marked, stained, repaired and remade it is possible to connect with the intense emotions of mourning. Experiencing the trauma of mourning, melancholia and grief happens through the course of life and it is a trauma which indelibly marks our memory and can be understood through the medium of cloth. This chapter discusses Freud's theory of the work of mourning and the state of melancholia and the critique of it by Kathleen Woodward who suggests that it is possible to be suffering from an interminable grief that is not actual melancholia as defined by Freud, but a grief that 'is lived in such a way that one is still in mourning but no longer exclusively devoted to mourning.'[2] There will also be discussion of the work of a number of artists including Michelle Walker, Anne Wilson, and Chiyoko Tanaka to illustrate how using cloth in their practice can evoke memories of the deceased and facilitate the work of mourning. The chapter will conclude by drawing on my own practice and research including an investigation of the *Kesa*, the Japanese Buddhist robe, and my textile responses to the writings of Freud to demonstrate how different types of cloth are used to commemorate the deceased and create a robe redolent with a sense of mourning and memorial.

Key Words: Memory, grief, mourning, melancholia, trauma, cloth, textiles.

*****

1. Mourning and Melancholia

It has been said that 'grief is the price we pay for love' and mourning has been described as the process of coping with loss and grief.[3] Mourning the death of a loved one is something we will all experience. The intensity of the emotion and the length of time that it lasts will vary considerably from person to person. Phrases such as 'time is a great healer' are used to reassure the bereaved that eventually their grieving will one day end and life will go on as normal. In order to achieve this certain coping strategies are adopted in what Sigmund Freud described as 'Trauerarbeit' or 'grief work.'[4] Some people, however, find that it is impossible to bring their grieving to an end and in certain cases this can become detrimental to their mental health and they suffer from what was described by Freud as melancholia, but has also been described as 'pathological' or failed mourning, or in more recent times, 'complicated' grief.

In this chapter I will examine the definitions of complicated grief starting with Sigmund Freud's comparison of the two emotional states of mourning and melancholia and question whether these are still useful in our understanding of mourning today.

Within this context I will also examine the role of contemporary art in the facilitation of mourning particularly where artists use textiles as their medium. Textiles are a particularly evocative medium with which to explore this subject. Cloth is the first thing we are wrapped in when we are born and the last thing to cover us when we die and so our relationship with it lasts longer than a lifetime. There are few times when we are not in contact with cloth in some form or another – as such it takes on our shape, folds itself into creases and shapes which echo our form when we are no longer there. It also is able to retain the smell of the person who wore it. The intimacy that cloth has with the body often causes such an evocative and poignant reminder to loved ones when the corporeal body is no longer present. This is what makes cloth such a powerful metaphor for memory and loss.

The chapter will conclude with examples of artists work, including my own, which has been made to connect with the unresolved grief of the audience and to evoke an emotional response, and makes a connection with their unfinished work of mourning.

In his essay of 1917 Sigmund Freud describes the two states: 'mourning' and 'melancholia' as two reactions to the trauma of the death of a loved object – be that a person, an ideal or an abstraction such as freedom or fatherland.[5] In mourning, the bereaved gradually removes emotional ties of their libido to the deceased object by the 'testing of reality' – taking each memory and severing bonds with it, accepting that the object no longer exists.[6] Only when all bonds are severed can the work of mourning be completed and be 'overcome after a certain period of time.'[7] This is work which is painful and requires emotional energy and so may result in some lethargy and 'loss of interest in the outside world' on the part of the bereaved but this will eventually pass and the mourner is free to make new attachments.[8] The shared experiences with the deceased are examined and repeatedly remembered – music listened to together, places visited and everyday common experiences are all mentally held up to reconfirm that the person is no longer here. This can often be observed in bereaved people as they go through old photographs, look at old clothes and possessions, reminiscing but also re-confirming their loss.

The meaning of the term melancholia has changed over the centuries since Aristotle's definition of being the world weariness of the sensitive and creative person[9]. At the time when Aristotle was writing it was thought that a person's temperament was determined by the balance between the four humours of the body – bile, phlegm, choler and blood. A person who suffered from melancholy was thought to have too much black bile in their body as it was thought that 'if there was a black mood there must be a black substance.'[10] Aristotle questioned the association between brilliance and achievement and the diseases of melancholy.[11] He stated that this was because black bile can become too hot or too cold in the body-too hot leading to 'cheerfulness with song and madness,' too cold causing despondency and fear.[12] Robert Burton, writing in 1621 in his *Anatomy of Melancholy*, whilst acknowledging that the main symptoms of melancholy are 'sadness and fear without a cause,' also described its more positive attributes as 'humourous-ness, proneness to love and wit, wisdom and inspiration'.[13]

Whilst melancholy is associated with pensive sadness and having a gloomy character, melancholia has a much more destructive connotation. The German psychiatrist Wilhelm Griesinger writing in 1867 described the darker side of the state of melancholia as being the predominant effect, and it is not until the publication of Sigmund Freud's 'Mourning and Melancholia' in 1917 that the psychoanalytical interpretation of the emotion is fully explored. Freud's view of melancholia is that it displays an almost identical range of characteristics as mourning but that it also includes a large element of self-loathing and self-accusation. Jennifer Radden describes these emotions as 'a form of rage redirected from the loved object to the self'. She also suggests that Freud draws on previous definitions of melancholia by stating that it 'is characterised by loss of an object of which its subject may be unconscious'[14] thereby characterising melancholia as a state of fear or sadness without cause. Jennifer Radden suggests that Freud allows that 'melancholia may have a glamorous aspect' because he admits that someone suffering from melancholia may 'have a keener eye for the truth than others who are not melancholic.'[15] Judith Butler argues that when mourning 'one accepts that by the loss one undergoes one will be changed, possibly for ever'.[16] If, in melancholia, we are unconscious of what we have lost, then there is an enigmatic element to the loss – not knowing, echoing Robert Burton's characteristic trait of melancholy - sadness without reason.

Melancholia has been described by Freud as unsuccessful, failed, pathological mourning and a disorder or disease. Freud describes mourning as 'coming to a spontaneous end' like a wound that has now healed and gone.[17] In contrast melancholia is described as an 'open wound' which cannot be healed.[18]

In her paper 'Freud and Barthes: Theorizing Mourning, Sustaining Grief' Kathleen Woodward proposes that Freud's distinction between the two states is too abrupt. She suggests that there is another place – between 'a crippling melancholia and the end of mourning'. It is this space, when one is suffering from an interminable grief that is not actual melancholia as defined by Freud, but a grief that 'is lived in such a way that one is still in mourning but no longer exclusively devoted to mourning.'[19]

Roland Barthes, writing about the death of his mother comments that the accepted view of the work of mourning should mean that eventually the pain of loss is reduced and comes to an end. However, he disagrees with this and states that time only 'eliminates the emotion of loss (I do not weep), that is all. For the rest, everything has remained motionless.'[20] Kathleen Woodward suggests that he is 'theorizing the possibility of sustaining the in-between of mourning and melancholia'[21] She also describes the idea of 'refused mourning' which the psychoanalytic theorists Nicholas Abraham and Maria Torok have likened to a 'split off crypt located psychically inside the body containing what cannot be forgotten.' This has also been described by the French philosopher Jacques Derrida as 'the very thing which provokes the worst suffering'.[22] This allows the mourner to keep himself in mourning and 'retain his psychic pain'. Kathleen Woodward also quotes Jean-Bertrand Pontalis as describing psychic pain as 'the state halfway between anxiety and attachment to others' and so suggests that this is the 'middle position between mourning and melancholia.'[23]

This halfway state may be a common experience for us all – it is hard to imagine a complete resolution of mourning where the memory of the deceased no longer causes any pain or sadness at all. Is it possible then, to be in a state of continuous unresolved (unsuccessful?) mourning without being melancholic?

In fact it is questionable whether the completion of the work of mourning as described by Freud is a desirable state. This would suggest that all the attachment for the deceased has gone and all feelings fully transferred to another person or object. Judith Butler questions whether it is possible to know when one has fully mourned another person.[24] In her own interpretation of Freud's work she states that she does not believe that successful grieving should imply 'that one has forgotten another person or that something else has come along to take its place, as if full substitutability were something for which we might strive.'[25] She describes the way in which we are changed by loss - 'the transformative effect of loss - which cannot be charted or planned.' And that 'one will be changed, possibly for ever'[26]. That there may be beneficial outcomes for society in the holding on to grief is argued by both Judith Butler and Kathleen Woodward, Butler positing that it may heighten awareness of the vulnerability of others. An example of when textiles have been used in this way would be the creation of AIDS memorial quilts known as The Names Project. This began in 1987 to raise awareness of the impact of AIDS and now has more than 48,000 panels marking the deaths of over 91,000 people. Woodward suggests that grief can actually give us strength 'as a sustaining force' against the terror of the State.[27] An example of this was when a memory cloth was created after the forced removal, by the apartheid regime, of 60,000 people from District 6 in Cape Town from 1968 to 1982. This cloth incorporated the signatures and stories of the people who were removed. These were not just been written but were embroidered onto the cloth to ensure that they do not fade and that they are not lost.

Other historical interpretations of the state of melancholia include that it was a mark of creative genius – indeed in the Elizabethan era, a melancholy man could have been a poet or a scholar and melancholy was an attribute which was affected in order to lend an aura of brilliance and to be considered fashionable. Julia Kristeva discussed the link between art and melancholia in her book *Black Sun* and John Lechte also comments that artists 'tend towards the melancholic pole of the psychical spectrum.'[28] Kristeva suggests every artistic work 'even those geared to provoke a strong emotional response, is executed with a certain detachment.' She describes the continuity between the artist's life and his work as a 'comportement', not that the artist's life is represented in the work but that 'the work is *part* of the artist's life.'[29]

2. Bereavement as Trauma

For an event to be described as a trauma, there are certain criteria that, according to the psychologists Richard Tedeschi and Lawrence Calhoun, it should fulfil. Firstly, the term trauma suggests that the event comes as a shock to the person because they have not had the time to prepare themselves psychologically for the event. The perceived lack of control over events is also more likely to make the person feel traumatised and change their psychological well-being, as does the event being 'out of the ordinary.' The death of someone close through old age is less likely to be deemed traumatic than suicide or other sudden death. The extent to which the person feels to blame for the event and the time of life at which the event occurs are also factors which determine how difficult the trauma is to cope with.[30] All these criteria defining trauma can be met by the experience of bereavement and the accompanying grief and mourning. William Worden has described in his book *Grief Counselling and Grief Therapy* how different 'mediators of mourning' may determine whether a bereavement is considered traumatic. These include factors such as who the person who died was; the nature of attachment to the bereaved; how the person died; previous experiences of death and the mourner's personality traits as well as social support and other stressful events which may be in the persons' life when the death occurs.[31] The development of post-traumatic stress disorder and complicated grief after traumatic bereavement is also discussed in Yao Xu's chapter on the frequency of mental health morbidity after the death of a child in the Sichuan earthquake in 2008.

Judith Butler has argued that being bereaved may increase one's sensitivity to the vulnerability of others,[32] and similarly, Richard Tedeschi and Lawrence Calhoun have found that those who suffer from trauma may be more likely to offer support to others in return. Bereaved parents in particular share their grief with other bereaved parents and this 'promotes a sense of having completed a substantial portion of the healing process.'[33]

The difficulties and negative psychological effects of trauma can include not only thoughts and emotions - e.g. anger, guilt, fear and depression but can also include physical problems, stress and psychiatric problems. The work of Tedeschi and Calhoun however, suggests that it is possible to survive and indeed thrive in the wake of trauma.

There have been many occasions where a traumatic event has caused artists to create work that acknowledges the impact of the trauma on the immediate community or society. As Langlands and Bell have commented 'Creating work in response to living history is possibly the greatest challenge for an artist and one of undeniable responsibility.'[34] An example of this was when the Colombian artist Doris Salcedo created a spontaneous work in 1999 after the murder of the Colombian humorist Jaime Garzon. Salcedo and her fellow artist friends made 'a ritual act of mourning' by pinning 5,000 roses on a 150 metre wall in Bogota in front of the house where Garzon had lived (which was already the focus of mourning by the public who had pinned messages on it). The roses were left to wither and die and became 'an ephemeral site of memory.'[35] Although Salcedo describes her initial action as an act of homage rather than the creation of an artwork by saying – 'when someone dies, one brings flowers' – it was this that 'operated in the social sphere' and prompted the students to act in a similar articulation of mourning when later in that year a professor was murdered on campus and the students spontaneously covered the walls of the campus with flowers.[36]

The increasing trend for leaving flowers at the roadside and of public displays of grief has been criticised by journalists and writers who comment that grief should be a privately not publicly displayed emotion. Tony Walter suggests that the 'British way of grief' is one of emotional reserve with words such as 'respectful' and 'dignified'being used to describe traditional mourning and funerals which celebrate the life of the deceased rather than focussing on the loss of life.[37] Having been accused of manipulating the emotions of the public over the death of Diana, Princess of Wales, writers in the media are now joining in the cry to stop this 'pornography of grief.'[38] Patrick West, writing for *Civitas* suggests that such displays of empathy 'do not help the bereaved' and that our 'culture of ostentatious caring concerns rather, projecting ones ego and informing others what a deeply caring individual you are.'[39] He also states that as a nation we are suffering from 'mourning sickness.'[40] Darian Leader in his book *The New Black* suggests that this is missing the point entirely – he argues that no-one can

> ...seriously argue that these tears are for the dead figures themselves. Rather it is precisely the public framework that allows people to articulate their own grief for other, unrelated losses.

In this way the 'public facilitates the private'[41] There would seem to be a need for the expression of grief and mourning which is not currently fulfilled by existing secular processes and rituals, for example, the action of creating roadside memorials and the taking of flowers to the grave of a stranger. The transient nature of these floral tributes means that they soon become unsightly and are removed – only to be replaced with more which in turn decay. It would seem that there is a space for the possibility for a more considered material approach. Textile work made to evoke the emotion of grief, loss and mourning could be used as a facilitator for the viewer to connect with their own grief and make some progress towards resolution of those feelings.

Nancy Guildart has commented on the spontaneous creation of 'artistic actions' following the terrorist attack on the World Trade Centre in 2001.[42] These are, she suggests, immediate expressions of grief and act as a way to channel outrage and fear alongside loss and sadness. With the move away, in recent decades, from the church into a more secular society we have seen the emergence of new rituals of mourning and expressions of grief such as the placing of flowers at roadside memorials. These activities have been criticised with the pejorative phrases 'conspicuous compassion',[43] 'mourning sickness'[44] and 'recreational grieving', but if we are all carrying with us a degree of unresolved mourning then perhaps this can be accessed through identification with the grief of another and empathy.[45] Did the visitors to Soham, the home town of murdered English schoolchildren Holly Wells and Jessica Chapman, who said to their parents 'I feel your pain' really mean that literally?[46] It would seem more likely that they were expressing empathy with them because they too were grieving for their own losses.

Darian Leader argues that it is not the content of works of art that have been made as a result of loss, which is the significant factor. He states that it is simply the fact that they have been made 'from an empty space, from an absence' and he suggests that creating something ourselves will allow us 'access to our own grief and to begin the work of mourning.'[47] The creation of art either by ones-self or by an artist would therefore appear to have a role in the facilitation of the work of mourning. This has been described by Peter Sacks with reference to the writing of an elegy. The act of writing removes the bereaved from what he called bereaved despair to resolution. In describing the loss of the person, a distance is created between the lost object or person and the means by which he expresses this loss. I would suggest that this could be applied to any artistic practice or creative process in which the sense of loss is conveyed.

In contrast to the positive emotion generated by creating what Nancy Guildart describes as 'textile actions' the journalist Karal Ann Marling writes that 'fine art takes too long to serve a useful purpose in a crisis,' but textile based actions which spontaneously occur following a personal or public loss are a response to people's basic needs to deal with loss immediately to and start to grieve.[48] 'Loss must be marked and it cannot be represented.' it is about immediacy of expression rather than good design and as such acts as a channel for outrage, fear, doubt and sorrow.[49] The results often lack aesthetic appeal, but the need to do something means people reach for what is close to hand for materials that allow them to express solidarity and grief and in doing so create 'space to remember.'[50] After the terrorist attacks on the World Trade Centre in New York in 2001, tributes to the police officers who died were written on an American Flag. David W. Chen reported in the New York Times that eventually there was no space left on the flag as 'in cursive script and block print the messages capture cathartic expressions of grief and gratitude in language that veers from the personal to the political.' Interestingly this 'impromptu, communal, memorial cloth' has now been sent to Afghanistan as an 'inspirational and emotional memento' to the American troops fighting there.[51] If mourning is never fully resolved and we are all in some way marked by the trauma of bereavement, viewing art that has at its core the communication of the emotion of grief may allow the viewer to progress their own work of mourning. In my own work, the showing of pieces intended to evoke the emotion of mourning and grief has resulted in a variety of responses. Viewers have commented on feelings from a reconnection to their grief through to deriving a cathartic comfort from the work. A common factor is the tendency to want to talk about and share their personal story of bereavement and their journey through their grief work.

3. The Importance of Cloth

The act of making private grief public could be illustrated by a number of artists but this chapter will focus on those who have used cloth as their medium. The use of cloth in rituals of mourning has a long history. In its simplest form cloth is used to wrap the body of the deceased as well as playing an important role in the social conventions of dress in mourning rituals – particularly in the Western world during the Victorian era. Cloth is described by the writer and curator Pennina Barnett as a 'second skin, a metaphor for the layer between ourselves and others.'[52] This long association of cloth with the body during and after life means that it is a uniquely placed medium to be used as a metaphor for grief, loss and mourning in contemporary art practice.

The fact that cloth maintains an intimate association with the body means that the clothes and textiles of the deceased have a special significance. One of the most difficult things to do after the death of someone close is to remove their clothes from the family home. Garments or textiles used by the deceased become precious to the bereaved and can take on a relic-like importance. As Peter Stallybrass writes, 'cloth *is* a kind of memory, when a person is absent or dies, cloth can absorb their absent presence.'[53]

The artist Louise Bourgeois recorded an anecdote in her notebook about a newly widowed woman who collects the unwashed underwear of her late husband and

> makes a doll with elastic and places it in her bed in his place.
> Smell of sweat - it is the symbol of life

Smell of feet and caress of feet related to bring my slippers
Smell of lavender lotion for the hair stirs palpitations after past a
half century. [54]

At the end of life textile objects such as clothes can become a link to the deceased in a similar way to how young children retain a link to their mother through a transitional object. Transitional objects are typically textile such as blankets, pieces of cloth, or soft toys. They provide an intermediate developmental phase between the psychic and external reality at a time when a child is beginning to understand the separation between itself and its mother. Until this time the child sees the mother and itself as a whole. Understanding this separation causes the child to feel that it has lost something and the object is used to represents all types of mothering. The transitional object is the first 'not-me' possession that the child owns and is particularly important at bed-time and as a defence against anxiety. Later in life when a person dies, their clothes are often kept by the bereaved as a way of keeping the person close, of maintaining a connection with them. Most importantly, cloth will retain the smell of the person and may come to substitute for the person themselves. Margaret Gibson states that transitional objects 'express the anguish and militate against the mother's absence as a primary figure and corporeal site of absence and loss.'[55] She also suggests that transitional objects can work in this way in grief as they become 'both a means of holding on and letting go.' The garments or fabrics of the deceased chosen to be kept are then associated with the first moments of mourning and so signify the memory of that devastating and overwhelming feeling as well as the memory of the deceased person. These become what she describes as 'melancholy objects' which act to memorialise the intense immediate mourning period and signify the incomplete nature of mourning – that it never really goes away.

The textile artist Anne Wilson uses hair to repair holes in traditional household linens. In the work 'Lost, misplaced, found', made after the death of her father, she used hair couched onto a shroud length of linen to represent the lost body for whom the shroud was made. Her work implies the presence of the body without it being physically present and reaffirms the sense of loss and mourning in its absence. The mending of linens with hair echoes the tending and mending processes undertaken by the family who owned the cloths. Repeatedly used, washed, ironed and mended, time and time again, cloths used for celebrations and family gatherings, the history of the family is contained in these possessions. Stitching with hair onto these cloths to repair the holes recalls the painstaking labour of mending, and creating a new cloth, a shroud to hold the memory of the family. Wilson uses a combination of the pure and the abject in her work. The pure represented by the use of white cloth, linen, and the patient labour of women in the laundering and repair of the cloth. This is contrasted by the use of hair – a reminder of the abject absent body, the holes suggesting the orifices and wounds rife with disease or decay. Writing about Ann Wilson, the writer and critic Tim Porges suggests that like other artists of the 'Art Fabric movement' such as Eva Hesse and Claes Oldenberg, her work stands in an in-between space, 'between depiction and abstraction, placed between mind and body' and suggests that work which 'intercedes between mind and body' tends to a profound sadness.[56]

The artist Michelle Walker has created work as an act of mourning for her mother who died from Alzheimer's disease. In particular the piece 'In memoriam' is a quilt which is pieced together from layered plastic sheeting and wire wool. Made in the tradition of a Commemorative quilt, the stitching of the clear plastic surface layer is based on the pattern of creases in Walkers own skin which is used as a metaphor for decay. The physical pain Walker experienced in working with the wire wool in creating the quilt was an embodied manifestation of the emotional pain of losing her mother to the disease. The border of the quilt is of knotted wire wool as a fringe and references the way her mother used to continually twist her hair in the latter stages of her Alzheimer's disease. The quilt is traditionally an inherited item passed from generation to generation and retaining memory but Walkers quilt is used instead to mark the loss of that memory through disease. The study for this piece also includes a piece of her mother's wedding veil looped into the shape of remembrance ribbons adopted by many charities. The veil is another textile which is handed down the generations reflecting the hopes and dreams of the women starting their married life. Sue Prichard, the textiles curator of the Victoria and Albert Museum wrote of this work that

> In this case, the creation of a tangible memorial to a lost family member or friend provides succour in the aftermath of a personal tragedy; the physical act of stitching also acts as a lynchpin on the therapeutic road to emotional recovery.[57]

The Japanese artist Chiyoko Tanaka stained the fabric she used to create a *kesa* in memory of each of her parents. *Kesas* are traditional robes worn by Buddhist monks and nuns after they have been ordained. They can also be made to honour the memory of a deceased person and are made either from sumptuous fabrics donated to the temple by the family of the deceased or can be made from rags. The use of rags follows the Buddhist tradition of not owning anything of intrinsic value. The Great Master Dogen – the Japanese Zen Buddhist teacher and founder of the Soto school of Zen in Japan - lists in the *Kesa-Kudoku* (The Spiritual Merits of the Kesa) chapter of the Shobogenzo, the ten sorts of rags suitable to be used: - those chewed by an ox or rats, rags scorched by fire, rags soiled by menstruation and childbirth, rags offered at a shrine or a dead persons clothing left at a graveyard, rags offered in petitional prayer or shrouds brought back from a funeral and rags rejected by the kings officers when they are promoted to a higher rank.[58] If new fabric is donated to the temple for a *kesa* to be made in memory of a deceased family member, once the *kesa* has been made there is a staining ceremony to make it 'not new.' Chiyoko Tanaka takes these traditions and transforms them into her own work of mourning. Using clothes that have been worn before and so contain trace elements of the previous owner, she layered the pieces of cloth as she layered 'an occasional memory' of her parents into her mind emptied by grief.[59]

In her article 'On Cloth, Stigma and Shame' Jenni Sorkin argues that stains elicit the idea of shame, and draws the distinction between the embarrassment caused by self-staining – nosebleeds, vomiting, bedwetting etc with staining by another, for example

> that which is inflicted by another. That which is forced [...]To stain another is to mark. To be marked is dark. This darkness is constant foreboding and permanent grief.[60]

Elizabeth Hallam and Jenny Hockey describe how the image of a painful memory of the death of a loved one is often likened to 'breaches in the skin which defy the supposed healing power of time.'[61] In his essay 'Mourning and Melancholia' Freud suggested that melancholia could be thought of as an 'open wound' whereas mourning is a healing process but one which marks us forever, leaving an emotional scar.[62] As Elizabeth Jennings wrote in her poem *Words about Grief*

> Time does not heal,
> It makes a half stitched scar
> That can be broken and you feel
> Grief as total as in its first hour.[63]

The physical presence of a scar is an indication of life experience – a textile analogy for this is the visible patching and mending of fabrics, giving a sense of repair and making whole. The mending of fabric through patching and darning, can be seen in the *Boro* textiles in Japan. These garments were made by the poor from a limited supply of fabrics and repeatedly mended and patched to keep the family warm – made from love and a need to protect – a practical version of Anne Wilson's repair of family linens.

As a textile artist, these ideas have raised questions in my own practice in which I have been investigating how I can make work which evokes the emotions of mourning and loss and make connections with the experience of the bereaved viewer. In previous work I have used materials associated with burial – lead and linen – to encourage a focus on the emotional dimensions inherent in the words grief, loss and absence. I have also been researching the use of the *kesa* as a way of expressing loss of childhood, both as a child grows into adulthood and leaves home but also the loss of the inner child as one ages. Using the measurements of my own body I created a fragment of a *kesa* and incorporated a small child's dress as a signifier of loss. Using ash as a covering to embed the dress into the fabric of the *kesa* integrates the piece into a whole in the same way that memories of a trauma embed themselves into the psyche of a person.

Image 1: From the nigredo series 2010. Photograph by Richard Brayshaw.

As part of an exploration of creating work which conveys the emotions of grief and loss, I have constructed a 'wall of mourning' which completely covered five metre wall within an exhibition space. Small patches of black linen were sanded and waxed and then pieced together to show a sense of the remembering, repeating and working through of memories as described by Freud. The patches of fabric were stitched together in a rhythmic way with the stitches evenly spaced and the patches overlapping. It was a repetitive and meditative process with the surface then covered in a web of larger stitches as evidence of the way one can be caught up in the emotion and find it difficult to move on.

Image 2: 'Remembering, repeating and working through'. Installation at Salts Mill August 2012. Photograph by Beverly Ayling-Smith.

One visitor to the exhibition who had recently been bereaved wrote about this piece:

> On first sight of 'remembering, repeating, and working through'
> I was aware of the somewhat ragged air about the piece, a
> somewhat not quite got-togetherness. It reflected my own sense
> of not quite togetherness following the death of Pat, my wife, and
> the love of my life for sixty years. There was no symmetry to the
> black patches or groups of patches, nor any sense of order to the
> tearing revealing the white beyond the black surface, whilst a
> network of threads criss-crossing the piece appeared to be
> constraining impending breakup. A metaphor for my grieving,
> for my state of emotional destruction and my efforts to find my
> 'way through'. I saw myself on that black wall. It spoke to the
> bruised and raw ME within me, wallowing in the damage to that

mutual love of sixty years; love that had been obliterated. It also spoke of the glimmers of brightness appearing from time to time, fragments of beautiful memories, easily lost to that ever present 'black wall', of memories out of reach for the time being.[64]

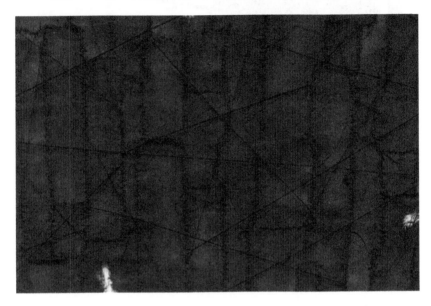

Image 3: Remembering, repeating and working through (detail) Photograph by Richard Brayshaw/

I have also created three pieces which show the journey from the darkness of the initial rawness of grief through healing to a sense of the wound of mourning being embedded in the experience of the bereaved. Wounds that are stark and obvious in 'remembering, repeating and working through' are, in the 'healing series', repaired and gradually fade to scarring in the cloth as a metaphor for the way the fabric of a person is marked by their life experience. These three pieces progress in colour from black to grey to white. The first shows a Y shaped tear in the fabric, referencing the shape of an autopsy incision and mended with lead sutures. The slashes in the fabric themselves are a bruised purple colour with the surrounding fabric black and textured with charcoal and pastel. The second piece suggests the healing of the rents but progresses from black to grey in the way scars heal and fade with time. Some are still the purple bruised colour but are stitched closed. The final piece in this series is white with no tears but traces of the stitching can be seen embedded in the surface of the piece in gesso and wax.

Image 4: Healing series 2012. Photograph by Beverly Ayling-Smith

Artists are accustomed, in their own practice, to the idea of making the private public – whatever their concept, subject matter or sphere of work. Artists strive to make a connection with their audience in order to convey a message, an emotion or thought. Evoking an emotional response from the viewer may connect with an unresolved grief. Using cloth as a medium – with its very tangible connection to the body and the deceased - to convey this emotion provides a creative strategy to facilitate the work of mourning.

Notes

[1] Jenni Sorkin, 'Stain: On Cloth, Stigma and Shame' *Third Text* 53 (2001): 77-80.
[2] Kathleen Woodward, Freud and Barthes: Theorizing Mourning, Sustaining Grief *Discourse* 13 (1990): 93-110.
[3] Colin Murray-Parkes and Holly G. Prigerson, *Bereavement: Studies of Grief in Adult Life* (Penguin 2010), 6.
[4] Sigmund Freud, 'Mourning and Melancholia', in *On Murder, Mourning and Melancholia* (Penguin Modern Classics, 2005), 204.
[5] Ibid., 203.
[6] Ibid., 204.
[7] Ibid.
[8] Ibid.
[9] Jennifer Radden, *The Nature of Melancholy: from Aristotle to Kristeva* (Oxford: Oxford University Press, 2002), 58.
[10] Jennifer Radden, *Moody Minds Distempered: Essays on Melancholy and Depression* (Oxford University Press, 2009), 63.
[11] Jennifer Radden, *The Nature of Melancholy*, 55.
[12] Ibid., 58.
[13] Radden, *Moody Minds Distempered*, 60.
[14] Radden, *The Nature of Melancholy*, 282.
[15] Ibid., 283.
[16] Judith Butler, *Precarious Life: The Powers of Mourning and Violence* (London, New York: Verso, 2004), 21.
[17] Sigmund Freud, 'Transience' in *On Murder Mourning and Melancholia* (Penguin Modern Classics 2005), 199.
[18] Freud, *On Murder, Mourning and Melancholia*, 212.
[19] Woodward, Freud and Barthes, 96.
[20] Roland Barthes, *Camera Lucida* (London: Vintage, 2000), 75.
[21] Woodward, Freud and Barthes, 98.
[22] Ibid., 99.
[23] Ibid., 100.
[24] Butler, *Precarious Life*, 20.
[25] Ibid., 21.
[26] Ibid.
[27] Woodward, Freud and Barthes, 105.
[28] John Lechte, *Julia Kristeva* (London: Routledge, 1990), 35.
[29] Ibid.
[30] Richard Tedeschi and Laurence Calhoun, *Trauma and Transformation: Growing in the Aftermath of Suffering* (Sage Publications, 1995), 17.
[31] J. William Worden, *Grief Counselling and Grief Therapy* (London: Routledge, 2010) 57.

[32] Butler, *Precarious Life*, 30.

[33] Tedeschi and Calhoun, *Trauma and Transformation*, 37.

[34] printed on wall of Tate Britain gallery during the Turner Prize exhibition 2004. http://www.tate.org.uk/whats-on/tate-britain/exhibition/turner-prize-2004/turner-prize-2004-langlands-bell viewed 23rd January 2013

[35] Nancy Princenthal, Carlos Basualdo and Andreas Huyssen, *Doris Salcedo* (London: Phaidon 2000), 33.

[36] Ibid.,

[37] Elizabeth Hallam, Jenny Hockey, *Death, Memory and Material Culture*, Oxford, Berg, 2001), 99.

[38] Carol Sarler, 'This New and Peculiar Pornography of Grief.' *The Times*, 7 September 2007. London.

[39] Patrick West, *Conspicuous Compassion: Why Sometimes it Really is Cruel to be Kind* (Civitas, 2004), 1.

[40] Ibid.

[41] Darian Leader, *The New Black* (London: Penguin, 2008), 77.

[42] Nancy Guildart, 'Torn and Mended' in *The Object of Labor: Art, Cloth and Cultural Production* eds. Joan Livingstone and John Ploof (Cambridge USA: MIT Press 2007), 239.

[43] West, *Conspicuous Compassion*, 1.

[44] Ibid., 7.

[45] Tom Coghlan, 'General Fears 'Mawkish' View of Military', *The Times*, 13 November 2010.

[46] Charlotte Wyatt, 'Don't Get Me Started.' VHS recording. *Rosie Boycott on False Grief*. Channel 5, August 30, 2005.

[47] Darian Leader, *The New Black* (London: Penguin 2008) 207.

[48] Nancy Guildart, 'Torn and Mended', 252.

[49] Judith Butler, 'After Loss, What Then?' in *Loss: The Politics of Mourning*, eds. David Eng and David Kazanjian (University of California Press, 2003), 467.

[50] Nancy Guildart, 'Torn and Mended', 253.

[51] David W. Chen, 'Flag to Carry Sentiments From Ground Zero to Afghanistan', *New York Times*, 26 November 2001.

[52] Pennina Barnett, 'Stain', in *Shame and Sexuality*, ed. Claire Pajaczkowska and Ivan Ward (London: Routledge, 2008), 203.

[53] Peter Stallybrass, 'Worn Worlds: Clothes and Mourning', in *Cultural Memory and the Construction of Identity*, ed. Dan Ben-Amos and Lillian Weissberg, (Wayne State University Press, 1999), 30.

[54] Germano Celant, *Louise Bourgeois The Fabric Works* (Milan: Skira, 2010), 116.

[55] Margaret Gibson, 'Melancholy Objects' *Mortality* 9 (2004): 288.

[56] Tim Porges, *Anne Wilson* (Winchester: Telos Portfolio Collection, 2001), 20.

[57] Sue Prichard, 'Keepsakes of Identity: Michele Walker Memoriam', *V and A Online Journal* 1 (2008) Viewed 15th October 2012
http://www.vam.ac.uk/content/journals/research-journal/issue-01/keepsakes-of-identity-michele-walker-memoriam/
[58] Great Master Dogen, *Shobogenzo* (Shasta Abbey, 2007), 965-966, viewed 14 November 2012,
http://www.urbandharma.org.pdf/Shobogenzo.pdf.
[59] Lesley Millar, *Chiyoko Tanaka* (Winchester: Telos Art Publishing, 2002), 38.
[60] Sorkin, 'Stain: On Cloth, Stigma and Shame', 79.
[61] Hallam and Hockey, *Death, Memory and Material Culture*, 36.
[62] Freud, *On Murder Mourning and Melancholia*, 212.
[63] Hallam and Hockey, *Death Memory and Material Culture*, 36.
[64] Alan Firth in email to author 8th August 2012. Alan Firth purchased this piece in memory of his wife Pat and it will be shown at the Whitworth Art Gallery in February 2013.

Bibliography

Barnett, Pennina. 'Stain'. In *Shame and Sexuality: Psychoanalysis Visual Culture*, edited by Claire Pajaczkowska and Ivan Ward, 203-215. London: Routledge, 2008.

Barthes, Roland. *Camera Lucida* London: Vintage, 2000.

Basualdo, Carlos. 'Carlos Basualdo in Conversation with Doris Salcedo'. In *Doris Salcedo*, edited by Nancy Princenthal, Carlos Basualdo, and Andreas Huyssen, 8-35. London: Phaidon, 2000.

Butler, Judith. 'After Loss, What Then?' In *Loss: the Politics of Mourning*, edited by David Eng and David Kazanjian, 467-473 California: University of California Press, 2003

Butler, Judith. *Precarious Life: The Powers of Mourning and Violence* London: Verso, 2006.

Celant, Germano. *Louise Bourgeois:The Fabric Works* Milan: Skira 2010.

Clewell, Tammy. 'Mourning Beyond Melancholia: Freud's Psychoanalysis of Loss.' *The American Psychoanalytic Journal* 52 (2004): 43-67

Coghlan, Tom. 'General Fears Mawkish View of Military'. *The Times*. 13 November 2010.

Dogen, Great Master. *Shobogenzo*. Shasta Abbey 2007. Viewed 14 November 2012. http://www.urbandharma.org/pdf/Shobogenzo.pdf.

Freud, Sigmund. *On Murder, Mourning and Melancholia*. London: Penguin Modern Classics 2005.

Gibson, Margaret. 'Melancholy Objects'. *Mortality* 9 (2004): 285-299.

Guildart, Nancy. 'Torn and Mended'. *The Object of Labor: Art Cloth and Cultural Production*, edited by Joan Livingstone and John Ploof, 239-254. MIT Press, 2007.

Hallam, Elizabeth and Jenny Hockey. *Death, Memory and Material Culture*. Oxford: Berg 2001.

Hockey, Jenny, John Katz and Neil Small. *Grief, Mourning and Death Ritual*. Open University Press, 2001.

Howarth, Glenys. *Death and Dying*. Polity Press, 2007.

Kristeva, Julia. *Black Sun: Depression and Melancholia*. Translated by Leon S. Roudiez. New York: Columbia University Press, 1987.

Leach, Neil. *Camouflage*. Massachusetts MIT Press, 2006.

Leader, Darian. *The New Black: Mourning, Melancholia and Depression*. London: Penguin, 2009.

Lechte, John. 'Art, Love and Melancholy in the Work of Julia Kristeva.' In *Abjection, Melancholia and Love: The Work of Julia Kristeva*, edited by John Fletcher and Andrew Benjamin, 24-41. London: Routledge, 1990.

Millar, Lesley. *Chiyoka Tanaka*. Portfolio Volume 12 Winchester: Telos Art Publishing 2002.

Murray-Parkes, Colin, and Holly G. Priegerson. *Bereavement: Studies of Grief in Adult Life*. London: Penguin, 2010.

Porges, Tim. *Anne Wilson.* Portfolio Volume 6. Winchester: Telos Portfolio Collection 2001.

Prichard, Sue. Keepsakes of Identity: Michele Walker Memoriam'. *V and A Online Journal* 1 (2008). Viewed 15th October 2012. http://www.vam.ac.uk/content/journals/research-journal/issue-01/keepsakes-of-identity-michele-walker-memoriam/

Radden, Jennifer. *The Nature of Melancholy: From Aristotle to Kristeva.* Oxford University Press, 2002.

Radden, Jennifer. *Moody Minds Distempered: Essays on Melancholy and Depression.* New York: Oxford University Press, 2009.

Sarler, Carol. 'This New and Peculiar Pornography of Grief.' *The Times.* 7 September 2007.

Sorkin, Jenni. 'Stain: on Cloth, Stigma and Shame.' *Third Text* 53 (2001): 77-80,

Stallybrass, Peter. 'Worn Worlds: Clothes and Mourning', *Cultural Memory and the Construction of Identity*, edited by Dan Ben-Amos and Lillian Weissberg, 27-44. Wayne State University Press, 1999.

Tedeschi, Richard and Laurence Calhoun. *Trauma and Transformation : Growing in the Aftermath of Suffering.* Sage Publications, 1995.

Till Barry and Paula Swart. 'Elegance and Spirituality of Japanese Kesa'. *Arts of Asia* 27 (1997): 51-63.

West, Patrick. *Conspicuous Compassion: Why sometimes it Really is Cruel to be Kind.* Civitas, 2004.

Woodward, Kathleen. 'Freud and Barthes: Theorizing Mourning, Sustaining Grief'. *Discourse* 13 (1990): 93-110.

Worden, J. William. *Grief Counselling and Grief Therapy.* London: Routledge 2010.

Wyatt, Charlotte. 'Don't Get Me Started.' VHS recording. *Rosie Boycott on False Grief.* Channel 5, August 30, 2005.

Beverly Ayling-Smith is a post-graduate research student at the University for the Creative Arts, Farnham, Surrey, UK. Her main research interest is in the use of cloth in contemporary art practice to materialise the work of mourning.

Indigenous Girls and Women in Canada: Collective Trauma, Survivance and Participatory Research

Johanne N. Fleming-Saraceno

Abstract
In view of historical conditions and ongoing policies, practices, and discourses in Canada, Indigenous girls continue to be vulnerable to sexualized and racialized violence. On the West Coast of Canada, high rates of sexual exploitation and numerous cases of missing or murdered Indigenous girls and women reflect a perpetual intergenerational trauma. Engaged and participatory research offers a possible venue for Indigenous girls to map out systemic violence as well as strategies of resistance and perseverance in the face of collective trauma. Furthermore, this approach offers opportunities for Indigenous girls to begin to disrupt normalized practices of sexualized and racialized violence in their communities.

Key Words: Indigenous girls, Canada, colonisation, collective trauma, survivance, participatory research

*****

1. Introduction

This chapter engages in a critical and timely discussion of the extreme disparities existing for Canada's Indigenous peoples, its girls and women in particular. Most significant to the issue was the announcement, coming at the close of 2011, that the United Nations Committee on the Elimination of Discrimination Against Women (CEDAW) would investigate the high numbers of missing Indigenous women in Canada following appeals from the Native Women's Association of Canada (NWAC) and the Canadian Feminist Alliance for International Action (FAFIA). These appeals were in response to the limited efforts of the Canadian government and policing agencies to investigate and resolve the numerous cases since 1990 of missing Indigenous women across Canada[1]. Furthermore, the United Nations Child Rights review in 2012 chastised the federal government of Canada for failing to meet its commitments under the *Convention on the Rights of the Child*[2]. In particular, the review emphasized the need for the government to address the discrimination against Indigenous children and youth in the areas of health, education, justice, and child welfare[3].

This discussion is informed by my research and counselling practice, those of my colleagues, and current and relevant readings in the field. My analysis is informed by Indigenous, critical, and postcolonial feminist theories. This chapter will highlight the historical and ongoing oppression enacted in a normalised, systematic manner in the colonial Canadian context and the ensuing collective trauma which continues to mark the lives of Indigenous people across the country. This critique intends to map out existing inequities in the hope that with increased knowledge those outside traumatised Indigenous communities can better stand alongside and support Indigenous community initiatives to reclaim language and economic autonomy and to re-integrate traditional practices for healing. Non-Indigenous supporters must mobilize for legal and policy reform and the complex and multi-layered systemic change required to disrupt the cumulative trauma lived in Indigenous families and communities. Indigenous girls and women bear the brunt of this trauma due to the prominence of Euro-western values of hetero-patriarchy[4] which normalise the use and abuse of women's bodies.

In addition to mapping out the historic and ongoing sexualisation and exploitation of Indigenous girls and women, this chapter will discuss the potential benefits of participatory and engaged approaches to research and practice. This potential will be illustrated by a case example from my own research. For my master's thesis research, I facilitated a Photovoice study with four local Indigenous adolescent girls. I employ the term 'participant-researchers' rather than 'subjects' intentionally, to reflect the dynamic and democratic research process wherein the participants and lead researcher are on par. Critical, feminist participatory research can support and encourage girls and women to identify and mobilize existing resources in their communities. Additionally, participatory research offers possibilities to facilitate the identification, naming, and sharing of the practices of resistance that sustain Indigenous girls and women in the face of persistent and entrenched racialized discrimination.

2. Colonialism in Canada

In considering the topic of trauma as it relates to Indigenous girls and women, it is impossible to ignore the historic and ongoing context of colonial imperialism which disrupted, through legally justified measures entrenched in the Indian Act[5], Indigenous peoples' ability to live in accordance with their own sophisticated and balanced social and economic codes.

The Indian Act further entrenched the growing colonial power and legalised the new government of Canada's agenda of assimilation. This is an agenda that has not wavered to this day—as evidenced by the current status of Indigenous people in Canadian society and the recently passed paternalistic legislation of Bill C-45 which promotes Prime Minister Stephen Harper's assimilationist plans.[6] When the Indian Act came into effect in 1876, 'Indian self-government was abolished and finance and all social services, including education were placed under federal control.'[7] Furthermore, diverse communities and distinct tribes or nations were forced together onto restricted tracts of land the settlers found less desirable, resulting in the 'theft of Native lands and the forceful segregation of Natives away from mainstream society.'[8] The trauma of this forced displacement has very real, continued consequences on Indigenous communities today. As Razack states,

'Canada is a settler society with a history of genocide and colonization ... place and landscape are not inert but actively participate in the identity formation of the individual.'[9] Even in urban areas without prescribed reserves this segregation of Indigenous from European-descended Canadians persists. Intentionally segregated reserves or urban settings reinforce the devaluing of Indigenous people in relation to mainstream Canadian society.[10]

The trauma of forced exile and loss of economic autonomy was further compounded by the assimilationist legislation requiring the mandatory attendance of Indigenous children in residential schools—including the forcible removal of children from their communities to attend these schools.[11] The residential school mandate was directed by an assimilationist policy intended to sever the ties to traditional ways of knowing and being: 'the stated purpose of residential schools was to strip aboriginal children of their culture.'[12] In these residential schools, children were forbidden from speaking their mother tongue and often from interacting with their siblings. Many legal cases have gone before the court, and it is now widely known in Canada that many generations of Indigenous children were subjected to all forms of abuse while residing in these government and church-sanctioned institutions.[13]

For Indigenous people in Canada, trauma has occurred at multiple levels, across many generations, and impacted entire communities. This renders individualised conceptualisations of trauma inadequate. The situation of Indigenous girls and women in Canada certainly fits Evans-Campbell's proposed criteria for identifying collective trauma: 'Many people in the community experienced it, the events generated high levels of collective distress, and the events were perpetuated by others with a destructive intent.'[14] The extent and complexity of the effects of historic and intergenerational trauma can perhaps be glimpsed but is still not fully understood.[15] Diagnoses such as post-traumatic stress disorder are still inadequate to address collective trauma as the focus remains on the individual and does not account for social and environmental responses.[16] In order to support Indigenous girls, women, and communities in reclaiming autonomy and healing, it will be imperative to follow the lead of Indigenous expertise and look to localized Indigenous wisdom and strategies rather than assuming that the theories and interventions of Western society will be relevant and most effective. In fact, it is critical to question whether Western interventions do not further contribute to the assimilation of Indigenous ways of being into colonial Canadian norms.

3. Colonialism and the Collective Trauma of Indigenous Girls and Women

The objectification, racialization, and sexualization of Indigenous women combined with economic disempowerment, have rendered Indigenous girls among the most vulnerable to violence and discrimination in Canada.[17] It is critical to consider systemic racism as it intersects with sexualized violence in examining the collective trauma experienced by Indigenous girls and women. Indigenous women and girls have been systemically devalued and sexualized and their bodies abused and degraded for more than two centuries. Historically, in Canada, following early contact, European men who moved to Canada to profit from the exploitation of natural resources such as fur would often buy or take a woman from an Indigenous community.[18] As discussed by Anderson, Native women have long been seen by the colonial man as tied to the land and thus, as another conquest to be won[19]. This practice of buying women marked the beginning of the sexual exploitation of Indigenous women and girls in Canada, and exploitation that continues today.

Another policy that contributed to the trauma specific to Indigenous women and girls was the effective denial of their right to membership in their respective First Nations communities and their right to enjoy 'Indian status.' The Indian Act did not recognise many First Nations women, and their offspring, as citizens with their own rights and entitlements.[20] The historical disenfranchisement of Aboriginal women meant that until 1985, a First Nation woman who married a non-First Nation man lost her membership and identity (status) as an 'Indian;' whereas, if a First Nation man married a non-First Nation woman, his partner gained First Nations membership and status. The impact of these discriminatory provisions was partially ameliorated by the 1985 amendments to the *Indian Act* (Bill C-31); however, as many authors have commented, discrimination against the children of reinstated First Nations women continues.[21]

The findings of my own study further emphasize the link between colonial constructions of Indigenous women and girls and sexual exploitation. The experiences recounted by the participant-researchers conveyed feelings of being diminished, ignored, embarrassed, unseen, and vulnerable to inappropriate sexual attention from men anytime, anywhere. As Downe states, Indigenous girls are 'connected through a pervasive colonial ideology that sees these young women as exploitable and dispensable.'[22] Mainstream discourses of Indigenous womanhood construct Indigenous women as dirty and lazy and as sexual property, and reinforce colonial power dynamics that position Indigenous women as consumable sexual objects for a white man's pleasure and dominance.[23] Historically, a Western dichotomy of virgin-whore was imposed upon Indigenous women's identity through the princess-squaw imagery.[24] Razack and Maracle identify how various constructs perpetuate the stereotypes of Indigenous women as 'rapeable'.[25] Anderson recounts stories from Indigenous women elders throughout Canada who tell of their own encounters as children and youth with white men and sexualized violence. She introduces the concept of the *Triangle of Oppression*, developed by the Doris Marshall Institute, which is a model for conceptualising the link between these colonial discourses and the sexual exploitation of Native women in their everyday lives.[26] This model positions 'dominant ideas, assumptions, and values' at the top of the triangle, 'individual behaviour (name calling, sexual abuse)' at the base of the triangle at the right point and 'structures, systems (courts, healthcare system)' at the left point. Underneath the base of the triangle is the 'impact on

Native women's lives (low self-worth, violence, sexual abuse).'[27] This model illustrates the inextricable link between the policies and actions of dominant colonial society and the ongoing oppression of Indigenous girls and women in every day contexts.

The extent to which Indigenous girls and women are vulnerable to sexual violence is evidenced by two tragedies experienced by British Columbia communities: The Pickton murders[28] and the Highway of Tears, a stretch of Highway in Northern British Columbia[29]. The Pickton case pertains to numerous missing and murdered women, many of who were Indigenous, from the downtown east side (DTES) of Vancouver, B.C. through the 1990's and early 2000's. The DTES is an area renowned for its extreme poverty, drug use, and sex trade. A disproportionate number of residents in the DTES are Indigenous. 'Historical poverty and cultural dislocation have tended to place this group among the most marginalized, making them particularly vulnerable to the social dysfunctions evident in the neighbourhood.'[30] A recent review of the police investigation of this case indicated that systemic sexism in the Vancouver police and the RCMP resulted in a lack of thorough police work due to the devaluation of the victims because they were sex workers. "The women were poor, they were addicted, vulnerable, aboriginal' Oppal told a news conference Monday afternoon, 'As a group they were dismissed."[31]

The *Highway of Tears* refers to a stretch of Highway 16 in remote British Columbia which has earned its title following more than three decades in which numerous girls and women, predominantly Indigenous, have gone missing while travelling along or near the highway. Many murdered women's bodies have been found along Highway 16.[32] In both cases, large numbers of Indigenous women, many of whom worked in the sex trade industry, disappeared.[33] Despite these tragedies, until recent years, the government, media, and local authorities effectively ignored the cases of these missing women.[34] There was little interest in acknowledging the systemic victimization of members of Canada's most vulnerable population further. These examples highlight the social invisibility of Indigenous girls and women.

As the literature spanning the last decade illustrates, the colonial constructions of Indigenous females as dirty, consumable sexual objects is ongoing.[35] This is the legacy of Indigenous women's identity that the participant-researchers have been exposed to growing up. One participant-researcher said, that based on her life experience, she had noticed that women are, metaphorically, 'at men's feet.'

McNinch, in his critical examination of the trial of the adult men who sexually assaulted a twelve year-old Saulteaux girl in Saskatchewan in 2001, critiques a justice system in which white men are inherently entitled, while Indigenous girls are devalued as sexual objects. The following paragraph highlights how these discourses are enacted both implicitly and explicitly through the justice system, and therefore sustain the broader social exploitation of Indigenous girls and women by white men.

> The defence gazed down on the 12-year-old girl and saw only one role for her, the Indian squaw or slut–a role substantiated because of questionable semen found on her underpants and allegations of family sexual abuse. Melissa compromised herself by 'wearing makeup,' looking and saying she was older than she was, accepting and drinking the beer offered to her... Under such blame the victim scrutiny, she is made into a precociously promiscuous deviant. The men are left with their 'natural' and hence understandable sexual appetite, their 'horniness,' their masculinity; their white privilege.[36]

As illustrated by this excerpt, hetero-patriarchal colonial values continue to dominate the structures of Canadian society maintaining a risk to Indigenous girls and women for further trauma. Indigenous girls in Canada today need support and spaces available to them so they can strengthen their resistance to the internalization of these restrictive, oppressive colonial discourses of Indigenous womanhood.

4. Race and Gender-Based Trauma: On-Going and Historical

It is important to pay attention to the role that historical context, policies, and law play in shaping Indigenous girls' experiences of sexual exploitation. Indigenous girls continue to be the most frequent victims of sexualized violence and are the most at risk for sexual exploitation.[37]

For Indigenous girls and women, the experience of being 'othered' is reinforced daily through their experiences and interactions with white peers, in a white, mainstream school setting and community, and in media that renders them invisible. As racialized girls, female Indigenous Canadians are limited by how others see them and by a lack of possibilities to see themselves beyond stereotypical representations. As Lesko states, 'another avenue for establishing the inferiority of subordinated peoples is the construction of psychological knowledges that portray the colonized as inferior.'[38] These negative psychological constructions are locally manifest in racial slurs and stereotypes such as 'chug', 'dirty Indian', and 'lazy' or 'welfare recipients'. These examples shared by research-participants resonate with Anderson's claim that 'Native girls begin to hear racial slurs from a young age, often before they even understand the terms themselves.'[39]

Indigenous girls live the collective trauma narratives of more than one hundred years of violence and discrimination. Sikka stresses that, 'with colonization, white settlers uprooted traditional spiritual and intellectual values accorded to Indigenous women and replaced them with notions of inferiority, hierarchy, and the paradigm of women as property.'[40] My own research also highlights how these historical events continue to undermine the safety and positive self-regard of Indigenous girls today.

Indigenous girls and women face multiple erasures; as racialized, gendered, sexualized, and classed subjects, they do not see their realities reflected in the dominant narratives which permeate their lived daily experiences.[41] The girls involved in my research expressed that they do not see themselves, as Indigenous females, represented in society. They noted that when their worlds are represented they are usually positioned against a white, middle-class normalised backdrop which then constitutes them as marginalised others. Even within mainstream literature, which exists to educate and train service providers such as teachers, social workers, and mental health counselors, 'erasures of racialized minority girls occur in dominant psychosocial representations of 'youth' and 'girlhood' that essentialize race, age, and gender.'[42] Girls are grouped into preset categories which erase nuanced differences. Jiwani, Steenbergen, and Mitchell note that constructions of girlhood 'include hegemonic femininities articulated through preferences which are race, class, ability, and sexuality-based.'[43] As Spears articulated,

> I grew up within an ideology that said I did not exist, because Native people did not exist, except as mascots or objects of desire. Through this process of symbolic annihilation, I ceased to exist as a Native person within my own mind.[44]

The stories and experiences shared by the participant-researchers of my study align with existing literature to indicate that a better understanding of the diversity and uniqueness of Indigenous girls' experiences is needed. In order to support Indigenous girls in their resistance of these narratives of collective trauma, educators and helping professionals must be able to acknowledge the biases and limitations they may be imposing on Indigenous girls with whom they are working.

In working with collective trauma and the historical and ongoing systemic devaluation and exploitation of Indigenous girls and women, it is critical to support continued efforts to actively promote changes to Canadian policy and dominant social values, while also supporting Indigenous girls and women as they enhance their existing capacities and resources and to come together to build solidarity.

5. Resistance, 'Survivance' and Engaged Participatory Approaches to Research

Critical feminist scholarship emphasizes that knowledge is socially constructed; Michelle Fine states that 'knowledge is rooted in social relations and produced in collaboration and in action,' and Moosa-Mitha sees the process of knowledge production as a viable 'site in the struggle for social justice.'[45][46] Critical engaged participatory research provides opportunities to facilitate linkages between individual experience and broader social forces. The decentralization of knowledge production is political, offering a site of resistance. A commitment to this as a core principle requires a process of facilitating community engagement with regard to research from the moment of conceptualisation. As Andrea Dyrness described, participatory research 'aims to transform the relationships between 'researcher' and 'subjects' and expand the capacity of participants to make change in their own communities.'[47]

Listening to girls' stories affords opportunities for practitioners, educators, and policy makers to better understand how they construct their subjective lived experiences. How do Indigenous girls continue to survive and thrive? Numerous Indigenous women scholars have taken up some form of the notion of survivance to foreground the importance of collecting and sharing stories in the spirit of strengthening community rather than further undermining it.[48] Rather than focus on deficiencies Vizenor, an Anishinaabe (Chippewa) scholar, advances the concept of survivance; this is distinct from survival: it is 'moving beyond our basic survival in the face of overwhelming cultural genocide to create spaces of synthesis and renewal.'[49] This notion of honoring strategies and practices that have allowed girls and women to thrive in face of deeply entrenched structural inequity underpins my own research with Indigenous girls.

Through my community practice, engaged research and personal relationships with Indigenous girls and women on the West Coast of Canada, it has become clear that strength, vitality, and spirit continue to persevere in the face of such potentially overwhelming and systemic oppression. Anderson, Maracle, and others recount the strength to be found in stories passed down from their grandmothers. According to Anderson, 'storytelling can help us transform our individual and collective experiences to create a new world...'[50] Vizenor also views storytelling as a mechanism of survivance with its 'active repudiation of dominance, tragedy, and victimry.'[51]

The participant-researchers involved who collaborated on my master's thesis research spoke of strategies present in their lives; these included attending school, not attending school, drinking alcohol, not drinking alcohol, taking up a sport or an art, and participating in traditional economic or cultural activities such as fishing, cedar bark stripping and weaving, etc. These girls have resisted through very personal strategies available to them according to their specific contexts. They have strong networks of support amongst one another and they rely on their families for support, encouragement, and traditional teachings. The participant-researchers shared that they gain enriched cultural ties through participation in various the traditions or ceremonies of their Nation / culture. These strategies enable Indigenous girls to preserve their dignity and move forward in their lives in spite of ever-present threats to their physical, emotional, and psychic security.

As scholars and practitioners we can support the ongoing disruption of the collective trauma within which Indigenous girls' experiences are located, facilitate opportunities for collective healing and for Indigenous girls to strengthen and express their voices. Participatory and engaged approaches to research that make direct links to relevant social change have the potential to achieve this.

Participatory research that engages Indigenous girls in conversation has the potential to open up spaces for discussions of racialized discrimination, the impact of racism on their day-to-day lives, their social positioning in the context of the broader community, and importantly, provide opportunities for the exchange of strategies and resources. Participatory and engaged research approaches can facilitate the development of narratives of resilience/resistance, break isolation and build solidarity.

6. Participatory Research: A Case Example

My engagement in research is motivated by a desire for social justice and thus I have sought to facilitate engaged, egalitarian approaches to research which open up space to deconstruct social stereotypes and constraints based on race, gender, class and age. Photovoice is a method of participatory action research developed by Caroline Wang to 'put cameras in the hands of individuals often excluded from decision-making processes in order to capture their voices and visions.'[52] The opportunity for participants to also be researchers by looking through the lens of the camera and then thinking and talking about their photos provides a 'means of catalysing personal and community change.'[53] Using the camera to document their experiences participants become active researchers, exchange stories and co-produce knowledge to potentially facilitate change in their communities.

In this participatory research project, the participant-researchers were able to reflect on how broader structural issues were relevant to their own lives and to formulate the questions that would guide the photo-taking process. Interactive and experiential exercises were useful to provoke reflection and dialogue and to promote connection, engagement, and ownership. The process of selecting and taking photographs and then exchanging their thoughts about the messages, symbolism, or stories represented within their selected photos allowed the girls to develop an understanding of the clear links between theories about sexism, racism, and colonialism and their everyday lived experiences.

Throughout the discussions and the subsequent photo analysis, the girls unpacked some of the forms of sexualized and racialized violence they had come to expect as inevitable in their young lives. Some of the stories the girls shared related to acts perpetrated by strangers: walking home from school as a young girl and being followed by an unknown man in a car offering a ride; being followed by men or hearing them make obscene comments when walking home alone; standing outside a youth drop-in space (up to that point a safe space) after school waiting for it to open and being approached by an older white man soliciting sex.

Many of the participant-researchers' stories involved incidents facilitated by the internet: being 'chatted up' by someone eventually discovered to be an adult male on a social media site geared to preteen girls, being added as a 'friend' by random men on *Facebook* or on *MSN*, and being pressured to remove clothing in front of the 'webcam'.

Furthermore, many of the stories the girls shared involved acts perpetrated by known and trusted individuals. One girl recounted being approached by her older brother's adult friend in the bathroom of her home while her brother and the other adults were either intoxicated or absent. She recounted that when she told her family, she was teased as though she should be flattered by his attention. This behaviour from her brother's friend was ongoing and she developed strategies to avoid being isolated by him whenever he visited her home. One girl recounted that her dad would send her to her room for the night when a certain uncle was over and started to get too inebriated. Another girl described how her sister had dated an older man who got her addicted to crack and then expected her to trade sexual favours to get money for him.

The girls' examples illustrate their awareness that their intersecting social locations as both girls and Indigenous rendered them further vulnerable to sexualized violence. They reported that they hear slurs such as 'dirty Squaw' and 'chug' (a local racial slur) regularly. The participant-researchers also shared many stories of racialized violence of a non-sexual nature from their day-to-day lives; they had all had frequent experiences in school settings of being discriminated against by teachers and peers because they are 'Native'. Again, the girls' stories illustrate that simply going about their day frequently put them on the receiving end of racial slurs by older, white and typically male community members driving or walking by.

Amidst these stories of victimization were layered many different examples of methods of resistance that the girls employ in their ongoing encounters with normalized, sexualized and racialized violence. The use of humour, avoidance, assertive communication, having a friend at your side, and telling an adult you trust were some of the individual strategies highlighted by the participant-researchers. Furthermore, the girls noted that increased awareness through education, for example, (having information that certain behaviours constitute abuse and solidarity and knowing that they are not alone in their experiences) are crucial to enhance resilience and support the preservation of dignity and integrity in the face of pervasive discrimination.

Through their engagement with this participatory research project, of which they were encouraged and supported to take ownership, the girls were able to articulate their experiences, recognise the commonality across their experiences (thus reducing isolation), and feel empowered to share their expertise with younger girls. For the final synthesis of their collective learning through engagement with the research, the participant-researchers created a photomontage for younger girls that would educate them about sexual exploitation, from the perspective of their peers. The photomontage consisted of various photos they had captured in the community interspersed with stock photos they selected from the Internet and set to segments of two popular Top 40 songs. The participant-researchers chose quotes to overlay images and accompany the music throughout the montage. Overall, the participant-researchers achieved a greater confidence in themselves and their knowledge-base with regard to sexualized and racialized violence. With this they developed a desire to share this knowledge. They wanted to help ensure that younger sisters and cousins could prevent such things from happening to them, or that they could at least be aware that it is part of a societal problem and not their fault if they experience such exploitation.

7. Conclusion

Euro-Western colonialism and its inherent sexism and gender-based discrimination persist in twenty-first century Canadian society. Within existing structures Indigenous girls have few opportunities to share their voices, thoughts, opinions and expertise or contribute in productive ways to social policy and dialogue. Educators, psychologists, social workers, mental health clinicians, and policy makers can only benefit from informing our approaches to intervention or social policies with direct input from those for whom our programs and services are intended. Most importantly, participatory and engaged approaches to research enable participant-researchers to benefit from their involvement with research. Empowered, they articulate their thinking and express it, use their voices, and involve themselves in local activities of community change that can affect change in their individual lives.

I strongly advocate for engaged, participatory research, which facilitates and supports authentic engagement and ownership of the research process and outcomes by the participants. It provides valuable opportunities for girls, including Indigenous girls, to develop their analysis and contribute to public discussions and community processes that impact their lives. Though the process of engaged, participatory research is more complex and dynamic than that of traditional research, the outcomes are deeply meaningful for the participant-researchers and, certainly, from my own experience, more enriching for the research facilitator.

Participatory research, in particular for Indigenous girls and women who take part in such a process, can lead to further solidarity-building and mobilization in the community. Alongside persistent paternalistic federal policies, this is an era of reclaiming culture, language, and economic autonomy; many Indigenous people across Canada are taking a stand with regard to access and control of land, resources, health, and education in First Nation communities. These young women will have insights to contribute to local activities that resist colonial imperialism (for example, pipeline blockades, clean water advocacy, vigils for missing and murdered women) and will impart further awareness to their peers, families, and eventually their own children. They will recognise and share the survivance stories that have enabled them to persevere and ultimately work towards social justice.

Notes

[1] Tanya Talaga, 'U.N. to Investigate Missing Aboriginal Women,' *TheStar.com*, Last modified January 6 2012, http://www.thestar.com/news/insight/article/1111907--un-to-investigate-missing-aboriginal-women.

[2] 'Convention on the Rights of the Child', *Unicef.org*, Last modified May 26 2012, http://www.unicef.org/crc/.

[3] Meagan Fitzpatrick, 'Ottawa Accused of Failing Aboriginal Children,' *CBC News*, Last modified October 24 2012, http://www.cbc.ca/news/politics/story/2011/10/24/pol-rights-child-united-nations.html.

[4] Andrea Smith, 'Queer Theory and Native Studies: The Heteronormativity of Settler Colonialism,' *GLQ* 16 (2010).

[5] Judith Sayers and Kelly MacDonald, 'A Strong and Meaningful Role for First Nations Women in Governance,' *First Nations Women, Government, and the Indian Act* (Ottawa: Status of Women Canada, 2001), Viewed May 17 2011, http://dsp-psd.pwgsc.gc.ca/Collection/SW21-85-2001E.pdf.

[6] Jesse Winter, 'First Nations Slam Bill C-45,' *Yukon News*, Last modified December 12 2012, http://www.yukon-news.com/news/31466/.

[7] Murray Sinclair, Nicholas Bala, Heino Lilles and Cindy Blackstock, 'Aboriginal Child Welfare,' in *Canadian Child Welfare Law: Children, Families, and the State*, eds. Nicholas Bala et al. (Toronto: Thompson Educational Publishing, 2004), 202.

[8] Wesley Chrichlow, 'Western Colonization as Disease: Native Adoption and Cultural Genocide,' *Canadian Social Work Journal* 5 (2003): 91.

[9] Sherene Razack, 'When Place becomes Race,' *Race, Space and the Law: Unmapping a White Settler Society* (Toronto: Between the Lines, 2002), 1-20.

[10] Ibid.

[11] Sinclair, Bala, Lilles and Blackstock, 'Aboriginal Child Welfare'.

[12] Alan Wade, 'Resistant Knowledges: Therapy with Aboriginal Persons Who have Experienced Violence', *Canadian Western Geographical Series* (1995): 171.

[13] Wade, 'Resistant Knowledges.'

[14] Elizabeth Fast and Dauphine Collin-Vézina, 'Historical Trauma, Race-Based Trauma and Resilience of Indigenous Peoples: A Literature Review,' *First Peoples Child and Family Review* 5 (2010): 131.

[15] Ibid.

[16] Teresa Evans-Campbell, 'Historical Trauma in American Indian/Native Alaska Communities: A Multilevel Framework for Exploring Impacts on Individuals, Families, and Communities,' *Journal of Interpersonal Violence* 23 (2008).

[17] Justice for Girls, 'Justice for Girls Voices Opposition to the Proposed Safe Care Legislation,' *BC Awareness*, Viewed November 23 2012, http://www.justiceforgirls.org/publications/pos_safecareact2.html.

[18] Lee Maracle, *I am Woman* (Vancouver, BC: Press Gang Publishers, 1996).

[19] Kim Anderson, *A Recognition of Being: Reconstructing Native Womanhood* (Toronto, ON: Sumach Press, 2000).

[20] Sayers and MacDonald, 'A Meaningful Role for First Nations Women'.

[21] Ibid.

[22] Pamela Downe, 'Aboriginal Girls in Canada: Living Histories of Dislocation, Exploitation and Strength,' in *Girlhood Defining the Limits*, eds. Yasmin Jiwani, Candis Steenbergen, and Claudia Mitchell (Montreal: Black Rose Books, 2005), 3.

[23] Anderson, *A Recognition of Being*; Maracle, *I am Woman*; James McNinch, 'Queer Eye on Straight Youth: Homoerotics and Racial Violence in the Narrative Discourse of White Settler Masculinity,' *Journal of LGBT Youth* 5 (2008); Razack, 'When Place becomes Race'; Anette Sikka, *Trafficking of Aboriginal Women and Girls in Canada* (Ottawa: Institute on Governance, 2009).

[24] Anderson, *A Recognition of Being*; Razack, 'When Place becomes Race.'

[25] Maracle, *I am Woman*; Sherene Razack, 'Gendered Racial Violence and Spatialized Justice: The Murder of Pamela George,' *Canadian Journal of Law and Society / Revue Canadienne droit et société* 15 (2000).

[26] Anderson, A *Recognition of Being*, 111.

[27] Ibid.

[28] 'Police Reluctant to Probe Native Disappearances', *CBC News*, Last modified April 12 2012, http://www.cbc.ca/news/canada/british-columbia/story/2012/04/03/bc-pickton-inquiry-aboriginal.html.

[29] 'Highway of Tears,' Viewed November 23, 2012, http://www.highwayoftears.ca/.

[30] Joji Kumagi and Judy McGuire, *Vancouver's Downtown Eastside: A Community in Need of Balance*, Last modified August 10 2011, http://strathconabia.com/wp-content/uploads/2012/08/DTES-A-Community-in-Need-of-Balance.pdf, 6.

[31] 'Pickton reports Highlights Tragedy of Epic Proportions', *CTVNews.ca*, Last modified December 17 2012, http://www.ctvnews.ca/pickton-report-highlights-tragedy-of-epic-proportions-1.1082679.

[32] 'Highway of Tears'.

[33] Rebecca Aleem, *International Human Rights Law and Aboriginal Girls in Canada: Never the Twain Shall Meet* (Justice for Girls International, 2009).

[34] Aleem, *International Human Rights*
[35] Ibid.
[36] McNinch, 'Queer Eye', 94.
[37] Downe, 'Aboriginal Girls in Canada'; Sethi, 'Domestic Sex Trafficking'; Sikka, 'Trafficking Aboriginal Women.'
[38] Nancy Lesko, 'Denaturalizing Adolescence: The Politics of Contemporary Representations,' *Youth and Society* 28 (1996): 465.
[39] Anderson, *A Recognition of Being*, 105.
[40] Sikka, 'Trafficking Aboriginal Women,' 7.
[41] Sandrina de Finney, *It's About Us: Racialized Minority Girls Transformative Engagement in Feminist Participatory Action Research* (Victoria, BC: University of Victoria, 2007).
[42] Ibid., 57.
[43] Yasmin Jiwani, Candis Steenbergen and Claudia Mitchell, 'Girlhood: Surveying the Terrain,' in *Girlhood: Redefining the Limits*, eds. Yasmin Jiwani, Candis, Steenbergen and Claudia Mitchell (Montreal: Black Rose Books, 2005), xiii.
[44] Shandra Spears, 'Strong Spirit, Fractured Identity: An Ojibway Adoptee's Journey to Wholeness,' in *Strong Women Stories: Native Vision and Community Survival*, eds. Kim Anderson and Bonita Lawrence (Toronto: Sumach Press, 2003): 83.
[45] Michelle Fine, et al., 'Participatory Action Research: From within and beyond Prison Bars,' in *Working Method: Research and Social Justice*, eds. Lois Weis and Michelle Fine (New York, NY: Routledge, 2004): 95.
[46] Moosa-Mitha, 56.
[47] Andrea Dyrness, 'Research for Change vs. Research as Change: Lessons from a Mujerista Participatory Research Team,' *Anthropology and Education Quarterly* 39 (American Anthropological Association, 2008).
[48] Anderson, *A Recognition of Being*; Anderson and Lawrence, *Strong Women Stories*.
[49] Vizenor, *Manifest Manners*, 53.
[50] Kim Anderson, 'Speaking from the Heart: Everyday Storytelling and Adult Learning,' *Canadian Journal of Native Education* 28 (2004): 126.
[51] Eve Tuck, 'Breaking up with Deleuze: Desire and Valuing the Irreconcilable,' *International Journal of Qualitative Studies in Education* 23 (2010): 639.
[52] Pennie Foster-Fishman et al., 'Using Methods that Matter: The Impact of Reflection, Dialogue, and Voice,' *American Journal of Community Psychology* 36 (2005): 277.
[53] Caroline Wang, 'Photovoice as a Participatory Health Promotion Strategy,' *Health Promotion International* 13(1998): 75.

Bibliography

Aleem, Rebecca. *International Human Rights Law and Aboriginal Girls in Canada: Never the Twain Shall Meet*. Justice for Girls International, 2009. Accessed on November 23 2012. http://www.justiceforgirls.org/international_hr/International%20Human%20Rights %20of%20Indigenous%20Girls.pdf.

Anderson, Kim. *A Recognition of Being: Reconstructing Native Womanhood*. Toronto, ON: Sumach Press, 2000.

Anderson, Kim. 'Speaking from the Heart: Everyday Storytelling and Adult Learning'. *Canadian Journal of Native Education* 28 (2004): 123-129.

Anderson, Kim and Bonita Lawrence. *Strong Women Stories: Native Vision and Community Survival*. Toronto, ON: Sumach Press, 2003.

Battiste, Marie and Helen Semeganis. 'First Thoughts on First Nation's Citizenship: Issues in Education'. *Citizenship in Transformation in Canada*, edited by Yvonne Hébert. Toronto: University of Toronto Press, 2002.

Crichlow, Wesley. 'Western Colonization as Disease: Native Adoption and Cultural Genocide'. *Canadian Social Work Journal* 5 (2003): 88-107.

Downe, Pamela. 'Aboriginal Girls in Canada: Living Histories of Dislocation, Exploitation and Srength'. *Girlhood Defining the Limits*, edited by Yasmin Jasmin, Candis Steenbergen, and Claudia Mitchell. Montreal: Black Rose Books, 2005.

Evans-Campbell, Teresa. 'Historical Trauma in American Indian/Native Alaska Communities: A Multilevel Framework for Exploring Impacts on Individuals, Families, and Communities'. *Journal of Interpersonal Violence* 23 (2008): 316-338.

Fast, Elizabeth and Dauphine Collin-Vézina. 'Historical Trauma, Race-Based Trauma and Resilience of Indigenous Peoples: A Literature Review'. *First Peoples Child and Family Review* 5 (2010): 126-136.

Fitzpatrick, Meagan. 'Ottawa Accused of Failing Aboriginal Children'. *CBC News*. Last modified October 24 2012. http://www.cbc.ca/news/politics/story/2011/10/24/pol-rights-child-united-nations.html.

Gross, Emma. 'Native American Family Continuity as Resistance: The Indian Child Welfare Act as Legitimation for an Effective Social Work Practice,' *Journal of Social Work* 3 (2003): 31-44.

Kumagi, Joji and Judy McGuire. *Vancouver's Downtown Eastside: A Community in Need of Balance.* Last modified August 10 2011. http://strathconabia.com/wp-content/uploads/2012/08/DTES-A-Community-in-Need-of-Balance.pdf.

Lesko, Nancy. 'Denaturalizing Adolescence: The Politics of Contemporary Representations'. *Youth and Society* 28 (1996): 139-161.

Maracle, Lee. *I am Woman.* Vancouver, BC: Press Gang Publishers, 1996.

McNinch, James. 'Queer Eye on Straight Youth: Homoerotics and Racial Violence in the Narrative Discourse of White Settler Masculinity'. *Journal of LGBT Youth* 5 (2008): 87-107.

Moosa-Mitha, Mehmoona. 'Situating Anti-Oppressive Theories within Critical and Difference-Centred Perspectives'. *Research as Resistance: Critical, Indigenous, and Anti-Oppressive Approaches*, edited by Leslie Brown and Susan Strega, 37-72. Toronto, ON: Canadian Scholars Press, 2005.

Razack, Sherene. 'When Place becomes Race'. *Race, Space, and the Law: Unmapping a White Settler Society* Toronto: Between the Lines, 2005.

Razack, Sherene. 'Gendered Racial Violence and Spatialized Justice: The Murder of Pamela George'. *Canadian Journal of Law and Society / Revue canadienne droit et société* 15 (2000): 91-130.

Sayers, Judith and Kelly MacDonald. 'A Strong and Meaningful Role for First Nations Women in Governance'. *First Nations Women, Government, and the Indian Act.* Ottawa: Status of Women Canada. Viewed on May 17 2012. http://dsp-psd.pwgsc.gc.ca/Collection/SW21-85-2001E.pdf.

Sethi, Anupriya. 'Domestic Sex Trafficking of Aboriginal Girls in Canada: Issues and Implications'. *First Peoples Child and Family Review* 3 (2007): 57-71.

Sikka, Anette, *Trafficking of Aboriginal Women and Girls in Canada*. Aboriginal Policy Research Series. Ottawa: Institute on Governance, 2009.

Sinclair, Murray, Nicholas Bala, Heini Lilles and Cindy Blackstock. 'Aboriginal Child Welfare'. *Canadian Child Welfare Law: Children, Families, and the State*, edited by Nicholas Bala, M. Zapf, J. Williams, R. Vogl and J. Hornick. Toronto: Thompson Educational Publishing, 2004.

Smith, Andrea. 'Queer Theory and Native Studies: The Heteronormativity of Settler Colonialism'. *GLQ*, 16 (2010): 41-68.

Spears, Shandra. 'Strong Spirit, Fractured Identity: An Ojibway Adoptee's Journey to Wholeness'. *Strong Women Stories: Native Vision and Community Survival*, edited by Kim Anderson and Bonita Lawrence, 81-94. Toronto: Sumach Press, 2003.

Talaga, Tanya. 'U.N. to Investigate Missing Aboriginal Women'. *TheStar.com*. Last modified January 6 2012. http://www.thestar.com/news/insight/article/1111907--un-to-investigate-missing-aboriginal-women.

The Canadian Press, 'Police Reluctant to Probe Native Disappearances'. *CBC News*. Viewed November 23 2012. http://www.cbc.ca/news/canada/british-columbia/story/2012/04/03/bc-pickton-inquiry-aboriginal.html.

Tuck, Eve. 'Suspending Damage: A Letter to Communities'. *Harvard Educational Review* 79 (2009): 409-427.

———. 'Breaking up with Deleuze: Desire and Valuing the Irreconcilable'. *International Journal of Qualitative Studies in Education* 23 (2010): 635-650.

Ungar, Michael, *Nurturing Hidden Resilience in Troubled Youth*. Toronto: University of Toronto Press, 2004.

Vizenor, Gerald. *Manifest Manners: Post-Indian Warriors of Survivance*. Middleton, CT: Wesleyan University Press, 1994.

Wade, Alan. 'Resistant Knowledges: Therapy with Aboriginal Persons who have Experienced Violence'. *Canadian Western Geographical Series* 31 (1995): 167-206.

Wang, Caroline, Wu Kun Yi, Zhan Wen Tao and Kathryn Carovano. 'Photovoice as a Participatory Health Promotion Strategy'. *Health Promotion International* 13 (1998): 75-86.

————. *Highway of Tears.* Viewed November 23 2012. http://www.highwayoftears.ca/.

————. 'Pickton Report Highlights Tragedy of Epic Proportions'. *CTVNews.ca.* Last modified December 17 2012. http://www.ctvnews.ca/pickton-report-highlights-tragedy-of-epic-proportions-1.1082679.

Johanne N. Fleming-Saraceno holds a Master's of Arts from the School of Child and Youth Care (CYC) at the University of Victoria, Victoria, British Columbia. She is currently pursuing her doctoral degree with the School of CYC. She has over fifteen years of experience in psychotherapy and community development and has worked alongside Indigenous girls and women for over a decade on the West Coast of Canada. She has co-authored a number of publications which discuss the systemic racialized discrimination of Indigenous children, youth, and women in Canada.

Afterword

Peter Bray

1. Trauma in the World

The implications of trauma are universal. In the last century alone 'genocides and other mass murders killed more people ... than all the wars combined'.[1] Repeated images of suffering and death contribute to our collective cultural consciousness and we are all uneasily implicated in its realisation. No longer a discrete speciality within emergency medicine or psychoanalysis, modern trauma studies emerged, to quote Marshall McLuhan, at the same time as 'television brought the brutality of war into the comfort of the living room.'[2] Just as the Holocaust engaged generations of survivors in a painful reawakening from its traumatic nightmare, so a decade of war in Vietnam, Laos and Cambodia exercised an unprecedented inquiry into the meaning and impact of the terrible events of the 1960's. With the addition of the diagnostic criteria for posttraumatic stress disorder (PTSD) to the classification of medical health the field of trauma studies legitimately expanded into a multidisciplinary and interdisciplinary industry.[3] In the field of medical humanities, for example, the dramatic arts, cultural and media studies, history, and psychology now find themselves engaging with trauma theory in discourses concerning human subjectivity and experience through historical and political agendas and contexts. Studying trauma has established influential methodologies for understanding the pervasive and complex impact of contemporary crisis events on human beings across the lifespan.

As our ability to access global digital technologies increases and we are able to observe the raw and the extreme experiences of others we are confounded and bewildered by our genuine incredulity and impotence in the face of trauma's real and epidemic presence. Interdisciplinary interest in the experience, theory, practice and expression of trauma has grown to incorporate almost every aspect of human behaviour and aspiration. Trauma permeates our lives and trauma research into the origins of post-traumatic stress and assessing who is most at risk, has led to breakthroughs in the neurobiology of trauma, brain imaging and gene science. This in turn has accommodated a re-conceptualisation of trauma that has freed itself from the harness of Cartesian dualism previously dominating thought and practice in this work. Thus, both human biology and human behaviour influence the role of family, community, and nations in shaping our neuro-biological responses to trauma and stress, expanding those fields particularly concerned with human thought and response. Emerging research in medicine and mental health, for example, now studies the efficacy of early and brief interventions that might prevent PTSD, the use of neurology in memory management, the biomarkers of stress injuries and the risk of health disorders following trauma, and how vulnerable populations such as the elderly, disabled and children are effected by traumatic experiences.[4]

There has been a re-balancing, or blending, of those central and hitherto prevailing notions of trauma that describe and treat the emotional effects of psychological trauma in terms of mental health disorder, or illness, with emerging research that now directs its attention to aspects of trauma that support wellness. This refreshing re-visioning of earlier research in exploring coping and resilience have encouraged the academy to admit to the positive potential of trauma and its role in the promotion of psychological wellness and growth. This orientation suggests an expansion, not only of our knowledge of trauma but, more significantly how we might modify, understand, and apply this knowledge to the present PTSD criteria. Thus for some survivors trauma's woundings, rather than precipitating PTSD, can provide unlikely benefits and experiences, and birth new understanding and opportunities.

2. Trauma in this Book

Many of our expert contributors reflect the ongoing concerns of trauma studies through their perceptive consideration of culturally significant literatures and critical theory. In this volume they draw deeply from the narratives, accounts, testimonies and texts of African and Latin American, Australian, and Scottish authors interrogating female and postcolonial perspectives and contexts. Their work also broadens trauma research and scholarship by drawing attention to the wartime victimization and oppression of female non-combatants and their families in the Middle East and Africa, from Nigeria, Rwanda, and French-Algeria to Beirut, Biafra, and the Lebanon. In their exploration of physical and psychological responses to trauma and survivor support the authors underline the importance of understanding the diversity of cultural perspectives in trauma narratives that negotiate politically and racially motivated acts of genocide, violence, and oppression which foster silence, disenfranchisement and shame. Their work that details the post-traumatic impact on families of state-sanctioned oppression, manipulation, and a conspiracy of silence following the intentional wholesale slaughter and transportation of Alevi and Zaza Kurds in the Dersim region of Turkey juxtaposed with the telling argument supporting the work of the Gacacas courts in the wake of the Rwandan genocide of Tutsis speak powerfully together. There is no doubt that the intentional stifling of discourse, the forced silence, in the former between the non-combatant survivors and their descendants about these genocidal atrocities have resulted in the intergenerational suffering of a nation – motifs that repeatedly occur in this collection. Thus, in the interests of healing and truth, the Gacacas by their examination and disclosure of suffering, power, and social conventions bring the private and secret into a public domain that links individual with national trauma.[5] It is suggested that healing is best served by community systems of justice – where 'justice' is subjective – and bound to the legitimacy of the survivors' claims and trust in their governments' and communities' commitments to understanding and reparation. Healing is also found in intimate relationship, therapeutic listening, in supportive family structures, and through the re-stabilisation of fractured societies drawn together through processes of reintegration and growthful reconciliation in post-conflict recovery.

A further theme that threads through this collection deals with the ongoing development of trauma theory in areas of cultural difference. Authors suggest that for dealing with clients from different cultures there can be no standardised norms and they call for conceptually realistic ways of seeing or narrating, symbolising or describing trauma from perspectives that specifically recognise and support the diversity of Indigenous and non-Western cultural experiences. By understanding the cultural context, beliefs and practices of individuals and communities we are introduced to the impact of trauma and its management from the inside. Furthermore, it is important to note that it is not enough to incorporate this localized Indigenous knowledge and expertise into colonial norms but to invite participatory research that will more effectively equip everyone with tools that are tailored to the specific needs of particular communities at a particular time.[6]

The broadening of research emphasis from psychopathological ways of seeing trauma toward these more positive outcomes of trauma will no doubt help to reconceptualise the field and how those risk and resilience factors, deployed in personal and community adversity are examined in the future. This collection has highlighted the challenges and difficulties engendered by long-term, intergenerational, and socio-culturally transmitted experiences of trauma, the affects of post-traumatic distress and the significance of memory in the articulation and release of trauma, whilst also celebrating the human capacity to endure, to find meaning, to be supportive, and to creatively emerge from trauma in self-actualisation. The future of our work lies in recognising that there exists a balance between light and shadow in trauma that influences experience and outcome.[7] However, that is not to suggest that there is a place where the painful reactions and behaviours of trauma can be discarded as irresolvable.[8]

Whilst celebrating human resilience and its exploration through the self-soothing imperatives of creative expression such as performance-making, artistic works and installations, film, and theatre our authors also alert us to those questionable or darker inflictions imposed by artists and authors, directors and performers upon themselves and their audiences as a result of wedding traumatic experience with the Arts. Here creative re-enactment and reiteration, sometimes in the guise of entertainment that intentionally exploits the event, the survivor, and the perpetrator in these personal violations and painful entanglements, poses questions that reveal the complexity of our ongoing socio-cultural relationship with trauma.

Trauma is a personal experience, the only authority, which trauma studies often translate into universal experiences. Exposure to traumatic events engages a multiplicity of biological, cultural, and psychological responses, and social support factors and therapeutic interventions used to support survivors should be unique in each case.[9] Perhaps the next great step in trauma research is to recognise, assess, and incorporate interdisciplinary and holistic approaches. As researchers engaging with unexpected responses we might for a while suspend our belief in the predictable, medically authorised nature of the human condition, emphasised in the universality of trauma events, and work with the uniqueness of the individual's trauma experience. It has been suggested, for example, that we still have very little 'Cosmic' understanding of the philosophy and science of the universe, the spiritual dimension of trauma, and therefore we are unaware of the full impact of the existential pain – the 'most crucial traumatic stress injury' - that persists after physical recovery has been achieved.[10]

3. The Day-to-Day Afterwards of Trauma

Human crises like the Tōhoku earthquake and tsunami, the Thailand floods, and the 'terror attacks' in 9/11 bear overt witness to the best and the worst qualities of mankind in traumatic circumstances. For those who live in countries where the risk of genocide, politicide, and mass atrocities is a reality the re-experiencing and struggle to understand trauma is relentless. Where day-to-day, lives are cheapened by violence and abuse, or distress is compounded or complicated by ongoing stress from loss of jobs, housing, and suitable health care trauma is relentlessly cycled and recovery delayed. These are the places where trauma research may sometimes hope to reach because often the perpetrators are the powerful gate-keepers to the unrecorded, unwitnessed and stigmatising experiences of trauma that are held silently in the minds and bodies of disenfranchised individuals, in trans-cultural memory and in its daily reiteration reaching beyond the lives of present survivors into those of future generations.

As we realise the totality of trauma's influence across disciplines so we understand that the longer we study trauma 'the more it seems to incorporate the essence of human experience–both the adversity and the growth, the horror and the beauty.'[11] It is because trauma defies us to explain it that it will always be a challenge to get the focus right between our understanding of the trauma event, our experience of the event, and the later ways in which it is transmuted by our cultures, politics and histories. Thus, in the *nachträglichkeit*, the 'afterwardsness' of the appalling event it is not the event itself that makes the trauma but the way in which it comes to be understood and lived out in our everyday existence.[12] To understand trauma we may need to expand how we conceptualise it and how we talk about it as theoreticians and survivors. If we can allow ourselves not to be too ransomed to the facts of the traumatic event, or at least not allow pre-traumatic history and the post-traumatic truth to become impediments to their integration, we make it possible to site the meaning of these experiences in our immediate, everyday lives.

Without exception the contributors to this volume draw attention to the psychophysical impact of trauma upon those who are disenfranchised and challenged by appalling international disasters such as the earthquake in Sichuan and the national horrors of civil disorder and war. In their detailed work they attest to the importance of a supportive environment post-trauma in which processes of retrospective representation and reconstruction of emergent life narratives are safely engaged through a meaningful witnessing, memorialising and understanding of these events enabling the integration and management of experiences. In their revealing presentations our authors examine these human questions and implicitly challenge our ability to be academically impartial or neutral when discussing the real experiences of trauma survivors. As persons who actually live in the world we cannot avoid being implicated in and transformed by trauma's causes and resolution. However, as scholars and researchers, readers and recorders of trauma we are powerfully challenged and charged with originating and realising theory through practice and research. Observing and witnessing the injustice and inevitability of trauma in people's lives, we risk ourselves in asking the hard questions that demand the delivery of support and hope to survivors, and raise humanity's consciousness.

Notes

[1] 'The International Alliance to End Genocide Kosovars'. Viewed February 3 2013,
http://www.genocidewatch.org/alliancetoendgenocide/about.html.
[2] Marshall McLuhan, *Montreal Gazette*, 16 May, 1975.
[3] American Psychiatric Association, *Diagnostic and Statistical Manual of Mental Disorders: DSM-III-R* (Washington: American Psychiatric Association, 1987). It is important to note here that not everyone who has trauma has PTSD.
[4] Charles R. Figley, Introduction to the *Encyclopaedia of Trauma: An Interdisciplinary Guide* by ed. Charles R. Figley (London: Sage, 2012), xxiv.
[5] Anne Rothe, *Popular Trauma Culture: Selling the Pain of Others in the Mass Media* (New Brunswick: Rutgers University Press), 87-98.
[6] In her work on trauma and memory Kali Tal makes a useful rejoinder to Cathy Caruth's work and her claim that trauma links different cultures. Kali Tal, *Worlds of Hurt: Reading the Literatures of Trauma* (Cambridge: Cambridge University Press, 1996), Viewed February 10 2013,
http://www.kalital.com/Text/Worlds/Chap3.html#fn8.
[7] Stephen Joseph, *What Doesn't Kill Us: The New Psychology of Posttraumatic Growth* (London: Piatkus, 2012).
[8] Pittu Laungani, *Asian Perspectives in Counselling and Psychotherapy* (Hove: Brunner-Routledge, 2004), 222-229.
[9] John Briere and Catherine Scott, *Principles of Trauma Therapy: A Guide to Symptoms, Evaluation, and Treatment* (Los Angeles: Sage, 2013), 286.
[10] Figley, *Encyclopaedia of Trauma*, xxiv.

[11] Ibid., xxiii.
[12] Robert Eaglestone in discussion with Dan Stone, 'Trauma and History: Approaches to the Holocaust', Viewed January 24 2013, http://backdoorbroadcasting.net/2010/10/robert-eaglestone-and-dan-stone-trauma-and-history-approaches-to-the-holocaust/.

Bibliography

American Psychiatric Association. *Diagnostic and Statistical Manual of Mental Disorders: DSM-III-R.* Washington: American Psychiatric Association, 1987.

Briere, John and Catherine Scott. *Principles of Trauma Therapy: A Guide to Symptoms, Evaluation, and Treatment.* Los Angeles: Sage, 2013.

Caruth, Cathy. *Unclaimed Experience: Trauma, Narrative, and History.* Baltimore: The Johns Hopkins University Press, 1996.

Figley, Charles R. ed. *Encyclopaedia of Trauma: An Interdisciplinary Guide.* London: Sage, 2012.

Joseph, Stephen. *What Doesn't Kill Us: The New Psychology of Posttraumatic Growth.* London: Piatkus, 2012.

Kaplan, E. Ann. *Trauma Culture: The Politics of Terror and Loss in Media and Literature.* New Brunswick: Rutgers University Press, 2005.

Laungani, Pittu. *Asian Perspectives in Counselling and Psychotherapy.* Hove: Brunner-Routledge, 2004.

Rothe, Anne. *Popular Trauma Culture: Selling the Pain of Others in the Mass Media.* New Brunswick: Rutgers University Press, 2011.

Tal, Kali. *Worlds of Hurt: Reading the Literatures of Trauma.* Cambridge: Cambridge University Press, 1996.

—

Lightning Source UK Ltd.
Milton Keynes UK
UKOW06f0911030614

232704UK00010B/45/P